Coaching and Mentoring Supervision: Theory and Practice

Second edition

Coaching and Mentoring Supervision: Theory and Practice

Second edition

Tatiana Bachkirova, Peter Jackson
and David Clutterbuck

Mc Graw Hill

Open University Press

Open University Press
McGraw Hill
8th Floor, 338 Euston Road
London
England
NW1 3BH

email: enquiries@openup.co.uk
world wide web: www.openup.co.uk

First edition published 2011

First Published in this second edition 2021
Copyright © Open International Publishing Limited, 2021

A catalogue record of this book is available from the British Library

ISBN-13: 9780335249534
ISBN-10: 0335249531
eISBN: 9780335249541

Library of Congress Cataloging-in-Publication Data
CIP data applied for

Typeset by Transforma Pvt. Ltd., Chennai, India

Praise Page

This volume is edited by three of the world's leading experts in coaching and mentoring supervision and in that sense a guaranty for solid work, professionalism and expertise in practice. The division in four main sections with a focus on the needs of the field, on theory, on methods and on practical modalities is well thought-out. This book is a central contribution to the further professional development of coaching and mentoring, where supervision should play a central role that cannot be underestimated.

> *—Reinhard Stelter, accred. coaching psychologist and professor of coaching psychology at the University of Copenhagen*

The overarching strength of this book is the abundance of stimulation justifying this as an essential read on the topic of coaching and mentoring supervision. The title says exactly what to expect between the covers with chapters written by credible authors known for expertise in the field – a union of multiple perspectives expertly woven into one reference point. If you're seeking rationale you'll find supervision immersed within theoretical frameworks. The popular inclusion of models and techniques refreshes the familiar alongside new creative concepts with the final chapters portraying supervision in a collection of applications focused on practitioner development.

> *—Dr Lise Lewis, Founder of Bluesky International provider of EMCC Accredited Coach and Author of* Relational Feedback

An outstanding book, updated to 2021. This new edition contains contributions from the most names in the field, including David Lane, Robin Shohots, Michael Cavanagh, Tammy Turner, Peter Hawkins, Erik de Haan and Damian Godvarg. This second edition has been skilfully edited by three thought leaders in coaching supervision to create a coherent and integrated review of the field. This book is an essential read for those undertaking training in coaching supervision, as well as a useful addition to every practitioners coaching library.

> *—Professor Jonathan Passmore, Director Henley Centre for Coaching, Henley Business School, UK*

This is a well-researched and multidisciplinary-grounded book by leading authors in the field who offer theoretical and practical knowledge for coaching practitioners to rethink, reset, and continue their professional development through supervision. It provides a foundation for the coaching profession to raise the bar and inspire excellence in coaching, bringing a line of sight into coaching practice through guided reflection. At a time when unexpected changes happen more rapidly, the authors underscore the impact of effective coaching on individuals and organizations. Coaching and Mentoring by Supervision: Theory and Practice is the sourcebook for coaches and supervisors. It is highly recommended for academic coaching programs, coaching supervision training as well as coaching practitioner groups who serve as peer supervisors.

—Charline S. Russo, EdD, Senior Lecturer, Organizational Dynamics Program, University of Pennsylvania

Combining the complementary expertise of world-class practitioners, researchers and educators, this book advances coaching supervision as a profession and a discipline. It articulates contributions on perspectives, theories, models, contexts in coaching supervision, systematically providing meaningful illustrations, insightful questions for reflection and promising research avenues. Our assumptions about how to practice, think about and research supervision are both challenged and enriched. I appreciate that emerging issues such as the use of AI in supervision, and sensitive topics such as ethics and taboos in supervision fully find a home in this corpus.

—Pauline Fatien, Grenoble Ecole de Management

Coaching and mentoring practices have evolved significantly over the past two decades and, with them, the supervisory requirements of practitioners. This second edition responds to these needs while also advancing the field with new contributions in the emerging areas of team coaching and systemic work. Written by a 'who's who' of coaching supervisors, if you're not currently in supervision, this book is a call to action to get started. If you've experienced coaching supervision already, there's lots of gems in this book for you too.

—Declan Woods, CEO, teamGenie®, Top Team Coach and Registered Supervisor Global Head, Team Coaching Standards and Accreditation, Association for Coaching (AC)

Contents

Notes on contributors

Coreene Archer, Principal Leadership Coach, The Tavistock Institute of Human Relations.

Dr Eliat Arram, CEO, The Tavistock Institute of Human Relations.

Prof Tatiana Bachkirova, Professor of Coaching Psychology, Oxford Brookes University.

David Birch, Associate faculty at Ashridge Centre for Coaching, Hult International Business School.

Dr Michael Cavanagh, Deputy Director, Coaching Psychology Unit, The University of Sydney.

Christine K. Champion, Founder, Acumen Executive Coaching.

Prof David Clutterbuck, Special Ambassador, European Mentoring & Coaching Council.

Bernard Cooke, Business Psychologist, Leaderspace.

Dr Sue Congram, Director, EB Centre for Engendering Balance and Inclusivity in Leadership.

Prof Erik de Haan, Director of Ashridge Centre for Coaching, Hult International Business School and Professor of Organisation Development, VU University, Amsterdam.

Dr Ty Francis, Director, Meus.

Dr Damian Goldvarg, President, Goldvarg Consulting Group, Inc. and Co-leader Americas Coaching Supervision Network.

Monica Hanaway, Lecturer, Regent's University, Coach and Mediator (private practice).

Prof Peter Hawkins, Emeritus Professor, Henley Business School, Chairman of Renewal Associates.

Julie Hay, Managing Director, Psychological Intelligence Foundation CIC.

Dr Alison Hodge, Executive Coach and Supervisor, Alison Hodge Associates.

Dr Peter Jackson, Co-Director, International Centre for Coaching and Mentoring Studies, Oxford Brookes University.

Florence Lamy, Cergy-Pontoise University, France.

Prof David A. Lane, Professor, Professional Development Foundation.

Dr Paul Lawrence, Principal, Centre for Coaching in Organisations and Associate Lecturer, Sydney Business School.

Dr Carmelina Lawton Smith, Associate Lecturer and Consultant, Oxford Brookes University.

Michelle Lucas, Principal Executive Coach and Supervisor, Greenfields Consulting Limited.

Alison Maxwell, Independent Coach and Coach Supervisor, Alison Maxwell Coaching Ltd.

Lis Merrick, Managing Director, Coach Mentoring Ltd.

Dr Michel Moral, Cergy-Pontoise University, France.

Dr Mike Munro Turner, Leadership Coach and Supervisor, Jericho Partners Ltd.

Dr Sean O'Connor, Director, Coaching Psychology Unit, The University of Sydney.

Kate Pinder, Director, Piaffirm.

Prof Andrey Rossokhin, Professor, Department Head, HSE University, Moscow.

Gil Schwenk, Coach and Supervisor, Managing Director of Lifetrek Ltd.

Dr Louise Sheppard, Partner and Executive Coach at Praesta LLP.

Robin Shohet, Co-founder, Centre for Supervision and Team Development, London.

Michael Soth, Psychotherapist, Integral-Relational Body Psychotherapy, Supervisor, Coach Trainer and Organizational Consultant.

Dr Paul Stokes, Principal Lecturer, Sheffield Hallam University.

Eve Turner, Visiting Fellow, University of Southampton/Henley Business Schools; Chair, APECS.

Tammy Turner, Master Team and Individual Coach, Supervisor and Author, CEO Turner International.

Carol Whitaker, Executive Coach and Supervisor, Whitaker Consulting, Co-chair AC SIG Supervision.

Angela Wright, Partner, Coach and Supervisor, CEC Global LLC.

Series editor's preface

A warm welcome to this excellent new second edition of *Coaching Supervision* as part of the Supervision in Context Series. Supervision of coaches, mentors and consultants has grown up more recently than supervision in many of the people professions such as counselling, psychotherapy, psychology, social work and nursing. Although a minority of coaches had been receiving supervision for many years, this was mostly delivered by supervisors trained in counselling, psychotherapy or psychology, and supervision in coaching lacked its own distinctive approach, relevant to its own unique challenges. This lack of specific coaching supervision was a major factor, as many in the field were reluctant to take up supervision and there was a good deal of resistance to its development (Hawkins and Schwenk 2006). It did not help address what the authors of this book describe as the 'blurred boundary between coaching and counseling'. The first research and the first book specifically on supervision for coaches, mentors and consultants was not published until 2006 (Hawkins and Smith 2006, 2nd edition 2013) and the first training specifically for supervisors of coaches and mentors did not start until 2003. Yet in the last 10 years much has been done to develop this fast-growing field, of which this new edition is the latest very welcome addition. This book brings together a remarkably rich array of contributions. These show how supervision has developed for coaches beyond the UK and a few other European countries as represented in the first edition to many other parts of the world. It addresses the differing needs of internal and external coaches, mentors and consultants, and for those coaching individuals, groups, teams and wider systems. This new edition also pays attention to the different mediums of supervision, whether it is done one to one, in groups, in peer groups or delivered virtually.

Coaching supervision draws on many of the supervision models and approaches developed in other professions that each of the chapters in Section 2 elucidate. However, supervision of coaches has significant differences from those supervising other helping professionals. Whereas the counsellor, nurse and social worker have clear individual and group clients that they bring to supervision, those who are carrying out executive coaching, paid for by organizations, always have to serve multiple clients. Those coaching managers and leaders in organizations have the challenge of serving the individual coaching client, the organization in which the coaching takes place, the relationship between the two, and the wider systemic and stakeholder contexts. It is all too easy for the coach to be more focused on the individual they are with in the coaching room and pay less attention to the organization, and yet the organization has an investment in the coaching relationship and its outcomes. When the coach comes to supervision, the supervisor needs to hold in mind the coach and their development, the coach's individual and team clients, the organizations investing in the coaching and the wider systemic connections. This requires a sophisticated, systemic and sensitive form of supervision.

Tatiana, Peter and David also point out other extra challenges for the coach supervisor; namely that coaches are often less well trained to 'identify mental-health issues impinging on the boundaries of coaching'; and 'less prepared to identify the effect of their personal process on their work because they are not required . . . to undertake . . . counselling or other personal development'. These put extra responsibility on the coaching supervisor who needs to combine expertise on the coaching craft, understanding of adult development and psychological processes, and a wide-ranging understanding of business, systems and organizational dynamics. This requires specific supervision skills on top of the coaching skills they will have already acquired.

One of the great strengths of this particular book is that Tatiana, Peter and David have brought together contributions from practice, teaching and research as well as the growing body of theory in the field, while providing a lively and practical text that help both the new coaching supervisor and those who have been practising for many years. They have also added new chapters that address such important areas as supervising team coaching, organizational transformation, using constellations in the supervision process and supervising virtually. There are also very useful new chapters on the ethical and legal aspects of supervision, and a new seminal chapter by Tatiana Bachkirova on how one can work pluralistically, across the diversity and complexity that the work must embrace.

This new edition sits proudly alongside the other books in this series, which include:

> *Supervision in the Helping Professions* by Peter Hawkins and Aisling McMahon (now in its 5th edition)
> *Clinical Supervision for Nurses* by Meg Bond and Susie Holland (now in its 2nd edition)
> *The Social Work Supervisor* by Allan Brown and Iain Bourne
> *Coaching, Mentoring and Organizational Consultancy: Supervision and Development* by Peter Hawkins and Nick Smith (now in its 2nd edition)
> *Psychotherapy Supervision* by Maria Gilbert and Ken Evans
> *Supervision in Action: A Relational Approach to Coaching and Consulting Supervision* by Erik de Hahn
> *Clinical Supervision in Medical Settings* edited by David Owen and Robin Shohet
> *Supervision in the Psychological Professions* edited by David Lane, Mary Watts and Sarah Corrie

All of these have very useful models, approaches and research that would be helpful to those supervising coaches and mentors and many of these authors are included in this new edition.

This whole series focuses on how to create, develop and sustain helping relationships, through providing quality supervision to those who work broadly in the people and helping professions. Quality supervision is fundamental in helping practitioners link what they learn in theory with what they learn and do in practice and is therefore at the core of all continuous personal and professional development.

At its best it serves and benefits the professional being supervised, their current and future clients, the organizations in which they and/or their clients work, the organization's stakeholders and the learning and development of the profession. In today's world no helping professional can afford to be without supervision and this book also provides an excellent frame for coaches, mentors and consultants to know what they should be demanding as part of sustaining the quality and development of their practice.

I am confident that this new edition will significantly take forward the development of supervision in this young and developing profession.

Professor Peter Hawkins, Series Editor
October 2020

Introduction

The field of coaching and mentoring supervision has changed significantly since the first edition of this book. Supervision is now an established practice supported by most professional bodies and served by a growing cohort of well-trained supervisors. The most noticeable and welcome shift has been in the status of the coaching discipline and, by extension, in the growth of literature and research on coaching supervision. It could be said that coaching and mentoring supervision is now emerging as a discipline in its own right. Even though the extent of research on coaching supervision is still rather limited, recognition of supervision's importance and its increasing uptake have been consistently identified across the coaching field (Bachkirova et al. 2020; de Haan 2017; Hawkins and Turner 2017).

To support the development of the discipline of coaching supervision, this second edition of the book aims to provide a conceptual foundation for various strands of the field with a clear commitment to an academically rigorous, fully referenced and evidence-based approach. We hope that this text can provide a retrospective and prospective overview of the state of knowledge on supervision as a multidisciplinary field. The first edition of the book was developed with this vision in mind. The second edition builds on its strengths and also creates a fresh perspective on both the fundamentals of supervision and new emerging ideas and methods. The goal of the book is to be a primary point of departure for students, educators and practitioners who wish to engage with current research and new and established ideas for practice.

We are very pleased that so many authors of the first edition of the book have agreed to review and update their chapters. We are also happy to welcome into the collection contributions from newcomers from different parts of the world, each with their own different theoretical background and different contextual experience. It is their generosity with ideas and time and their willingness to rise to the challenge of high expectations and stringent criteria of quality that makes this book one of the most comprehensive representations of the coaching supervision field.

In this Introduction we also wish to indicate what, in our view, is changing in the field of coaching supervision: which specific new developments are worth mentioning and some current issues that need attention at this stage. Then we are proud to introduce the chapters in this volume, including 13 completely new chapters to this edition, five under new authorship and therefore fully re-written, and eight updated and refreshed by the authors who collaborated with us in the first edition. We finish this Introduction with an appeal to researchers by suggesting examples of research topics and questions generated in this volume.

What is changing in the field of coaching supervision?

Education and training of supervisors

During the period of growth and development between the first edition of this book and the current time, the education and training of supervisors has both reflected and contributed to the discipline. Casting our mind back to the time of the first edition, it was still less than a decade since the first postgraduate qualifications in coaching had been developed in the UK (though the pioneering work of the Coaching Psychology Unit at the University of Sydney was a little earlier). Tony Grant's important review of coaching literature (2012) identified only 13 academic papers between 2000 and the beginning of 2011 that dealt with supervision even tangentially. Only seven of these papers had supervision as their primary focus. In contrast, 10 years later, Bachkirova et al. (2020: 35–36) identified 58 peer-reviewed articles as well as eight collections containing relevant chapters and 12 monographs discussing coaching supervision. This is a testament to the growing interest in supervision, its practice, its evidence base and the development of theory.

The contributors to the first edition of this collection were invited to present at an inaugural Coaching Supervision Conference at Oxford Brookes University. Since then, the annual conference has included discussions of the education and training of supervisors, including exercises, workshops, debates around competencies and the philosophy of education. Contributors have represented work taking place at universities such as Oxford Brookes, Henley, Ashridge and Sydney, as well as regular contributions from training providers such as Bath Consultancy Group and the Coaching Supervision Academy (both UK), the Centre for Coaching in Organisations (Australia), Goldvarg Consulting Group (US) and Undici (France). This not only attests to the spread of training and education, but also to the seriousness with which providers are approaching the issues of disciplinary research and evidence-based practice.

Recognition and regulation of supervision by professional bodies

During this same period there has been a healthy interaction between those developments in education and training on the one hand and the attitudes and developments of the professional bodies on the other. An interesting checkpoint is provided by the European Economic and Social Committee Professional Charter for Coaching and Mentoring, which was originally drafted in 2011 by a collaboration of the International Coach Federation (ICF) and European Mentoring and Coaching Council (EMCC), and later subscribed to by the Association for Coaching (AC) and Société Française de Coaching. The charter itself made reference to 'supervision' in only one of its articles: Part 3, Item 6 specified that any breach of the charter may result in sanctions including 'additional and/or specific supervision' and that 'authority to supervise' may be suspended. At this time, the requirement to participate in supervision was included in the EMCC competence framework and ethical framework, and a definition of supervision was provided. Fast forward to the present day and the ICF recognizes supervision and its contribution to professional development (though it is not mandated), while both AC and EMCC now provide a comprehensive definition, guidance for coaches and accreditation for both individual supervisors and supervision trainings. The Société Française de Coaching describes supervision as a professional imperative; it is incorporated into the ethical framework and is a requirement for accreditation.

Assessment and accreditation of supervisors

As professional bodies acknowledge the importance of supervision in coaching, they have developed processes that provide a rite of passage to the profession parallel to those they have for coaching. For example, AC, EMCC and the Association for Professional Executive Coaching and Supervision (APECS) have developed assessment and accreditation procedures for supervisors, leading to official recognition by the respective bodies. These assessment schemes include sets of competences that supervisors should demonstrate over and above those that they have as coaches. Some academic institutions, such as Ashridge and Oxford Brookes University, also provide accreditation opportunities that are based on the holistic evaluation of supervisors' capabilities.

We are glad to see that these accreditation schemes do not involve gradation of supervisory expertise as it is often done in coaching (for example, differentiating a 'Master' level). We take a cautious view on these kinds of gradations as they are not confirmed by any relevant research. However, we support the efforts of professional bodies to regularly evaluate and re-evaluate these competence schemes, as this is in line with the dynamic changes in the field of supervision and growth of knowledge through research and advanced conceptual studies.

New ideas and initiatives in the field

Transitioning to virtual space

When planning a collection such as this, we tend towards downplaying current affairs that may turn out to be of less historical significance than it seems at the time. As we approach our writing deadlines, any doubts that the COVID-19 pandemic might not change our previously 'normal' ways of working are fast evaporating. We have already seen over recent years an acceleration of the adoption of videoconferencing for both coaching and supervision, particularly in geographies where great distances discourage travel. Even in smaller and more densely populated regions such as the UK, both government policy and social movements towards decentralization have highlighted the economic downsides of travelling significant distances to carry out relatively short conversations. Added to this, concern for the environmental impact of travel has become much more overt over the last 10 years. Technology during this time has developed in step: more bandwidth, more processing power and more choice of applications for users. The inclusion of a chapter to deal with this issue was already overdue. Then, by virtue of the pandemic, we all experienced large parts of our communications turning to videoconferencing: day-to-day work-related conversations and meetings, education, virtual conferences, as well as coaching and supervision. For the most part, we suspect that supervisors have found that more is certainly possible 'online' than they perhaps would have thought previously. With the changes of expectations and infrastructure it has, in many cases, ceased to be an 'alternative' and become the first choice. In the coming years, the agenda may be about how we take advantage of the opportunities offered by the medium, rather than coping with the switch. In the same way that business information systems initially reproduced paper systems before becoming a capability in their own right, we expect there to be a growth of research into how online coaching/supervision has its own characteristics that are way beyond simply reproducing the experience of physical presence.

Extended use of supervision

Supervision is spreading into more and more new areas. In the context of team coaching, where coaches typically work in pairs, supervision increasingly occurs with the two coaches together. An unusual aspect of this is that the coach dyad is expected to role model teamwork, so a focus of the supervision is their co-development. A challenge for supervisors is that relatively few have extensive knowledge and experience of group and team dynamics or knowledge of its underpinning theory. Hodge and Clutterbuck (2019) found in a survey of the field that there is much room for improvement.

Another innovation occurred through the Ethical Coach project, which was aimed at creating an indigenous coaching capability in a developing country (Ethiopia) and brought to life by a large number of voluntary participants. Local coaches-in-training were paired with highly experienced international coaches and these coach dyads were in turn supervised by volunteers from the Global Supervisor Network.

New forms of coaching, such as well-being coaching and ethical mentoring (where coaches are given tools to help clients work through ethical dilemmas), also pose new challenges for supervisors. The broadening diversity of coaching practice brings to the fore the critical question: 'To what extent does a supervisor need to have relevant experience as a coach in that context?'

Use of AI in supervision

The increasing use of coachbots in coaching and team coaching brings both opportunities and challenges. Coachbots provide an intermediate step between electronic administration of a questionnaire and an AI, which adapts and learns to work with a coach. Supervisors now need to have sufficient familiarity and comfort with the technology to explore with coaches how they use these digital aids. Is the coachbot a practical and helpful time saver, able to conduct semi-intelligent interviews and extract useful data? Or is it a crutch that debilitates the coach's intuitive abilities?

As coachbots become more sophisticated and able to learn more efficiently, to what extent might they supplant the supervisor by analysing the coaching conversation, critiquing the approach and showing the coach the link between their interventions and the client's reactions? We can predict a scenario, where both coaches and supervisors bring their AIs to a supervision session, with the AIs communicating with each other in the background and feeding prompts to their respective partners. The question then arises: 'Who is leading the conversation – the coach and supervisor or their AIs?'

Supervision for working with children

One of the fastest growing areas of coaching is in secondary education. While, in theory, effective coaching requires a level of socio-emotional and cognitive maturity associated with adulthood, in practice it appears that children in their teens (and sometimes younger) can pick up the coaching mindset more rapidly than adults. One of us is on a mission to train 5 million school age coaches over a five-year period, across the world. The impact of child coaches is perceived to be partly related to the fact that children are typically influenced by their peers. Longer term, learning these skills and behaviours early may help them have more purposeful, successful careers – and save employers from having to 're-educate' junior managers, who have learned traditional command and control leadership styles. Supervision for these young coaches is typically a form of pastoral oversight from teachers, whose own coaching skills may be limited. How do we provide supervision in this context, given that the relative immaturity of the coaches and coachees raises a whole raft of new formative, normative and restorative challenges?

What is problematic? What requires attention and further research?

Issues and 'taboo' topics in supervision

The noticeably growing uptake of supervision is a positive feature of our time, but, unfortunately, any positive movement may be accompanied by new challenges. For example, as supervision is now a pre-requisite for accreditation as a coach with the main professional bodies, some coaches take supervision only reluctantly and do not use it in full measure. For example, there has been a growth in the number of 'everything-is-fine' coaches coming to supervision (Bachkirova 2019). These are coaches who present as very happy with their practice, with little or nothing to bring to supervision. Apart from the number of psychological explanations of this phenomenon, there is also a structural one: if the supervisor is the one to provide an all-important reference to the coach, this creates a natural reluctance in the coach to be completely open about their shortcomings. The other side of this situation is a 'taboo' topic that the supervisor would rather not face. If they believe that the coach is not able to perform to the standards they should vouch for, they may be very reluctant to bring such news to the coach. Supervisors can be seen to use all the explanations in the world to avoid the fact that some sort of evaluation is a part of their role.

There are a number of other topics that are not often on the supervision table because of reticence on the part of the coach, the supervisor or both of them. These topics include becoming stale, losing enthusiasm in the work they do, not believing in the client, feeling disillusioned and emotionally drained. These are just some examples of topics that are often avoided because of the shame and fear of being judged as they do not conform to the ideal image of practitioner in our field as someone devoted to the job and full of energy.

A topic that has become unusually challenging, considering the generally well-developed experience of coaches and supervisors in issues of diversity, is a frank conversation about attitudes to racial difference and their effect on coaching and supervisory relationships. It is becoming increasingly clear that a 'trained' way to respond to the challenges associated with race is often just a platitude. Training programmes need to openly discuss these difficult issues and taboo topics and consider the consequences of avoiding them in a coaching and supervisory relationship.

Impact of supervision

Although it is pleasing to report that a growing number of studies demonstrate that coaching supervision makes a difference, there is a great need for further research. In a recent systematic literature review on coaching supervision (Bachkirova et al. 2020), the benefits of supervision were identified in 13 empirical studies. While this may look like a very small number, in the light of the early stage of the discipline's development, and the complexity of empirical research on supervision, we still have good reason to celebrate. It is important, though, to be wary of overestimating the *effectiveness* of supervision when what has been measured is *perceived value* or 'benefit'. Because the *effect* of supervision is not once or twice but three times removed from the work-related outcomes of coaching, there are immense practical difficulties of designing a study that can demonstrate the effectiveness of supervision using traditional quantitative designs. And that is before considering that the conceptualization of the effectiveness of supervision is still very much work in progress. Nonetheless, the results of these 13 studies, most of which were conducted quite recently, are offering hope that evidence of the impact of coaching supervision might be forthcoming.

Five of these studies use approaches that quantify data in their methodology, while eight papers reported on the use of qualitative methodologies. All these studies identified the value of supervision from the perspective of coaches rather than other stakeholders, understandably given the difficulties already mentioned. At the same time, the findings suggest a wide spectrum of benefits of coaching supervision in relation to all three main functions of supervision, for example:

- The restorative function of supervision (Graßmann and Schermuly 2018)
- 'the development of insights and new perspectives' (Grant 2012: 21)
- 'continual growth and development of my practice' (Jepson 2016: 137)
- 'helping maintain the delivery of a good quality coaching particularly in dealing with difficult cases' (Grant 2012: 21)
- The buffer effect on coaches' job satisfaction when they experienced a high amount of work-related mental strain (Müller, Kotte and Möller 2020)
- The opportunity to be challenged and to validate one's practice (e.g. Lawrence and White 2014)
- Promoting continuing learning (e.g. McGivern 2009)
- The development of reflexivity (e.g. Hodge 2016)

- Being part of the community that enables learning and support (e.g. Robson 2016).

We urge aspiring researchers to consider research questions and potential methodologies that are recommended in this systematic literature review (Bachkirova et al. 2020) when they choose the focus and design of their studies.

Overview of the sections of the book

Section 1 Supervision meeting the needs of the field

The purpose of this section is to demonstrate how supervision serves the needs of coaching and mentoring practice. It goes beyond traditional functions of supervision (normative, formative and restorative) by extending them in a much more comprehensive way. Engagement with this section should help coaches and mentors develop their practice by being able to work with the complexity and uncertainty of their work systemically and pluralistically in a reflexive, ethical and professionally rigorous way.

In the very first chapter Paul Lawrence addresses the issue of complexity head on and specifically in the context of organizations, as this is what supervisors need to deal with on a regular basis. Tatiana Bachkirova argues that what follows from the recognition of complexity is *diversity in the ways we work*. This requires that supervisors adopt a pluralistic attitude and the skills for such an approach. The next chapter is on the importance of reflexivity in coaches and supervisors, and Peter Jackson discusses reflexivity as a deep and organic capability of practitioners. This is demonstrated in the next, unusual, chapter in which Robin Shohet provides a fascinating example of high reflexivity working with a focus on both the self of the coach and of the supervisor. The following two chapters take us back from internal to external complexity by focusing on the parameters within which this profession can legitimately function. First, David A. Lane and Michael Cavanagh engage us with a useful framework for understanding ethical issues that supervisors encounter. Then Angela Wright and Sean O'Connor highlight even stricter legal parameters for our work, which at the same time raise many concerns that we, as supervisors, should recognize.

Section 2 Supervision grounded in theory

The purpose of this section is to present different theoretical perspectives that are useful in coaching and mentoring supervision. The chapters allow supervisors to deepen their understanding of their own practice and provide practitioners with a critical insight into the range of practices available. The contributors offer six different, but extensively used perspectives: psychoanalytic by Andrey Rossokhin; Gestalt by Sue Congram; existential by Monica Hanaway; person-centred by Bernard Cooke and Louise Sheppard; transactional analysis by Julie Hay; and organizational psychology by Carmelina Lawton Smith. It is our view as editors that, while supervisors may choose to incorporate one or more of these approaches into their practice, an *understanding* of all of them is essential in choosing and developing the supervisor's own, unique approach. We can argue that effective supervision requires the ability to both be grounded in specific approaches and at the same time pluralistic in awareness of and capacity to draw upon a wider range of approaches.

Section 3 Models and methods of supervision

The purpose of this section is to introduce the reader to a variety of well-established as well as novel models of supervision practice. It also provides readers with insight into practical ideas and approaches of coaching supervision.

The seven-eyed model is popular and effective. It reflects many of the perspectives and issues introduced in Section 1. For this edition Peter Hawkins and Gil Schwenk have updated their chapter to reflect the model's development in recent years. Mike Munro Turner's 'three worlds four territories' model and David Clutterbuck's 'seven conversations' model are also retained and updated from the first edition. Michael Soth, in the first of three new chapters in this section, explores much more deeply the nature of the 'implicit' in the supervision system. Soth discusses the implicit as bodymind, as unconscious and as a parallel process, highlighting the challenges and opportunities that this presents in supervision. Staying with the theme of the 'implicit', Ty Francis's chapter on using constellations in supervision sets out the history of constellation work as well as the principles and qualities of working with constellations. As a capstone to this section, Michelle Lucas explores the process by which we might select our interventions as supervisors. Lucas's framework will help supervisors make sense of what will always be a complex and uncertain process of in-the-moment decision-making.

Section 4 Contexts and practical modalities of supervision

In this section the reader can engage with issues relating to specific contexts and modalities of coaching supervision. It shows the growing range of uses of supervision and demonstrates differences and nuances of supervising in each context. Our great challenge here was selecting a representative sample of contexts from the constantly evolving applications of coaching and mentoring. We could, for example, have incorporated a chapter on supervising in the context of ethical mentoring (coaches and mentors specializing in helping clients work through complex ethical dilemmas) or on the rapidly growing area of return to work coaching and mentoring. We concluded, however, that these and many other applications were not sufficiently mainstream as yet.

The first of these contexts we have chosen to illustrate is group supervision, where Eliat Arram and Coreene Archer present a Tavistock perspective. Peer supervision – explored by Tammy Turner, Michelle Lucas and Carol Whitaker – is gaining increasing traction as a low-cost alternative to supervision by a trained professional supervisor. Alison Hodge provides an overview of team coaching, where the complexity of the coaching role requires a corresponding expansion of the supervisor's ability to work with complex systems. This theme of complexity is continued in chapters on supervising organizational consultants by David Birch and Erik de Haan, and on supervising in organizational transformation by Michel Moral and Florence Lamy. Christine K. Champion, Alison Maxwell and Kate Pinder take us into the fast-growing area of supervising internal coaches.

Lis Merrick and Paul Stokes remind us that supervision is of equal value to mentors as to coaches. Lastly, Eve Turner and Damian Goldvarg investigate the implications and practicalities of the remarkable rapid shift from in-person supervision to virtual supervision as the dominant medium.

Finally, more about research

We hope that this book can inspire researchers and practitioners interested in research, to take on an important task of developing the knowledge base of coaching and mentoring supervision. To translate this inspiration into tangible research projects we, and the authors of this book, provide some questions and ideas for further research. This is just a selection of questions of a cross-sectional and meta-perspectival nature; questions with a more specific focus on individual topics can be found in the respective chapters.

- What are the essential elements of the supervision process that can allow a definition of supervision practice on the basis of empirical investigation?
- What is the relationship between different functions/process elements of supervision?
- What process elements of coaching supervision are associated with a higher value of coaching supervision for coaches and other stakeholders?
- What is the comparative value of receiving supervision in different modalities/ informed by different theoretical traditions?
- In what way are the differences in the delivery of coaching supervision in different cultural contexts manifested?
- What are the reasons for not undertaking coaching supervision?
- What are the challenges that coaching supervisors face?
- What are the typical challenges that coaches bring for supervision and what topics are avoided?

Enjoy your reading!

Tatiana, Peter and David

References

Bachkirova, T. (2019) *Supervising 'Everything Is Fine' Coaches*. Presentation at the 8th International Conference on Coaching Supervision, 11 May 2019, Oxford Brookes University, Oxford.

Bachkirova, T., Jackson, P., Hennig, C. et al. (2020) Supervision in coaching: systematic literature review, *International Coaching Psychology Review*, 15(2): 31–53.

De Haan, E. (2017) Large scale survey of trust and safety in coaching supervision: some evidence that we are doing it right, *International Coaching Psychology Review*, 12(1): 37–48.

Grant, A. (2012) Australian coaches' view on coaching supervision: a study with implications for Australian coach education, training and practice, *International Journal of Evidence Based Coaching and Mentoring*, 10(2): 17–33.

Graßmann, C. and Schermuly, C. (2018) The role of neuroticism and supervision in the relationship between negative effects for clients and novice coaches, *Coaching: An International Journal of Theory, Research and Practice*, 11(1): 74–88.

Hawkins, P. and Turner, E. (2017) The rise of coaching supervision 2006–2014, *Coaching: An International Journal of Theory, Research and Practice*, 10(2): 99–101.

Hodge, A. (2016) The value of coaching supervision as a developmental process: contribution to continued professional and personal well-being for executive coaches, *International Journal of Evidence Based Coaching and Mentoring*, 14(2): 87–106.

Hodge, A. and Clutterbuck, D. (2019) Supervising team coaches: Working with complexity at a distance, in D. Clutterbuck, J. Gannon, S. Hayes et al. (eds) *The Practitioner's Handbook of Team Coaching*. London: Routledge.

Jepson, Z. (2016) An investigation and analysis of the continuous professional development and coaching supervision needs of newly qualified and experienced coaches: a small-scale practitioner-based study, *Coaching: An International Journal of Theory, Research and Practice*, 9(2): 129–142.

Lawrence, P. and White, A. (2014) What is coaching supervision and is it important? *Coaching: An International Journal of Theory, Research and Practice*, 7(1): 39–55.

McGivern, L. (2009) Continuous professional development and avoiding the vanity trap: an exploration of coaches' lived experiences of supervision, *International Journal of Evidence Based Coaching and Mentoring*, Special Issue 3: 22–37.

Müller, A.A., Kotte, S. and Möller, H. (2020) Coach and no regrets about it: on the life satisfaction, work-related mental strain, and use of supervision of workplace coaches, *Coaching: An International Journal of Theory, Research and Practice*, 13(1): 16–29.

Robson, M. (2016) An ethnographic study of the introduction of internal supervisors to an internal coaching scheme, *International Journal of Evidence Based Coaching and Mentoring*, 14(2): 106–122.

Section 1

Supervision meeting the needs of the field

1 Supervision for working systemically

Paul Lawrence

Introduction

> The world as we have created it is a process of our thinking. It cannot be changed without changing our thinking.
>
> Albert Einstein

As the world continues to encounter complexity and crisis, so we are increasingly urged to think more 'systemically'. Coaches and coach supervisors must think more systemically because they work with leaders, those we perceive to have a particular responsibility for addressing complex issues. This presents a challenge for the coach supervision community. Fifteen years ago, Hawkins and Smith (2006) suggested that 'the most difficult new skill that supervision requires is what we call the helicopter ability' (p. 147). As we are called upon to be more 'systemic', this seems to be what is meant; a capacity to think more holistically. The most recent version of the seven-eyed model, for example, prompts coach and supervisor to think beyond the two-way relationship between coach and coachee, to include the role of supervisor and various dimensions of the wider 'system', including stakeholders, society and culture, and the 'ecological context' (Hawkins and Turner 2020).

The first purpose of this chapter is to enable coach supervisors to recognize how much more complex and demanding is the call to think systemically. Frameworks such as the seven-eyed model are useful, but mostly 'theory-neutral'. Accordingly, Hawkins (2011) suggests we all take responsibility for developing our own personal 'epistemologies' (or knowledge base). This is important, because if we do not challenge the way that we think, we remain unaware of the limitations of that thinking, as do the coaches we supervise and their clients. Coaches cannot help leaders think differently without accessing new ways of thinking themselves, and coach supervisors have an important role to play in facilitating that process. The second purpose of this chapter, therefore, is to provide a roadmap for coach supervisors interested in building their own personal knowledge base as it applies to systems thinking. To further build that knowledge base is an ongoing task.

There are many different systems theories offering quite different perspectives on how organizations-as-systems operate. It is outside the scope of this chapter to present a comprehensive account of the history of systems thinking. Instead, the chapter is structured around five broad categories of theory. Key distinctions between the five categories are highlighted in terms of theory and the practice of supervision. The focus is primarily on individual supervision, although a brief commentary on the supervision of team coaches is provided at the end.

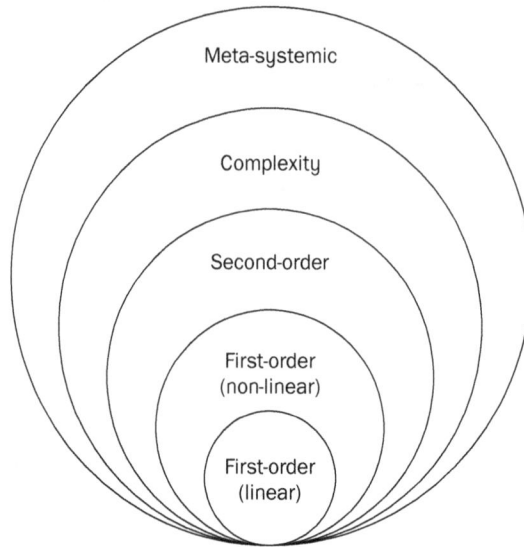

Figure 1.1 From *Coaching Systemically. Five Ways of Thinking About Systems* by Paul Lawrence (Routledge 2021)

Figure 1.1 shows five different ways of thinking about systems. In reviewing these five categories, the reader is invited to consider not 'which category am I?' but instead, 'which ways of thinking do I have access to?' These five categories are just one way of simplifying an immensely deep, rich and complex literature. As you read through the chapter, I would encourage you to define your own philosophy and to refine that philosophy over time as you continue to explore for yourself what it means to be a 'systemic' supervisor.

Five ways of thinking about systems

First-order (linear) thinking

The 'first-order (linear)' perspective on organizations is based on the notion of organization-as-machine. The notion of organization-as-machine became popular in the early twentieth century with the work of Frederick Winslow Taylor, pioneer of Scientific Management (Morgan 2006; Taylor 1911). Taylor was an engineer who observed people engage in manual work, and redesigned tasks to be more efficient. Scientific Management principles include the idea that responsibility for the organization of work sits best with the manager, not the worker. The manager designs roles, trains people to perform those roles, and monitors performance to ensure workers perform their roles correctly. Twenty years later, Elton Mayo, at the Hawthorne Plant of the Western Electric Company in Chicago, found that working groups performed at their best when their members were motivated (Mayo 1933; Morgan 2006). The task of the manager thus became binary. The manager was now responsible not only for designing efficient tasks but also for ensuring that the people performing those tasks were motivated. This binary scoping of the leader's role is still popular today, such as definitions of leadership based upon the individual leader's ability to 'get the job done' and 'bring people on the journey'.

Norbert Wiener's early theories of cybernetics are consistent with the idea of organization-as-machine (Morgan 2006; Stacey and Mowles 2016; Wiener 1961). Cybernetics emphasizes the importance of negative feedback loops in guiding intelligent behaviour. Cybernetic principles are reflected in traditional goal theory. The coachee sets a goal and an action plan. She implements the action plan and seeks feedback from others. Based on the feedback received, she makes changes to her action plan and keeps doing so until the goal is achieved. It is implicitly assumed that there is a simple linear relationship between input and output.

These are three slants on the idea of organization as machine. The leader is the custodian of the machine and the coach's role is to accompany the leader in stepping back to diagnose the 'system' and make any changes required to ensure smooth functioning of the machine. People perform two roles in the first-order system. Most people are passive, required to follow the rules if the system is to operate as intended. Leaders, however, also stand outside the system and tweak its design. The coach is external to the system: a neutral observer. The only change that emerges from within the system is entropic, as people slowly depart from the detailed expectations of their roles. Purposeful change is initiated by leadership. Maintaining equilibrium is an objective and conflict is seen as a threat to stability and efficiency. A coach supervisor thinking through this lens will, in effect, co-create this linear approach to addressing issues.

Box 1.1 Case illustration

Angela comes to supervision to talk with David about Andy, her coachee. Andy says he lacks confidence. He received feedback from senior management saying he needs to speak up more in meetings. He needs to demonstrate his ability to engage and influence. If he doesn't succeed in changing his behaviour, then he will find it hard to advance further in the organization. Angela outlines the strategy that she and Andy came up with to address the issue. Andy has ring-fenced 20 minutes before every team meeting to calm himself down and prepare himself to make sure he always says something within the first 10 minutes. In coming up with this strategy, Angela and Andy have made an implicit assumption; that the extent to which senior management perceive Andy to be influential is directly related to how often he speaks up. This strategy might work, in which case the assumption is practically valid. But it may not work, in which case Angela and Andy can either pursue further linear solutions, or else choose to think differently about what might be going on.

First-order (non-linear) thinking

This second perspective is still based on the idea of organization-as-machine, but the relationship between component parts is no longer assumed to be simple and linear. Senge et al. (1994) identified five disciplines required by a learning organization, one of which was systems thinking. Systems thinking, thus defined, looks beyond simple cause and effect. The non-linear practitioner looks for archetypal patterns that are a consequence of positive feedback and causal loops. A causal loop exists when inputs and outputs depend on each other.

A coach supervisor thinking through this lens will recognize a temptation to move too quickly to deciding what is going on in any given scenario. She will, over time, come to recognize archetypal patterns of more complex cause and effect that typically show up in organizational settings.

Box 1.2

Talking further, Angela and Andy work out that when Andy goes to meetings and doesn't speak up, Susan, his line manager, gets frustrated. She glares at Andy, which further inhibits him from speaking up. This leads Susan to become even more frustrated, and she glares even harder. Susan's level of frustration with Andy doesn't grow steadily. For a while, she is tolerant of Andy's behaviour, but once he hasn't spoken for more than 10 minutes, she may explode. This catches Andy by surprise, shocking him into further silence. Angela and David realize they need to think about the scenario more deeply. Andy may need to consider the way he responds to Susan's frustration and learn to look for early warning signals of her becoming frustrated. As supervisor, David slows things down, giving Angela time to think more deeply about Andy's predicament.

Second-order thinking

In contemplating the limitations of conventional thinking, Bateson was impressed by the work of Warren McCulloch, who demonstrated that what the frog sees is limited by the design of its optic system (Kobayashi 1988). A frog sees what moves. If a thing doesn't move, the frog doesn't see it. This discovery captured neatly for Bateson the essence of the issue; Man is no different to the frog, incapable of experiencing reality directly. Yet Man assumes his perception of events to be real. This is one of three key ideas underpinning Soft Systems Methodology (Checkland 1994, 2000, 2012; Checkland and Haynes 1994). Checkland believed that attempts to identify general rules that could be mathematically modelled and applied to all systems fail because the world is too 'complex, problematical and mysterious' for any one of us to understand, not least because we are incapable of objective analysis.

A coach supervisor thinking through this lens still regards the organization as a real system but is not concerned with conducting a definitive analysis as to how the system works because she recognizes that organizations are too complex for us to understand in any 'real' sense. The supervisor can, nevertheless, work with the coach to think about how the system *might* be working, leveraging multiple perspectives through the construction of a collective perspective. The supervisor is compelled to enquire how others view the world. She will be interested in how others create their versions of reality, including the coach, the coachee and other players in the system. Indeed, she will be constantly curious as to her own mental modelling and how that may impact her interpretation of the coach's story and her response to it.

Box 1.3

Angela and David think about Andy's predicament differently. Angela recognizes she is thinking about Andy's issue through quite a solution-focused lens. David confesses that he is most attracted to thinking about Andy's predicament through a psychological lens, exploring the role of parents and other authority figures in Andy's response to senior leaders, especially Susan. The two of them deliberately discuss what might be going on through various modalities. Between them they construct a theory with elements of family systems and solutions-focused thinking that Angela finds useful. Angela wonders aloud if she might start attending some of David's group supervision sessions, curious as to what other coaches might think.

Complexity thinking

There are many complexity theories (Stacey and Mowles 2016), of which Complex Adaptive Systems (CAS) theory has been most discussed in the context of coaching (e.g. Cavanagh 2006; Cavanagh and Lane 2012). Theories of CAS depict the system as comprising multiple agents. Each of these agents behaves according to its own rules, rules that determine its response to the behaviour of other agents. Change is constantly emerging from multiple loci across an organization. To understand what is happening at an organizational level therefore requires an exploration of what is happening at the local level. Changes at the local level interact to create organizational patterns of change that may appear random. These organizational patterns impact local patterns and a complex dynamic pattern of behaviours is created. If this is how change works, then the leader can influence change, as can anyone else, but she cannot control change. The leader cannot step outside the system to plot an intervention, for that very plotting is part of the overall pattern. Other people are having conversations at the same time and all these different local interactions constitute the system.

Behavioural patterns can flip as the system falls under the influence of different 'attractors'. I may have experienced an example of this during the COVID-19 crisis. I was working with an organization, one of whose leaders publicly declared how impressed he was that people in different divisions were working together. He said that the organization had been trying for years to get people to work across silos and he was delighted that those silos had finally been broken down. From a complexity perspective, however, this may have been the flipping of a system that may well flip back once the crisis is over. Pre-COVID-19, various factors in the system drew people to behaving in the way that they did, focusing on the achievement of relatively narrow objectives. During COVID-19, people found they simply couldn't achieve their goals without working with others. The pattern flipped. If the system reverts to old policy and process after COVID-19, then we might expect to see patterns of behaviour flip back as well.

Through the complexity lens, the organization is still a system, with subsystems and boundaries, but this is a system that cannot be directed or controlled. Conversations between coach and leader, or coach and executive team, are just examples of conversations happening inside the system. There are many other local conversations happening across the organization at the same time, and each plays a role in the emergence of new patterns of behaviour. The coach is as much an active co-creator of change as anyone else. The idea that positional power is absolute is lost. The leader cannot control behaviours in the system. The leader can, however, influence. She can travel the system to engage in conversation with people in different parts of the system and what she says and does *will* influence what happens next. But what happens next is still, to a great extent, unpredictable.

The coach supervisor recognizes emergent properties of change. Change is a social phenomenon that can be influenced, but not controlled. Leaders are therefore not autonomous. Leaders can influence through their participation in relationships, but they cannot determine outcomes without the involvement of others. Positional power is still relevant, but multiple other forms of power exist as well.

Box 1.4

Angela recognizes how important it is to understand who else Andy is talking to in making sense of his dilemma. She thinks to suggest to Andy that she might join him in some of those conversations, with his line manager for example, colleagues and direct reports. She becomes interested in conversations taking place at senior management level. This idea that Andy is quiet and lacks influencing skills – how did this story emerge and how is it being perpetuated? How might Andy gain greater visibility of these conversations, and how might he seek to influence the ongoing evolution of those conversations? What is it about the functioning of the organization as a whole that means Andy's behaviour is being perceived in this way? How else might his behaviour be perceived were other aspects of the system to change? David supports Angela in reflecting upon Andy's predicament through this lens and asks questions to help her find new insight.

Meta-systemic thinking

Most versions of complexity thinking focus on the behaviour of individual agents, operating in local environments or subsystems. Mathematicians seek to model the functioning of complex systems by assigning rules to individual agents and observing the outcome of agent interactions. But people do not follow simple rules. People are conscious, emotional and spontaneous, capable themselves of observing the pattern of interactions within which they are operating and responding accordingly. The choices people make are often neither logical nor obvious, even to themselves. Because the way people behave cannot be reliably modelled, the idea of 'organization-as-system' may not always be useful. Stacey and Mowles (2016: 287) suggest: 'Organisations are not things at all, let alone living things. They are processes of communication and joint action. Communication and joint action as such are not alive. It is the bodies communicating and interacting that are alive.'

Stacey and Mowles (2016) suggest it is more useful to focus on the responsive manner in which humans interact with each other. Notions of autonomy and independence are seen ultimately as fictions. If people in an organization are interdependent, then no one person can choose what happens to all of them and action emerges from un-modellable human interaction. As Stacey (2012b: 91–95) says, with reference to leadership: 'All anyone can ever do, no matter how powerful, is engage intentionally, and as skilfully as possible, in local interaction.'

Stacey's theory of Complex Responsive Processes positions change as emerging from social interaction. He compares and contrasts his theory of Complex Responsive Processes with other ways of thinking and concludes that the complex responsive perspective is most useful. However, I would argue, all systemic perspectives can be useful. If we agree with Bateson that Man is largely incapable of understanding the complexity of the world (Kobayashi 1988), then we must recognize the value of simple frameworks and schemas that allow us to make sense of our environment. All the ways of thinking we have covered in this chapter may be viewed as efforts to simplify that which is complex. What is important is to recognize that we are simplifying and to hold that simplification as hypotheses. For these reasons I have not called this way of thinking 'complex responsive'. The meta-systemic perspective owes much to Stacey's theories *and* recognizes the value of thinking systemically. At the same time, it recognizes that, in responding to each other, people are usually responding through the lens of one or other ways of thinking systemically.

The meta-systemic supervisor, therefore, is happy to talk about organization-as-system, and about boundaries and subsystems, at the same time calling out these notions as metaphor when it feels useful to do so. For example, it could be useful if the supervisor feels that a systemic narrative is limiting the coach's exploration of interactions and relationships taking place within the broader social network. In exploring the broader social network, the meta-systemic way of thinking compels the supervisor to notice power dynamics. First- and second-order ways of thinking, in particular, may lead to the over-privileging of positional power. The supervisor, working with this perspective in mind, is curious as to the functioning of power dynamics, a field of enquiry some coaches may disdain in the name of avoiding getting involved in 'politics'. Morgan (2006) suggests it is a shame that so many people see politics as dysfunctional. The study of politics through the meta lens, is the study of power, and how different forms of power direct patterns of conversation.

The coach supervisor *thinking* through a meta-systemic lens may be open to working with a wide variety of existing tools and techniques. The supervisor may feel no need to devise a playbook of techniques specific to this way of thinking. To illustrate the point, consider as an example John Whittington's (2012) book *Systemic Coaching & Constellations*. In the book Whittington defines systemic coaching as 'that which acknowledges, illuminates and releases the system dynamics so that each element can function with ease. It is coaching that prioritises the system' (2012: 35). He writes about the limitations of rational thinking and linear thinking. A constellation, he suggests, depicts 'natural orders'; 'organizing principles' or forces that sustain systems. The first stage of a constellation is 'designed to support the client to stand in the truth of the current situation . . .' (p. 14). This way of thinking about systems would appear to be closest to second-order thinking. It isn't first-order linear because he says that causal relationships are more complex. It does not sound like first-order non-linear because he says that the functioning of the system cannot be understood only through a rational lens. The system may be mysterious, but it is real, sustained by a finite number of hidden forces, time, place and exchange. The creation of a constellation is a social process, in that multiple perspectives are engaged in service of finding the 'truth'. Let us suppose, only in service of illustrating a point, that the underlying philosophy behind Whittington's work is second-order. This does not mean that others cannot derive equal value from a process that entails people mapping their 'system' spatially. The coach supervisor may not go about the process in precisely the way that Whittington suggests, but can, nevertheless, usefully apply the processes he has developed, mapping out a social network in a way that yields useful insights for the coach.

Stacey (2012a) suggests that an important role of the coach is to 'explore how coach and client are together thinking about how they are thinking'. In a similar

---

Box 1.5

Angela and David recognize that their previous conversation may have overemphasized relationships within the organization. The stories Andy tells about himself and what is likely to happen if he speaks more in meetings, is co-created not only with others in the organization, but with family, friends, social media and society. The story about Andy constructed by senior leaders is influenced again by the functioning of social networks spreading far beyond the boundaries of the organization. David helps Angela to access this perspective by asking questions about the functioning of the broader network. He encourages her to slow down, to think aloud and explore not only Andy's dilemma, but how she and Andy are thinking about that dilemma.

way, the coach supervisor, thinking through the meta lens, may see their primary role as being to explore how supervisor, coach and client are all thinking about how they are thinking.

Summary

Table 1.1 summarizes the five ways of thinking in terms of example theories, core beliefs and practice. Again, in reviewing these five categories the coach supervisor is not being encouraged to consider 'which category am I?' Rather, you are invited to consider what ways of thinking you think you have access to, and what ways of thinking appear to be dominant by the coach and the people with whom you work. This table is also designed to help supervisors to explore if they can contribute more by considering their coach's issues through each of the five lenses.

A note on supervising team coaches

This chapter has focused mainly on supervising coaches working with individuals, but the implications for supervisors working with team coaches are just as significant. Viewed through a first-order lens, an effective team is a group of people with clearly defined roles. The team coach may focus primarily on clarification of purpose, intentions and roles. Through a second-order lens, the supervisor's attention is drawn to interactions between team members. Team dynamics are construed in terms of the coming together of different mental models, and the co-creation of a frame through which the team *collectively* makes sense of events. Through a complexity lens, the coach supervisor will be drawn toward the co-creation of intention. To understand the co-creation of intention again requires an understanding of team dynamics. From a meta-perspective there is no such thing as a team, and no real boundaries between team members and those outside the team. Whoever the coach is working with, she is working with people located in a complex social network, the properties of which neither she nor the people being coached will ever completely understand. The team coach works with whoever is in the room, on whatever that group wants to work on in the moment. These may all be useful ways of thinking and useful ways to work with teams, but the supervisor who has access to more ways of thinking may be most useful across different contexts and domains.

Guidance for further learning and research

Cavanagh and Lane (2012) acknowledge that the complexity perspective has significant implications for coaching research. While not dismissing the value of quantitative research methodologies, they point out that quantitative approaches implicitly assume relatively simple relationships between cause and effect, relationships that can be assumed to endure over time. It would appear paradoxical to leverage research approaches based on first-order principles to further study second-order and complexity perspectives and the functioning of complex responsive processes as defined by Stacey and Mowles (2016). Future research is therefore likely to at least include qualitative methodologies. The field of enquiry will be broad ranging, including not only coaching and coaching supervision specifically

Table 1.1 Five ways of thinking in terms of example theories, core beliefs and practice

	Ways of thinking				
	First-order (linear)	First-order (non-linear)	Second-order	Complexity	Meta-systemic
Theories (examples)	Scientific management (Taylor 1911) Management theory (Mayo 1933) Cybernetics (Wiener 1961)	Systems Dynamics (Senge et al. 1994)	Soft Systems Methodology (Checkland 1994)	Chaos theory Complex Adaptive Systems (various, e.g. Gell-Man 1994)	Complex Responsive Processes (Stacey 2012b)
Beliefs	The organization is a system Cause and effect are simple and linear The leader has control	The organization is a system Cause and effect can be hard to discern The leader has control	The organization is a system Functioning of the system is dark and mysterious Perception is subjective The leader has control	The organization is a system There is order in chaos Change emerges from local interaction, and from the interface between local interaction and broad patterns Everyone is a player in the system The leader cannot control but does influence	Organizations are not things and are therefore not systems Meaning-making is social 'All one can ever do . . . is engage intentionally, and as skilfully as possible, in local interaction'
Practice	Regard coach and coachee as external to the system Look for simple, linear cause and effect Focus on the impact of individuals	Regard coach and coachee as external to the system Look for archetypal patterns of complex cause and effect Focus on the impact of individuals	Regard coach and coachee as external to the system Explore multiple perspectives Explore mental models Focus on the impact of individuals	Recognize supervisor, coach and coachee as players in the system Explore the emergence of local meaning and behaviours Explore the relationship between what's happening at the local level and what's happening at the broader, organizational level Explore power dynamics	Recognize supervisor, coach and coachee as participants in social networks Explore the emergence of meaning through social interaction Explore power dynamics Look beyond the specific 'system'

but also more broadly how people think, how systems work, and how people collectively behave and respond to their environments. Research will also study implications for coach training and education and the role and the most useful function of coaching associations.

In closing this chapter, I leave you with four questions. These questions are framed with reference to the three Ps of supervision and coaching (Philosophy, Purpose and Practice) (Jackson and Bachkirova 2019). This is a reflective framework that encourages us to question which philosophies guide our practice and how those philosophies connect to our purpose for supervision and manifest in the practices we deploy.

Questions for reflection

- Which systems theories most resonate with you?
- With reference to those philosophies, why do you supervise?
- What does your approach to supervision look like through each of the five lenses?
- What will you do to further refine your philosophy and practice?

Further sources

Stacey, R.D. and Mowles, C. (2016) *Strategic Management and Organisational Dynamics*, 7th edn. Harlow, UK: Pearson. The first edition of this book was published in 1993. The most recent version of the book charts systemic ways of thinking in great detail, beginning with the origins of systems thinking during the Scientific Revolution, through first-order, second-order and complexity ways of thinking, through to complex responsive processing.

Stacey, R. (2012a) *Tools and Techniques of leadership and Management. Meeting the Challenge of Complexity.* Abingdon: Routledge. This much shorter book is a great introduction to Stacey's work. Of particular interest is the lengthy appendix that charts the evolution of his thinking over time, including the development and subsequent disavowal of the well-known Stacey Diagram.

Cavanagh, M. and Lane, D. (2012) Coaching psychology coming of age: the challenges we face in the messy world of complexity, *International Coaching Psychology Review*, 7(1): 75–90. Cavanagh and Lane cite the Stacey Diagram in differentiating between three types of system: simple, complex and chaotic. Stacey himself, as well as Bachkirova, Atkins, Drake, Hodge, Kuhn, Allan and Spence all then critique the article, in the process highlighting important theoretical and practical issues the reflective coach will find of interest.

References

Cavanagh, M. (2006) Coaching from a systemic perspective: a complex adaptive conversation, in D.R. Stober and A.M. Grant (eds), *Evidence Based Coaching Handbook: Putting Best Practices to Work for Your Clients.* Englewood Cliffs, NJ: John Wiley & Sons.

Cavanagh, M. and Lane, D. (2012) Coaching psychology coming of age: the challenges we face in the messy world of complexity, *International Coaching Psychology Review*, 7(1): 75–90.

Checkland, P. (1994) Systems theory and management thinking, *The American Behavioral Scientist*, 38(1): 756–791.

Checkland, P. (2000) Soft systems methodology: a thirty year retrospective, *Systems Research and Behavioral Science*, 17(suppl. 1): S11–S58.

Checkland, P. (2012) Four conditions for serious systems, *Systems Research and Behavioral Science*, 29: 465–469.

Checkland, P. and Haynes, M. (1994) Varieties of systems thinking: the case of soft systems methodology, *Systems Dynamics Review*, 10(2/3): 189–197.

Gell-Man, M. (1994) *The Quark and the Jaguar*. New York: Freeman Press.

Hawkins, P. (2011) Systemic approaches to supervision, in T. Bachkirova, P. Jackson, and D. Clutterbuck (eds) *Coaching and Mentoring Supervision: Theory and Practice*. Maidenhead: Open University Press.

Hawkins, P. and Smith, N. (2006) *Coaching, Mentoring and Organizational Consultancy*. Maidenhead: Open University Press.

Hawkins, P. and Turner, E. (2020) *Systemic Coaching: Delivering Value Beyond the Individual*. London: Routledge.

Jackson, P. and Bachkirova, T. (2019) The 3 Ps of supervision and coaching: philosophy, purpose and process, in E. Turner and S. Palmer (eds) *The Heart of Coaching Supervision*. Abingdon: Routledge.

Kobayashi, V.N. (1988) The self-reflexive mind: the life's work of Gregory Bateson, *International Journal of Qualitative Studies in Education*, 1(4): 347–359.

Mayo, E. (1933) *The Human Problems of an Industrial Civilisation*. New York: Macmillan.

Morgan, G. (2006) *Images of Organization*. Thousand Oaks, CA: Sage.

Senge, P.M., Kleiner, A., Roberts, C. et al. (1994) *The Fifth Discipline Fieldbook*. New York: Doubleday.

Stacey, R. (2012a) *Tools and Techniques of Leadership and Management: Meeting the Challenge of Complexity*. Abingdon: Routledge.

Stacey, R. (2012b) Comment on debate article: Coaching psychology coming of age: the challenges we face in the messy world of complexity, *International Coaching Psychology Review*, 7(1): 91–95.

Stacey, R.D. and Mowles, C. (2016) *Strategic Management and Organisational Dynamics*, 7th ed. Harlow: Pearson.

Taylor, F.W. (1911) *Principles of Scientific Management*. New York: Harper & Row.

Whittington, J. (2012) *Systemic Coaching & Constellations: An Introduction to the Principles, Practices and Application*. London: Kogan Page.

Wiener, F.W. (1961) *Cybernetics*. Cambridge, MA: MIT Press.

2 Supervision for working pluralistically

Tatiana Bachkirova

Introduction

The purpose of this chapter is to explore the importance of the pluralistic attitude in the practice of coaching supervision and the role of supervisors in developing pluralistic thinking of coaches. Pluralism is a philosophical perspective that positively values multiplicity in the world and in the ways we can know the world (Berlin 1953/1993; Novis-Deutsch 2018). In the context of this chapter, pluralism is considered in relation to multiplicity in individual differences, which requires a capacity for significant open-mindedness. Such open-mindedness is the result of recognizing complexity in the world and, therefore, accepting diversity and difference in all their forms.

In this context, pluralism is different from multiculturism, which is seen as an 'ideology of supporting cultural heterogeneity' (van de Vijver et al. 2008). Multiculturalism is often associated with recognizing and defending the rights of different social sub-groups that are perceived of as deviating from the norms of the majority. The divergence of these groups usually refers to collective identities such as race, age, sexual orientation, etc. and the importance of supporting these groups arises from the principles of equality and inclusion for all human beings regardless of their cultural differences. Notwithstanding the important role of this ethical commitment, pluralism, as such, is not limited to culture and ethnic diversity (Novis-Deutsch 2018). Pluralism is about recognizing differences in all shapes and forms as a reflection of the complexity of human nature being part of the complexity of the world. For example, the diversity of individuals can be recognized in terms of their psychological differences in beliefs, attitudes, learning styles, thinking strategies, motivations, drives, etc.

I believe that coaching supervision is a practice that cannot be conceived without acknowledging and engaging with multiplicity and complexity. This is not only about complexity of the cases that coaches bring to supervision; it is about multiplicity in terms of the individual differences of coaches who use supervision. Such differences include their level of experience and knowledge, their drives and values, and the ways they learn and accept feedback, to mention just a few. Individual differences in coaches are also amplified by the diversity of coaching genres. This implies that supervisors should be able to support coaches in ways that are appropriate to their individual characteristics. This is also important because the supervisors' explicit pluralism in supervision can model for coaches how they can engage with diversity in their clients. It could be argued that the development of pluralistic attitudes and thinking of coaches is an important part of the developmental function of coaching supervision. However, the development and application of pluralism in the supervisory context is not easy.

It is obvious that individuals can differ in many ways. In this chapter I introduce three features or dimensions of individual differences that are, in my view, particularly important in the context of supervision and that call on supervisors to work pluralistically:

- Theoretical perspective dimension (approach to practice and its underpinning theories)
- Psychological dimension (attitudes, drives and personality characteristics)
- Developmental dimension (stages of adult development).

Engagement with each of these dimensions involves specific challenges for coaching supervisors. Each section on dimensions includes 'ideas from research' and 'ideas for practice'. More general difficulties in the development of pluralistic thinking are then explored with suggestions for further learning.

Theoretical perspective dimension

This dimension of individual difference is about multiplicity in the way coaches conceive and structure their approach to practice. Coaches work with a view of what they want to achieve in their work. They have beliefs about why this purpose is important and accumulate tools/skills that allow them to achieve the results they want. All these elements constitute a model of their practice. We call these elements the 3Ps (Philosophy, Purpose and Process) of our practice (Bachkirova 2016; Jackson and Bachkirova 2019). The alignment of all 3Ps in coaches' professional actions can be provided by one or more theoretical perspectives that have been developed within different schools of knowledge and, when fully developed, include the following features:

- Main concepts and assumptions about human nature
- Conditions for change/development
- Tasks and goals
- Methods and techniques
- Essential processes/dynamics
- Pitfalls and limitations.

In coaching there are a number of theories that play a role in supporting a coherent approach to practice (Gestalt, solution-focused approach, adult development, etc.) (Cox et al. 2018). Some of them share key assumptions and can be seen as forming families of theories (e.g. humanistic). Some of them are compatible and some are not. The theories affect the work of supervisors in the same way as they do the work of coaches.

Hopefully, many coaches are aware what theories underpin their practice and can clearly formulate their three Ps if necessary. Sometimes coaches are not aware of their theories, which does not mean that their practice is atheoretical. It means that the assumptions they hold are not articulated and, therefore, most likely, not examined. Some coaches are able to indicate some of the theories that influence their practice, but claim that their approach is eclectic, as they 'use' multiple theories. This is not in itself a problem – there is no single theory or coaching modality that can offer optimum efficacy. However, complacency in this regard, with no attempt to create a coherent integration of theories, might indicate that the coach works using a 'trial and error' method that is questionable when calling oneself a professional. This can present quite a challenge should any of these coaches come for supervision expecting a supervisor to make sense of their difficulties and developmental needs. In order to see the level of this challenge please read the short description of an important piece of research in Box 2.1.

Box 2.1 Ideas from research

A study highlighting the role of theoretical frameworks

In his doctoral study, Myers (Myers and Bachkirova 2020) recorded a one-off coaching session by six different coaches with the purpose of exploring what can be observed in these sessions in terms of the process. The recording of each session was then shown to a group of other coaches. So, each coaching session received feedback on the process of coaching from three different standpoints: coach, client and a group of observers. In addition to the descriptive information about the process, all parties were asked to give a narrative view in response to a very open-ended question: 'What stands out for you in this session?'

The results of this study are very challenging for many areas of the coaching industry, including supervision. In a nutshell, they show interesting discrepancies. For example, the descriptions by all three parties of what was happening in the session in terms of the process were not significantly different. However, the narrative views show extreme and disturbing differences. All clients responded to this question in a largely positive way. They all benefited from coaching. All coaches were also reasonably satisfied with their session, mainly because they perceived the value of the session for the client. In contrast, observers tended to coalesce around a generally negative view of the session they observed. The comments varied from the mild: 'session lacked structure' and 'the coach gave unnecessary advice', to very strong: 'the coach colluded with the client' and 'the coach being unprofessional'.

These findings present a serious challenge for assessments of coaching sessions: whose perspectives on the session are more relevant in a case where there is a discrepancy between different standpoints? Professional bodies clearly prioritize the observers' view, which might not be always justified. Coaches themselves tend to rely on the view of their clients, which might also not be sufficiently informative.

Although the study by Myers (Myers and Bachkirova 2020) was not set up in the context of supervision, the implications of its findings for supervisors are important. One of them, relevant to the context of this chapter, is concerned with the fact that observers of these sessions were looking at them through different theoretical lenses. For example, NLP coaches were observing a person-centred coach, or the session by a Gestalt coach was observed by TA coaches. It is not surprising, then, that their assumptions of what is important to achieve and what is a good or not so good piece of work were not in agreement. In fact, in some cases these assumptions could not be more different. This highlights the challenge for supervisors who often work with coaches from different orientations without checking for this and without sharing their own assumptions. This can be a recipe for misunderstanding at best and serious misjudgements at worst.

The theoretical perspective dimension of individual differences creates the need for supervisors to be aware that they may be looking at the coach's practice from a particular perspective. This requires that supervisors examine their own 'lenses' in order to see what influences their contributions and evaluations. It is also important that supervisors are sufficiently informed of other theoretical perspectives, recognize differences between them and anticipate what kind of misunderstandings can arise when they and coaches hold different sets of assumptions. These are good reasons for initiating such a conversation as part of contracting.

Recognition of this dimension of individual differences shows that two main functions of supervision, normative and developmental, become more complex. First of all, it is important to state that it is entirely within the right of coaches to have their model of practice. Therefore, in performing the normative function (contributing to the quality of work and ethical decision-making) the supervisor has to be able to use the coach's lens to help them advance their work. Although there are some widely shared 'good practice' recommendations and clear signs that suggest the need for improving basic competences, these are not the typical issues that are brought to supervision. This simpler task is a domain of *mentoring* – providing support in learning basic competences, as, for example, the ICF (International Coach Federation) advocates. For novice coaches, mentoring might be a useful arrangement, as pointing out simple 'rules' and 'basic skills' will not confuse them unnecessarily. However, *supervision* for both novice and experienced coaches requires a more sophisticated and nuanced approach for addressing the issues that coaches wish to explore. This can only be done when supervisors are aware of how diverse coaches' beliefs and assumptions can be, and are able to recognize and, if necessary, stand back from their own position to help coaches make sense of their predicaments. This is a pluralistic approach to a normative function of supervision.

The pluralistic stance is also important for the developmental function of supervision (facilitating personal and professional development of the coach). When a coach becomes too comfortable working within their original theoretical framework and attached to a particular lens on their work, it might be a good time to consider if their original model may benefit from being expanded. As part of the developmental process, the supervisor may check if the coach is ready to extend their capacity for experimenting with multiple theoretical perspectives. This does not imply that the supervisor would start suggesting different interventions to try with their clients. A new theoretical perspective can be played with when coaches bring their specific issues/themes to explore and make sense of. For example, if a coach's main model of practice is positive psychology and working with strength, a supervisor might ask them to consider what the puzzling situation in coaching may look like if the actions of the client suggest self-deception. Box 2.2 offers some ideas for experimenting with a different lens.

Box 2.2 Ideas for practice

Expanding the range of coaches' theoretical frameworks

Many supervisors know a useful intervention to help the coach to stand back from their session in order to capture a spontaneous and, hopefully, more objective description (Hawkins and Schwenk 2011). The intervention involves variations on this question:

- If you are a fly in the room observing your own session what would you see?

Although the intention behind this intervention is valuable, it is most likely that 'the coach's fly' will see this session from his/her typical lens that comes naturally. In this case, you can extend this intervention for helping the coach to try a different lens by asking:

- What might you see if you were a different fly?

To make this intervention even more interesting and playful you might also choose to ask:

- What might you see if you were a psychodynamically (humanistically or existentially) trained fly?

Psychological dimension

Of the three dimensions explored in this chapter, the psychological dimension of individual difference is probably the most extensively studied in psychology and is widely used in applied disciplines and industries like coaching. There are numerous psychometric instruments that coaches include in their tool kits as the result of a widespread assumption that capturing individual differences of clients is useful. Many sponsors of coaching expect coaches to use psychometric instruments as a part of coaching interventions, believing that this is evidence for a scientific approach to the coaching process, which otherwise remains somewhat mysterious.

For coaching supervision, the psychological dimension is also useful. Supervisors are in a better position to understand how coaches work if they take into account differences such as whether the coach is an introvert or extravert, or what learning style is typical for them. Some supervisors start a new supervisory relationship by learning in depth their coaches' personal history, values and most influential drives. It is unusual for supervisors to use psychometric instruments to learn more about the coach, but they are often curious about how coaches identify their psychological characteristics when they volunteer such information.

However, many supervisors as well as coaches are aware of the criticisms often associated with the results of psychometric tests. Among these is a reluctance to label a person on the basis of methodologies that were developed for different purposes. Personality theories and instruments usually aim to understand the psychological nature of personhood on a large scale and to learn about patterns of individual differences using statistical methods and probability measures. Any claims about individuals on the basis of these tests are probabilistic and can be flawed. There is also a danger for practitioners to be perceived as experts in the client's psyche, thereby influencing the egalitarian quality of the relationship. This often happens if practitioners take the calculated scores as 'the truth' about the client, forgetting the many issues that exist with the way this data is generated. For example, completing a questionnaire in a different state of mind or for different purposes influences the result. Even such robust instruments as the Big Five test have been found to show different results on every one of the tested dimensions when people were asked to complete it in different roles (e.g. parent, student, friend) (Sheldon et al. 1997).

There is another reason that the critique of psychometrics is interesting, which is the recognition, particularly by coaching practitioners, that clients are much more psychologically complex than psychometric instruments allow. Coaches and supervisors are in a position to observe that our psychological features can be inconsistent, self-contradictory, manifesting differently in different contexts and sometimes changing even in the same context. This realization requires an explanation of the nature of this dimension of individual differences that can acknowledge some patterns but without diminishing the complexity of the human psyche.

A more useful explanation of psychological differences in individuals in the context of coaching is the theory of multiplicity of selves, which I have been developing in relation to coaching (Bachkirova 2011) following many other thinkers in various disciplines (e.g. Gallagher 2013; Gazzaniga 2012; Kurzban 2010). See Box 2.3 for further details.

Box 2.3 Ideas from research

Conceptualizing multiple selves

The idea of multiple selves in action has support from neuroscience, biology and evolutionary psychology. For example, the neuroscientist Gazzaniga (2012), on the basis of his seminal research, argued that the human brain has a modular-type organization. A huge number of relatively independent functioning units work in parallel frequently without our conscious awareness. 'All these modules are not reporting to a department head, it is a free-for-all, self-organizing system' (Gazzaniga 2012: 70). Each of these modules could be called a 'mini-self' because it 'does a job' that we imagine a whole self does, but for each particular purpose (Bachkirova 2011).

The idea of the multiple self provides a convincing answer to the question of why theories that postulate fixed and consistent psychological traits generate only partial descriptions of each individual self. According to this idea, the patterns of behaviours and feelings they identify might be relevant only to some mini-selves in some particular contexts under some particular circumstances. As each mini-self facilitates a person's interactive engagement with various tasks, they are involved in a constant interplay because the tasks and situations change. Kurzban (2010) argued that consistency in our engagements with situations is not a default. It takes careful engineering to keep systems consistent and every human mind has a different capacity for that.

In coaching there are occasions when a short-term oriented mini-self of the client may be in conflict with a long-term oriented one. We observe how strong and more vulnerable mini-selves may be present in the same session at different points of discussion. It does not help if the coach sides with only some of these mini-selves of the client and agrees with their desire (e.g. to eliminate their procrastinating mini-self). A supervisor would need to watch for a coach's tendency to do this and would invite the coach to pay attention to all of the relevant mini-selves of the client.

In the supervision process the role of the supervisor is therefore to be aware of the multiplicity of mini-selves. One of a coach's mini-selves might be driven by a fear of exposure and so be very tentative about disclosing what they see as mistakes. At the same time, their mini-self driven by love of learning would describe mistakes in spite of this fear. There could be a dynamic tension between other mini-selves, such as competitive and compassionate or open and manipulative. In relation to coaching practice, their 'competent' mini-self may overpower their 'dialogic' mini-self or the other way around (Bachkirova 2016). All of these mini-selves require attention if the supervisor works pluralistically.

Box 2.4 Ideas for practice

Inviting different mini-selves of the coach to a session

Some coaches might be limiting their mini-selves participating in the supervisory dialogue. It is useful for a supervisor to check from time to time:

- What are the typical mini-selves of the coach that are active in our sessions?
- What does it say about our relationship?
- Which mini-selves of the coach do I unwittingly encourage to come to the session and which of them might I discourage?

Developmental dimension

The developmental dimension of individual differences is often considered vertical (Cook-Greuter 1999) as opposed to horizontal, which for this chapter is psychological. It is called vertical because it cuts across the differences in the psychological dimension and identifies patterns in terms of our thinking, feeling, values and actions that change over time according to theories of adult development (e.g. Kegan 1982; Graves 1970). According to these theories, growth occurs in a logical sequence of stages from birth to adulthood; later stages are reached only through the earlier stages and each later stage includes all previous ones, analogous to the layers of an onion. This dimension is important for supervision because coaches in supervision may require attention to their different developmental needs at different stages of their working life and it is important that supervisors can recognize them as such and provide appropriate support.

Box 2.5 How to identify a developmental stage

Theories of adult development can be useful, and they are popular among coaches and supervisors. However, a standard criticism that is made against them is the need to use very complex and labour-intensive instruments for identifying stages for a particular client. To overcome this issue, I have developed an approach that can allow coaches to make use of this dimension of individual difference without using such instruments (Bachkirova 2011). The ideas behind this approach are:

a) Specific stages are not fixed but depend on context and individual circumstances.
b) Although some sort of gauging of where an individual's 'centre of developmental gravity' is might be possible, measurement and precision in this task is difficult and not always necessary. Instead, a tentative guess about the stage of the client can be sufficient for the coaching process.
c) This guess could be derived from a developmental theme – what the clients bring to the session. These themes usually indicate the types of difficulties that clients experience and wish to overcome. For example, one of the typical themes for unformed ego (Table 2.1) is the inability to say 'no', and for formed ego could be issues with delegation. In Bachkirova (2011), there is an extensive list of themes characteristic for each stage of development and they can be used as general guidance for their recognition, which is something that any coach can do without resorting to specialized instruments.

Developmental dimensions of individual differences in coaching can be utilized in supervision. Adult development theories postulate various numbers of stages. I have been arguing (Bachkirova 2011) that for the coaching clientele and, by extension for coaches in supervision, three stages (unformed, formed and reformed ego) may be most typical and therefore sufficient. Table 2.1 provides a short

Table 2.1 Description of adult developmental stages for a pluralistic approach in coaching supervision

Stages	Unformed ego (socialized mind, dependent)	Formed ego (self-authoring mind, independent)	Reformed ego (self-transforming mind, inter-dependent)
A cumulative description of the coach according to: cognitive style (Kegan 1982), interpersonal style (Cook-Greuter 1999), values (Graves 1970) and engagement in action (Bachkirova 2011)	Ability for abstract thinking and self-reflection; Need for belonging; socially expected behaviour in relationships; peacemakers/keepers; Importance of social acceptance, reputation; Reduced sense of control over themselves and environment. Higher dependency on others for action	Can see multiplicity and patterns; is critical and analytical; Responsible for their own choices; Importance of achieving personal goals according to inner standards; Capacity to take ownership of the past and act independently; 'Mind over body' control of action	Systems view and tolerance of ambiguity; Take responsibility; respect autonomy of others; non-hostile humour; Importance of individuality, freedom, self-understanding; Harmony between mind and body in action. Appreciation of complexity in the relationship between self and environment
Strength as a coach	Developing confidence in clients, providing support	Remaining focused on results and goals, challenging clients	Providing many perspectives on clients' issues
What they find difficult	Challenging clients, use of self as an instrument	Experimenting, letting go of the approach that works	Containing their influence
Self-deception tendency	For protection	For a gain	Subject of curiosity
How they judge quality of their work	By the way clients feel understood and supported	By degree of the client achieving his/her goals	By own criteria congruent with their philosophy
Expectations from the supervisor	To give emotional support, to help in finding their own style	To affirm, add value to practice and increase their efficiency	To challenge them more than they can challenge themselves
Need to learn in supervision	To believe in themselves	To expand perspectives on the issues	To understand and accept paradoxes
Example of challenge for supervisors	Sensitivity to critique, lack of criticality, being put on a pedestal	'Everything-is-fine coaches', competitiveness	For both, supervisor and coach: going off track, colluding

Modified and extended from Bachkirova (2016: 150)

description of these three stages and corresponding aspects of their practice – something that supervisors can pay attention to in service to their supervisees.

All aspects in the first column of Table 2.1 indicate features of the coach that can be useful in supervision in light of the difficulties they might face and their developmental trajectories. The final aspect postulates some difficulties a supervisor might have working with each type of coach. The developmental trajectory does not imply that the task of the supervisor is 'to move' coaches to the next stage. Coaches can be effective and add value to their clients at any stage of their own process. In fact, coaching might be popular exactly because there are different coaches who can meet many different needs of the coaching clientele.

There are also many caveats to keep in mind if the supervisor uses this table to identify an overall stage of the coach. First of all, it is important to know that these descriptions are not clear-cut in principle. According to the 'onion' metaphor, even coaches who have developed some mini-selves at the 'layer' of reformed ego can still act sometimes according to their unformed or formed ego mini-selves. Coaches with most mini-selves at the unformed ego stage can sometimes respond to a difficult situation as a formed ego. Supervisors would benefit from paying attention to what seems like the internal resources of the coach and the situation they are in, by taking a pluralistic stance towards them.

It is also important not to confuse the stages in this table with a coach's level of experience. The coach might be very experienced but working at the level of unformed ego most of the time. Similarly, a reformed ego coach may be at the beginning of their coaching career, still engaged in shaping their style and therefore needing this kind of support. However, the level of support provided in this case needs to be appropriate, with an appreciation of the internal resources already available.

Box 2.6 Ideas for practice

Supervising 'everything-is-fine' coaches

My guess is that a significant number of coaches, if not most, have the majority of their mini-selves at the formed ego stage. Venturing into a relatively new profession indicates the ability to be sufficiently confident, self-reliant and entrepreneurial. At the same time, these qualities can go together with a resistance to authority, self-assurance and competitiveness. This might explain the objections voiced against supervision in many sectors of the coaching community. Even if supervision is taken, as a requirement from professional bodies, this may generate a category of somewhat reluctant supervisees or those whom I call 'everything-is-fine' coaches.

It is therefore useful for a supervisor to be prepared for working with this type of coach. The challenge here is paradoxical. Many things work well: they have found their own style, receive good feedback from clients, know what they need and do not need. On the other hand, they do not bring real issues to discuss as 'everything is fine' in their practice and supervisors feel that 'they work harder than these coaches'. In a way, supervisors have to make these coaches unhappy when they are happy.

Here are some suggestions for working with these coaches:

- Contract and regularly re-contract with them in terms of their aims for supervision and their responsibility for the results of the sessions.
- Ask them to bring recordings of the actual sessions.
- Work 'hypothetically' – if they have managed a particular intervention well with a client, ask them how they would deal with it under different, more difficult circumstances or with different clients.
- If they are satisfied with their own explanation of the situation, ask them 'in what way might they be wrong?'
- Work developmentally, e.g. expanding the comfort zone, asking 'how can they see more in the situation and what it demands?'

Guidance for further learning and research

For researchers, pluralism is both an opportunity and a challenge. As an opportunity, it allows for richer explanations of many phenomena in coaching and supervision. As a challenge, it shows again how difficult it is to make evidence conclusive and to come to 'one size fit for all' recommendations for practice.

For supervisors, this topic implies a dual responsibility: to work on their own pluralistic thinking and to help coaches to embrace pluralism. What helps is the fact that coaches generally accept the idea of complexity in our practice. It is just important to realize that complexity and diversity are intrinsically connected. The more complex the processes that we are engaged with are, the more variety there is for approaching them successfully. Put simply: there are many different ways to do a good job. This is why many very different coaching styles work, and many different coaches and supervisors can deliver good results.

For supervisors' own personal and professional development, it is useful to consider what can help in developing pluralistic attitudes and thinking and what prevents them. Various studies show (see Novis-Deutsch 2018, for an overview) that pluralism can be enhanced cognitively by practising 'both/and' in addition to 'either/or' reasoning, recognizing the importance and validity of multiple perspectives and related values, and acknowledging contradictions without the urge to resolve them. On a personal level, pluralism goes together with an openness to experience and tolerance of ambiguity and uncertainty. Research also shows that recognition of the complexity and multiplicity of one's own self can add to pluralistic thinking (Novis-Deutsch 2018). On the other hand, there are tendencies that diminish our ability for pluralistic thinking, for example, the desire for unity and the comfort of familiarity with what we already know. The desire for harmony at the cost of recognizing contradictions may lead to 'difference-blindness' (Novis-Deutsch 2018: 444) – something to watch for if we aim for pluralism in supervision.

Questions for reflection

- What are your theoretical preferences as a supervisor and how can they affect your work with coaches?
- Which of your mini-selves are aligned with pluralism and which resist it?
- How can you recognize the situation when the coach you supervise is 'over your head'?
- What do you see as challenging for enhancing pluralistic thinking of the coaches you supervise?

Further reading

Cox, E., Bachkirova, T. and Clutterbuck, D. (eds) (2018) *The Complete Handbook of Coaching*, 3rd edn. London: Sage. This book can be suggested for the dimension of theoretical differences. The first section of this volume provides a concise introduction to 13 theoretical traditions that can increase the breadth of the supervisor's familiarity with them and support an appreciation of theoretical multiplicity.

Lawrence, P. (2018) A narrative approach to coaching multiple selves, *International Journal of Evidence Based Coaching and Mentoring*, 16(2): 32–34. A good start for exploring the psychological dimension of differences in the context of coaching.

Bachkirova, T. (2011) *Developmental Coaching: Working with the Self*. Maidenhead: Open University Press, various theories supporting the developmental dimension of difference and multiplicity of self are explored in the context of coaching.

References

Bachkirova, T. (2011) *Developmental Coaching: Working with the Self*. Maidenhead: Open University Press.

Bachkirova, T. (2016) The self of the coach: conceptualization, issues, and opportunities for practitioner development, *Consulting Psychology Journal: Practice and Research*, 68(2): 143–156.

Bachkirova, T. (2018) Psychological development in adulthood and coaching, in E. Cox, T. Bachkirova and D. Clutterbuck (eds) *The Complete Handbook of Coaching*, 3rd edn. London: Sage.

Berlin, I. (1953/1993) *The Hedgehog and the Fox: An Essay on Tolstoy's View of History*. Chicago, IL: John Murray.

Cook-Greuter, S. (1999) *Postautonomous Ego Development: A Study of Its Nature and Measurement*. Doctoral dissertation. Cambridge, MA: Harvard University Graduate School of Education.

Gallagher, S. (ed.) (2013) *The Oxford Handbook of the Self*. Oxford: Oxford University Press.

Gazzaniga, M. (2012) *Who's in Charge? Free Will and the Science of the Brain*. London: Constable & Robinson.

Graves, C. (1970) Levels of existence: an open system theory of values, *Journal of Humanistic Psychology*, 10(2): 131–155.

Hawkins, P. and Schwenk, G. (2011) The seven-eyed model of coaching supervision, in T. Bachkirova, P. Jackson and D. Clutterbuck (eds) *Supervision in Coaching and Mentoring: Theory and Practice*. Maidenhead: Open University Press.

Jackson, P. and Bachkirova, T. (2019) The 3 Ps of supervision and coaching: Philosophy, Purpose and Process, in E. Turner and S. Palmer (eds) *The Heart of Coaching Supervision: Working with Reflection and Self-care*. Abingdon: Routledge.

Kegan, R. (1982) *The Evolving Self: Problem and Process in Human Development*. London: Harvard University Press.

Kurzban, R. (2010) *Why Everyone (Else) Is a Hypocrite: Evolution and the Modular Mind*. Princeton, NJ: Princeton University Press.

Myers, A. and Bachkirova, T. (2020) The Rashomon effect in the perception of coaching sessions and what this means for the evaluation of the quality: a grounded theory study, *Coaching: An International Journal of Theory, Research and Practice*, 13(1): 92–105.

Novis-Deutsch, N. (2018) The one and the many: both-and reasoning and the embracement of pluralism, *Therapy & Psychology*, 28(4): 429–450.

Sheldon, K., Ryan, R., Rawsthorne, L. and Ilardi, B. (1997) Trait self and true self: cross-role variation in the Big Five personality traits and its relations with authenticity and subjective well-being, *Journal of Personality and Social Psychology*, 73(6): 1380–1393.

van de Vijver, F., Breugelmans, S. and Schalk-Soekar, S. (2008) Multiculturalism: construct validity and stability, *International Journal of Intercultural Relations*, 32(2): 93–104.

3 Supervision for enhancing reflexivity

Peter Jackson

Introduction

Reflection, reflective learning and reflective practice are familiar to coaches and supervisors, and quite widely discussed in the coaching and coaching supervision literatures; the concept of reflexivity, however, seems to be 'below the radar'. There are remarkably few explicit references to reflexivity in many standard collections, even if in many conceptualizations of the purpose and practice of coaching, the capacity for the coach to be reflexive is implicit. It is implicit in coaching concepts from fundamental skills of listening (see the descriptions of 'generative' listening, for example, in Hawkins and Smith 2013) to advanced psychodynamic concepts such as countertransference (see Rossokhin, this volume, for an excellent discussion of this and other interpersonal dynamics).

If supervision is often about making the implicit explicit, it seems equally important to address this gap by clarifying the concept of reflexivity. I will address this in the first section of the chapter, where I will expand and explain my choice of the following definition:

> *Reflexivity is the ability to notice, understand and use constructively one's own processes of thinking and feeling as well as the psychological, social and systemic influences that condition them.*

Reflexivity in this definition sounds a tall order, but in the same way as many aspects of personal and professional development, it is an ongoing and progressive pursuit, not a black and white competence. After all, any embryonic inkling of theory of mind – the idea that the other is separate from ourselves, with their own motivation and rationales – is a level of reflexivity.

Once I have established what is meant by reflexivity, I explore how it contributes to coaches' process of helping others. My premise here, in common with many others, is that coaches practise most richly from where they are as a person. Finally, I will outline some strategies and considerations for supervisors in order to work effectively at developing reflexivity in their own and in their clients' practice.

In the process of expanding on these three areas, I hope to demonstrate that the development of the coach's reflexivity already underpins much of the practice of supervision. Conceptualizing reflexivity as a key component of supervision encourages a constructivist approach to the development of the coach, ensures a commitment to their autonomy, and enables them to access a safe environment to explore their own feelings and responses to client work. All these have the effect of improving practice.

What is reflexivity?

Despite the relative lack of explicit discussion in coaching and coaching supervision, reflexivity is considered an important concept in some other disciplines. These more developed discussions in other disciplines are useful to inform thinking in coaching and supervision. In particular, perspectives from qualitative research, critical management studies and learning help us to understand the range of meanings of reflexivity and how it might be useful. Some or all of these fields may be familiar to postgraduate coaching students and academics – they are chosen partly because they are quite natural bedfellows to coaching studies.

Taking the first of these fields, reflexive research is characterized by a questioning approach towards the taken-for-granted. For Alvesson and Sköldberg (2009), reflexive research has the following characteristics:

- A scepticism towards the necessity of direct relationship between empirical material and 'reality'
- An acceptance that all processes of knowledge production are in part a process of interpretation
- An acknowledgement that the researcher is therefore an interpreter
- A view that social science 'is a social phenomenon embedded in a political and ethical context' (p. 13)
- And, finally, following from the above, the position that in a post-modern sense all texts (including attempts to interpret data) may be political representations.

One or two parallels with coaching and supervision immediately stand out. For example, does the client's/coach's narrative reflect an objective reality, or might it be as much an expression of their state of mind? Could their feelings be conditioned by habits and experiences outside of their current awareness? When the supervisor is asking themselves these questions, they are already playing a reflexive role in the discussion.

Academic supervisors are familiar with postgraduate students' requests for very concrete guidance on how to 'do' reflexivity in their own qualitative research, and for sure a number of steps can be specified relating to one or other of the characteristics described above. In the research domain, strategies to make the implicit explicit include the researcher reflecting in writing on their previous knowledge of the research topic; recording and reflecting on the procedural and (particularly) analytical choices they make in the research process; and presenting their forming ideas to a critical audience who may help identify tacit assumptions and premises. These steps help develop reflexive insights and a reflexive capacity. But by the same token, persuasively reflexive research writing is consistently characterized by an *aura* of reflexivity rather than the presence of specific steps. It becomes a habit or part of the practice.

Critical management studies is a field that focuses on querying the taken-for-granted, critiquing underlying power structures and recognizing the construction of discourse (qualities that may be familiar in some supervisors' practice). Critical management scholars look at both the practice of management and organizations, as well as management education. Cunliffe underlines that in management action and decision-making, as in qualitative and particularly interpretative research, there is no 'view from nowhere' (Nagel 1989). We are always subject to our previous experience and that reflexivity is an attempt to manage this relativity constructively. She argues:

> In examining [. . .] assumptions [underlying our actions], we can uncover their limitations and possibilities, become less prone to becoming complacent or ritualistic in our thoughts and actions, and develop a greater awareness of different perspectives and possibilities and of the need to transform old ways of theorizing and managing. (Cunliffe 2016: 748)

Finally, the field of learning provides arguments for a constructivist approach to developing reflexivity. This is relevant to supervision, as it helps explain why the supervisor's work towards building capacity in their coach/client is not well served by directive methods. Cunliffe notes that traditional educational practices actually discourage reflexivity. She cites Paulo Freire's description of the 'banking' approach in which declarative knowledge is simply accumulated in order for it to be applied 'objectively'. Freire then contrasts this to 'critical pedagogy' that 'transforms reality and unites critical thinking and dialogue to develop a more humanistic approach to learning' (Cunliffe 2016: 750). This parallels the supervisor's responsibility to help develop independent, flexible and responsive thought in the coach. Similarly, Brookfield (2005) describes reflexivity as dialogic: 'we learn to question and challenge everyday practices or social arrangements by discussing with others the extent to which these can be justified' (p. 250). Supervision is dialogue, in which this critical perspective is crucial.

To return, then, to the definition of reflexivity outlined in the introduction to the chapter:

> *Reflexivity is the ability to notice, understand and use constructively one's own processes of thinking and feeling as well as the psychological, social and systemic influences that condition them.*

Drawing from the brief observations on research, critical management studies and learning above, I would now add that it is an active capacity applied to the taken-for-granted knowledge, action and one's own development and that is built through critical dialogue embracing multiple perspectives. It seems to me that supervision provides the space in which this is enabled to happen. Before looking at how this can be addressed in supervision, I review the significance of reflexivity for coaches.

How does reflexivity relate to the work of coaches?

Although the way coaching is defined and practised varies widely, a number of characteristics that are fairly common across practices can be used to highlight the significance of reflexivity. Here we are discussing supervising *for* (the coach's) reflexivity, so the main focus is on why the coach and/or their clients might benefit from their reflexivity. Therefore, in this section I will look at some key features of what coaches do, and will explore how their own reflexivity might enhance this practice. I do not intend here to be comprehensive in reviewing all features of all conceptualizations of coaching. Rather, by providing some examples drawn from the most common assumptions of what we think coaching is, I aim to draw out a pattern that is not always explicit in the literature, handbooks or trainings. Namely, that an approach to coaching that moves beyond the mechanistic is underpinned by reflexivity.

Any number of books, chapters and competency frameworks present variations on familiar themes and perhaps particular concepts and techniques that are unique to their approach. Nonetheless, in descriptions of different practices, key concepts emerge time and time again. Common descriptions include skills of listening, facilitating the development of thoughts and feelings of the client, holding a safe environment and playing back (and maybe challenging inconsistencies) in the client's sense-making. It is fair to say that most conceptualizations of coaching include something similar to these features. Some then add aspects of a client's less explicit experience such as imagination (art making, metaphor and symbolism) and embodied experience (strongly present in Gestalt, somatic and mindfulness-based approaches).

Taking just the first three uncontroversial features from this list, we can illustrate how reflexivity as defined in the previous section may be significant.

Listening

Listening in its everyday sense could be considered a passive activity, though descriptions in coaching literature always include certain attitudes and internal decision-making processes in addition to just hearing. In Hawkins and Smith's (2013) four-level structure, even the first level of 'attending' involves 'emptying oneself' in order to be 'more available in the moment' (p. 252) by putting aside the busy-ness of your own concerns. But it is not the case that we listen with a completely hollow mind, so how do we know what to empty and what not to empty? What is it important to put to one side? At one extreme, we might want to remember where we are and what time it is, while at the other we might want to avoid running through imaginary arguments with our nearest and dearest while the client is talking about what is on their agenda. We are urged to '[give] the right non-verbal signals of attention and interest' (p. 252), but the Rogerian principle might suggest we avoid giving non-verbal signals of disapproval, for example. So we are already applying a filter at this level. The filter relies on a practised self-awareness of our habitual thoughts so that we can separate our professional skills from our feelings about our own experiences in order to avoid projecting those feelings as judgements on the experience of the other: our completely autonomous client.

Hawkins and Smith's structure progresses through reflecting back content, empathic reflection, to 'pure listening' where the listener 'play[s] back the thoughts and feelings that are at "the edge" of the awareness of the speaker' (p. 254). This clearly involves sufficient self-awareness (and emotional self-management) to avoid attachment to pet theories arising from our own experience. It requires being able to hold lightly our own perspective in among an infinite number of possible perspectives, yet to hold it, nevertheless, in order to ensure that we are able to bring to the session the necessary quality of human interaction.

Facilitating the development of thoughts and feelings of the client

Facilitating the development of the client's thoughts and feelings is implicit in basic models of the coaching process ('explore' in CLEAR; 'reality' in GROW) as a step in the process towards decision-making and action. Clarifying the thinking process itself is given more emphasis in cognitive-behavioural approaches (where it might be examined for flaws). Also, becoming more acquainted with one's own emotional process is given a central role in Gestalt-inspired and embodied practices.

We do this by initiating lines of enquiry (asking questions), encouraging deeper exploration and potentially using techniques to highlight whether or not the thoughts/feelings are valid, useful or, perhaps (often in relation to feelings), somewhat neglected. Again, these can be reduced to mechanical techniques (ask open questions, not closed questions; reflect back what has been said). Experienced practitioners, though, will probably have witnessed somewhere in their professional development, the artless application of techniques. The artful practitioner, even at early stages of their practice, is able to shift away from the orthodox. But as with listening, as we move into the realm of more intuitive decision-making, the practitioner must now engage with the uncertainty of navigating *in the moment* a path between their own habits of mind and the interests of their client.

Holding a safe environment

It is clear that appropriate contracting and protocols of confidentiality are essential to creating an environment where the client can explore their situation and their responses to it without fear. However, the client's sense of safety is further enhanced by how they see their coach responding to events. Lee and Roberts (2010) describe an environment where 'established patterns of identity and their associated defences can be loosened'. They suggest that 'above all it is the coach's capacity to stay curious and reflective that builds rapport and trust, and eventually the belief that this is a space where difficult thoughts and feelings can be held, examined and ultimately transformed' (Lee and Roberts 2010: 24).

In the advanced practice of holding a safe environment then, as noted above, we may want to avoid reacting to the client following our own preferences and values (which may be perceived as judgemental), while not ignoring or casting aside such reactions. We do not want to become automata; a strategy that would not enhance rapport and trust. There will be times when we use these reactions (our intuition) to powerful effect as they may provide an alternative perspective, an illustration of how the client's behaviour may affect others. Furthermore, this openness about our own process provides a demonstration of an honest relationship with the client, creating trust and role-modelling reflexivity.

I have intentionally here looked at three fundamental aspects of coaches' practice. These examples illustrate first, that the coach's reflexivity underlies a dynamic and adaptable, as opposed to mechanical, practice; and second, that this core function of reflexivity is not necessarily made explicit in much practice guidance. We can also note here that some very accessible mechanical skills – such as repeating the last thing the client has said – can be adopted, which effectively *simulate* the reflexive decision-making without actually *being* reflexive.

This mechanical approach, however, is likely to result in a limited or inflexible practice. As Schön (1983) argues, complex professional action cannot be arrived at through the model of 'technical rationality', and that such an approach to professional development leads to over-specialization and an unhelpfully narrow view.

How does the supervisor help coaches develop and exercise reflexivity?

Previously, I outlined the nature of reflexivity for the practitioner as being able to reflect critically on one's own processes and the influences that condition them. It is both an opportunity and an important part of the supervisor's responsibility to encourage and develop this reflexivity in the coach. Indeed, it is inherent in many widely used definitions of supervision that this should be the case. To take just one example, Hawkins and Smith (2013: 169) talk about 'understanding better both the client system and themselves as part of the client-coach/mentor system and transform their work'. The current section looks at how this might be done. As reflexivity and developing reflexivity in the coach is such an inherent part of supervision, the actions we might take may be very familiar already. However, thinking about this work in terms of reflexivity is an important perspective as it opens up the opportunity to focus on what is a key capacity underpinning a more sophisticated practice.

The constructivist learning principle: experiential learning and autonomy

The foundation of developing reflexivity is to take a constructivist learning approach. I have found Kolb's (1984) theory of experiential learning an extremely helpful starting point in this respect. Kolb's theory is often depicted as a cycle consisting of what Kolb calls 'concrete experience', 'reflective observation', 'abstract conceptualization' and 'active experimentation'. Kolb's own description emphasizes the chaining of these activities rather than a cycle, arguing that the longer the chain, the 'deeper' the learning. In simple terms, we switch between thinking and doing activities, each informing the next iteration of the other. The coaching and supervision space provides a natural pause for thought (which may be difficult to come by otherwise) and this is already a contribution. But Kolb also reminds us that learning is equally about real-world challenges and action. In this respect, every tricky decision, setback and disappointment really does become an opportunity to learn.

In practical terms, using Kolb as a model implies consciously extending the experiential 'chaining' of the learning activities. The theory argues that the activities that are concerned with gaining material (concrete experience and abstract conceptualization – often depicted as a vertical axis in graphic representations), should be followed by activities concerned with processing that material (active experimentation and reflective observation – often depicted as a horizontal axis). It follows therefore that in our helping we can use two quite simple strategies. First, we can prompt these switches through our questioning ('are there any theories that guide us here?'; 'is that really what happens when you try it out?'; 'what actually happened?', and so on – see Fig. 3.1). Second, we can encourage our client

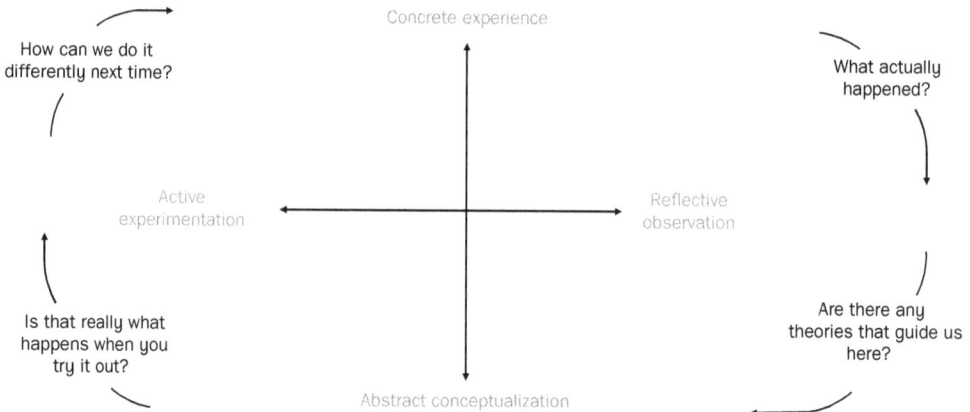

Figure 3.1 A simplified version of Kolb's model showing sample supervision questions to shift learning mode

to exercise those activities that are less habitual for them. I believe this not only serves to improve the reflective analysis, but develops the client's learning capacity and flexibility (Jackson 2004).

There are critiques of Kolb's model, but as a humanist and a pragmatist a great strength of his model from a coaching perspective is that the learning is generated by the individual and embedded in their own experience. This naturally has the effect of enhancing the autonomy of the learner. They are not being told what to want, what to think, or what to do. This is of profound importance for reflexivity. In developing coaches' reflexivity, we are always aiming to generate autonomy and make our input redundant.

Yet Kolb's model does not explicitly bring out two dimensions that are important to the step from reflective/experiential learning to reflexivity. These are criticality and the self. The differentiation between them is implicit in the discussion of 'what is reflexivity' set out earlier. In the next section, where I look at how we might we add those elements to the learning process, it is useful to treat criticality and the self separately.

Adding 'critical reflexivity' to reflection and reflective learning

Criticality can be thought of as operating at a number of levels and in all cases relates to the taking of perspectives. First, we may take a simple approach of enquiry or scepticism: 'do we know for sure that it's going to turn out that way?', or 'what other views might there be of this situation?'. Second, we can consciously apply different perspectives by putting ourselves in the place of specific others, or different positions: 'what would you say about this if you were the client's work colleague?', or 'what would be a quality management view of this?'. This might be extended to consciously taking a perspective from a particular world view. I like to relate this directly to the coach themselves rather than an abstract, so I will tend to explore questions like, 'what is the pragmatist *in you* wanting to say here?'.

In particular, it can be useful to explore the perspectives of underrepresented or less prominently vocal groups. Taking systemic perspectives is particularly useful (see Lawrence, this volume; Hawkins and Schwenk, this volume). Finally, we can select specific dynamics that serve to suppress different perspectives as an analytical stance: power, structures, (organizational) culture, professional ethos, gender, ethnicity. 'What is in play here in relation to (for example) power?'

In relation to Kolb, we can see these strategies as differing ways of surfacing working assumptions about the world, of which we may be otherwise unaware. Following Kolb's model without the additional dimension of criticality, it is quite possible that, for example, the process of 'reflective observation' may not extend to genuinely different perspectives: the stance taken in reflection can be conditioned by the same assumptions as prevailed in the action under observation. Similarly, the process of 'abstract conceptualization' – theorizing and exploring theory – may be conditioned by the same underlying (unexamined) preferences. The learning may be significant, but the frame of reference can remain unchallenged.

Adding 'self-reflexivity' to reflection and reflective learning

Cunliffe and Jun (2005: 229) described self-reflexivity as, 'transforming self, continuously emerging and changing as we interact with others and our environment'. It is the attention we give to our own thinking and feeling processes, learning where our responses emerge from, and ultimately how they affect our interactions. In order to do this, Cunliffe (2002) suggests paying attention to the 'reflex interaction' in the reflective dialogue. These are the automatic, unplanned responses we have in discussion. I would add that in reviewing colleagues' practice in supervision, the same enquiry can be applied to our reflex *action*, that is, how we behave in unplanned ways in the moment. These reflex actions and interactions will be conditioned by beliefs, experiences and narratives about them which we have internalized. They encompass intuitions, gut feel, prejudices and, as Argyris and Schön (1974) termed them, 'theories-in-use'. Thinking in these terms, the question for supervision therefore becomes twofold: how are our assumptions and theories-in-use about the self articulated in our thinking and practice; and/or what does our thinking and practice tell us about our assumptions and theories-in-use about the self.

Where criticality is more of a cognitive process, theories-in-use about the self are more embedded and embodied. Although we still apply our rational capacity to analysis, the material of self-reflexivity is more in the realm of intuition and felt experience. Rossokhin (this volume) relates reflexivity to the developing ability of the coach to separate their response from their analysis. This separation is quite naturally the work of psychotherapy and exploration of psychodynamics through supervision (as described in that chapter) is invaluable. Or, as De Haan (2012: 27) notes: 'Supervision is about taking an independent and frank look at the supervisee's practice, including his failures, shame, doubts and unprocessed or poorly processed experiences.' So now, without stumbling into the realm of psychotherapy, we might, at the very least, be exploring the unexplained barriers to action, the emotional content of coaches' interaction with clients, and recurrent patterns of relating: 'what are you trying not to say here?' 'What is at stake emotionally?' 'How does this serve you? And what part of you does it serve?'

Accessing the material of reflexivity

In my own practice, the starting point of all the enquiries I have described above is the coaching case. Sometimes coaches also need a space to discuss and explore professional themes and methods to use in their practice. This is quite a reasonable function of supervision. However, my own view as a supervisor is that the 'reflex' action/interaction is better accessed by discussion of real, experienced casework. Sometimes this is more difficult for less experienced coaches, with less experience of supervision. Sometimes I am led to wonder if discussing the practicalities can be a way of diverting our attention away from the difficult, unformed, inchoate intuitions about our practice. The 'self' can be a place of uncertainty and even discomfort. In a group I was working in once, I found myself hesitant to express how a case really made me feel. Eventually, I was able to say that there was an 'ugly thought'. The group supervisor – also, conveniently, a psychodynamic psychotherapist – exclaimed 'yes, yes, the ugly thought . . . that's what we want to work with!' Not all such thoughts need be 'ugly', but they are often disguised or discomfiting. (The inhibition that this might create in group situations will be explored by other contributors to this collection.)

A number of strategies described by Gray (2007) are useful here. Gray includes activities that are already built into the supervision process (reflecting on critical incidents; reflective dialogue), but also highlights some others. These are likely to be familiar, but I repeat them here to highlight the logic of their use in facilitating reflexivity:

- Storytelling – According to Gray, storytelling facilitates the 'Creative exploration of values, novel ideas, organizational norms or contradictions and individual viewpoints (including alternative perspectives) [. . .] self identity and characterization – we are "told" by stories' (Gray 2007: 500).
- Reflective journaling – A reflective journal, where it includes not just events but thoughts, feelings and analysis, provides a practice ground for reflexivity. In my own practice, I encourage clients (whether of coaching or supervision) to write entirely privately; that is, I commit to not asking them about the content of their journal. This allows the client to release themselves from social norms and mores about the content without fear of someone else's judgement.
- Concept mapping – Many coaches will use concept maps or mind maps quite routinely as a way of articulating their thoughts. Gray (2007: 503) says that concept mapping, 'Makes cognitive frameworks explicit for subsequent analysis and discussion'. However, Buzan's mind mapping approach (Buzan and Buzan 2006) is explicitly intended as a medium for exploring more intuitive and embedded sense-making processes. Some people will be reluctant to engage with the aesthetic aspects of Buzan's method, perhaps not appreciating the value of doing so, or because of reticence about their artistic capability. In these cases, I would stress the value of it as a *process* rather than as a *product*.

Guidance for further learning and research

Most coaches and most supervisors will have been working on their own reflexivity as a natural consequence of their training. By understanding it more deeply as a concept, I believe that supervisors will be better resourced to develop their coach/clients' reflexivity, and in turn their coach/clients' capacity as coaches. As Clutterbuck et al. (2016: 108) put it: 'The greater our own self-awareness, the less likely that our own issues will interfere with the dynamics of a client session.' It is not just a hygiene factor, however. In our view, 'coaches need to grow in terms of reflexivity: to understand themselves, to find out their values and principles of change and development in order to build a practice that is congruent with who they are' (Jackson and Bachkirova 2018: 21).

In our own supervisor development programmes, we use a version of an exercise drawn from Moon (2013), itself an excellent review and resource for reflective and experiential learning. Moon has scripted four reflective accounts from the viewpoint of a medical General Practitioner. They each concern a specific experience in the GP's practice, but are written to demonstrate different depths of reflection. In the exercise, we ask small groups to compare the accounts to identify any qualitative shifts. For example, the narrator progressively becomes more able to separate his emotional response from his analysis of the situation; he is progressively more aware of how his own circumstances affect his responses in the moment; he starts to look at issues such as power dynamics. In a facilitated review we surface the dimensions of change that participants have noticed. This exercise could be completed individually, but it is in groups that I am constantly reminded of the richness of other people's sense-making: no two cohorts come up with exactly the same set of dimensions. There are alternative sets of reflections in the appendices of Moon's book and explanations of her own concept of the qualities of deepening reflection.

We also encourage both coaches and supervisors to work on making explicit the assumptions, values and beliefs that underlie their model of practice. A full description of this approach can be found in Jackson and Bachkirova (2018).

Questions for reflection

- Reflecting on your understanding of 'reflexivity', when do you think you have been more reflexive? What circumstances helped facilitate your reflexivity?
- Where and when in your coaching or supervision have you wished you had raised an issue? What stopped you, and would you 'miss your chance' again if it came up?
- Which are the functions and activities in your coaching or supervision where you feel least your 'self'?
- Are there practices in your repertoire where you are more mechanistic than your level of experience would predict?

Further sources

Kolb, D.A. (1984) *Experiential Learning: Experience as the Source of Learning and Development*, 1st edn. Englewood Cliffs, NJ: Prentice Hall. As discussed in the body of the chapter, I have found Kolb's model of experiential learning invaluable in my own practice. It is also very accessible in its writing and the theory he presents is more subtle than many summaries written elsewhere give it credit for.

Schön, D.A. (1983) *The Reflective Practitioner: How Professionals Think in Action*. New York: Basic Books. Schön's book describes how effective practice in complex problem-solving environments is enhanced by the reflective approach. It is clear and readable.

Cunliffe, A.L. (2004) On becoming a critically reflexive practitioner, *Journal of Management Education*, 28(4): 407–426. The literature on reflexivity itself is less readable than the two books I have recommended above. For a deep and comprehensive understanding, however, this paper is excellent and is written by a very highly regarded author.

References

Alvesson, M. and Sköldberg, K. (2009) *Reflexive Methodology: New Vistas for Qualitative Research*. London: Sage.

Argyris, C. and Schön, D.A. (1974) *Theory in Practice: Increasing Professional Effectiveness*. San Francisco, CA: Jossey-Bass.

Brookfield, S. (2005) *The Power of Critical Theory for Adult Learning and Teaching*. Maidenhead: Open University Press.

Buzan, T. and Buzan, B. (2006) *The Mind Map Book*. London: Pearson Education.

Clutterbuck, D., Whitaker, C. and Lucas, M. (2016) *Coaching Supervision: A Practical Guide for Supervisees*. Abingdon: Routledge.

Cunliffe, A. (2002) Reflexive dialogical practice in management learning, *Management Learning*, 33(1): 35–61.

Cunliffe, A.L. (2016) On becoming a critically reflexive practitioner. Redux: what does it mean to be reflexive, *Journal of Management Education*, 40(6): 740–746.

Cunliffe, A.L. and Jun, J.S. (2005) The need for reflexivity in public administration, *Administration & Society*, 37(2): 225–242.

De Haan, E (2012) *Supervision in Action: A Relational Approach to Coaching and Consulting Supervision*. Maidenhead: McGraw-Hill Education.

Gray, D.E. (2007) Facilitating management learning: developing critical reflection through reflective tools, *Management Learning*, 38(5): 495–517.

Grey, C. and Willmott, H. (2005) *Critical Management Studies: A Reader*. Oxford: Oxford University Press.

Hawkins, P. and Smith, N. (2013) *Coaching, Mentoring and Organizational Consultancy: Supervision, Skills and Development*, 2nd edn. Maidenhead: Open University Press.

Jackson, P. (2004) Understanding the experience of experience: a practical model of reflective practice for coaching, *International Journal of Evidence-based Coaching and Mentoring*, 2(1): 57–67.

Jackson, P. and Bachkirova, T. (2018) The 3 Ps of supervision and coaching: Philosophy, Purpose and Process, in E. Turner and S. Palmer (eds) *The Heart of Coaching Supervision: Working with Reflection and Self-Care*. Abingdon: Routledge.

Kolb, D.A. (1984) *Experiential Learning: Experience as the Source of Learning and Development,* 1st edn. Englewood Cliffs, NJ: Prentice Hall.

Lee, G. and Roberts, I. (2010) Coaching for authentic leadership, in J. Passmore (ed.) *Leadership Coaching. Working with Leaders to Develop Elite Performance.* London: Kogan Page.

Moon, J.A. (2013) *A Handbook of Reflective and Experiential Learning: Theory and Practice.* London: Routledge.

Nagel, T. (1989) *The View From Nowhere.* New York: Oxford University Press.

Schön, D.A. (1983) *The Reflective Practitioner: How Professionals Think in Action.* New York: Basic Books.

Supervision for working with the self

Robin Shohet

Introduction

In this chapter I am focusing on two aspects of the supervision work. First, I describe the supervisor's use of self in their work with their supervisees. Second, I show how the supervisor can facilitate the supervisee's use of self with their coachees. I am doing it mostly in the form of a partly imagined dialogue between supervisor and supervisee to capture some of the immediacy of the supervisor's use of self. I believe that the purpose of any supervision intervention is to enable the supervisee to be more present with their coachee. To this end, the supervisor has to model being very present to the supervisee. They need to be aware of what is happening for them as they sit with their supervisees, and be willing and able to share their responses in the here and now.

The supervisor's use of self has informed the core of my supervision work. As a supervisor, I feed back what is going on inside me as I listen, not censoring or trying to make sense of what I am experiencing. I also apply this to group supervision, group members feeding back their reactions as a supervisee is presenting. In the seven-eyed model (Hawkins 1985; Hawkins and Shohet 2012) this is mode 6, supervisor's use of self. Counter-intuitively focusing on myself as I supervise seems to bring me into contact with the supervisee, and also often mirrors some aspect of the supervisee's coachee and also the coachee/coach relationship.

I also discovered that any issue that was being presented by the supervisee led back to a block in them. I noticed that helping a supervisee access their block freed them up, and the client, who had formerly been seen as a problem, no longer appeared in that light. In the terminology of Appreciative Inquiry (e.g. Bushe 2011), we are seeing the client or coachee as a mystery to be embraced rather than a problem to be solved.

The focus of this chapter will be on modes 4, 5 and 6 of the seven-eyed model (the self of the supervisee, the supervisee/supervisor relationship and the self of the supervisor). Many coaches are used to focusing on their coachee, or finding strategies to work with an issue, or looking at the wider system. All these have their place but as Bachkirova (2016) states, they belong to aspects of the competent self as opposed to the dialogic self. The former is perhaps more concerned with action, results and evidence; the latter is more concerned with both parties making meaning together. I have found that if I start with this approach, we see the coachee or the issue being brought with fresh eyes and unexpected solutions begin to emerge.

The chapter will start with an example from my supervision practice that is an amalgamation of various sessions. Next, I will describe some ideas to help make meaning of this example and to put it in the context of some traditions of coaching and supervision. The chapter concludes with suggestions that supervisors can take on board if they wish to enhance their ability for using themselves as the instrument of their practice. The chapter is written from a first-person perspective as it seems most appropriate for the topic on the self.

An example of working with self of supervisor and self of supervisee

Supervisee:	I want to bring this coachee that I saw last week. Shall I tell you a bit about them?
Robin:	Yes, in a minute. But we could start somewhere else?
Supervisee:	Like where? I usually start with a description of the client and why I am bringing them
Robin:	I would like to try something different. I am going to tell you how I feel right now and see if it has any resonances for you. Right now I am feeling irritable.
Supervisee:	Well, I was beginning to feel this towards you. I thought where does he want to take me? And, I definitely feel irritated with my coachee.
Robin:	Now I notice something strange – my mouth wanting to go into a sneer.
Supervisee:	That is interesting. He thinks he does not need coaching. He has been almost pushed into it by HR and he thinks there is nothing wrong with him.
Robin:	Now even stranger. I am starting to feel sexual. And I feel very uncomfortable.
Supervisee:	This feels spooky. My client heads a team and has been reported for inappropriate behaviour to a couple of women on the team – lewd comments that he says are 'harmless'. So you have picked up his inappropriate use of sexuality and their uncomfortableness.
Robin:	Now I want to hit you – I hope you realize this is not personal but trust you can make sense of that. And suddenly I feel really sad.
Supervisee:	Of course the women want to hit him. But the sadness really interests me. I can feel it too now. Or am I being suggestible?
Robin:	Stay with it a moment. Perhaps visualize your session with him.
Supervisee:	Just as he was leaving he knocked over his glass of water and was very apologetic. I saw something different behind his façade. You are going to think this strange, like a boy who was frightened of being told off by his mother. And then he made a joke and said, 'At least it wasn't coffee or tea.' But, hey, I am not a therapist and that is not my contract with him. Where is this taking us?
Robin:	I am glad you mention the therapy word. Even therapists ask me about therapy and supervision. The way I see it is that my job is to help you be present with your coachee. This means I have to role model being present with you, which is where I started. And here we have an interesting paradox around the use of self. By focusing on myself I was present to you. I think we might be taught to focus on the other. This has an important place, like watching changes in facial expression, breathing, etc., but my experience is that sometimes coaches can focus on the other person and help with strategies and not use the most immediate source of data, which is use of self. Actually, I have even seen coaches who say it is

wrong to share anything about oneself – we are here for the other. I am saying that I can be more present to you if I am present to myself. I do an exercise where the supervisor keeps sharing what is going on with them as I did with you and people report feeling very connected.

Supervisee: As I did with you. But you haven't really answered the question about therapy.

Robin: Well I am going to try and support your clearing whatever stops you being present with your coachee, as I mentioned. It might touch on areas like relationships between sons and mothers but we just raise awareness and don't work on them. By the way, a moment ago I noticed I was feeling a little guilty that I had gone into teaching mode and we abandoned your client.

Supervisee: You know I was feeling guilty that I had been so judgemental of him. I feel softer, although I can't say I am looking forward to our next session.

Robin: Well we have made a beginning. And now for what could be seen as the most challenging bit. I need to ask your permission

Supervisee: Well, so far it has been fine. What had you in mind? I notice I am feeling nervous.

Robin: Thank you for sharing that. So I will start with there is no coachee.

Supervisee: I don't get that. I can tell you his age, his job, how long he has been working in the company. That makes no sense.

Robin: Yes, all true, but you see all that is not him. How might his wife or superior or an old school friend describe him? We pick certain facts and think we are describing the person. Often, they are presented through an issue – a 47-year-old man abusing his power. That immediately identifies the problem and leads me to think of him in a certain way and then limits the interventions I might suggest, like suggesting he go on a sexual awareness course to try and fix the issue. When you suddenly felt sad you opened up other possibilities.

Supervisee: I don't get that. I agree I softened a bit, but I still don't want to see him and, to go back to an earlier point, I am relieved that this is not therapy so I don't have to work on him and his mother.

Robin: But you might have to work on you and your mother. Just teasing. But I do hold the position that where our client is blocked is where we might be blocked. I feel a little tense now. I wonder, have I been insensitive in some way?

Supervisee: I felt wrong in some way. That I had not seen who he was. Could that be how he feels – wrong in some way?

Robin: Quite possible.

Supervisee: So you are giving me an opportunity to feel like him?

Robin: Well, not deliberately. I just reported how I felt and, yes, it did cross my mind there might have been parallels with him. I'd like to take this further. I am not altogether sure I explained well enough there is no client – there is only the client seen through your eyes, and you are seeing him through the HR's eyes.

Supervisee: But that is true for everyone – we can never see the whole of a person.

Robin: Exactly. So what we see can just be a problem to be fixed. And the difficulty of that is that at some level we are using the other to make ourselves be effective. We need a result. But often it is the clients with whom we have the most difficulty that will teach us the most.

Supervisee:	But this is not about us
Robin:	Again, a paradox. If we make it about us as a starting point, we clear ourselves out of the way so we can be more present to them. But we come with so much baggage – a male who is abusive who needs sorting is not the best place to start.
Supervisee:	So should I have refused?
Robin:	No, because you didn't. Let's assume we all have something to learn here.
Supervisee:	Like what?
Robin:	Like how we are similar to him. I include myself.
Supervisee:	But I am nothing like him. In fact, women say how safe they feel with me.
Robin:	Tell me three things you don't like about him
Supervisee:	He is arrogant. He abuses power. He doesn't want to learn.
Robin:	I can find all of those in me. I guess you have never been any of those things?
Supervisee:	OK, I can be like that. But . . .
Robin:	I know it's different when you are like that.
Supervisee:	Touché. You've just called me arrogant, abusive and unwilling to learn and I am smiling.
Robin:	There is a school of thought that says our clients have come to heal us. If we have any difficulty in them, they are mirroring a part of ourselves that is not integrated.
Supervisee:	But lewd comments when you are the boss is not right.
Robin:	And do you think sitting there in judgement is going to help the work? At best, he will adapt.
Supervisee:	So?
Robin:	Now we are focusing on you (and I haven't done anything to do with therapy like asking about you and your mother, although I would give myself permission if I felt the work needed to go in that direction), I would like you to picture seeing him again as part of yourself – a young part who is vulnerable. No, before I do that I will give you some theory. I am pretty sure he feels very vulnerable. How do I know that?
Supervisee:	Because you are spooky.
Robin:	Thank you. No, it is my belief that we do to others what others have done to us. Let me explain. This man has apparently made two women feel very uncomfortable. He has abused power and doesn't want to recognize that. What we have not been able to integrate into ourselves we do to others. So someone who is full of fear, gets others to feel their fear – we know this because we know bullies are cowards. They can't face their fear so get us to feel it. Or a very sweet person constantly gets others enraged because they have repressed their anger. Or I know someone who had a very deprived childhood who is now very successful and gets others to feel envious of him. I feel deprived suddenly with what I have.
Supervisee:	So my coachee feels powerless and gets others to feel that.
Robin:	I can't know, but it is a good hypothesis.
Supervisee:	And I did see it for a second. So, noticing how I feel in someone's presence can give me a clue about what is unintegrated in them, but also in me because I am bothered by it.
Robin:	Exactly.

Supervisee:	So you are encouraging me to use myself much more than I would ever have believed possible and you are role modelling that. And by recognizing our similarities, you, me, him we join whereas judging keeps us separate.
Robin:	Yes. And you have hit a very important point. That every problem is not the problem itself – that is content, and there will always be different problems for ever. But it is the framing of the problem, the process, that goes to the source of any problem. When you see him as less separate from you, you sit together in a space of not knowing and see what emerges.
Supervisee:	I can't do that. We don't have unlimited time to sit and wait.
Robin:	Have you heard the expression today's problems are a result of yesterday's solutions? Well, we are increasingly going for short-term solutions, which create problems for the future. So, because we cannot take the time to reflect, we 'solve' a problem, which creates trouble further down the line so we have less time to deal with what is in front of us because of the accumulated backlog of 'solved' problems.
Supervisee:	Are you saying even with limited time we should slow down?
Robin:	Absolutely. I want to tell you about a brilliant analyst called Wilfred Bion. He said you should go into a session without memory, desire or understanding. I will explain. Without memory, you see him new each time and don't hold the picture of how he was. Desire – you have no need for him to change. A big one when we feel a contract could be at stake. And understanding. Well, I think we have established how understanding is an illusion.
Supervisee:	Then I would have nothing to hold on to.
Robin:	And then something new and unexpected can arise, not limited by yours or their history. You have created an empty space to be filled with what needs to happen.
Supervisee:	This is sounding quite metaphysical.
Robin:	Well I hate to say it, well not really, this is quite practical. I said that I hate to say it, because I don't want to be caught in the web of needing a result. And paradox, by not needing an outcome something can emerge which is beyond the rational mind.
	In a way, you are right there is a metaphysical element to this. It is about the illusion of separation and how the answer is in the joining with another. No, that is not quite right. We are already joined whether we like it or not. However, whenever we see anything as 'other' it will create a certain amount of fear and need to control this 'other'.
	The journey I have wanted to go with you is my use of self to be with the you, you understanding your self to find out your blocks so you can see your coachee more clearly, and finally invite the possibility of no separate self but a sort of joining beyond individuality. I/Thou instead of I/It in the words of Martin Buber.
Supervisee:	My head is spinning. But I feel excited at seeing this client again. You are right. He does not feel so 'other' and I have less need for him to be 'fixed'.
Robin:	Good. And I will do one final push. Imagine him in your mind's eye. Can you do that?
Supervisee:	Yes.
Robin:	Now I want you to apologize to him for not being open to his essence.

Supervisee:	That is a step too far.
Robin:	And try it.
Supervisee:	OK. Then I think of all the other people I could apply this to.
Robin:	Then thank him for giving you so many opportunities.
Supervisee (smiling):	I start with a coachee who is seen by some of his staff as a sexist bully and HR ask me to work with him. He is totally resistant, and then you ask me to find the arrogant, resistant, abuser of power in me, help me to remember that he is vulnerable, and help me to own how I felt judgemental and that it would be quite natural for him to resist me. And now I feel quite chilled about seeing him and might even share some of the work I have done with you with him. Do you always mess with people's minds like this?
Robin:	As much as I can.

Making sense of this example

Challenge and judgement

In the above session the supervisee is open to having their thinking challenged. The problem has not been fixed, but the supervisee is more willing just to be present with the coachee. From there, something new has the space to emerge. And this might be a hefty challenge. I have found that I can be more challenging when I feel compassionate as then there is no judgement in the challenge. On the other hand, I hold back when I feel critical because I know there is more of my baggage there. So I have role modelled being able to be challenging in a way that comes alongside the supervisee. This could, in turn, help the supervisee challenge their coachee.

In our work and in life we are taught to be non-judgemental. This is often easier said than done, and we learn to repress our judgemental side, which the coachee/client might well pick up unconsciously. Instead, I try and raise awareness of possible judgements and then go to their source. This is usually a non-acceptance of part of oneself, which is then projected, an observation that is also made in the psychodynamic approaches (e.g. Lee 2018) and Gestalt (e.g. Bluckert 2018). This is relevant for both supervisor and supervisee, and is a useful insight that can be carried into life generally. It is why I think that all supervision and coaching training should include a large component of working on self. What parts of ourselves can we not bring to our sessions and why? What can this difficult client/situation teach me about a possible blind spot, in me, in them, which is stopping us seeing as clearly as possible.

We all have blind spots and a willingness to be challenged in supervision can lead to the coach developing their use of self. Self-deception seems to be part of the human condition (Heffernan, 2011; Bachkirova 2015), and supervision can play an important role in dismantling some of the ways we try and keep our world view intact in an unhelpful way. Supervision can pave the way for a possible reframing.

Reframing

I have come to believe that any problem can be reframed. The issue is not the problem out there, but the way it has been framed by the supervisee. I see the work of both supervision and coaching as raising awareness to what stops us being present. This enables the supervisee to see their coachee/situation with fresh eyes. It is not therapy, digging into the past, although the past will have had an impact, but bringing to awareness how much that past is still with us, and in doing so enabling us to make new choices.

In the middle of writing this, I am supervising a student online. She says she is not earning any money. I am surprised. Earlier, she has mentioned that she is like her father. I try a hunch. Are you being loyal to your father by not earning? She is quite emotional on hearing this and says he always undercharged and was a giver and could not receive. I suggest she writes a letter to him, thanking him for what he has given her, but saying she needs to also break free of something she has learnt from him. Is this therapy? It was certainly therapeutic, but I see it as a reframe of her issue about not earning money into a loyalty towards her father. It took about three minutes.

Guidance for further learning and experimenting

In terms of use of self, if we are willing to look at ourselves, then we will not fear and unconsciously block the other person from going where they need to go. There might be a fear of bringing up powerful feelings, which can result in over-focusing on the coachee or strategies in supervision. If the supervisor is willing to use the 'here and now', their own responses and to comment on the relationship between them and their supervisee, they are modelling for the supervisee being able to do that with their coachee. It is not that we don't also focus on the coachee in supervision, or strategy or the wider system or the contract, but we have prepared the ground by using our responses in the 'here and now', which is our use of self. In doing so we are modelling for supervisees being able to use themselves with their coachees.

What might help the supervisor in this process? I will share some thoughts on this based on my own learning and experimenting. Bachkirova talks about the complexity and unpredictably of the coaching process (2016) in proposing the idea of self as the main instrument of coaching. She posits the importance of understanding the instrument, looking after the instrument, and checking the instrument for quality and sensitivity. I wonder if there could be a fourth condition that is relevant to use of self? That is learning to play by ear and improvising with another's instrument so they can 'jam' together. In other words, creating an environment where both parties are willing to risk vulnerability, not knowing and suspend a need to come away with a product. This approach has a lot in common with improvisation drama (Johnstone 1979), done for the love of it, or indeed other modalities like jazz. Could something like this be included in coach/supervisor training? (See Wiener 1994.)

The role of relationship in the coaching and supervisory relationship has been well researched (e.g. de Haan and Gannon 2017). Taking this further, Bachkirova (2016) states, 'For the dialogic self, the relationship is not a means to an end; it is a purpose in itself'. I suggest that allowing the relationship to be an end rather than a means creates the conditions for something new and unpredictable to emerge. We move from a finite game – wanting a result, to an infinite game, played in the recognition that life is far more than we can consciously know (Carse 1986).

There is a problem if programmes for education and continuing development of coaches are mainly concerned with skills and knowledge required for delivery of coaching (Bachkirova 2016). What can happen with this approach is that the exclusive emphasis on skills can be used for hiding the self, the so-called objective approach favoured by behaviourists, classic analysts and some coaches. This keeps the supervisor or coach safe, and no doubt effective work can be done. However, I believe that it is impossible to keep the self out of the relationship, because even in the attempt to do so, we are putting that philosophy of some kind of objectivity into the equation. In psychoanalytic terms, it is impossible *not* to have countertransference to our work. In terms of my philosophy I have drawn heavily on Gestalt (feeding back the 'here and now') and psychoanalysis (transference, countertransference and projective identification) and believe in the value of these ideas for working with the self.

Perhaps what supports me most in my work is a core belief that there is a part of everyone that wants to learn about themselves. If this is the case, the issue brought to supervision or coaching will be seen in a different way. My job as a supervisor is to somehow make an alliance with that part that wants to learn about themselves, and I have found using myself and my here and now responses to be an effective way of doing this. It has provided a rationale and a methodology for my work as a supervisor. It allows something new, unexpected and unpredictable to emerge. And it provides a foundation on which to build other interventions like focusing on the coachee, or looking at interventions that coach has made, or looking at the wider system. In other words, the other modes from the seven-eyed model (Hawkins and Shohet 2012).

Supervision can be described as being in a relationship (supervisee/supervisor), on a relationship (supervisee/coach), about a relationship (coachee/their system). As such, the immediacy of 'here and now' use of self can be an effective tool and a role model for enhancing relationship at all levels of the system that supervisee and supervisor are working with.

Questions for reflection

- In the dialogue above, I fed back irritation and sexual feelings. Both are outside the norms of everyday conversation and even regular supervision. What might stop you from feeding back what is going on with you in the here and now? Name at least four core beliefs. For example, 'the supervisee would get very upset or take it personally, etc.'.
- As a supervisor, what would you most like a supervisee to say to you (e.g. you are the best supervisor I have ever had) or least like a supervisee to say to you (e.g. you are useless)? These could lead you to see how much you want to guide a supervisee in a certain direction (admire me, find me useful), and stop your being present to what is.

- Is there a challenge in your relationship you are not making? What story do you tell yourself to justify it?
- What areas have you decided are taboo? Was this done explicitly or implicitly and if the latter, how can you make it explicit?

Further sources

Shohet, R. and Shohet, J (2020) *In Love with Supervision*. Monmouth: PCCS Books. Chapter on 'Paralleling in the supervision process' (pp. 211–215). A simple explanation of the paralleling process, an understanding of which the authors believe is important for both supervisors and supervisees to have.

Tolle, E. (2001) *The Power of Now*. London: Hodder and Stoughton. A classic inviting us to go beyond our analytic mind and move into the here and now in a different way to improvisation drama, but with the same philosophy of inviting presence.

Wiener, D. (1994) *Rehearsals for Growth*. New York: W.W. Norton and Co. Showing how improvisation drama can be used for all aspects of life as well as coaching and supervision. (See also Shohet and Shohet, pp. 225–227 for a summary.)

References

Bachkirova, T. (2015) Self-deception in coaches: an issue in principle and a challenge for supervision, *Coaching: An International Journal of Theory, Research and Practice*, 8(1): 4–19.

Bachkirova, T. (2016) The self of the coach: conceptualization, issues, and opportunities for practitioner development, *Consulting Psychology Journal: Practice and Research*, 68(2): 143–156.

Bluckert, P. (2018) The Gestalt approach to coaching, in E. Cox, T. Bachkirova and D. Clutterbuck (eds) *The Complete Handbook of Coaching*, 3rd edn. London: Sage.

Bushe, G.R. (2011) Appreciative inquiry: theory and critique, in D. Boje, B. Burnes and J. Hassard (eds) *The Routledge Companion to Organizational Change*. Abingdon: Routledge.

Carse, J. (1986) *Finite and Infinite Games: A Vision of Life as Play and Possibility*. New York: Free Press

De Haan, E. and Gannon, J. (2017) The coaching relationship, in T. Bachkirova, G. Spence and D. Drake (eds) *The SAGE Handbook of Coaching*. London: Sage.

Hawkins, P. (1985) Humanistic psychotherapy supervision: a conceptual framework, *Self and Society*, 13(2): 69–79.

Hawkins, P. and Shohet, R. (2012) *Supervision in the Helping Professions*, 4th edn. Maidenhead: Open University Press.

Heffernan, M. (2011) *Wilful Blindness: Why We Ignore the Obvious at Our Peril*. New York: Bloomsbury.

Johnstone, K. (1979) *Impro: Improvisation and the Theatre*. London: Faber and Faber.

Lee, G. (2018) The psychodynamic approach to coaching, in E. Cox, T. Bachkirova and D. Clutterbuck (eds) *The Complete Handbook of Coaching*, 3rd edn. London: Sage.

Shohet, R. and Shohet, J. (2020) *In Love with Supervision*. Monmouth: PCCS Books.

Tolle, E. (2001) *The Power of Now*. London: Hodder and Stoughton.

Wiener, D. (1994) *Rehearsals for Growth*. New York: W.W. Norton and Co.

5 | Supervision for working ethically

David A. Lane and Michael Cavanagh

Introduction

Our understanding of the importance of supervision in professional practice has gradually taken a central place in coaching. Ethical codes for coaching were established by professional bodies very early and codes for supervision followed. This was helped in part by the emergence of associations (Association of Coaching Supervisors – ACS, Association of National Organisations for Supervision in Europe – ANSE), which saw supervision as a distinct practice and which built their codes accordingly. However, ethics is not simply about following an external code.

While many words have been devoted to the importance of ethical practice, the main thrust in the teaching of ethics has been defensive. In other words, ethics is seen as primarily targeted towards clarifying and fortifying the boundaries within practice to avoid negative outcomes and ethical complaints. We suggest that this is only one component of ethical practice. A second purpose of equal (and perhaps increasing) importance in our complex world positions ethics as a positive driver of effective practice. In other words, ethical reflection can be used to help determine goals and interventions in both coaching and supervision. In this approach, supervision moves beyond quality assurance towards a developmental and transformative process shaped by ongoing ethical reflection.

This chapter will briefly outline the emergence of supervision in its context within the coaching industry. We ask the question of what purposes ethics serve. This will lead to an exploration of the purpose of supervision in coaching as an essential process for ensuring ethical working. We further argue that, in complex contexts, ethical engagement positively contributes to establishment of goals and processes used to reach those goals, and to coach, coachee and supervisor development. Continuous ethical reflection provides a key pathway to enhance human and professional development and client benefit. Core perspectives on ethics will be critiqued. This will include the use of external codes and in particular universal codes of practice, developing towards the idea of an internal moral compass or ethical maturity that guides practice and the concept of ethics as a relational practice. The process by which supervision can enhance ethical practice will be examined to assist in building ethical ways of working. Brief cases and exercises will provide examples of the use of different ethical perspectives and the reader will be asked to consider how they might create a framework for their own ethical practice. It is not enough to say 'I work to a particular ethical code'; we need to be able to frame our practice as an ethical endeavour. Guidance for further reading in the area will be provided with a focus on how a supervisor can critique their own practice and build their ethical awareness to face emerging challenges to our discipline. As you, the reader, work through this chapter, keep in mind how you draw upon your experience, and use your own sense of ethics to monitor and guide your practice.

The purposes of supervision and their ethical implications

Supervision in coaching is a relatively new field. Along with positive development of this practice, not every coaching community responds enthusiastically to this process. This is in large part due to differences in what is understood as the purposes of supervision. Is it to oversee practice and hence provide *quality control*? Is it a relationship where coach and supervisor are engaged in a dialogue to enhance skills and knowledge, thus a *developmental process for the coach*? Or is it a process to challenge assumptions and maybe the coach's worldview thereby *transforming practice*? Is it about the individual coach, or the wider relationships in which they engage or even the even wider systems they impact? Thus, does it draw upon individual, interpersonal or systemic perspectives? Who is it for, the novice coach learning their trade, the competent coach wanting to maintain effective practice or the expert looking to gain a bigger perspectives on the world, or the coachee or wider stakeholders whose lives may be changed by supervision?

All of the above purposes are valid reasons for undertaking supervision. However, clarity about the purpose behind supervision has important implications for the ethical basis of our supervision practice and assessment of its outcomes. Experienced peers offering developmental support to each other in a supervision group, experienced practitioners working with apprentice coaches in training and expert-to-expert supervision are faced with different levels of ethical exposure and commitment. If supervision is about quality control, development or transformation of practice, the ethical responsibilities of the supervisor change. So far, the implications of these ethical differences have not been widely explored in the literature.

Box 5.1 Case illustration

John was coaching Helen, a senior executive who had been assigned an international project as part of a planned process of movement towards a board level position. Helen was a perfectionist who had a long history of success and had never experienced failure at school, university or work. As the coaching progressed, Helen raised concerns about elements of her context that were getting out of control. She started expressing concerns that colleagues were making negative comments about her work and very quickly started to make disparaging comments about her own competence and increasingly low mood. John felt she was becoming depressed and perhaps using over-exaggerated judgements about the project and how she was seen by others. He decides he needs to take this to supervision.

This case demonstrates how ethical considerations would be affected depending on the conceived purpose of supervision and specific situation in which it is used.

What ethical responsibilities are held and what challenges arise for John and his supervisors in the following contexts?

1. John is part of a peer-to-peer supervision group.
2. John, while he has an established practice, is taking an advanced university course and is under one-to-one supervision from an experienced trainer.
3. John is an expert in coaching but not therapy and is working with an expert coach supervisor who is also a therapist.

If we are to take an 'ethics as defence against poor practice' perspective, the above contexts have different implications and consequences. As part of a peer-to-peer group we have to consider what is included in their contract for working together, assuming they have agreed one. The ethical responsibilities they have contracted to cover are likely to include something about confidentiality and to be largely developmental. They may raise questions about the risks, but are unlikely to have agreed to provide quality control and therefore assume responsibilities for client welfare.

If John is being supervised in training, the supervision will almost certainly include quality control as part of the contract. There will, therefore, be a need to explore John's responsibilities, those of the supervisor and their shared responsibilities to the training establishment as well as the client and the employers. In the expert-to-expert case the supervisor will be under an obligation to more than one professional code of ethics. They will have to balance what is and what is not coaching and where the boundaries sit. The ethical purpose, perspectives and process adopted in these different scenarios to address the issue vary by context in which they are working, and the content matter covered by their supervision contract. Hence, the extent of the supervision required and ethical dilemmas presented in the above three scenarios are both context and content dependent.

The difficulty with the defensive approach to ethics (i.e. ethics as a bulwark against poor practice) is that it is first shaped by the parameters of the contracted conversation. These determine the boundaries around the purpose of the supervisory conversation, and whose interests are to be preferred. Ethical attention is drawn to considerations associated with the parties identified in the contract, to the relative exclusion of others in the wider ethical systemic context. For example, in the above illustration, peer group supervision focuses on John's development to the relative exclusion of ethical obligations to John's client or the impact on others working in her team.

In reality, all ethical considerations are interconnected. John's development is intimately bound up with client safety, obligations to the profession and wider society. While each of the supervision contexts outlined above focuses on part of the ethical conversation, there remains a critical responsibility to enter into a fuller ethical refection about what is to be done. As supervisors (peer, expert or otherwise) we cannot contract away the ethical imperative of assisting John to critically reflect on the implications of his actions for the human flourishing of all likely to be touched by them.

Indeed, as Corrie and Lane (2015) assert, we have a professional, moral and legal responsibility to protect the public from poor practice even where this conflicts with the remit of advancing the learning and development of an individual coach. Simply asserting that one has acted within the boundaries of a contract or complied with a professional code does not satisfy true ethical practice. Contracts and codes of conduct cannot cover the subtlety of practice or matters that arise at the boundary of right and wrong in our ambiguous and complex world. For this, a wider, more systemically inclusive dialogue is needed. Fortunately, for John, this wider reflection has the potential to open new possibilities for action and positively shape the goals John has for his practice, the goals he develops with the client and the interventions taken to achieve these ends. This perspective will be explored more fully when we consider the relational approach to ethics that stems from the principles of ethics that we discuss next.

Our overarching perspective on the question of 'Why be ethical?'

At its heart, ethics seeks to answer the question, 'what is the good?' in both general terms and in particular contexts (McIntyre 1998; Carroll and Shaw 2012). The answers we find satisfying will depend in large part on the assumptions we make about what it means to be human and the nature of the world in which we exist. In a complex, diverse and ambiguous world, agreement about what constitutes 'the good' is increasingly difficult to find. Calls for strict adherence to particular moral and ethical codes and extreme moral and ethical relativism are two responses that seek to resolve this question and the tension it brings.

While we do not intend to present a treatise on the nature of ethics, we think that both of the above responses represent an understanding of ethics that is at once both too universal and too narrow. Rather than seeking a final resolution to a universal question of 'the good', based on our particular beliefs, we hold that the purpose of ethics is to create the conditions in which human beings can flourish. Being human is a fundamentally social condition. Hence, we hold that the purpose of ethics and ethical behaviour is to ensure sufficient trust exists for us to be able to negotiate a shared pathway to human flourishing in our complex world. In other words, the purpose of ethics is to enable social intercourse and shared action.

From this perspective, ethics can be seen as an ongoing iterative conversation about the quality of what we will do, how we will behave and how to respond in the contexts in which we find ourselves. In this conversation there are many possible 'goods', the adequacy of which will depend on their coherence with intended purpose, the unintended consequences they produce (both social and individual) and the timeframe deemed relevant to assess these factors.

Supervision is a conversation in which we collaboratively reflect on what is to be done in pursuit of the good in the complex contexts in which we find ourselves. It can take many forms depending upon the skills of those in the conversation, and the explicit and implicit agreements they form for the conversation. In large part, these agreements and the way we conceptualize the supervision conversation will determine how well it functions to achieve the overarching ethical imperative of reflecting on what is to be done in pursuit of human flourishing and for whom.

In light of this overarching perspective we consider three main approaches to ethics in supervision discussed in the literature. We evaluate them and particularly argue for the importance of the third relational approach. Examples of the use of each approach and a combination of all three depending on the context are described in the following boxes.

Approaches to dealing with ethical concerns in coaching supervision

There are many ethical approaches outlined in the philosophical and academic literature. Three approaches are: the external, internal and relational (Corrie and Lane 2015).

1. *External* – Ethical decisions derive from a universal set of principles that are externally mandated and with which we are required to comply.
2. *Internal* – Ethical decision-making rests on ethical maturity; that is, practitioners' internal sense of moral behaviour, which includes a sensitivity to ethical dilemmas and willingness to engage with them.
3. *Relational* – Ethical issues as dilemmas arise in the context of a relationship with others where we are required to negotiate what is moral in order to arrive at a shared understanding and judgement of an appropriate course of action.

Ethics as an external perspective – Professional body codes of conduct are aimed to be consistent with common principles of law since the latter takes precedence in any court proceedings. They include a more general duty of care, which is to act competently and not negligently, to reasonably fulfil our contractual obligations to our clients and build on general principles of law such as equity, proportionality, good faith and human dignity (Voigt 2008; Lane et al. 2018).

The Universal Declaration of Ethical Principles for Psychologists (International Union of Psychological Science 2008) provides an example built on general principles. They state there are four principles covering all professional work:

1. Respect for the dignity of persons and peoples
2. Competent caring for the well-being of persons and peoples
3. Integrity
4. Professional and scientific responsibilities to society.

You might find it helpful to apply these four principles to any ethical dilemmas that you have encountered in your practice. Box 5.2 describes an example of how these four ethical principles might be manifested in practice.

Ethics as an internal perspective – In contrast to the view of ethics as a set of external universal principles, Carroll and Shaw (2012) use the concept of ethical maturity, which is required for ethical decision-making. Smith (1761) sees judgement as the ideal to which we hold ourselves accountable. Judgement is, in his view, a form of deliberative thought that is fair, open-minded and free of prejudice, grounded in ethical commitment and responsible action and appropriate to the situation in which it is deployed. In short, judgement requires more than an ethical code. Carroll and Shaw (2012) understand ethical issues as generated by our personal (internal) moral decision-making and our ethical maturation as professionals.

Box 5.2

In the context of a supervision training programme for experienced coaches, you are supervising a coach who consistently passes formal assessments. Yet in your work you have increasing and persistent doubts about their approach to practice.

What issues of respect, competence, integrity and responsibility does this raise? Think about this for a moment before reading further.

Your doubts as supervisor (which, given they are passing their assessments, may possibly not be shared by others) raise an integrity issue: you have to decide whether or not to voice your concern. If you raise it there is the issue of how competence is being assessed and why that fails to capture your concerns. How can it be raised in a way that respects the supervisee's dignity, who is, after all, diligently applying themselves and passing assignments? If you choose not to raise it, the ethical dilemma becomes your failure to address professional and scientific responsibilities to society.

A similar but less developed position on ethics as an internal moral compass is proposed by Corrie and Lane (2015). There are six components to the Carroll and Shaw framework:

1. *Ethical Sensitivity* – Awareness of self, of harm, of consequences, of impact of behaviour, of intention
2. *Ethical Discernment* – Reflection, emotional awareness, problem-solving process, ethical decisions
3. *Ethical Implementation* – What blocks me/what supports me, how to implement decisions
4. *Ethical Conversation* – Defending the decision, going public, connecting to principles
5. *Ethical Peace* – Living with the decision, support networks, crisis of limits, learning from the process, letting go
6. *Ethical Growth and Development of Character* – Utilize learning to enrich moral self-knowledge, to extend ethical understanding, become more ethically attuned and competent.

Box 5.3 describes how these six components might be manifested in practice.

Ethics as a relational perspective – It is clear that ethical dilemmas happen in relationship with others. Ethics can, therefore, be considered as a relational matter. Supervisors become aware of issues through the relationship and contacts with their wider group.

We can view ethics not as precepts but as matters of dialogue and collaboration within a relationship (Gergen 2001). Collaboration becomes the central concern. In other fields, such as therapy, there is an emphasis on the perspectives of therapist and client to develop a shared understanding (Dudley and Kuyken 2014;

Box 5.3

You are supervising a coach who has just completed a workshop on the use of the technique of paradoxical intention. In this technique, the client is instructed to act in a way they have previously avoided in order to gain new information and experience that might assist them towards their desired goal. For example, a socially anxious client might be asked to be assertive or even provocative in a meeting in order see that this behaviour is unlikely to end in the social ostracization they fear. The coach is intent on 'trying out' the technique on a client. Using the perspectives above, where might the ethical issues arise?

In relation to Ethical Sensitivity, the question arises of the extent to which the coach shows insufficient awareness of self, doing what they want rather than putting the needs of the client foremost, of potential harm to the client. What is missing is the coach's analysis of potential downsides of the intervention and of their intention in making the decision. Ethical Discernment could be developed by helping the coach reflect on the process by which they decided to use this technique with this particular client. Was it anything more than 'I want to try this'? What Ethical Conversation needs to happen to ensure that the coach has a full understanding of their decision and its defensibility both publicly and privately? In having these conversations with the coach, the supervisor can use this situation to promote Ethical Growth. These are just a few of the ethical issues that arise in this example.

Meichenbaum 1977; Corrie and Lane 2010). We can apply the idea of a shared understanding to an ethical dilemma in supervision. A relational perspective would imply seeking through dialogue to come to a shared understanding, rather than resolving the issue by looking externally to a code. The process of relating, itself, becomes the focus (Gergen 2001). Drawing on the work of Epstein (2006) one might consider:

1. How in the dialogue do we respect the supervisee's constructions of the world?
2. What can we do to avoid unilateral authority-based decisions?
3. How might we broaden the circle of those participating in the dialogue?
4. How can we hold our focus on the relationship, not just the issue before us?
5. What can we do to ensure no personal blame?
6. How might we place an emphasis on affirmation – positions we share to enable consideration where we do not agree?
7. How can we consistently and collaboratively reflect on the participatory process itself?

Box 5.4 describes an example of how the use of these seven questions can be manifested in practice.

Box 5.4

You are the line manager to a team of internal coaches and also responsible for their supervision. An issue has arisen in the group supervision that you run where a member of your team refuses to consider ideas from outside their preferred model of practice (and the one taught to the team by your organization). This happens even when you believe that it is inappropriate to the client being considered and unethical in that it may cause harm. While you are a member of a professional body and subject to an external code of ethics, your supervisee is not. How might you use dialogue to address the ethical tensions that are emerging in the supervision sessions?

You might start by reaching out to fully understand their values and perspectives. This would require that you do not impose your 'expert' view on the supervisee. Rather, you encourage the group to reflect on the broader context of the work you do together and invite them to consider other positions, unintended consequences for the client and the wider range of stakeholders. You also ask them to reflect on how these decisions might play out over time. You remain an active participant in this dialogue and are open to hearing new information and perspectives that may change your position. You would emphasize your ongoing commitment to sustain your working alliance and invite others to do the same. You should avoid labelling the resistance to your view and seek actions that build rather than undermine the confidence of the supervisees to explore other perspectives. In this way you can encourage a process in which all feel enabled to fully engage.

Combining the external, internal and relational approaches to ethics in supervision

In a discussion of different approaches to ethical issues in supervision, Corrie and Lane (2015) make the point that supervisory relationships exist within boundaries. These define what is and is not part of our supervision practice and consequently identify issues within or outside our boundary of competent and responsible activity. If a matter of concern clearly sits outside the boundary, it is in another domain, for example, when an act is illegal or in obvious breach of a code of conduct requiring it to be referred to statutory authorities. The difficulty occurs when we are near the boundary. We recognize that we have to respond but cannot readily identify how to do so. These marginal dilemmas cause us most trouble in deciding how to act. However, using the internal, external and relational lenses may help to clarify ethical courses of action. Box 5.5 provides an example for dealing with such dilemmas.

Guidance for further learning and research

Supervision was not previously at the top of the agenda of the coaching associations, but has grown rapidly in importance. We are also seeing developmental

---

Box 5.5

Consider a supervision case where you felt uncomfortable about the practice of a coach you were supervising and believed that you were confronted with an ethical dilemma. Make a detailed note of the case or use the case notes you previously recorded. Take the external, internal and relational approaches in turn.

1. What considerations does each approach enable?
2. What considerations might be neglected by using that approach?
3. What consequences might flow from each of the approaches for the full range of stakeholders affected by the decisions taken. Who gains, who is disenfranchised, etc.?
4. Finally, reflect on what you have learned by using the different perspectives and how you might apply this to enhancing your future practice or that of your service.

Some possible issues that might have arisen in this activity include:

External perspectives – This might raise issues such as respect and responsibility and be a productive way to help the supervisee think about what any action might mean for those involved.

Internal perspectives – Were issues of ethical maturity present? What ethical blind spots seem to exist? Is the supervisee able to articulate a clear, coherent rationale for their approach that takes into consideration the full range of stakeholders and impacts likely to emerge? Consideration of the different components of ethical maturity might enable the supervisor to identify specific areas of ethical development that need to occur.

Relational perspectives – You might decide that collaborative dialogue offers options if the issue does not fit well within an external code (often at a boundary margin). A process of negotiation in relation to different worldviews could usefully occur. It is in approaching these tensions that new, more expansive and inclusive perspectives can be found. These perspectives often open up the possibility for a wider range of responses that serve higher ethical purposes and avoid some of the unintended consequences that flow from decisions based on more narrow understandings.

---

models being used more in coaching supervision, enabling a more focused consideration of the needs of coaches and supervisors at different stages. While there is a lack of research breadth and depth specific to coaching supervision, this is highly developed in other fields and should be seen as a valuable resource for coaches. Coaching-focused supervision research is also needed to attend to the specific ethical issues generated by different modes of supervision – including one-to-one (individual and peer) and group supervision (expert led and peer led). As these modes become more widespread, we need to understand their limitations and benefits.

Coaching associations have their own codes of ethics, which they see as both a guide to good practice and as part of professional standards. Most now either recommend supervision or make it mandatory. Yet the negative effects are under-researched. As our understanding of supervision develops, the importance of going beyond a defensive approach to ethics, or simple adherence to external codes becomes ever more pressing. Growing ethical maturity and the development of an ever more finely tuned individual and collective moral compass is needed if the coaching industry is to assist those we coach to navigate a changing, complex and ambiguous world. The relational approach to ethical goal setting is also critical if we are to avoid the false comfort of occupying the high moral ground, to the detriment of building the trust and safety required for genuine ethical development and collaborative action.

We are beginning to understand more of ethics as relational practice. Given the importance both coaching and supervision place on relationships, this is a welcome development.

To assist with your further development as a supervisor or when you are in supervision a series of suggestions follow.

In relation to external bodies (look back at the external ethical stance above):

- Develop awareness of the code of conduct or standards of practice and any guidance available from the relevant professional body as well as those of the organization where you work. Consider the implications for your supervision practice.
- Also consider the limitations of these codes, and how their implementation in different contexts and under different conditions might enable or constrain social cohesion and collaborative action.
- Consider the sources of support that might be available to you from your training establishment or place of work or professional body should you feel your supervisor/supervisee might be transgressing ethical boundaries. Become aware of what you can and cannot expect.

For reflection on your practice (look back on the internal ethical stance above):

- Consider what differentiates ethical issues in supervision and coaching.
- Consider a past experience of an ethical dilemma:
  - What assumptions and values were brought to awareness? How did these make you feel?
  - What helped you to manage the dilemma?
  - What principles or guidelines influenced your response?
  - Who benefitted most from this response – who was most disadvantaged by it?
  - In terms of the concept of ethical maturity, which of the six components were the most challenging to apply?
  - What did you learn about yourself, the way you work or your values?

In your relationships with those you supervise (look back at the relational ethical stance above):

- Regularly jointly monitor your supervisory relationships and the supervision contracts.

- Consider what you might do to assist your supervisor/supervisee in helping you explore ethical issues.
- Depending on the nature of the supervisory relationship, it might be useful to ask your supervisor/supervisee about any ethical dilemmas they have faced and how they have managed them.

Questions for reflection

- How will supervision develop and with what implications for ethical practice? How will organizations balance internal and external supervision of their coaching faculty?
- Will supervision become a sub-profession of coaching or a profession in its own right?
- How standardized will supervision become globally? Will it develop in different directions, depending on the national context? If it becomes standardized, what will this imply for ethical codes?
- Does supervision require its own set of ethical standards and should these be based on universal principles, separate professional body codes or locally negotiated?

Further sources

Carroll, M. and Shaw, E. (2012) *Ethical Maturity in the Helping Professions: Making Difficult Life and Work Decisions.* London: Jessica Kingsley. Excellent discussion of ethics and professional practice, a thoughtful and engaging read.

Gray, D.E., Garvey, B. and Lane, D.A. (2016) *A Critical Introduction to Coaching and Mentoring.* London: Sage. A practical and comprehensive book that adopts a critical discourse perspective. It includes extensive discussion of supervision and ethics. It offers a guide to the dilemmas that we will face in the future.

Lane, D.A., Watts, M. and Corrie, S. (2016) *Supervision in the Psychological Professions: Building your Own Personalized Model.* London: Open University Press. Looks at supervision in different psychological professions including coaching. Useful reflective tool provided for building your own model of practice.

Additional relevant sources

ANSE Code of Ethics (2012) Available at: http://www.anse.eu/about-anse/standards (accessed 18 August 2020).

Association for Coaching (2005) *Association for Coaching Supervision Report.* Available at: www.associationforcoaching.com (accessed 18 August 2020).

Association for Coaching (2020) *Supervision guide.* Available at: https://cdn.ymaws.com/www.associationforcoaching.com/resource/resmgr/accreditation/coach_accreditation/supporting_documentation/ca_supervision_guide.pdf (accessed 18 August 2020).

Corrie, S. and Lane, D.A. (2015) *CBT Supervision.* London: Sage.

Carroll, M. and Shaw, E. (2012) *Ethical Maturity in the Helping Professions: Making Difficult Life and Work Decisions.* London: Jessica Kingsley.

Dublin Declaration on Coaching (2008) Available at: https://www.pdf.net/assets/uploads/Dublin-DeclarationandAppendicesFINALEnglish.pdf (accessed 18 August 2020).

Dudley, R. and Kuyken, W. (2014) Case formulation in cognitive behavioural therapy: a principle-driven approach, in L. Johnson and R. Dallos (eds) *Formulation in Psychology and Psychotherapy.* Hove: Routledge.

Epstein, R.M. (2006) Mindful practice and the tacit ethics of the moment, in N. Kenny and W. Shelton (eds) *Lost Virtue: Professional Character Development in Medical Education.* Oxford: Elsevier.

Gergen, K.J. (2001) Relational process for ethical outcomes, *Journal of Systemic Therapies,* 20(4): 7–10.

Grant, A. (2012) Australian coaches' views on coaching supervision: a study with implications for Australian coach education, training and practice, *International Journal of Evidence-based Coaching and Mentoring,* 10(2): 17–33.

Hawkins, P. and Schwenk, G. (2011) The seven-eye model of coaching supervision, in T. Bachkirova, P. Jackson and D. Clutterbuck (eds) *Coaching and Mentoring Supervision: Theory and Practice.* Maidenhead: Open University Press.

Lane, D.A. (2011) Ethics and professional standards in supervision, in T. Bachkirova, P. Jackson and D. Clutterbuck (eds) *Coaching and Mentoring Supervision: Theory and Practice.* Maidenhead: Open University Press.

Lane, D.A., Stelter, R. and Stout-Rostron, S. (2018) The future of coaching as a profession, in E. Cox, T. Bachkirova and D. Clutterbuck (eds) *The Complete Handbook of Coaching.* London: Sage.

MacIntyre, A.C. (1998) *A Short History of Ethics: A History of Moral Philosophy from the Homeric Age to the Twentieth Century.* Notre Dame: University of Notre Dame Press.

Meichenbaum, D. (1977) *Cognitive Behaviour Modification: An Integrative Approach.* New York: Plenum Press.

Ronnestad, M.H. and Skovhot, T.M. (1993) Supervision of beginning and advanced graduate students of counselling and psychotherapy, *Journal of Counselling and Development,* 71(4): 396–405.

Schermuly, C.C. (2014) Negative effects of coaching for coaches: an exploratory study, *International Coaching Psychology Review,* 9(2): 165–180.

SGCP (2006) *Guidelines on Supervision for Coaching Psychology.* London: BPS.

Smith, A. (1761). *Theory of Moral Sentiments* (2 ed.) Strand & Edinburgh: A. Millar; A. Kincaid & J. Bell.

Stoltenberg, C.D. and Delworth, U. (1987) *Supervising Counselors and Therapists.* San Francisco: Jossey-Bass Publishers.

WABC (2020) Available at: http://www.wabccoaches.com/includes/popups/professional_standards.html (accessed 18 August 2020).

Voigt, C. (2008) The role of general principles in international law and their relationship to treaty law, *Nordisk Juridisk Tidsskrift,* 31(2): 3–25.

6 | Supervision for working legally

Angela Wright and Sean O'Connor

Introduction

As coaching continues to evolve to encompass a broader, more systemic frame, attention increasingly turns to the context in which coaching takes place (Cavanagh 2013). Clients, coaches and supervisors are all systems embedded in a hierarchy of systems – systems that are both seen and unseen. It has been argued that one of the main aims of supervision is to help a coach 'see' more than they can currently see, in themselves, others and the systems in which they work (Bachkirova 2008; Wright et al. 2019). This chapter considers the often unseen, and rarely discussed, complex legal context in which supervisors operate.

The last five years have seen some significant shifts in the field of coaching supervision, including the publication of specialist books, a growing cohort of trained supervisors, recognition by most of the coaching bodies and an increasing requirement for supervision by organizations using coaching services. Despite these shifts, and aside from discussions around ethics (Lane 2011), there appears to be very little literature on professional or legal issues in coaching supervision as a distinct practice. The purpose of this chapter is to contribute to this literature by discussing the importance of an understanding of legal issues in coaching supervision and the role supervisors may play in developing the legal thinking of coaches.

First, this chapter provides an overview of some of the literature on coaching, supervision and the law. Acknowledging the difficulty of identifying relevant legal issues across multiple global jurisdictions, we explore a number of legal principles, as examples of the type of considerations that coaches and supervisors may need to be mindful of in their practice. Then we identify ways in which supervisors may support the functions of supervision through the development of legal awareness, knowledge, sensitivity and judgement. Next, through a discussion of recent developments in coaching, we aim to highlight the critical importance of supervision and the development of legal thinking if coaches are to remain relevant and fit for purpose. Finally, guidance for further learning and research will be provided.

While engaging with this chapter, we invite you to consider how, and in what ways, the law might have an impact on coaching and supervision in the jurisdictions in which you work; the level of your own legal awareness, knowledge, sensitivity and judgement; and how incorporating the development of legal thinking might contribute to your supervision practice.

The state of literature on coaching supervision and the law

The increasing emphasis on professional issues in coaching is evidenced in a number of recent publications (e.g. *The Sage Handbook of Coaching* and *The Complete Handbook of Coaching*), which include chapters on the development of coaches and the evolution of the coaching industry. These include discussions around: coach education, training and development; the assessment and accreditation of coaches; developing ethical capabilities; adapting and working with new technologies; mental health issues in coaching and the future of coaching as a profession. In contrast, there is a paucity of literature on legal issues in coaching.

As far as the authors are aware, there are no substantive texts on legal issues in coaching supervision. Rogers (2011) explores legal issues such as establishing a coaching business, advertising and marketing, contracting, confidentiality and data protection in one chapter. While the focus of the book is the law of England and Wales, it also touches on European law. More recently, Hawkins and McMahon (2020) discuss a number of key areas of legal responsibility in a chapter on ethics and law, including confidentiality, legal responsibility for the supervisee's practice, data protection and record keeping and responsibility for continuity of care. In Australia, Spence, Cavanagh and Grant (2006) report the initial findings on the diversity and practices of Australian coaches. Through hypothetical examples they explore the legal ramifications of failing to recognize mental health issues in coaching and consider the degree to which coach training assists coaches in discharging their duty of care. Ethical and legal issues are explored from a US perspective by Williams and Anderson (2006). This book includes chapters on ethical issues in coaching (including an ethical choice-making process), confidentiality, competence, multiple roles, legal matters and the future of coaching. The book has a strong bias towards the International Coach Federation (ICF). For example, it holds out ICF accredited training programmes as the gold standard in coach education despite critiques that there are more rigorous approaches to educating coaches (Bachkirova and Lawson-Smith 2015). It also makes the assertion that coaches should hire a Master Coach for supervision. We do not accept such assertions for a number of reasons, including legal considerations surrounding a coach's competence and requisite standard of care.

Legal issues in coaching supervision

No chapter on the legal aspects of coaching supervision could do justice to the myriad of complex legal issues coaches and supervisors face in our global and multi-jurisdictional coaching industry. It is incumbent on all coaches and supervisors to consider not only the local laws in the location in which they are based, but all jurisdictions in which they work. Legal considerations arise in almost all aspects of coaching and supervision practice, from establishing businesses, marketing coaching services, contracting with clients, safeguarding confidential information, intellectual property and personal data, to the retention and disposal of documents post engagement.

There may also be additional considerations in light of the nature of the coaching or supervisory relationship. For example, the duty of confidentiality is an established common law principle that applies in some jurisdictions. Common law is derived from the judicial decisions of courts or similar tribunals. The duty applies in relationships involving trust and confidence, where there is a public interest in protecting confidence or where there is a reasonable expectation that confidences will be kept. Examples of such relationships include the relationship between doctor/patient, lawyer/client and trustee/beneficiary. These relationships, known as fiduciary relationships, also create a duty to exercise good faith. It may be possible that the coach/coachee and supervisor/supervisee relationships may be similarly characterized. A duty of confidentiality usually applies in fiduciary relationships unless there is specific exception, including where the client consents to the disclosure of confidential information, where there is the potential for harm to self or others or some other serious illegality. For example, in the UK the Terrorism Act 2000 requires disclosure of all information connected to acts of terrorism. Outside of a fiduciary relationship, in some jurisdictions there is no duty of confidentiality unless a specific statute provides otherwise.

Given the coaching industry is still in its infancy relative to more established professions, there are limited legal precedents either in the form of interpretations of statutory obligations or resulting from legal disputes and litigation. A supervisor may, however, draw on general legal principles and statutory obligations that have been applied in similar situations or closely related fields. While we will touch on a number of areas of law throughout this chapter, our focus will be on the law of contract and the Tort of Negligence.

The law of contract

It is important for all coaches and supervisors to understand the basic legal principles related to the law of contract, including the requirements of a valid contract. In most common law jurisdictions, the first element of a valid contract is that there must be real consent. While there are a number of other legal requirements including the requirement of consideration (an exchange of something of value), one requirement that may be of particular interest in coaching and supervision is that the parties to the contract have the legal capacity to enter into an agreement. For example, one of the parties may lack capacity due to a disability or mental health issue.

Consider also the organizationally mandated coachee, the reluctant team member who does not wish to engage in team coaching or the cautious internal coach who prefers not to participate in group supervision. In a situation where their job, promotion, or their career progression may be at stake, perceived coercion and/or felt internal pressure to participate is a clear possibility. It is of note, however, that in most organizational assignments the coachee (or supervisee) is not usually a party to any formal written contract. The question arises, however, whether the coachee/supervisee is party to any other verbal (or written) agreement and how that interacts with any formal written contract. To what extent do these agreements form part of the contract between the parties? And how might they impact the issue of consent? These potential scenarios have a multitude of legal implications, not only for any coach or supervisor, but also the organization using their services.

Importantly, there is usually no requirement that a contract be written; contracts may be oral or implied by conduct of the parties. That said, it is best practice to have a written record of the essential terms of an agreement. While no contract can cover all possible situations that emerge in the course of a coaching or supervisory engagement, it helps to set expectations, clarify methods of working, identify boundaries and agree how issues such as confidentiality will be dealt with.

The Tort of Negligence

Another crucial area pertinent to coaching and supervision is the Tort of Negligence. Torts are civil wrongs that cause a claimant to suffer loss or harm. Negligence is an 'omission of doing something a reasonable and prudent person, guided by ordinary considerations that regulate human affairs, would do; or in doing something a reasonable and prudent person would have refrained from doing under the same or similar circumstances' (Williams and Anderson 2006: 117). There are typically four elements required for a claim in Negligence, including:

1. *A duty of care* – The presence of a legal duty not to cause harm
2. *Breach* – Failure to live up to that duty
3. *Causation* – The breach has legally caused loss
4. *Damage* – The claimant (known as a plaintiff) suffered damage.

Duty of care and breach

A duty of care is a legal obligation that is imposed on an individual requiring adherence to a standard of reasonable care while performing any acts that could foreseeably harm others. In determining the duty owed by a coach (or supervisor) regard would likely be had to that which has been 'assumed' (or taken on) by the coach/supervisor, which, in turn, will be derived from the terms of the engagement (including any written contract) and all of the circumstances of the case. For example, if a coach or supervisor has not entered into a formal written contract, a court would likely have regard to the course of dealings between the parties in determining the nature of the agreement between them.

In the absence of any universal standards or body of law, when determining the scope of the duty, the requisite standard of care owed by a coach (or supervisor) and whether a duty has been breached, a court is likely to want to hear evidence as to what a reasonably prudent coach/supervisor would have done in a particular circumstance. Regard will likely be had to other coaches possessing the same skill or knowledge in the same community, or what is customarily done in the same situation. This may be difficult given there is no single agreed definition of coaching or universally accepted practices. It is also important to note that what is customarily done is not always deemed reasonable. A court is also likely to be interested in what has been promised in any coaching agreement and how the coach has 'held themselves out'.

The concept of 'holding out' may be particularly important in determining the standard of care that may reasonably be expected of coaches and supervisors. For example, a trainee is likely to be held to the same standard as a qualified or experienced practitioner. A specialist, on the other hand, will likely be held to a higher standard. This becomes problematic given the many poorly defined and unregulated labels littering the coaching marketplace with confusion (e.g. 'Master Coach').

One question often asked in the context of law and supervision relates to the responsibility a supervisor might have to their supervisee's client. Under the law of Negligence, we owe a duty to members of a class of person who might be foreseeably harmed by our conduct. It could be argued that the end client is reasonably foreseeable. While the legal principle of Privity of Contract (we only owe a duty to those with whom we have a contractual relationship) may apply in some jurisdictions there has been a general policy shift away from this principle. In some jurisdictions the parties need not be in a contractual relationship for a duty to arise. It would therefore be judicious for a supervisor to assume that there is at least the possibility of liability to the end client.

In a recent online critique of supervision vis-à-vis mentor coaching, Krapu (2019) contended that unlike mentor coaching (in the US at least), it has been established that 'supervisors' in various capacities, but especially in psychotherapy, bear some legal responsibility for the actions of their supervisees and, as such, coaching supervisors will be assigned legal liability because it comes with the title. In our view this is debatable. Werth et al. (2009) have suggested that, for mental health professionals in the US, liability of the supervisor is inversely proportional to the therapist's degree of skill and experience. If a therapist is in training, then the supervisor may be responsible for the well-being of the client and any harm to a third party arising out of a duty to protect. Conversely, if the therapist is an experienced practitioner, the supervisor would have very little responsibility for the therapist's action. This suggests that the situation in which a supervisor may be liable (i.e. trainee/expert) is arguably more akin to a coach mentoring model rather than a coaching supervision model. Nevertheless, it may be wise for a coaching supervisor to make it clear in their written contract that supervision is a co-created dialogue between two trained professionals. Whether, of course, this would protect a supervisor from such a claim remains to be seen.

Causation and damage

In addition to establishing that a coach/supervisor owed and breached their duty of care, the claimant must also prove that they caused the damage alleged and that the damage was not too remote. When considering whether a coach or supervisor has caused the claimant's loss, one legal doctrine that may be of relevance is the 'eggshell skull' (or thin skull) rule, which considers the issue of a hypersensitive claimant. The rule states that we must take our victims as we find them with all their uniqueness and particular vulnerabilities. More specifically, the unexpected frailty of the person who is alleging harm is not a valid defence to the seriousness of any injury caused to them. This may be of particular concern as it relates to the mental health of a coachee/supervisee. Importantly, the rule applies irrespective of intention or knowledge. To say that we did not intend to do harm (e.g. that this is coaching not therapy) or that a mental health issue was unknown may not suffice.

Issues may also arise at the boundary between coaching, mentoring and consulting. It is in this context that the concept of the 'shadow' director may apply in some jurisdictions. While there may be exceptions for those providing advice in their professional capacity (e.g. Corporations Act 2001 in Australia and Companies Act 2006 in the UK), it is prudent for any coach/supervisor to understand this principle to ensure that they do not unintentionally fall foul of this rule. Whether this would mean coaches who profess not to provide 'advice' – to 'ask not tell' – fall outside the professional advice exception is an interesting question.

Those who employ coaches and supervisors should also be mindful that an employer may be vicariously liable for the actions of their employees. In some jurisdictions this may include sub-contractors depending on the level of control the organization has over the sub-contractor's work. Given recent changes to the law in California (Assembly Bill 5 (A5) 2020) regarding the designation of sub-contractors as employees, it may be unwise, at least in the US, to assume that defining a coach or a supervisor as a sub-contractor prevents those for whom they work from being held vicariously liable.

Developing legal awareness, knowledge sensitivity and judgement

Despite a proliferation of coach education, training and development programmes, there is limited understanding of the approaches to learning and development being used. We suspect that there are very few programmes that address the legal implications of practicing as a coach or supervisor in any meaningful way. While legal issues should be a core aspect of the education and training of both coaches and supervisors, this can only ever be at the level of guidance. Similar to the necessary limitations of ethical codes, the law is complex, coach education can never cover the plethora of situations that a coach or supervisor is likely to encounter. It is in this context that supervision has an essential role to play.

In our discussion below we aim to demonstrate how legal awareness, knowledge, sensitivity and judgement may be developed through the accepted functions of supervision (normative, developmental and restorative).

Normative function

An important consideration for any industry or profession is the issue of ethical standards. The development of various codes of ethics by coaching bodies attests to this. Yet ethics and law are inextricably linked. The law is not just about following external rules, avoiding liability, litigation or disputes, it has a key contribution to make to effective and professional practice. Developing reflexivity and critical thinking around the legal implications of our practice is not only part of our commitment to quality, integrity, accountability, rigor and high levels of service, but also our professional responsibility to the broader coaching industry and the clients and communities we serve. Supervision, through its accepted normative function (contributing to the quality of work and ethical decision-making), may help identify legal issues of which a coach may be unaware (e.g. in Box 6.1).

Box 6.1

Debra has been working as an external coach for about 5 years. Prior to that she had a 20-year career in Human Resources. Her marketing materials describe her as a Master Coach with 25 years of experience. Debra may be unaware that she may be held to a higher standard (whether she is more qualified, experienced, competent or not) through use of the title Master Coach. Similarly, she may be unaware that her marketing materials may be misleading (she does not have 25 years of coaching experience). This could potentially lead to a case of Misrepresentation, and in some jurisdictions, a breach of various Trade Practices laws.

Developmental function

Supervision is about more than quality assurance. Reflection on legal issues may help coaches enhance their capacity to face challenges that emerge in their practice. In this way, supervision may enhance a coach's legal thinking as part of the Developmental function. While education and training may be useful for learning basic legal literacy, supervision allows for a more nuanced approach to the development of legal awareness, knowledge, sensitivity and judgement through exploration of real and hypothetical examples (e.g. in Box 6.2).

Box 6.2

Eli is working with a coachee who appears to be under a significant amount of work-related stress. He has a sense that the coachee might benefit from undertaking some form of therapy. He also takes the view that if the coaching is to continue, it should, at least initially, focus on the coachee's well-being rather than the agreed performance goals. This situation raises a number of potential legal issues. For example, how will Eli raise this issue and what considerations around confidentiality and referrals might arise? And is he competent to support the coachee in developing her well-being? Eli has also contracted to provide the coachee with 360-degree feedback. He now believes, however, that delivery of the feedback should be postponed given its very negative content. Supervision may provide Eli with the opportunity to think through the ramifications and any unintended consequences of his decisions, including whether he will be breaching his contract if he does not provide the feedback or breaching his duty of care if he does – since he may be knowingly causing harm.

Restorative function

Litigation, disputes, conflicts of interest, allegations of improper conduct, negligence, unethical or unprofessional practice, however unfounded, can cause tre-

---

Box 6.3

Vijay has been working as a coach for over 20 years. After three sessions with a coachee, he received a call from his coachee's direct manager asking for specific feedback on the progress of the coaching. He refused to provide the feedback. The manager became furious and threatened to terminate his contract and sue him for breach. This not only raises the question of breach of contract but also questions around confidentiality. Vijay was upset by the conversation and wishes he had handled the situation differently. This has shaken him somewhat and he is now second guessing himself. Supervision may help Vijay see different perspectives in the situation. For example, through normalizing his response, recognizing his positive intent and acknowledging what he might look back at and be proud of in the future.

---

mendous anxiety and stress for a coach. A supervisor may support a coach when navigating such issues as part of the Restorative function (e.g. in Box 6.3).

It may also be wise for coaches to seek the support of a supervisor as evidence of any assertion that the coach has taken all reasonable steps to uphold and discharge their duty of care (Werth et al. 2009).

Legal aspects of recent developments in coaching

In 2006 it was observed that 'As coaching evolves, as the number of coaches proliferates, and as the economic impact of coaching grows, heightened attention will be given to the legal aspects of coaching because boundary questions with other fields will intensify' (Williams and Anderson 2006: 176). We identify below three areas where the evolution of coaching is likely to raise increasingly complex legal issues.

Systemic coaching

In recent years, there has been a growing interest in systemic coaching (Cavanagh 2013; Lawrence and Moore 2019). Systemic approaches to coaching require coaches to understand and work with multiple complexities in a system and to take and integrate multiple perspectives – perspectives on themselves, others and the world. This may raise complex legal issues about a coach's level of competence and development, managing and integrating stakeholder perspectives and questions about confidentiality and who is the client – the coachee, the client, or the system.

Developmental coaching

There has also been a similar increase in developmental coaching (Bachkirova and Baker 2018; Lawrence 2016). Drawing on theories of developmental psychology, developmental coaching is aimed at enhancing a client's ability to meet current and future challenges more effectively as a result of the development of an increasingly complex understanding of self, others and the systems in which they operate (Cavanagh 2013). The blurring of boundaries between coaching and therapy, the identification of mental health issues (Bachkirova and Baker 2018) and the question of a coach's own level of development may be more complex in developmental coaching, which may raise similarly complex legal issues.

Artificial intelligence in coaching

The introduction and use of new technologies, including artificial intelligence (AI) in coaching (Terblanche 2020) will also raise unique legal questions. For example, who owns, who may access, and for what purposes may data be used? To whom is confidentiality owed and in what ways might a coachee be open to manipulation? How will liability be determined where multiple stakeholders are involved in the creation of the new technologies? What biases might be inherent in any algorithms used and what discriminatory practices and decisions might this lead too?

Given the growth and evolution of coaching, we believe that supervisors are likely to have an increasingly important role to play in the development of legal thinking if coaches are to remain relevant and fit for purpose. This may be even more important for internal coaches where legal issues may be particularly complex given overlapping boundaries, responsibilities and roles.

Guidance for further learning and research

While coaching is an unregulated industry (Spence et al. 2006) with no universal standard of practice, code of ethics or independent oversight, the coaching industry is still 'bound by' the laws that apply to professional practice in the jurisdictions in which a coach may operate. Indeed, for those practitioners who are members of various coaching bodies, this requirement is clearly articulated (for example, by the Association for Coaching, the European Coaching and Mentoring Council and the ICF). Beyond the requirement to abide by applicable laws, as far as we are aware, no significant legal education is provided as part of the training programmes accredited by coaching bodies. This is particularly important since there is an established legal principle in most jurisdictions that ignorance is no defence. This also raises some interesting legal questions for coaching bodies around their own responsibility and potential legal culpability in endorsing and accrediting such programmes.

Legal issues are present and will emerge in coaching and coaching supervision. Legal considerations and implications for coaches and supervisors are complex and multi-directional. This highlights the imperative for supervisors to develop their own legal literacy. We believe that there is a critical need for supervisors to understand their own legal obligations and have an awareness of the obligations of coaches with whom they work. In this way, they will not only ensure that they discharge their own legal obligations but may also be able to support the development of legal thinking in others. Moreover, this co-created dialogue may help both the coach and supervisor increase their reflexivity, criticality and their ability to see potential legal issues. This may, in turn, develop their capacity for greater levels of complexity in legal thinking.

In the same way that diagnosing mental health issues is not the role of coaching, it is not suggested that supervisors, or indeed coaches, become experts in law. Rather, to develop sufficient legal awareness, knowledge, sensitivity and judgement to recognize the red flags that indicate the relevance of legal issues, determine their capability of working with the level of complexity the issues present, and know where to refer should specialist legal advice be required.

Many people see the law as a set of rules or norms about right and wrong behaviour, duties, obligations and responsibilities – a controlling force that is oppressive and limiting. The law is often expressed as an independent, external requirement that warrants attention and specialist advice should a particular need arise. We believe that law is relational. That is, those subject to the law interact as part of the network of forces that create the social norms from which laws emerge (Friedman 1975). Seen in this way, the law is socially constructed. This then raises questions for the coach and supervisor as to what role they play in co-creating the law and what this means for the longevity and credibility of the coaching industry.

Undertaking research will help us better understand the importance and implications of legal issues in coaching and supervision. Questions for consideration may include:

- How prevalent are legal issues in coaching and supervision and how do they emerge?
- How do coaches and supervisors view the relevance of legal issues in their practice?
- What legal training and education should coaches and supervisors undertake?
- To what extent do coaches and supervisors recognize and understand legal issues when they appear?
- What do coaches and supervisors currently do when they encounter potential legal issues?
- How do they decide when a situation is inappropriate for supervision and requires specialist advice?
- What specific legal issues might be generated by new approaches to coaching?

Researching legal issues in coaching and supervision is not without its challenges since we can only bring to (or recognize in) supervision that which is within our current awareness.

In this chapter we have considered a very limited selection of potential legal issues. These have necessarily been discussed at a very general level given the global audience of this text. The following texts may help coaches and supervisors enhance their understanding of the importance of legal issues in coaching and supervision. Those working in other jurisdictions are encouraged to explore texts relevant to their context. It should be noted, however, that the law is always evolving; legal texts become quickly out of date. Moreover, in industries experiencing rapid growth and change, many legal questions have yet to be considered.

Questions for reflection

- How might you support the development of legal awareness, knowledge, sensitivity and judgement in yourself and others? And what value might this add to your practice?
- How as a coach or supervisor might you develop your own capacity for legal thinking and what are the implications of this for discharging your own duty of care?
- What legal responsibility may you have assumed in working as a supervisor and is it different for individual, group or peer supervision?
- If we assume that the law is socially constructed, what impact might you have on the development of the law?

Further sources

Hawkins, P. and McMahon, A. (2020) *Supervision in the Helping Professions*. London: Open University Press. This chapter highlights a number of legal issues for supervisors generally, including a section on the General Data Protection Regulation, 2018.

Spence, G.B., Cavanagh, M.J. and Grant, A.M. (2006) Duty of care in an unregulated industry: initial findings on the diversity and practices of Australian coaches, *International Coaching Psychology Review*, 1(1): 71–85. This article aims to raise awareness about the obligations of coaches by exploring the potential links between coaching, mental health and the law.

Terblanche, N. (2020) A design framework to create artificial intelligence coaches, *International Journal of Evidence Based Coaching and Mentoring*, 18: 152–165. This article explores some of the ethical and legal issues raised by the use of AI in coaching.

References

Bachkirova, T. (2008) Role of coaching psychology in defining boundaries between counselling and coaching, in S. Palmer and A. Whybrow (eds) *Handbook of Coaching Psychology: A Guide for Practitioners*. New York: Routledge.

Bachkirova, T. and Baker, S. (2018) Revisiting the issue of boundaries between coaching and counselling, in S. Palmer and A. Whybrow (eds) *Handbook of Coaching Psychology: A Guide for Practitioners*. Abingdon: Routledge.

Bachkirova, T. and Smith, C.L. (2015) From competencies to capabilities in the assessment and accreditation of coaches, *International Journal of Evidence Based Coaching and Mentoring*, 13(2): 123–140.

Cavanagh, M.J. (2013) The coaching engagement in the twenty-first century: new paradigms for complex times, in S. David, D. Clutterbuck and Megginson (eds) *Beyond Goals: Effective Strategies for Coaching and Mentoring*, New York: Routledge.

Friedman, L.M. (1975) *The Legal System: A Social Science Perspective*. New York: Russell Sage Foundation.

Hawkins, P. and McMahon, A. (2020) *Supervision in the Helping Professions*. London: Open University Press.

Lane, D. (2011) Ethics and professional standards in supervision, in T. Bachkirova, P. Jackson and D. Clutterbuck (eds) *Coaching and Mentoring Supervision*. Maidenhead: Open University Press.

Lawrence, P. (2016) Coaching and adult development, in T. Bachkirova, G. Spence and D.B. Drake (eds) *The SAGE Handbook of Coaching*. Los Angeles: Sage.

Lawrence, P. and Moore, A. (2019) *Coaching in Three Dimensions*. New York: Routledge.

Rogers, K. (2011) Legal considerations in coaching, in J. Passmore (ed.) *Supervision in Coaching*. London: Kogan Page.

Spence, G.B., Cavanagh, M.J. and Grant, A.M. (2006) Duty of care in an unregulated industry: initial findings on the diversity and practices of Australian coaches, *International Coaching Psychology Review*, 1(1): 71–85.

Terblanche, N. (2020) A design framework to create artificial intelligence coaches, *International Journal of Evidence Based Coaching and Mentoring*, 18: 152–165.

Werth, J.L., Jr., Welfel, E.R. and Benjamin, G.A.H. (eds) (2009) *The Duty to Protect: Ethical, Legal, and Professional Considerations for Mental Health Professionals*. Washington, DC: American Psychological Society.

Williams, P. and Anderson, S. (2006) *Law & Ethics in Coaching: How to Solve and Avoid Difficult Problems in Your Practice*. Hoboken: Wiley.

Wright, A., Walsh, M.M. and Tennyson, S. (2019) Systemic coaching supervision: responding to the complex challenges of our time, *Philosophy of Coaching: An International Journal*, 4(1): 107–122.

Section 2
Supervision grounded in theory

7 Psychoanalytic approach to coaching supervision

Andrey Rossokhin

Introduction

Do coaches and their supervisors need psychoanalytic knowledge? We are aware of the concerns from all sides that coaching is not psychotherapy, and certainly not psychoanalysis. To question this assumption from the very beginning, I will consider one of the main postulates of non-psychoanalytic coaching: that the coach should always follow the client. This technical rule, which is often monitored by supervisors, seems unquestionable, since otherwise the coach might impose their own agenda on the client's enquiry. Using a psychoanalytic approach, we will immediately discover the insurmountable contradiction to this rule. I like to tell my students that when they meet a client, they are faced with at least two people. The first – the developing self of the client that formulates an enquiry and hopes to find a solution to it – believes and wants to develop their professional competencies; but the second is the hidden protective self, which will do everything possible to ensure that no or minimal changes occur. As soon as the coaching process brings the client closer to potential changes, his protective self immediately comes to the foreground and pushes the developing self into the background. If the coach, according to the rule, continues to follow the client, they will actually enter into an unconscious collusion with this protective self, which leads in the exact opposite direction to that intended: pretending that changes are happening while remaining in the usual protective comfort zone. This is a well-known resistance to change, which psychoanalysts have been taught how to understand and be able to work through for more than a hundred years. Should, then, supervisors understand these simple pitfalls? Could they help coaches who have fallen into them without psychoanalytic knowledge?

Here is another example that many coaches will recognize. A male client chooses a female coach who he feels believes in him and his success. The results of the first sessions are very encouraging. The client talks about his achievements and results and receives supportive feedback from the coach. However, there is no change without resistance. The client begins to find it difficult to implement the action plan developed with the coach. Sometimes it does not work out at all, and sometimes he feels even less capable than before coaching. He cannot talk about these problems to his coach, because she believed in him so much and expected good results from him. He also cannot disappoint her, so session after session he is forced to tell her about his imaginary successes. He goes through several sessions like this and declares that they can finish the work, because, thanks to the coach, he has achieved all the results he needs. If these sessions were supervised, would the supervisor be able to help the coach identify the client's resistance and understand the reason for it? Would it help the coach to work through his own resistance and defences? To do this, the supervisor should know about transference, a key psychoanalytic phenomenon. Choosing as a coach a woman who believed in him, the client may have unknowingly fallen into the clutches of maternal transference. He had a mother who believed in him, admired his success and his brilliant grades, but who always became discouraged and disappointed if he failed. The client unconsciously chose this particular coach, perceiving her as 'his mother who believed in him'. While the shallow changes were taking place, he was inspired and basked in the coach's (mother's) admiration. But at the moment when he began to have difficulties, he could not share these with the coach. To do this would be to face the disappointment in the coach's (mother's) eyes again and to experience the pain of losing the mother's admiration and love again. He could not afford to allow that to happen.

The supervisor could ask why in this situation the coach blindly followed the client? Was it important for the coach to get a positive coaching result? Did the coach deliberately not pay attention to the client's dull eyes? Not to say that this was intentional. Rather, he would have been caught in a countertransference that blinded her professional self. Countertransference is another psychoanalytic phenomenon that is an unconscious emotional reaction of the specialist to the client's transference. Could a supervisor without awareness of countertransference help coaches recognize the impasse and get out of it?

Here I have illustrated just three (resistance, transference, and countertransference) of the many psychoanalytic phenomena that coaches could struggle with in every coaching process. These and others deserve the attention of the coach with the help of their supervisor.

In this chapter I will review the process of the development of the psychoanalytic tradition in supervision and the tasks of coaching supervision in light of this tradition. I will also explore an important aspect of supervision in relation to development of the self of the coach with some ideas for research and further learning about this approach.

Development of the psychoanalytic tradition in supervision

Supervision in psychoanalysis has more than a century of history. Reflecting on psychoanalysis as an important element of psychoanalytic education in universities, Freud wrote that the future analyst can get supervision and guidance from more experienced colleagues (Freud 1919). In 1922, for the first time the International Psychoanalytic Association made supervision an integral part of education, along with personal analysis and theoretical training. At that time, the 'teacher–student' model of supervision was dominant.

From the 1930s, psychoanalysts began to develop different supervision concepts that were often in conflict with each other (Caligor 1981). The Budapest Group insisted that supervision should be an extension of personal analysis and performed by the same analyst. Thus, the analysis was focused on the exploration of transference, and supervision on the countertransference. Another approach to supervision was developed in Vienna by Bibring (1937), who required a complete separation of analysis and supervision with the latter aimed at didactic training. The supervisor here actually taught the supervisee the technique of ana-lytical work – what and how to work through, when to interpret, in what words, and so on. The contradiction between these approaches is clearly reflected in the simple 'treat or teach' dilemma – whether the supervisor should treat the super-visee or teach them. In effect, this means choosing between a psychoanalytic study of the unconscious and a rational pedagogical approach to supervision. In the latter the knowledge and skills are transferred from the mentor to the student, who forms the required competencies and necessary skills through the supervi-sion process.

Leader (2010) describes the purpose of supervision from a pedagogical per-spective as 'the enhancement of the supervisee's professional development, taking place in a supportive context of education and "coaching". This benevolent atmo-sphere, it is also claimed, should include a "monitoring" function of the supervis-ee's work' (p. 228). Critiquing this model of supervision, he points out that psychoanalysis completely disappears in such 'coaching', namely the understand-ing of the unconscious dynamics of interaction between the therapist and the patient. Leader believes that supervision should not involve rational learning or skill transfer, but rather the analyst's ability to understand the underlying motives of the patient's actions and behaviour.

In the French psychoanalytic school, supervision is similarly not considered as a form of training for skills and gaining knowledge. Instead, it helps the analyst maintain their professional self in confusion and helplessness, while retaining and evolving the psychoanalytic process (Lebovici 1983). Lebovici, looking for a balance between 'teach' and 'treat', insisted that supervisory relationships should never be dogmatic or imperative. The supervisor provides support for the psy-choanalytic process instead of teaching analysis technique.

In keeping with Lebovici, Leader (2010) notes that the supervisor is neither the therapist's educator nor the patient's advocate. The supervisor is the warden of the analytic process, the main tool of psychoanalysis. The supervisee is expected to use the supervision to solve the problems that arise in the analysis on their own rather than asking the supervisor for such help. Supervision is not the transfer of experience and knowledge to the practitioner, but their further learning through the exploration of their work in the presence of the more experienced colleague, whose questions and sometimes interpretations are not a direct guide to action, but the way to advance the practitioner's understanding of the client and the ongoing psychoanalytic process.

Objectives of psychoanalytically oriented coaching supervisors

Freud insisted that a specialist of any profession can become a psychoanalyst if they complete a special psychoanalytic education, which includes personal anal-ysis and supervision in addition to theory. He meant that what matters for the future psychoanalyst is not so much the theoretical knowledge of psychology and psychiatry as understanding the complex and multidimensional aspects of unconscious interaction with another person. Freud was aware of how easily one can 'go wrong' or even seriously harm a person, relying only on theoretical ideas or, on the contrary, on his intuition. That is why, I would argue, an additional psychoanalytical education is necessary not only for psychoanalysts or psychotherapists, but also for coaches and their supervisors. This psychoanalytic component of training (personal analysis and supervision) is that 'fifth element', without which, in my opinion, it would be difficult for a coach to provide professional help to another person. The following example of coaching supervision demonstrates the significance of such knowledge in relation to the task of *developing insight*.

Box 7.1 Case illustration

A 38-year-old CEO of a family business came to coaching no longer able to work in an atmosphere of constant rudeness and offensive behaviour from the proprietor. Entering her office, he would immediately attack her with words like, 'Why are you just sitting and picking your nose, start working. Now.' She told the coach that when he was scheduled to visit the office, she would shrink in her chair from the very first thing, trying to become invisible. It was even worse when his visits were unexpected, with no time for her to prepare for them. Then, she reported feeling like a trapped butterfly whose wings were being torn off.

She was actually a very efficient leader and was unable to understand why he treated her so unfairly. She spent the entire first session crying, and the coach, not daring to put in a single word of his own thoughts, chose to listen to her carefully. The client ended the session with a request: 'I have to leave this job, and you have to help me do it.' During the second and third sessions, the same pattern was seen: crying, accounts of episodes of insults and bias against her, ending with an expression of desire to quit the job. The coach's suggestion that she was hurt because the proprietor behaved like this in front of her staff was not confirmed. 'This is his communication style with everyone, including his wife. She is also a co-owner, but just technically. When they come to the office together, he communicates with her in the same way. And anyway, why do I care how rude he is to my employees or his wife! He shouldn't treat me like this!' The coach's attempts to ask her if she was looking for another job led to an angry outburst and accusations directed towards the coach: 'Why should I leave? I gave this job 15 years, built everything here and now I have to give it up?' As a result, the coach began to feel more and more at an impasse, experiencing loss of competence, helplessness and powerlessness. With these feelings, the coach came to supervision.

In this situation, a psychoanalytic lens had the potential to offer the coach a way of helping the client recognize the kind of internal conflicts that she unconsciously brings to her business reality and play out there. Even in this short case description the client's regression to certain childhood states is tangible. For some reason, a successful manager loses her adult professional condition and turns in the presence of the owner into a little offended child, unable to assert her rights and request respect for herself. Obviously, this painful relationship with the owner has a certain hidden meaning for the client, which needs to be understood in order to help her.

The coach, by attempting to create a safe and caring container for the client, was gradually dragged into the client's enquiry without realizing it. Along with the client, he fell into a state of helplessness and was unable to take a more active position. This is the unconscious countertransference, which, in fact, does not have to prevent the coach from working and can potentially be one of his main instruments. The client's emotions can be compared to a lasso that is thrown at the coach, snags them, and draws them into replaying the client's actual conflict. All this happens completely unconsciously for both client and coach. That's why the participation of a third person – the supervisor – who is not involved in their interaction and so can recognize what is happening in coaching sessions, is so important. Drawing an analogy with the theatre – we also experience what is happening on stage while sitting in the audience, but we are still less emotionally involved in the action that is happening on stage.

Dealing with emotions

Does the coaching process always feel so emotionally charged? The answer is quite simple. If the client's enquiry does not affect the coach emotionally, this is most likely to be a sign of a fake protective enquiry, which conceals the real one. As the real inquiry unfolds, there will inevitably be anxiety and other distinct feelings. Should the coach then respond emotionally to the client's experience? From the standpoint of more than a century of theory and practice of psychoanalysis, the answer to this question is also simple: it is not in our power to allow, prohibit, or consciously control our emotional responses to the client's feelings (or their apparent absence). This usually happens outside of our wishes, completely unconsciously. What we are aware of and experience in a session is nothing more than just the tip of a huge emotional iceberg. A coach who feels nothing during a session is in a defence position, which is not an optimal coaching condition. This can be a result of the coach's personal unprocessed internal conflicts and poor emotional intelligence, or it can be a defensive reaction to some of the client's difficult emotions. It could also be both. These are questions that the supervisor should ask and try to explore with the coach. Does the client experience something disturbing in the present business reality? This is the first layer. Then the client comes to the coach and brings these feelings to the coaching process. This is the second layer. And the third layer is when the coach brings these emotional experiences to the supervisory process. So, the supervisor also cannot avoid an emotional challenge that is not only related to the client's enquiry, but also to the coach's enquiry. In psychoanalysis, this is called a parallel process. What could not be consciously worked out in coaching, what the coach did not want to notice and feel, will finally be shown during his supervision, and the supervisor will have the opportunity to see and feel it. Through this process, the supervisor can better help the coach understand the depth of the client's enquiry and discover new mental resources, by developing which the client will benefit. The following example shows how this case might develop.

Box 7.2 Case illustration

In an effort to express his feelings at the supervisor's request the coach suddenly said: 'I feel rejected, she doesn't want to listen to me . . . she doesn't need me . . . I can't attract her attention.' He instantly recognized these feelings as his own empathic identification with the client's experience: 'it's like I'm turning into a small child who needs the parent's attention and their love, but who can't get it.' The supervisor asked: 'If we assume that you are experiencing exactly what the client unconsciously encourages you to feel, then how could your work process might change?'

Thanks to the realization of his countertransference, the coach was able to see for himself and therefore help the client to discover a completely different unconscious layer of the client–owner relationship that was hidden until that moment. Instead of a clear request for a job change, the coach was able to hear a hidden request: 'How can I not fall into these painful states, learn to protect myself, build the appropriate boundaries with the boss and save the job that is important to me?' The coach's simple question to the client turned out to be the most resourceful: 'You mentioned a butterfly that gets its wings torn off. Do you remember anything about this?' The client burst into tears. She said that as a preschool child she and her father loved to catch butterflies. He collected them by pinning them. One day, he carelessly took a butterfly out of a net and tore its wing off. She recalled the horror she had felt at the time and added that the colouring of the butterflies helps them not to be caught. 'Be invisible?' – the coach asked.

These and other connections between the content from the present business situation and childhood memories helped the client clearly realize that for all these years she unconsciously treated her relationship with her boss like that with her father. After her admission to school, their warm relationship broke rapidly. Her father became very demanding, checking her grades every day and irritably scolding her for mistakes. Only later did it become clear that something else caused such a change and she could do nothing to influence it.

In this example, we can clearly see how psychoanalytic theory can support coaching without turning it into psychotherapy. In psychotherapy, subsequent work would be focused on deepening the understanding of the client's childhood experiences and fantasies in the relationship with the father (and mother) and thoroughly working out the corresponding internal conflicts. Instead, in coaching, the discovery of the connection between internal and external, child and adult realities is aimed solely at helping clients to solve their enquiry, develop a plan of specific actions and make the changes they desire. There is no goal of working through deep internal conflicts in coaching, but often even a simple awareness of their impact on the present reality helps the client's adult professional self to maintain and develop its activity, while not allowing the child self to jump out from behind the scenes to occupy the entire mental scene.

Indeed, one of the supervisor's most important objectives is to help the coach not to be seduced by psychotherapy content of the session and not to lose the focus on the business context.

However, the client's simple discovery and awareness of replaying a painful childhood relationship in the workplace is still only a potential resource for change. This resource has yet to gradually germinate and become stronger in the present corporate environment like a seed planted in the ground. At this next stage of the coaching process, supervision plays an important role, since it is that stage where resistance to change takes place, which often neither client nor coach want to work through.

Dealing with resistance

For example, even if they have planned a conversation with the boss on establishing a correct and respectful relationship, the client may find many apparently legitimate reasons for postponing it to a later date. If the coach is too insistent in encouraging the client to follow the plan, the client may sharply interrupt and terminate the coaching or even pretend that the conversation with the boss has already taken place and everything is now fine (and furthermore, since the result has been achieved, they can complete the coaching). How frequently we experience apparently 'positive' coaching results like this, coaches can only judge for themselves, but my more than 25 years' experience as a supervisor shows that ignoring resistance to change, and coaches' silent consent to this resistance, is very common. Therefore, an important task of the supervisor is to help the coach recognize the manifestations of resistance to change of all kinds and work through them diligently. Any explicit or gentle nudging by the coach usually works against the changes in cases of client resistance. All the major anxieties, fears and fantasies about the negative consequences of changes must be well worked through before the client can escape from usual behavioural patterns.

There can be no real change without resistance. So, the most reliable and accurate indicator of the effectiveness of the coaching process is the *presence* of resistance to change in the client rather than its absence. The supervisor should pay maximum attention to various aspects of resistance, putting emphasis on its absence, ignoring it, or delays in working through it. The phenomenon of resistance and how to work with it are comprehensively described in the psychoanalytic literature.

Dealing with termination of coaching engagements

Finally, perhaps one of the most important stages of the coaching process is its termination. The main objective of the supervisor at this stage is to help the coach start the process for a client to own the results of coaching. Until termination, the coaching process is a co-creative one. It is a joint work of the coach and the client, where internal resources are found and insights are born in order to solve the enquiry. Then new patterns of behaviour, communication, new leadership styles, and new purposes of work and engagement with it are developed. All this is a joint result. Simply telling the client to take ownership of the results obtained or insistently repeating 'this is yours, not mine' often reflects the professional incompetence of the coach and is a clear manifestation of their own resistance to the actual transfer of coaching results to the client. This prescriptive message captures the coach's dominant position, who indicates what the client should do. Ignoring this problem often leads to maintaining a client's internal, hidden dependence on the coach. If there are new problems or complex development opportunities, the client will be forced to appeal to the coach again and again. From the psychoanalytic coaching perspective, an effective ending of the coaching process and the client's taking ownership of its results is only possible when the client has formed their own 'coaching self' in the process of working together, thus enabling them to continue the development and respond to new challenges independently.

The client's coaching self is gradually formed through the unconscious identification with the main competencies of the coach – their ability to listen, feel, analyse, understand, become more aware of limitations and internal conflicts, find connections between past and present experiences, detect replays of the same situations, generate insights, recognize resistances, work through them, slowly nurture changes and so on. In fact, the main result of psychoanalytic coaching is the birth of the client's own coaching self and so the real possibility for them to choose between old and new behavioural and growth patterns. Therefore, the supervisor should specifically pay special attention to the coach's work aimed at the generation, development and strengthening of the client's coaching self. In order for the client's coaching self to take ownership of the results at the final stage, the coach's activity must gradually decrease from session to session, giving more space for the client to work in the session. This starts the process of separation by splitting the client's coaching self and the coach's professional self. The client feels more and more able to solve all problems independently and effectively and implement action plans.

Coaches sometimes find it psychologically difficult to 'let go' of a client in this way. This can be exacerbated by the lack of experience of understanding the unconscious and its impact on the client and the coaching process itself. The coach's own unprocessed internal conflicts can lead to a negative countertransference that has nothing to do with the client's experience. For example, an insecure coach may begin to please the client, to show them that they are completely at their disposal. A coach with narcissistic issues may unknowingly retain an important client who raises the coach's status in the professional community. Sometimes you can hear coaches using any opportunity to either complain about their clients or, on the contrary, boast about them. This confidentiality violation is also a consequence of the coach's personal problems, which destroy the coaching process. It is therefore a critical objective of the supervisor to detect the coach's demonstrations of such destructive and dangerous countertransference. However, the supervisor does not have the task to therapeutically elaborate the coach's countertransference. Often, it is enough to help the coach in understanding their experiences so that they do not bring them into the work with the client. In other cases, the supervisor should recommend the coach to start their own therapy to better understand and work through the unconscious conflicts that interfere with their work. It is important to point out that the coach is unlikely to be able to help the client in forming a coaching self, if the coach in turn has not developed his own professional coaching self during supervision sessions.

Development of the coaching self through supervision

The discussions that divide psychologists and coaches on the criteria of 'internal–external' and 'past–future' did not arise out of nowhere. Indeed, practitioners whose competencies are focused on working with personal problems can easily lose track of the client's initial enquiry and 'move on' in a direction they know. In psychoanalysis, this is considered to reflect the consultant's resistance to work with the present. It does not occur just to those fascinated by the past. The same avoidance of working with the present can push practitioners to work with the future. Sometimes it is much easier and more pleasant to help a client build a plan for achieving specific results than to thoroughly explore their enquiry in the present business reality. The opposite is also true, of course. A psychoanalytically oriented coach may unconsciously prefer the most in-depth and therefore prolonged (over a significant number of sessions) clarification of the request, rather than to switch focus at the right time onto how the client can implement what has been done and achieved in their current situation. Therefore, the supervisor should be very attentive to such deviations from the present concerns.

The process of developing and formulating the coach's competencies influences the development of the profession. Coaching as a profession requires individual mastery, which is not developed once and for all, like receiving a diploma, but needs constant attention, losing and finding new perspectives. This is an important and dynamic process of professional growth, which inevitably has its conflict stages.

We have seen above that one of the coach's most important competencies is their ability to maintain a working state in which they can simultaneously feel and reflect. It is in the process of supervision that the coach learns to do this. An external dialogue with the supervisor allows the coach to gradually form a reflexive split of their self into an analytical coaching self and an emotional self that can be open to the emotions of the client. The latter, in some cases, can be captured by defence mechanisms or, in other cases, by the coach's own emotions, anxiety or excitement. The most important for the coach in this case is not to identify with the supervisor, which would only lead to the emergence of a 'clone' of the latter, but to aim for better understanding and feeling of the coaching process focused on the client. The gradual formation of a reflexive split in supervision will allow the coach to avoid identifying completely with either his analytic self or his emotional self, but to take the third position – the professional coaching self that supports a productive dialogical interaction between them. As the supervisory process progresses, the coach becomes more and more capable of both recognizing and independently working through their own defences and maintaining focus on the client's enquiry when emotional experiences capture their selves. This is extremely important, since the coach's own emotional responses are usually a 'litmus test' that helps clarify the client's hidden limitations and resources that are relevant to the enquiry.

From the coaching self to the supervisor-coaching self

The secret of effective coaching seems to lie in the development of the professional coaching self, allowing it to be truly open to the client's experiences and resistances, as well as the coach's own feelings and defences, while retaining the ability to actively think and explore everything that happens in a coaching process. This key competence is formed not only in continuous supervision but can be significantly enhanced and developed through personal therapy or psychoanalysis. Due to the fact that such development is not common in coaching communities, the entire workload can end up on the supervisory process, where supervisors are forced to take on the role of therapist to some extent – to 'teach and (just a little) treat'. I would advocate that in the future there is a stricter separation of these roles and stronger requirement for certain personal therapy in coaching education. For now, supervision is the highest level of regulation of our profession.

The coaching self, flexible internal boundaries, active listening without excessive anxiety to fall into emotions, the ability for self-reflection and internal dialogue – these and many other important coaching competencies are born, grown and polished through supervisory regulation. In the course of this work, a new internal supervisor-coaching self should emerge on the basis of the coaching self, capable of sufficient supervisory self-regulation without the permanent assistance of an experienced supervisor. This, however, does not eliminate the need for further growth and discussion of coaching cases in professional groups with peers. The endless cycle of regulation and self-regulation of our profession – what could be more exciting and interesting!

Guidance for further learning and research

Coaching helps the client to get out of their comfort zone towards the development of more satisfying behavioural and leadership strategies. The task of the coaching supervisor is to help the coach to do this as effectively as possible. But are we good at our own developmental processes? Could it be the Achilles heel of classical coaching, its comfort zone and resistance to development? As we have seen above, the personal and the professional are inseparable in our clients, and if we really want to help them, we need first to explore the same relationship in ourselves. Our professional coaching competencies relate to our personal unconscious conflicts and limitations, and our personality influences the coaching process with our clients. We should stop telling ourselves that, unlike psychotherapists, coaches have no psychological influence on the client, and face the fact that we have. This has to be faced not just theoretically and through gaining intellectual knowledge, but through exploring our own unconscious and its influence on ourselves through psychotherapy or even psychoanalysis as a client. This is the main challenge facing supervisors. Changes in the profession begin with us. As soon as we begin to explore our unconscious, it immediately becomes psychoanalytic learning through experience, and together with the study of literature, it opens up a vast space of professional development in coaching and supervision. To do this, the first step is to leave our comfort zone.

Questions for reflection

- Do my feelings and fantasies interfere with or help me in supervising and coaching? Can I use them to better understand the coach's supervision enquiry or the client's coaching enquiry?
- How attentive am I to the coach's resistance to deeper investigate the hidden aspects of its client's request? Do I notice 'fake' elements in the results achieved by the coach and its client?
- What is my own knowledge as a supervisor about psychoanalytic concepts, their history and application?
- What is the balance in my supervisory work between transferring my experience and knowledge and building a space where the coach can deepen his/her own understanding of the clients and their enquiry?

Further sources

Kernberg, O.F. (2010) Psychoanalytic supervision: the supervisor's tasks, *The Psychoanalytic Quarterly*, 79(3): 603–627. This paper reviews key aspects of psychoanalytic supervision, including the psychoanalytic supervisor's objectives, the supervisee's countertransference exploration, the dynamics of supervision and supervisor's professional responsibility.

Kets de Vries, M.F.R. (2006) *The Leader on the Couch: A Clinical Approach to Changing People and Organizations*. Hoboken, NJ: John Wiley & Sons Ltd. This book is one of the most recognized introductions to psychoanalytic coaching and its use for working with business leaders.

Ogden, T.H. (2005) On psychoanalytic supervision, *International Journal of Psycho-Analysis*, 86(5): 1265–1280. The author provides both a theoretical context for, and clinical illustrations of, the way in which he works as a psychoanalytic supervisor.

Acknowledgement

*The chapter is translated from Russian by Feodor Loktev.

References

Bibring, E. (1937) III Report of the International Training Commission, *Bulletin of the International Psycho-Analytic Association*, 18: 365–372.

Caligor, L. (1981) Parallel and reciprocal processes in psychoanalytic supervision, *Contemporary Psychoanalysis*, 17: 1–27.

Freud, S. (1919) *On the Teaching of Psycho-Analysis in Universities. The Standard Edition of the Complete Psychological Works of Sigmund Freud*, Volume XVII (1917–1919), London: Vintage.

Leader, D. (2010) Some thoughts on supervision, *British Journal of Psychotherapy*, 26(2): 228–241.

Lebovici, S. (1983) Supervision in French psychoanalytic education: its history and evolution, *Annual of Psychoanalysis*, 11: 79–89.

8 | Supervising with Gestalt principles in mind

Sue Congram

Introduction

Gestalt-informed supervision offers a way of working that is creative, interconnective and systemic. Rooted in a relational discipline (Bentley and Congram 2020; Clemmens 2020; Chidiac 2018; Jacobs and Hycner 2008), supervision becomes a learning partnership where both supervisor and coach take responsibility for making the supervision work. As an established Gestalt practitioner, teacher and supervisor, I have found that Gestalt provides a rich and colourful tapestry to support and strengthen the work of coaches, whether the coach is Gestalt-based or not. I also believe there are many valuable components of Gestalt that supervisors can readily build into their thinking and practice. In support of this view I explain three core principles that sit at the heart of a Gestalt way of working:

- Dialogic process
- Phenomenological method
- Holistic field.

These three components distinguish Gestalt as a *process* methodology, with a focus on psychological patterns, or forces that influence the way people interact with each other and their environment. Characteristic of Gestalt, and building on these three components, is a creative means of inquiry (Spagnuolo Lobb and Amendt-Lyon 2003), working with what is embodied, the emotional field and subtleties in language. What this means in Gestalt supervision is that the holistic nature of being human is central to the work:

- Body responses are as important to attend to as the way that we think about and perceive our world.
- Emotions emerging between the coach and the supervisor inform the supervision.
- The language used to talk about the coaching offers structure, metaphor, nuances and focal points.

From this holistic view the supervisor and coach explore emerging themes in the coach's professional practice, where the role of the supervisor is to raise awareness of ethical practice, relational and conditioned patterns, shifts in behaviour, emotions, sensations, images and metaphor, as the narrative of client work is told. Drawing on the immediacy of the moment being one of the most powerful skills that comes into play. I will describe one of my own case studies to illustrate how this works:

Box 8.1

My client comes for regular supervision on her coaching. On one occasion, she tells me about a difficulty that she is having coaching a woman who is stressed by what she describes as emotional bullying at work. She narrates in detail how her coaching proceeded.

It is worth mentioning at this point that as Gestalt is informed by the phenomeno-logical method, the content of what a coach brings to supervision is of less concern than *how* they present their case material, *how* they do their coaching and, staying true to the learning partnership approach, *how* the coach and supervisor relate to each other in the here-and-now. The bullying case story therefore briefly describes observations of *how* the coach was presenting her client work and my response to that, rather than the story itself:

Box 8.2

I noticed as the coach was telling me about the client that she became more animated and descriptive when she talked about the bullying. When I shared my observation of this, she sidestepped it and drew attention to another issue of concern. I became even more curious. I referred back to her description of the bully, sharing my curiosity and inviting her to tell me again. This time she paid attention, eventually revealing a past experience of hers where she had been bullied at work and realizing that the issue had not been fully resolved.

My client had not made the connection between her own past experience and the client situation during her coaching. Her embodied emotional bruising had been forgotten or ignored. Through these reflections the coach was able to recognize how her own emotional reactions had become confused with the client work. With new awareness of this, she was able to see the client situation in a new light.

The dialogic aspect of supervision is continuous; it is demonstrated in this illustration through the sharing of my curiosity about the coach's animated behaviour, typically for a Gestalt-informed approach, that is reflected back without interpretation. The phenomenological method involved focusing on the here-and-now process of observation, while attending to the holistic field meant recognizing how something outside of the present situation could be entering and affecting the work in the moment. As such, the supervisor is in service to the coach, and the coach is in charge of shaping their own learning. The following sections describe these components in more detail.

The use of Gestalt theory in supervision

In this section I will briefly describe and illustrate the three main components of Gestalt in the context of coaching supervision. These interconnecting components of *dialogic process, phenomenological method* and attending to the *holistic field,* together provide an imaginative and creative process for reflection and transformative learning.

A commonly accepted view of supervision in the helping professions is that it is a reflective activity (Hawkins and Shohet 2000; Lahad 2000; Carroll and Tholstrup 2001; Carroll and Gilbert 2005; Hawkins and Smith 2006; Shohet 2008), a process where learning and evaluation of professional work takes place. Gestalt, too, is a reflective practice. In Gestalt supervision the supervisor and coach reflect on the professional practice and case studies of the coach through a holistic lens. What that means is that the client's concerns (now situated in the past) and the current reality of supervision are considered to be connected through the work; through the narrative of case studies told by the coach, the way that they bring their work to supervision and the interrelational dynamics between the supervisor and coach. The impact of this can be more fully understood in the section titled 'Holistic fields'.

Dialogic process

A dialogic attitude means being aware of and making choices on how the 'other' is perceived in the process of relating, engaging in an exchange that is inclusive and generative. This idea stems from the work of Buber (1937) who differentiated between 'I-it' and 'I-thou', where 'it' refers to a role, position, thing, profession, guru or a stereotype, where the other person is seen through the screen of 'it' (manager, teacher, leader, boss, client). 'I-it' usually implies that the relationship is hierarchical in some way. Whereas 'I-thou' is about seeing the other as a human being on mutual terms. Referring to the work of Buber and 'genuine dialogue', Jacobs (1989) describes three important elements: (1) presence, (2) genuine and unreserved communication and (3) inclusion, offering some indications of the richness of a dialogic process.

In Gestalt-informed supervision the supervisor and coach will likely achieve moments of exceptional 'I-thou' contact where something changes, as well as 'I-thou' dips in the relationship where contact seems more distant. The dips interest me in supervision, for in these dips may exist interruptions within the dialogue in the form of *confluence, projection* and *transference, which turn the dialogue towards I-it, and away from I-thou.* In Gestalt terms these are phenomena that occur naturally at the contact boundary between self and the environment (Mackewn 1997; Woldt and Toman 2005), which I discuss more fully in the next sections. The task in Gestalt supervision is to bring into awareness patterns that do not serve the coaching well but occur through habit rather than awareness, and in raising ethical subtleties. This may require the coach to reflect on their own fixed patterns and psychological conditioning.

Many professional relationships interweave between 'I-it' and 'I-thou'; the art of effective Gestalt supervision is to engage in genuine dialogue, pay attention to the moments when the dynamics of the relationship change, to be aware of such shifts and to make choices that can fulfil healthy and effective supervision.

Confluence

'Confluence' in Gestalt terms is a 'contact style'; it means merging together, where difference is not apparent and there is 'no appreciation of boundary' (Perls et al. 1951: 118) or 'sense of differentiation' (Mackewn 1997: 27). Often detected by the use of the word 'we', there are times when confluence is appropriate and enjoyable, such as in meditation, when two people are in love, or moments when a team is aligned, experiencing a sense of togetherness. Confluence can also interrupt dialogue when used to avoid difference or conflict.

When someone seeks coaching they are looking for a different voice, a new perspective, a way of expanding their own way of thinking in order to learn or change. If a coach becomes habitually confluent with their clients, their coaching ability will become limited, raising a number of ethical questions around their professional capabilities. Confluence in coaching lacks confrontation and there is an agreeable rather than challenging air about the work: wanting to 'be nice' or 'be good' for the client, acting in a way that keeps the dialogue safe, regularly engaging in a conversational style, fulfilling a need to belong, being what the client expects, avoiding conflict or a difference of opinion. When I am supervising I am constantly on the look-out for signs of confluence, to bring awareness of habitual patterns to the coach so that the coach can become more professionally competent, more integrated in the way they work.

Projection and transference

'Projection' in traditional Gestalt terms means denying or repressing a quality or feeling and attributing it to another person (Perls et al. 1951). As Joyce and Sills (2018) point out, there is today some confusion about this concept because the word is used in at least two other different ways: (1) to imagine what is not there, to anticipate a future; (2) and as transference, when projected material is historical and inappropriate. I would add two further usages: (3) where people make assumptions and expectations about others and the world around them, then act as though that is true; (4) as embedded in many forms of feedback.

Projection sits within a wide body of knowledge rooted in both Freudian (Gay 1995) and Jungian ideas (Samuels et al. 1986), and today has found its way into coaching (Rogers 2004) and supervision (Hawkins and Shohet 2000; Schaverien and Case 2007). In Gestalt supervision, the supervisor attends to what the coach may be projecting onto the client. For instance, when interpretation and meaning-making is narrow and rigid, a coach may be acting from a fixed projection. Other projective scenarios in coaching might be linked to role, gender, age and race, where attention is drawn to the role or stereotype, rather than the person. The link between 'I-it' and projection becomes more apparent when a client is better qualified and more experienced in their particular field of work than the coach, and the coach is intimidated or unconsciously affected by this.

If the coach projects onto the client 'better than me', then the coaching is unlikely to work well.

This leads to *transference* and *countertransference*, which are forms of projection rooted in the history of a person. A Gestalt perspective of transference is the way that a person organizes their *perceptual field* (Mackewn 1997); that is, they organize their thoughts through the lens of their history, key figures from the past, habitual behaviours, psychological conditioning and unfinished business, rather than through the current reality.

Transference and countertransference are part of life and social interaction. However, out of awareness it can become disruptive, or create co-dependence in relationships. Awareness of a transference brings choice and consideration for dealing with the current reality in a different way. In supervision, when the coach is troubled or seems confused about the work, I inquire into the transferential dynamics, inviting the coach to reflect on their relationship with the client. This may also involve explaining to the coach what transference is, what is happening, the value of transference and how to manage it. It has to be said that when coaching training does not include awareness of transference and countertransference, the coach may well fall into difficulties somewhere along the line and become perplexed by it. Complex as it may be, I consider this to be critical as well as ethical learning in coaching, and an essential part of supervision.

Phenomenological method

'Phenomenological method' in Gestalt is directly related to the holistic field (discussed in the next section), where attention is given to what comes into awareness within the flow of the here-and-now, described in Gestalt terms as 'figure/ground', where figure is the focus of attention and ground is the context (Burley and Bloom 2008).

Phenomenology is one of the strengths of the Gestalt method, taking the perspective that you can only really explore what is emerging and revealed in the present moment. There are three skills to phenomenological inquiry that have developed in the world of therapy and counselling (Mackewn 1997; Joyce and Sills 2018), which are particularly relevant in coaching supervision. These skills are *bracketing, describing* and *equalization*.

First, the supervisor is able to 'bracket off' their interpretations, judgements, concerns, ideas, and so on, in order to fully meet the coach. Working from a phenomenological frame-of-reference this is essential, but as Joyce and Sills (2018) point out, it is not so easy because we unconsciously interpret and judge the world as we meet it all the time. We have to become aware of our interpretations before we can begin to put them to one side.

The second skill, 'describing', is saying 'what is' – that is, what is noticed and observed as it is happening. Typically, this would be stated in language such as 'I notice that . . . (your voice has softened)'; 'You look . . . (flushed)'. What can happen in supervision is that both supervisor and coach fall into doing this together; noticing 'what is', is not only the responsibility of the supervisor, it is a skill that both supervisor and coach can develop.

The third skill is a process of 'equalizing', where emerging observations are treated with equal importance and tiny or big shifts are given equal consideration. It is worth noting that 'noticing the obvious', an aspect of equalizing, is really what a phenomenological method is interested in, yet the obvious can easily be obscured by the content of issues being discussed. What becomes obvious in supervision might not have been so obvious to the coach when working with their client, or treated with equal value alongside other concerns.

The phenomenological method is not so much a technique but an attitude, which particularly draws on the curiosity and open-mindedness of the supervisor. Joyce and Sills (2018) include *active curiosity* as one of the facets of phenomenological method. What it means is that the supervisor holds a position of interest and curiosity in situations arising in the room, as well as in the case stories told by the coach, 'being curious about how situations arise, how the client makes sense of them, how *this* fits with *that*, and what it means in the larger field' (Joyce and Sills 2018: 22). So, rather than giving answers or solutions, what brings supervision alive is the exploration of possibilities, bringing in questions and offering observations of gestures, voice tone, shifts in dialogue or body language, as well as the use of language.

Holistic fields

A Gestalt perspective in supervision takes into account multiple fields (Congram 2011), which serves supervision well when we consider the full extent of relationships that are impacting the supervision as it is taking place. To understand this concept better it is worth getting to know the work of Kurt Lewin (1946; 1947) whose idea of 'field theory' is deeply rooted in Gestalt. Describing a field as 'the totality of coexisting facts, which are conceived of as mutually interdependent' (Cartwright 1951: 240) he proposed that in order to understand people's behaviour it is necessary to look at the whole psychological, emotional and experiential field (situation) within which people act, behave and respond. This view has been more usefully explained by Parlett (1991; 1997), Staemmler (2006), and O'Neill and Gaffney (2008), describing how people are influenced by and are also influencers of the field. Applying this to supervision, the immediate field is co-created in the supervisor–coach relationship, whether the supervision is face-to-face, by phone or by video-conferencing. This supervisor–coach relationship is further influenced by the coach–client relationship and to some extent by the client–context field (Congram 2011), neither of which are physically in the room. In Gestalt terms this is *the absent presence in the room*. These three interconnecting fields of influence in supervision are illustrated in Figure 8.1.

A case example of how this can be seen in supervision, in this instance a supervision group, showed how the group unknowingly picked up and played out a pattern from the client system. A group member had been exploring a case, where a client was struggling to achieve recognition in her work. As she explored this in the group, incidents of 'feeling invisible' and 'lack of recognition' began to get played out between members of the group with each other. A situation known as 'parallel process' (in Gestalt and in a number of other disciplines), and an exam-

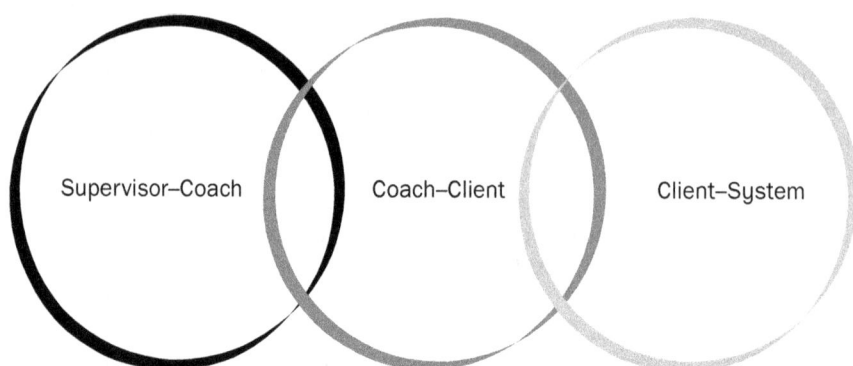

Figure 8.1 Interconnecting fields

ple of how powerful dynamics from one field can find their way into another. As a way of bringing awareness to this process, Gaffney (2008) asks a series of questions. 'How is that which is happening around us now entering the room? How have we brought it here with us? How are we playing it out?' (p. 29)

This field perspective is in some ways similar to the seven-eyed model of supervision described by Hawkins and Smith (2006), in that it takes into consideration the contextual field beyond the immediate work of the client in the room. Gestalt is different in the way that it attends to the wider processes: where the seven-eyed model helicopters over the different fields, dropping into each mode (pp. 171–172) to gain understanding, the holistic field perspective assumes an interconnection between them in which change in one field will have an effect on the other fields (Parlett 1991; O'Neill and Gaffney 2008). As such, the supervisor pays attention to field dynamics in the room that otherwise might go unnoticed.

When we look deeply into the holistic field, what we begin to see is that the interactive and psychological world of coaching and supervision is incredibly rich in information, connecting what's in the room with what is not in the room but exists as part of the unfolding work.

Box 8.3 Case illustration

Sara is an experienced coach. She coaches people at work, as well as offering in-depth coaching for people who meet difficulties in their lives, which she calls 'life coaching'.

Sometime after we had started working together, Sara brought to supervision a case story about a client who is the managing director of a family business, a role that he took over from his father three years ago. His father is now fully retired and yet makes his views clear about the way the business should be run. The client's sister also works in the business in a management role. The brother and sister do not get on particularly well. The situation is complex and often difficult. The client has asked for some coaching to try to deal with some staff issues. He wants to grow the business and believes that the current situation is not supporting growth. The sister has refused to take part in any intervention of this kind.

Sara is Gestalt trained. She is aware of overlapping boundaries between family life and business in the client situation. In supervision she was able to map out the multiple fields at the client's workplace and consider some of the themes being played out within each different field. Sara mapped them as 'emotional fields' (see Figure 8.2). In the client system a number of themes stood out, such as sibling rivalry, which was carried through splits within the organization; old and new staff, which brought tensions between traditional ways of doing things against modern practices; and loyalty to the retired father, which showed up as resistance to the son. These dynamics were getting in the way of business growth.

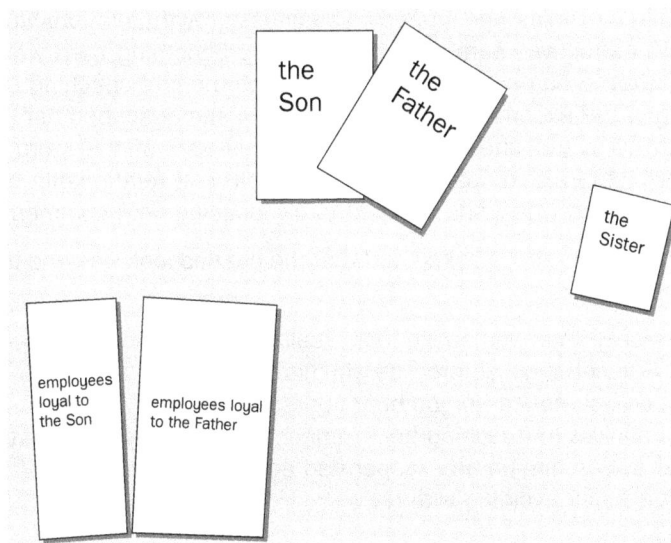

Figure 8.2 Emotional fields in family business

Sara then amplified this emotional map by using objects in my room to symbolize characters in the business, describing each one in colourful and descriptive ways. This narrative process amplified her understanding of power oppositions at play in the client system. Seeing this gave a much clearer perspective to Sara who, until then, had concentrated on emerging themes from her direct relationship with the client.

The phenomenological method discussed earlier maintains an approach where the clues for learning and growth are in the emerging process rather than the content of what is being said. So the mapping was held within a phenomenological frame as well as providing some insight into the holistic field. My attention was on the coach, her relationship with her client, how she maintained her attention, and what was happening in the here-and-now that might be relevant to the coaching work. This was not so much about what was evident, but what might be out of awareness yet influencing the holistic field. One aim in Gestalt is to bring into awareness what is otherwise unknown, on the basis that without awareness change cannot happen. The next step in this case illustration shows this, and how an experience from the past in the coach's own life was affecting the holistic field of coaching:

Box 8.4

In a later supervision Sara raised questions about her work with this same client. Although progress was being made, and her client had started to see the extent to which family dynamics were impeding business growth, relationships remained difficult and obstructive. Sara said that 'he was becoming hard work' and she didn't know what to do next. I invited her to recall the last coaching session – to tell the story of her experience with her client. As she described her client's relationship with his sister she appeared angry; this part of the story seemed to carry more vitality in it compared to the other difficult relationship between the client and his father, which she seemed to be focusing on. I commented on this.

Sara looked at me puzzled. I asked her what the puzzled look was and the following exchange took place:

Sara: It was only when you spoke that I realized my reaction. My feeling is that I want R to settle his differences with his sister.
Sue: What do you notice as you hear yourself say that?
Sara: I feel hooked in (touching her stomach), I feel a knot in my stomach. His sister avoids him (in an exasperated and questioning tone).
Sue: What are you avoiding with R . . . ?

[Long silence]

Sara: I think that I've diminished myself. I've put him in the role as managing director, as better than me and lost sight of him as a person.

My intervention of 'commenting' on Sara's shift in energy was a moment of describing and equalizing, both of which I explained earlier. This simple intervention led to a moment's reflection in which the exasperated comment 'his sister avoids him' suggested to me that there might be a projection around avoidance of R in the comment. I could have asked a number of questions at this point that would have raised awareness of this as a possible projection, or even questioned my own assumptions. But I felt that Sara had already sidestepped some issues regarding her client, so I decided to trust my intuition and ask the question with some directness.

Sara went on to tell me how she had often felt intimidated by men in senior roles when she was employed full time. She had never managed to overcome that fully, nor the discomforts that came with feeling belittled. This is an example of an 'I-it' shift described earlier, putting the client in an 'it' role of managing director with a further possible transference on the authority that the role carried. From a Gestalt perspective the coach will be less effective from this position. We agreed that Sara would take some time in supervision to explore her own projections and transferential patterns more fully – outlined earlier. She had a choice: she could have taken that issue and worked with it in therapy or coaching elsewhere.

Guidance for further learning and research

While the main canvas of Gestalt research is found in Gestalt therapy (Brownell 2008), the richness of Gestalt is in its totality of a number of underlying principles, practices and philosophies that can be applied to different sectors where personal, relational and systemic dynamics matter. A comprehensive text entitled *Relational Organisational Gestalt* by Chidiac (2018), provides a window into Gestalt as an approach for organizational work. She positions her thinking within the context of direct research, explaining why supervision is needed. Of particular interest here is that she highlights a wider range of research that underpins many of the facets that make up the 'gestalt' of Gestalt. She illustrates how Gestalt is not a single theory, but is informed by a multiplicity of theories, methods and philosophies that weave together in a particular way.

Strengthened by holistic and phenomenological methods, Gestalt supervision works well for individual work and supervision groups (Gaffney 2008). As already mentioned, the coaches who come to me for supervision are not all Gestalt-trained, and do not need to be. There are, however, a few factors that do make a difference:

- A reasonable capacity to self-reflect
- A strong sense of self and self-awareness
- A willingness to move away from content to appreciate the learning gained from process
- A willingness to step into a learning relationship and take joint responsibility for making supervision work.

With this in mind, a Gestalt supervisor could support a coach well where their practice has roots in existential ideas (Spinelli 2010), has concern for *ways of being* (Sieler 2010), and positive psychology (Zinker 1994; Kauffman et al. 2010). While Gestalt supervision is not so aligned with cognitive and transactional methods, it can complement these approaches well. I particularly wish to add, that where coaching training programmes do not include psychological competence, Gestalt-informed supervision is able to compensate for that, providing a psychological perspective that need not be difficult to grasp. In my view as a supervisor, coaching is strengthened when the coach has an ability to understand and work with psychological dynamics, as some of the concerns raised here will inevitably present themselves in coaching at some stage.

What Gestalt does not do is to provide professional knowledge and experience of different contexts, such as corporate work, educational experience, life coaching, executive coaching, groups and teams. It only provides a method that can be applied in these contexts. The supervisor's contextual experience is part of the skills, knowledge and wisdom that they bring to the work and to which they have applied their Gestalt knowledge. In other words, Gestalt alone is not the whole.

Questions for reflection

- In your supervision, how would you describe the dynamic field of your relationship? Does this serve the supervision well?
- Which of your supervision or coaching relationships are predominantly 'I-it' relationships? What can you do to change this? What do you think the benefit would be?
- What does it take to shift focus from the narrative content to in-the-moment observations? How can you learn that skill?
- Other than those mentioned in this chapter, what other ethical observations do you consider that Gestalt-based supervision could and would highlight?

Further sources

There are an increasing number of books becoming available on Gestalt-informed practice, especially beyond therapy. The list below offers a range within therapy and beyond, that would usefully feed into Gestalt-based supervision.

Chidiac, M. (2018) *Relational Organisational Gestalt*. Abingdon: Routledge. This is an excellent book bringing alive the relational perspectives of Gestalt within organizational settings. One of the strengths of this book is the way in which the ideas discussed are rooted in research.

Mackewn, J. (1997) *Developing Gestalt Counselling*. London: Sage and Joyce, P. and Sills, C. (2018) *Skills in Gestalt Counselling and Psychotherapy*. London: Sage, provide comprehensive texts of Gestalt in practice (in counselling and psychotherapy), which are easily digestible and translatable into coaching supervision.

Spagnuolo Lobb, M. and Amendt-Lyon, N. (eds) (2003) *Creative Licence: The Art of Gestalt Therapy*. New York: SpringerWien. This excellent collection provides an impressive array of the creative qualities of Gestalt that lead to in-depth work.

References

Bentley, T. and Congram, S. (2020, 2nd edn. due Autumn) *Gestalt: A Philosophy for Change*. Herefordshire: The Space between Publishing (original works published in the *Training Journal* 1996).

Brownell, P. (ed.) (2008) *Handbook for Theory, Research, and Practice in Gestalt Therapy*. Newcastle: Cambridge Scholars Publishing.

Buber, M. (1937) *I and Thou* (trans. R.G. Smith). London and New York: Continuum (original work published 1923).

Burley, T. and Bloom, D. (2008) Phenomenological method, in P. Brownell (ed.) *Handbook for Theory, Research and Practice in Gestalt Therapy*. Newcastle: Cambridge Scholars Publishing.

Carroll, M. and Gilbert, M. (2005) *On Being a Supervisee: Creating Learning Partnerships*. London: Vukani.

Carroll, M. and Tholstrup, M. (2001) *Integrative Approaches to Supervision*. London: Jessica Kingsley Publishers.

Cartwright, D. (ed.) (1951) *Kurt Lewin: Field Theory in the Social Sciences, Selected Theoretical Papers*. London: Harper-Torchbooks.

Chidiac, M. (2018) *Relational Organisational Gestalt*. Abingdon: Routledge

Clemmens, M. (ed.) (2020) *Embodied Relational Gestalt: Theory and Application*. New York: Routledge.

Congram, S. (2011) Narrative supervision – the experiential field and the 'imaginal', in J. Passmore (ed.) *Supervision in Coaching*. London: Routledge.

Gaffney, S. (2008) Gestalt group supervision in a divided society: theory, practice, perspectives and reflections, *British Gestalt Journal*, 17(1): 27–39.

Gay, P. (ed.) (1995) *The Freud Reader*. London: W.W. Norton & Company (originally published 1989).

Hawkins, P. and Shohet, R. (2000) *Supervision in the Helping Professions: An Individual, Group and Organizational Approach*, 3rd edn. Maidenhead: Open University Press.

Hawkins, P. and Smith, P. (2006) *Coaching, Mentoring and Organizational Consultancy*. Maidenhead: Open University Press.

Jacobs, L. (1989) Dialogue in Gestalt theory and therapy, *Gestalt Journal*, 12(1): 25–67.

Jacobs, L. and Hycner, R. (2008) *Relational Approaches in Gestalt Therapy*. New York: Gestalt Press.

Joyce, P. and Sills, C. (2018) *Skills in Gestalt Counselling and Psychotherapy*, 4th edn. London: Sage.

Kauffman, C., Boniwell, I. and Silberman, J. (2010) The positive psychology approach to coaching, in E. Cox, T. Bachkirova and D. Clutterbuck (eds) *The Complete Handbook of Coaching*. London: Sage.

Lahad, M. (2000) *Creative Supervision: The Use of Expressive Arts in Supervision and Self-supervision*. London: Jessica Kingsley.

Lewin, K. (1946) Behaviour and development as a function of the total situation, in D. Cartwright (ed.) *Kurt Lewin: Field Theory in the Social Sciences, Selected Theoretical Papers*. London: Harper Torchbooks.

Lewin, K. (1947) Frontiers in group dynamics, in D. Cartwright (ed.) *Kurt Lewin: Field Theory in the Social Sciences, Selected Theoretical Papers*. London: Harper-Torchbooks.

Mackewn, J. (1997) *Developing Gestalt Counselling*. London: Sage.

O'Neill, B. and Gaffney, S. (2008) Field theoretical strategy, in P. Brownell (ed.) *Handbook for Theory, Research, and Practice in Gestalt Therapy*. Newcastle: Cambridge Scholars Publishing.

Parlett, M. (1991) Reflections on field theory, *British Gestalt Journal*, 1(2): 63–81.

Parlett, M. (1997) The unified field in practice, *Gestalt Review*, 1(1): 16–33.

Perls, F., Hefferline, R.F. and Goodman, P. (1951) *Gestalt Therapy: Excitement and Growth in the Human Personality*. London: Souvenir Press (re-issued 1984).

Rogers, J. (2004) *Coaching Skills: A Handbook*. Maidenhead: Open University Press.

Samuels, A., Shorter, B. and Plaut, F. (1986) *A Critical Dictionary of Jungian Analysis*. Hove: Brunner-Routledge.

Schaverien, J. and Case, C. (2007) *Supervision of Art Psychotherapy*. London: Routledge.

Shohet, R. (2008) *Passionate Supervision*. London: Jessica Kingsley.

Sieler, A. (2010) Ontological coaching, in E. Cox, T. Bachkirova and D. Clutterbuck (eds) *The Complete Handbook of Coaching*. London: Sage.

Spagnuolo Lobb, M. and Amendt-Lyon, N. (eds) (2003) *Creative Licence: The Art of Gestalt Therapy*. New York: SpringerWien.

Spinelli, E. (2010) Existential coaching, in E. Cox, T. Bachkirova and D. Clutterbuck (eds) *The Complete Handbook of Coaching*. London: Sage.

Staemmler, F.M. (2006) A Babylonian confusion?: on the uses and meanings of the term 'field', *British Gestalt Journal*, 15(2): 64–83.

Woldt, A. and Toman, S. (2005) *Gestalt Therapy*. London: Sage.

Zinker, J.C. (1994) *In Search of Good Form*. San Francisco, CA: Jossey-Bass.

9 Supervising with the existential approach in mind

Monica Hanaway

Introduction

This chapter provides a flavour of the existential approach to coaching supervision and the challenges and opportunities it presents for coach and supervisor, respective of the central modality of the supervisee.

The first MA in existential coaching wasn't established until 2010, and we are just beginning to see its impact with graduates developing the approach further. As a model well suited for challenging times, focused on living meaningfully and creatively in an uncertain world, it generates interest in academic, business and coaching circles, with more people engaging in research and development, particularly in Europe (Berg 2006; Echeverria 2013; Hanaway 2020; Jacob 2019; Langle and Burgi,2014; van Deurzen and Hanaway 2012).

Existential coaching grew from the more established practice of existential psychotherapy, which draws on existential philosophy (Heidegger, Sartre, Kierkegaard, Nietzsche), and on phenomenology (Kierkegaard, Husserl, Heidegger, Merleau-Ponty). The phenomenological method presents a particular challenge, requiring us to 'bracket', or put to one side, our assumptions. These could include our belief in set theories and system-led training. The existential coach relies less on techniques and exercises, placing more emphasis on the lived relational experience. The coach studies the 'phenomena' of the moment; things as they appear in our experience, and the meaning we individually give to those experiences. Existential coaches cannot impose their own understanding, or seek diagnostic or test-driven reductive explanations, instead they explore the client's perception, thought, imagination, emotion, bodily awareness, embodied action, linguistic and social activity in relation to any presented dilemma.

Given that most coaching clients, and many coaches may not be sufficiently familiar with the approach, I start with an overview of what is understood by 'existential coaching', moving on to look at the unique challenges this presents for any coach, whether working as an 'existential coach' or seeking to incorporate elements of the approach into a more integrative model. These existential considerations are mirrored in the supervisee/supervisor dyad with greater emphasis on more 'philosophical' issues than some approaches.

I finish with a consideration of ways to incorporate an existential approach into supervision practice. In some coaching supervision the emphasis may be on the development of 'skills' a coach needs in their practice. In an existential approach the emphasis is on developing a certain supervisory approach and relationship, focused on an ethical and philosophical stance consistent with the values of existentialism.

Currently, there is little literature available for those wishing to know more about existential coaching and more specifically about supervision of this nature. This leaves scope for further research. To put the existential approach to supervision in context, in the following section I introduce some of the main themes to be found in existential coaching that form the core of supervising from an existential perspective.

What do we mean by existential coaching?

The existential approach is used in life, business and leadership coaching. It can be the main focus of the work or used within a more integrative model. To understand its emphasis, it is important to know a little about the key philosophical framework it draws upon.

Existential thought calls for acceptance of the uncertainty of our lives. It considers our existential task to be finding meaning within the limitations of our existential givens; those things we all share, no matter the context. Yalom (1980: 8) presents four existential givens that are described as 'certain ultimate concerns, certain intrinsic properties that are a part, and an inescapable part, of the human being's existence in the world'. The primary given is our temporality, and the inevitability of death. Second, we must accept that we have both freedom and responsibility making us the author of our life-choices and actions. Third, we are ultimately alone to grapple with the existential conflict between our innate awareness of our isolation, and our desire for continued contact with others – our need for relatedness. We are essentially beings-in-the-world-with-others who are both the same as, and different from, ourselves. We may experience others as enablers or obstacles to our existential projects. Finally, as meaning-seeking creatures we are thrown into a world with no meaning, requiring us to forge a meaningful existence for ourselves, while holding in mind the awareness of uncertainty and the inevitability of our temporal existence. How we find such meaning is unique to the individual and played out in all encounters with the world. Fortunately for the coach, another existential given is our need to be heard and understood in all our ambiguities and paradoxical thinking.

As befits an approach centred on uncertainty, existential coaching does not offer solutions but is primarily focused on facilitating an exploration of beliefs, values, attitudes, assumptions and behaviours that make up and maintain a worldview and a 'way of being' across all dimensions of existence. Many coaching approaches begin with a fairly speedy search for a solution to the client's presenting problem – their 'external reality – the outer game' (Bluckert 2006: 48). Arrogance and/or a desire to impress the client can lead to a quick belief that the coach has fully understood the complexities of the client's issues. Existential coaching seeks to illuminate and deconstruct these complexities rather than seek quick answers.

Instead of solution chasing, the existential coach seeks to understand their client in relation to key existential issues, including the level of authenticity in which the client engages with their dilemma and their wider way of being-in-the-world. The client's desire for or rejection of uncertainty will indicate how they interact with the world and their level of need for structure and universal truth. The coach will seek to clarify the client's relationship with self, others and their environment (relatedness). Centrally, the coach will seek to identify where the client finds meaning, relating this specifically to the issue brought to coaching.

The depth to which these issues will be explored is dependent on the nature and length of the coaching contract, the level of trust between coach and client, the relevance of these existential themes to the focus of the coaching, and the client's willingness to enter into discussion of these areas.

An existential approach to coaching supervision

Existential coaching supervision draws on models existing in existential psychotherapy (van Deurzen and Young 2009; Krug and Schneider 2016), which call for a dialogic approach (two people attending, listening and exploring), distinguished from monologue (one person speaks and the other listens) and duologue (two people speaking to each other but only superficially listening). Supervision has been described as 'a joint philosophical enterprise' (van Deurzen and Young 2009: 1) in which the supervisee and supervisor engage in a unique and embodied way. Ehrenwald (1991: 392) described this as meaning clients and supervisees 'need experiences not explanations'. Experiences call for an approach that doesn't fit neatly into any standardized model. Indeed, most existential thinkers such as Yalom (2002: 34) believe that standardization can make the work 'less real and less effective'. If we cannot look to generic supervision models, then the process is more challenging, calling for the supervisor to be a 'virtuoso' weaving together science, philosophy and art in a multifaceted approach (Bugental 1987: 264).

Existential belief starts with the uniqueness of each individual and each relationship individually interpreted and constructed. A supervisor can only experience the client through the supervisee's experience of their client, which itself is filtered through the coach's assumptions, modality, personal and professional experiences. Supervision provides a safe opportunity to explore doubts or concerns that affect the ability to fully and openly engage with the client and looks afresh at assumptions and biases in coach and client.

Existential supervision covers a wide orbit (Figure 9.1) focusing on the client's presenting issue, the supervisee and client's values and assumptions, level of comfort with uncertainty, importance given to meaning and level of authenticity. Krug and Schneider believe this calls for the supervisor to 'shine a spotlight on supervisees' patterns such as rescuing, judging or competing' (2016: 15) while modelling good practice, emphasizing that, 'presence, congruence, and empathy are ways of being; they cannot be taught, but they can be modeled and valued' (2016: 5). Given this is the case, they see a place for 'the supervisor to bring in examples from their own practice thus treating the supervisee as a fellow traveller and cultivate a collegial, non-hierarchical atmosphere' (2016: 60). As with all supervision models, the existential supervisor will facilitate the clarification of any ethical or professional problems.

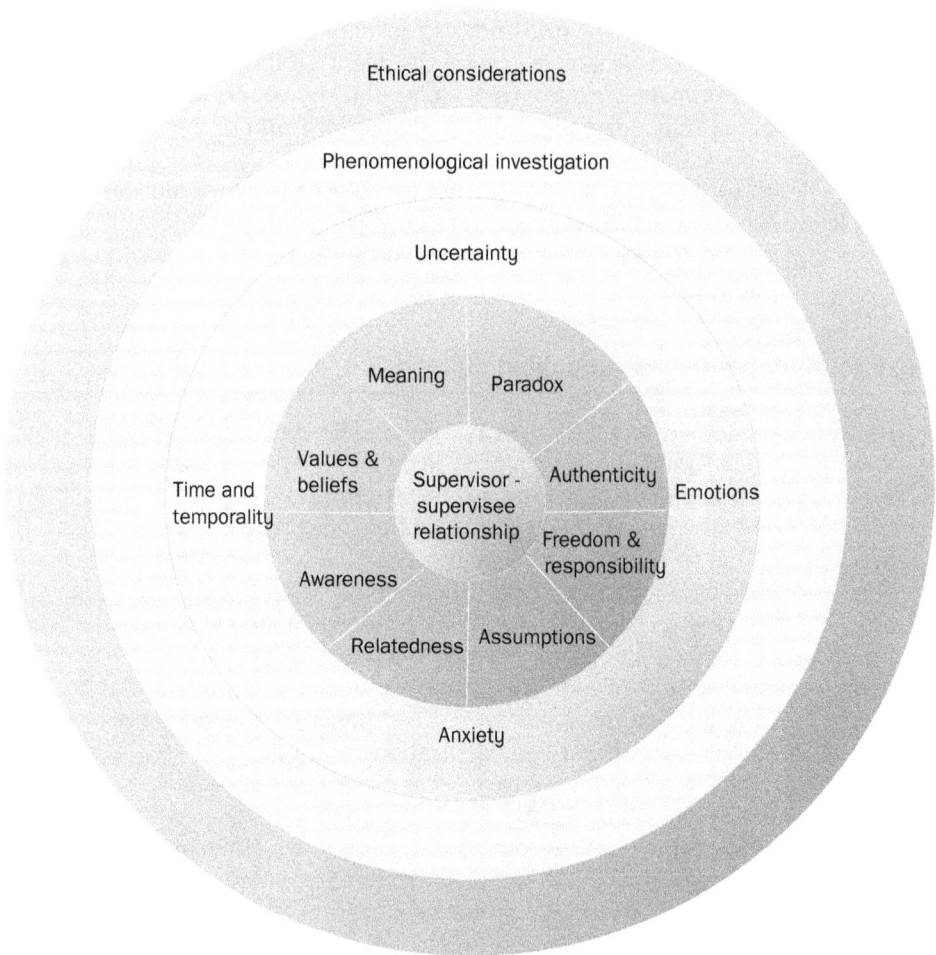

Figure 9.1 Orbit of existential supervision

Using phenomenological investigation

The supervisor will engage the supervisee in considering their work through a phenomenological lens. Central to this is the understanding that objects exist through the meaning that we give them. They do not carry a 'true' or 'correct' universal meaning. This is termed 'intentionality'. Husserl saw every act of intentionality as made up of two parts: noema and noesis. Noema is directional, '. . . the object (the what) that we direct our attention towards and focus upon' (Spinelli 1989: 13), while noesis is referential, the 'how' through which we define an object. This is the key to *phenomenological* listening. If we remain aware that noematic is made up of the content of what we are being told, and noetic is concerned with the individual's unique lived emotional experience of that content, then we begin to understand that we need to hear both aspects: the 'facts', and the way those 'facts' are experienced. The client and supervisee's unique experiences and beliefs will create these aspects. The supervisor seeks to understand how the supervisee has formed their understanding of an experience and will explore with them what they understand about their own and their client's assumptions, and the origins of those beliefs. Supervision provides a natural arena for a coach to develop their ability to challenge not only the client but their own prejudices and assumptions in order to understand and 'bracket' them and not impose them on the client. The supervisor is required to bring this open attentiveness to their practice and to model the Socratic questioning which the coach may use with their client.

Access to another's worldview and the assumptions held within it, comes from attentive listening from an open and humble place. This means reflecting back, paraphrasing and summarizing in ways that do not speak of certainty and authority but instead invite the client to consider and challenge the coach's offerings. Each challenge is a gift as it is usually followed by a further clarification of the client's true position, e.g. 'Well, I'm not sure you are right there . . . I guess it's a bit like that, but when I think about it more it is probably more like . . .'. The supervisor enables the coach to see that by being tentative and risking getting it 'wrong' they increase their chances of getting it 'right'. Where there is trust, the willingness

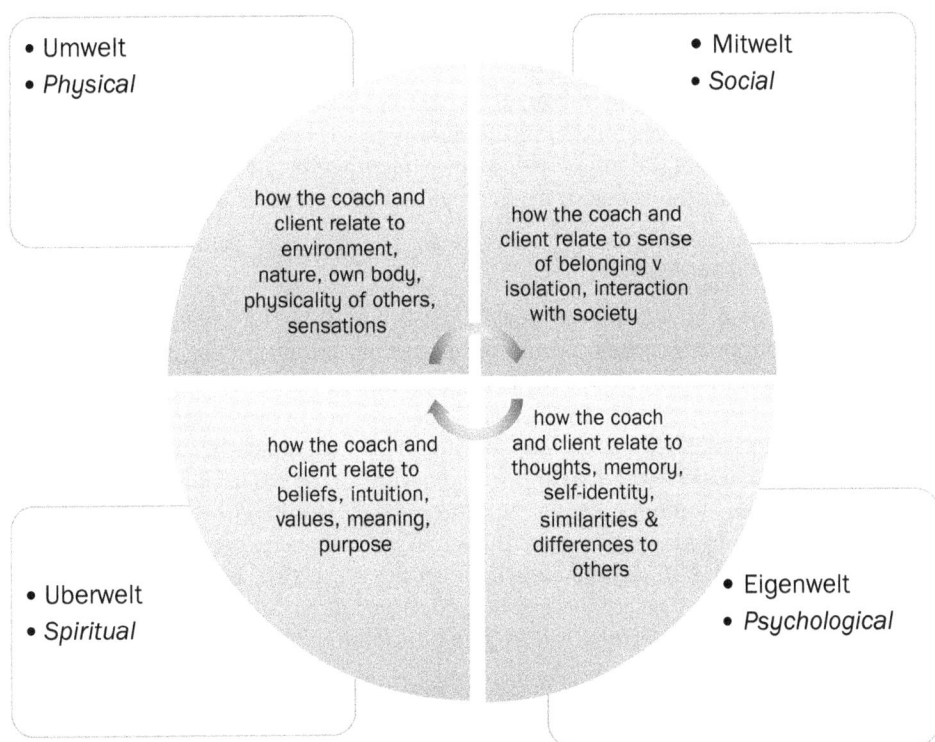

- Umwelt
- *Physical*

- Mitwelt
- *Social*

how the coach and client relate to environment, nature, own body, physicality of others, sensations

how the coach and client relate to sense of belonging v isolation, interaction with society

how the coach and client relate to beliefs, intuition, values, meaning, purpose

how the coach and client relate to thoughts, memory, self-identity, similarities & differences to others

- Uberwelt
- *Spiritual*

- Eigenwelt
- *Psychological*

Figure 9.2 Existential dimensions considered in supervision

to try, and at times get it wrong, shows a commitment to want to understand rather than appear to have knowledge or understanding which has not yet been reached. Feeling comfortable enough to disagree can enable greater clarity. This calls for a very trusting relationship between supervisor and supervisee.

Using existential dimensions

Existentialism doesn't divide people into types. It uses a description of different levels of experience and existence with which people are confronted. The way in which a person is 'in the world' at a particular stage can be placed on a 'map of human existence', which can be divided into four dimensions (Binswanger 1963; Yalom 1980; van Deurzen 1984).

An existential supervisor will start with this premise using the dimensions as places to find meaning. In some areas meaning may be easily identified, whereas others may be more problematic. The supervisor invites the coach to consider their understanding of their client through exploring four existential dimensions. These consist of the *Umwelt*, which is concerned with the physical world and promotes questions on how we relate to our environment, nature, physical body, the physicality of others and the world of sensations; the *Mitwelt*, which is concerned with social interactions, how we relate and communicate to others, our sense of belonging or of isolation and how we interact with society as a whole; the *Eigenwelt* or psychological dimension, is concerned with thoughts, memories, self-identity, similarities and differences from others, and the *Uberwelt* or spiritual dimension focuses on our beliefs, intuition, values, meaning and purpose. Through the use of existential dimensions, a coach can develop an understanding of a client's 'being', how they are in the world, and how they relate to it in all its complexity. This can be fed back to the client to provide a platform for them to understand and consider past and future action. If the informed client is content with only richly inhabiting some of their dimensions, it is not the role of the coach to try to change this, merely to identify it.

Using time and temporality

Each dimension is considered within the context of time. We experience time through the external measurement of hours, minutes and seconds, yet we also have an individual experience of time. As a child, a year seems very long but as we grow older years 'seem to fly by'.

Externally measured time may be important in issues brought to coaching. A client may feel pressured by imposed deadlines. The existential coach will work with these time elements just as any other coach would. However, an existential supervisor would also encourage the supervisee to consider the client's internal experience of time. If we consciously accept that our time is limited and will inevitably end in death, each day takes on added significance and leads us to consider how much time we are prepared to give to non-meaningful actions and worries.

Using emotions

When introducing the phenomenological method, I stressed that it calls for the coach to listen not just to what has happened to the client but also to how they experienced this emotionally (the noetic). In supervision, the supervisee will be asked to describe encounters with the client's material both factually and emotionally (those emotions shown by the client and those felt by the coach).

Emotions are always present. Even the person who seems most cut off and uncommunicative is feeling emotion, be it a desire for connection, or a strong sense of intrusion. For some clients, particularly those in the business context, it may seem strange for the coach to show an interest in emotional experiences. This is not the coach bringing psychotherapy into coaching. The coach never digs for emotions but will not ignore emotions that are present in the wording, tone or body language of the client. The sensitivity to, and exploration of, emotional content is needed in order for the coach to gain a deeper understanding of the client's experience. 'In emotion . . . We can rediscover the whole of human reality, for emotion is the human reality assuming itself and emotionally – directing itself towards the world' (Sartre 1962: 25). It is an area where one can fall into assuming that a described experience will be emotionally experienced in the same way one may experience it. As a dog lover, if someone tells me their dog has died, my assumption would be that this is a sad event. However, I must bracket that assumption, as it is equally possible that the death is experienced as a joyful release. The supervisor will enable the coach to avoid such assumptions.

All emotions are 'intentional', they are never in isolation but are attached to something and reveal the client's beliefs, values and assumptions. More than one emotion can be experienced at the same time, some in opposition, e.g. a client may hold strong feelings of anger and rejection at losing their job and yet also recognize feelings of relief. Exploring conflicting reactions can enable the client to make a better-informed decision about their next action.

Emotions may become stuck or 'sedimented' rather like the dregs of coffee left in a percolator. These need to be investigated so as not to be to the detriment of the client.

Using paradox

By nature, human beings are paradoxical. We can love and hate someone at the same time. We can want to move forward yet value the security of the status quo. Through enabling the client to see paradoxes inherent in their dilemma, the coach can facilitate the client's exploration of their values, identify their priorities, recognize the losses and gains in any decision and take responsibility for ensuing action and consequences.

The supervisor can enable the supervisee to identify any ambiguities, ambivalences and paradoxes in the client's material. In understanding that they cannot have everything, the client can then make use of their freedom of choice and take responsibility, knowing that most gains carry a loss.

Using CREATE and MOVER models

Hanaway and Reed (2014) drew together many existential concerns into two flexible frameworks for existential coaching practice, *MOVER* and *CREATE*. These were created to act as an aide-memoire for coaches' self-reflection but also work to give a structure for supervisors to explore supervisees' work.

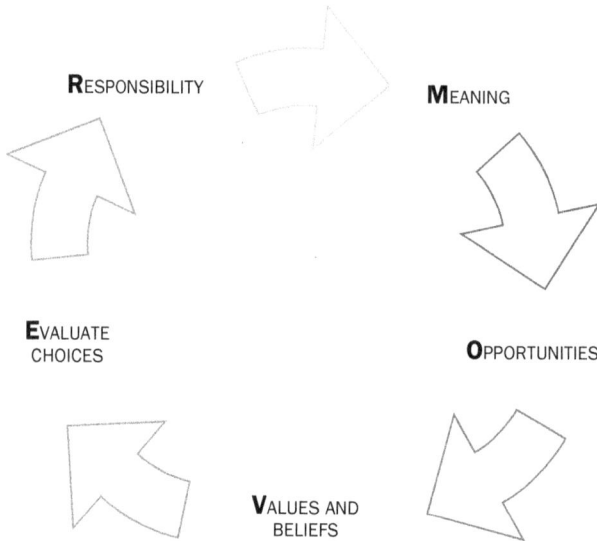

Figure 9.3 MOVER – existential coaching framework
(Hanaway and Reed 2014)

I shall focus on *MOVER*, which is concerned with the existential content of the work (Figure 9.3).

As the name suggests, it reflects the dynamic nature of the coaching relationship with its commitment to change and movement. Even if this results in an informed decision not to change or move, it is done with a considered acceptance of the implications of that decision for the client and others.

The framework considers *Meaning* as defined by the client. This is explored first by looking at the meaning that is given to the coaching relationship itself. This then moves to exploring where meaning sits within the presenting issue. Often people come to coaching because something which was once meaningful has subsequently lost its meaning. In considering the client's desired outcome the coach engages the client in considering what it would mean to achieve it, or indeed fail to achieve it.

In acting on any decision we encounter *Opportunities and Obstacles*. The supervisor and supervisee explore any obstacles in the client's dilemma. Understanding and acknowledging the temporality of the dilemma and the perceived obstacles is important to the process. Through reflective exploration, opportunities can be identified for new and creative action, and strategies developed for negotiating ways around obstacles, if indeed they are still perceived as such.

How obstacles and opportunities are defined is heavily influenced by *Values and Beliefs*. If strategies are offered that go against a person's values, then it becomes difficult to follow through on the agreed actions. Any attempt to do so may result in a deep sense of inauthenticity. To operate ethically within the existential approach, it is necessary to check whether:

> the proposed action works with or against the client's value system and to ensure that the client has sufficient space to consider the 'fit' of the action with their core beliefs and values and the implications of that action on not just the practical but also the psychological and emotional dimensions. (Hanaway 2020)

Once meaning, values, obstacles and ways forward have been identified, proposed actions need to be *evaluated* in relation to the existential givens and potential implications. This is undertaken in relation to the impact on existential dimensions and the client's state of being-in-the-world-with-others (relatedness).

When evaluations are completed, a decision to action can be taken, with acceptance of *responsibility* for any consequences for themselves and others. The process is completed through summarizing the journey, including any paradoxes, ambiguities or ambivalence identified, so that actions can be taken in full knowledge and with full existential responsibility. The supervisor is alert for any sign that the coach is taking over responsibility or overlying their own meaning instead of *exploring* what is meaningful for the client and the implications of their actions for authenticity, performance and achievement.

The temporal nature of coaching provides the opportunity to encourage *awareness* of existential anxiety attached to our temporal state. The supervisor will be alert for such existential content from the beginning until the end of the coaching contract. In the initial *contact* the supervisee may be concerned whether the client likes them, whether they like the client, whether they have the necessary skills, or whether the commissioning organization approves of their work. The supervisee will be encouraged to enter the coaching relationship openly by attending to the uniqueness of their client through a phenomenological approach and provision of a 'clean' psychological and moral state, bracketing any judgement or assumptions. The testing out of assumptions of all involved – coach, client, supervisor and commissioning organization–forms the foundations of the work.

The initial *'tuning in'* phase requires the building of trust through focusing on and reflecting back a holistic understanding of the client's worldview. When trust is sufficiently robust, the coach can bring in elements of their own perspective, knowledge and experience. These will not be hidden behind generic techniques or exercises, but will be acknowledged by the coach as their own thoughts, not universal truths. This is termed *'tuning out'* from the client's worldview, moving the focus to the original presenting issue. Supervisors provide an important check on when it is appropriate and necessary to move through these stages.

Coaching usually finishes when the allotted time or funding ends, or the client has achieved their intended goals. The *ending* of each session, and of the contract are reminders of our temporality. The supervisor will explore the supervisee's awareness of the client's different meanings, purpose and focus around endings. They will also look at the supervisee's own relationship with endings and how this may impact on their work.

Box 9.1 Case illustration

To ground these concepts in practice I offer an overview of my work as an existential supervisor with a coach from a different modality, keen to explore an existential way of working.

Stella was commissioned by a large organization to coach Jason, a middle manager, for three two-hour sessions over a three-month period. The first supervision took place before Stella met the client and she shared the information she had been given. Jason had worked successfully in his current organization in different posts before gaining promotion and managing a large team, some of whom had been his peers. His team complained that he was a poor communicator and had a bullying manner.

In a spirit of phenomenological enquiry we explored any assumptions Stella already held. These were noted down to revisit at the end of the work. Included in the assumptions was the possibility that Jason was an example of The Peter Principle (Peter and Hull 1964) in which a person rises to the level of their relative incompetence. Stella planned to undertake a SWOT analysis of his managerial skills and style and gain feedback from his colleagues through a 360-degree exercise. From there, she believed she could enable Jason to develop new management skills and recommend further relevant training.

Together, we drew up a set of questions for the 360-degree exercise with an existential focus and agreed Stella would use existential dimensions as a way of understanding Jason. We drew up a diagram of these dimensions as they revealed themselves over the sessions (Figure 9.4).

Stella elicited information through careful listening to noema and noesis, not attempting to be highjacked by her ego needs to rush Jason or keep him 'on point'. I reminded Stella that the client and the coach are equally aware of the temporality of the coaching contract and the client will be as keen, if not more so, to work to find a positive outcome within that time constraint. This meant it was unlikely anything Jason chose to speak about would be entirely 'off point' and was likely to offer something to the coach's understanding.

On their first meeting, Stella noticed that Jason dressed very formally, fitting for the stereotype of old-style manager, unusual for the organization. She experienced him as warm, yet tense. He was physically large, strong and fit and seemed comfortable in his body but careful not to intrude on Stella's space.

It transpired that a recent accident in which he had broken a leg had made him less sure of his bodily strength and at times he had needed to be reliant on others, something he found difficult. Previously, Stella would not have given any time to this, considering it irrelevant to the presenting issues. Given our previous discussion about the need to greet everything the client brought as potentially relevant, Stella decided to explore Jason's emotional experience of the accident. This non-censorship of content revealed how much of Jason's self-concept was invested

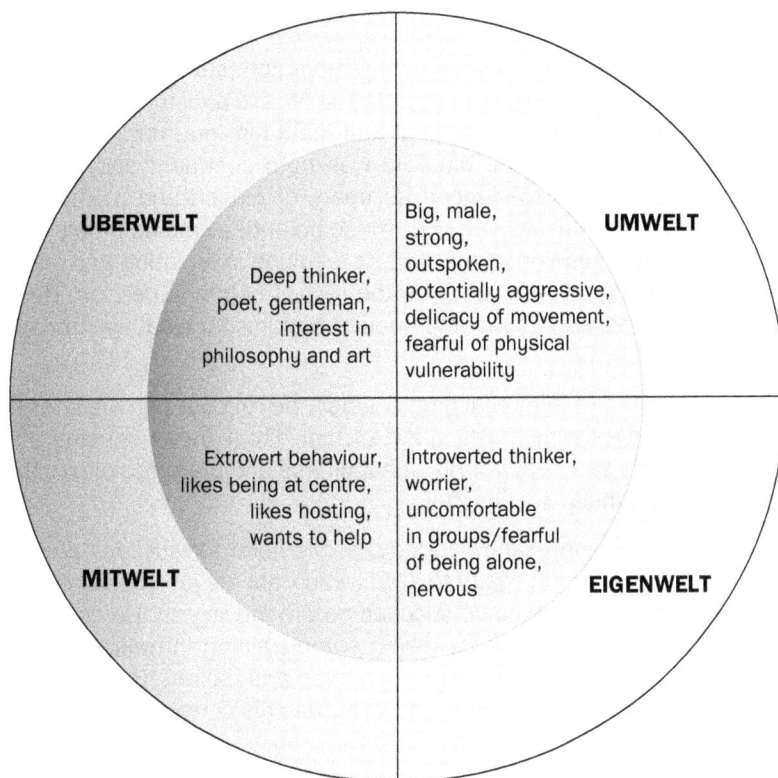

Figure 9.4 Jason's existential dimensions

in being male and strong, something he liked to demonstrate by helping with physical tasks and taking on leadership roles. He was conscious that he now limped when tired, and worried that those working to him would perceive this as weakness. He chose to remind them of his 'strength' and who was 'boss' through controlling behaviour, which the 360-degree feedback showed had been experienced as bullying. His increased awareness of physical vulnerability led him to think about ageing, temporality, dependence on others and, as he put it, 'the need to make something of myself before I am too old'. He wanted to continue moving quickly up the career ladder, not because he enjoyed the work, but because he feared mortality and wanted to leave a status legacy, proving that he had made something of his life. To remain in a post that he enjoyed, but carried little status, felt 'cowardly' and 'unmanly'.

In supervision we identified a number of Jason's paradoxes. Due to his competitive streak Jason had taken a risk in attaching himself to the ambitious polarity and desire to 'win'. In doing so he had paid a price, losing his previous sense of belonging and denying his real interests. His colleagues saw him differently from how he saw himself and how he wanted to be experienced, no longer seeing him as authentic and 'one of the boys', but as someone 'playing the role of manager' and 'a heavy one at that'. He considered himself to be a straightforward and confident leader but the 360-degree feedback allowed him to see the paradoxes in his position. He recognized he was a richer, more complex individual than he had considered himself to be, expressing interest in art and theatre, passions he believed would be considered 'unmanly' and mark him out as different resulting in colleagues losing respect for him. He was both confident and insecure. His straight talking could be experienced as open, or closed and manipulative. He needed people, yet feared dependence. These polarities caused problems for him and led to his current position of discomfort resulting in isolation and inauthenticity, which Kierkegaard considered to be the root of common despair. He realized that he could not have everything and needed to consider what was most important to him.

Between the second and third coaching session, he reflected on his priorities and discussed possibilities with those close to him. From these considerations he realized that his wife was aware of his unhappiness and preferred him to be happy rather than professionally successful.

In the final session Jason acknowledged that his need for success and competitive nature meant he was not ready to step away from his job. He wanted to prove to himself and others that he could succeed before moving on. He decided to give the job a maximum of three years, taking some training in management during that period, but also setting up a small bookshop and gallery. He accepted that it had been his decision to apply for the post, as was his current decision to stay on a temporary basis.

Discussing his plan with his wife, he had learnt that she was very excited by the idea and intended trying pottery classes in the hope that she might be successful and sell her products in the gallery. She welcomed the opportunity for them to spend more time together and for Jason to give more time to what made him happy. Jason used the rest of the session to explore what kind of manager he wanted to be, recognizing that it was important for him to develop a more collaborative and transformational way of working. He wanted work to be more creative and meaningful.

This brief summary shows how through supervision Stella covered elements in the *MOVER* and *CREATE* models, *tuning in* to Jason's *values*, identifying where he found *meaning*, increasing *awareness* of what was important and *tuning out* to identify and evaluate current and future choices enabling him to take full *responsibility*. All existential dimensions were covered. His *Mitwelt* highlighted his paradoxical need for both solitude and belonging and how he had placed competitiveness in the foreground which increased his isolation. Exploring his *Uberwelt*, he became proud of his interest in the arts and decided to create a future in which they were central. He accepted the physical changes to his strength which he experienced in his *Umwelt* and in the *Eigenwelt* he became more comfortable with differences.

Guidance for further learning

This chapter gives a flavour of the existential approach. There is very little written on existential supervision, but the texts below may be of interest to those wanting to know more about existential coaching and how existential supervision works in a coaching context.

Questions for reflection

- How comfortable are you working with a philosophical approach?
- What steps would you take if you felt the work was straying from coaching into therapy?
- What challenges does the need to bracket assumptions and theories present?
- How comfortable are you developing themes of existential concern with coaches?

Further sources

Hanaway, M. (2020) *Handbook of Existential Coaching Practice*. Abingdon: Routledge. Introduces key existential concepts related to authenticity, relatedness, freedom and responsibility, values and beliefs, and explores how these are relevant in the coaching process.

Jacob, Y. (2019) *An Introduction to Existential Coaching*. Abingdon: Routledge. Examines key themes in existentialism and how they show in the coaching space, including practical models and application to organizations and leadership.

Van Deurzen, E. and Young, S. (eds) (2009) *Existential Perspectives on Supervision*. Basingstoke: Palgrave. This edited book is written for psychotherapists but offers much in considering an existential coaching supervision.

References

Berg, M.E. (2006) *Coaching – å hjelpe ledere og medarbeidere til å lykkes*. Oslo: Universitetsforlaget.

Binswanger, L. (1963) *Being-in-the-World* (trans. J. Needleman). New York: Basic Books.

Bluckert, P. (2006) *Psychological Dimensions of Executive Coaching*. Maidenhead: Open University Press.

Bugental, J.F.T. (1987) *The Art of the Psychotherapist*. London: W.W. Norton & Co.

Echeverria, R. (2013) *Ontologia Del Lenguaje*. Spain: Granica Adelphi.

Ehrenwald, J. (1991) *The History of Psychotherapy: From Healing Magic to Encounter*. New York: J. Aronson.

Hanaway, M. (2020) *Handbook of Existential Coaching Practice*. Abingdon: Routledge.

Hanaway, M. and Reed, J. (2014) *Existential Coaching Skills: The Handbook*. Henley-on-Thames: The CH Group.

Heidegger, M. (1962) *Being and Time* (trans. J. Macquarrie and E.S. Robinson). Oxford: Blackwell.

Jacob, Y. (2019) *An Introduction to Existential Coaching.* Abingdon: Routledge.

Krug, O.T. and Schneider, K.J. (2016) *Supervision Essentials for Existential-Humanistic Therapy.* Washington, DC: American Psychological Association.

Langle, A. and Burgi, D. (2014) *Existentielles Coaching: Theorestiche Orientierung, Grundlagen Utd Praxis fur Coaching, Organistationsberatung und Supervision.* Vienna: Facultative Universitasverlag.

Peter, L.J. and Hull, R. (1964) *The Peter Principle: Why Things Always Go Wrong.* New York: Harper Collins.

Sartre, J.P. (1962) *Sketch for Theory of the Emotions.* London: Methuen.

Spinelli, E. (1989) *The Interpreted World: An Introduction to Phenomenological Psychology.* London: Sage.

Van Deurzen, E. and Hanaway, M. (2012) *Existential Perspectives on Coaching.* Basingstoke: Palgrave.

Van Deurzen, E. and Young, S. (eds) (2009) *Existential Perspectives on Supervision.* Basingstoke: Palgrave.

Yalom, I.D. (1980) *Existential Psychotherapy.* New York: Basic Books.

Yalom, I.D. (2002) *The Gift of Therapy: An Open Letter to a New Generation of Therapists and Their Patients.* London: HarperCollins.

10 Supervising according to person-centred principles

Bernard Cooke and Louise Sheppard

Introduction

The person-centred approach has its roots in therapy and has grown and adapted to the demands of coaching and coaching supervision. Many coaches and supervisors maintain that they adhere to the principles of person-centred coaching by regarding their clients as resourceful and capable of finding their own solutions – but a warm, generalized intent is not the same as a conscious application of a theory. It is valuable to dig deeper and examine our practice to see exactly how we are incorporating person-centred principles and to what effect. To date, there is little written about how these principles are adopted by supervisors in a coaching context but there has been recent research on the supervisee perspective and a framework for supervisee-led supervision with guidelines for supervisors. We will start by examining the principles of the person-centred approach and explore, with the help of a short case illustration, how the theory has been interpreted and applied in the practice of supervision. How one relates the underlying theory to practice can vary considerably but we will argue that a clear and conscious application of the approach can add a rewarding dimension to one's supervision. While reading this chapter, you may wish to reflect upon the extent to which you use a person-centred approach in coaching supervision.

Key principles of the person-centred approach

The fundamental assumption that underpins person-centred therapy is that people are intrinsically motivated to grow and develop into optimally functioning human beings. The approach was originally developed by the psychologist Carl Rogers (1961) as a form of psychotherapy, but the principles are now widely incorporated in coaching and coaching supervision. The *actualizing tendency* was viewed by Rogers as the central driving force of individuals to develop all of their capacities in the direction of maintaining and enhancing themselves. This fundamental belief of Rogers, that every individual can grow and develop into their 'optimal form', is central to the person-centred approach. However, *self-actualization* can only occur in an environment where the individual feels understood, valued and accepted for who they are and without conditions. If this is not the case, then the individual may actualize their personality in a way that is *incongruent* with their natural actualizing tendency and develop a *self-concept* that is more related to meeting the needs and expectations of others. This incongruence results in distress and dysfunction for the individual, as would be the case, for example, if someone's self-concept is based more upon some external evaluation of their worth ('you ought to be like this . . . ') than their real, underlying 'organismic' self, which is in line with their own experience ('I want to be like this . . . ').

Rogers' conditions within the context of person-centred supervision

For individuals to be able to self-actualize, Rogers maintained that six conditions have to be met. We have described these conditions within the context of the relationship between the coach (supervisee) and supervisor.

1. *Psychological contact between supervisor and supervisee* – Being aware of each other's presence and how our behaviour impacts the other. Without this, the following five conditions would be redundant.
2. *Supervisee incongruence* – Where the supervisee is conflicted between how to feel or behave and how this might be perceived.
3. *Congruence of the supervisor* – Where the supervisor is aware of the feelings that he has, accepts them and can share them with the supervisee if appropriate to do so.
4. *Unconditional positive regard* – The supervisor accepts the supervisee as they are, without imposing any conditions or judgement, seeing them as doing the best that they can.
5. *Empathic understanding* – The supervisor takes on board the supervisee's perceptions, experiences and concerns in order to step into their shoes.
6. *Perception* – The supervisee perceives the supervisor's genuine unconditional regard and empathy.

The use of person-centred theory in supervision

Let's examine how these principles might enable the key functions of supervision to occur, as defined by Hawkins and Smith (2006). The *developmental* function is facilitating the coach to reflect upon their work with their clients and to develop new skills, understanding and insight on their coaching practice. Clearly, the person-centred supervisor would work from an assumption that their supervisee has an innate capacity to develop, both as a person and as a professional coach and they would place their trust in them to take their own learning from the thoughts and reflections arising during the session. However, it can be argued that using a purely person-centred approach may present challenges for the supervisor depending on the developmental stage of the supervisee. Bachkirova and Borrington (2018) used the lens of adult developmental theories to explore the applicability of a pure person-centred approach in coaching and concluded that while at the 'unformed ego' stage, using a pure person-centred approach worked well for clients, other coaching approaches needed to be added for clients beyond this stage of development and they suggested augmenting a person-centred approach with a solution-focused approach for the 'formed ego' stage and using Gestalt or existential approaches for clients at the 'reformed ego' stage.

The *resourcing* function is concerned with helping coaches to face and remain working with difficult and often emotionally charged situations. As coaches will inevitably be affected by their work, the supervisor will help them to understand their responses better, sometimes surfacing feelings that relate to issues belonging to the coach rather than the coachee. With its emphasis on empathy, unconditional regard and congruency, the person-centred approach to supervision is highly compatible with this function. However, many supervisors also draw upon other theories such as psychodynamic to provide this function, and this raises the issue of compatibility with other approaches.

The *qualitative* function is concerned with the reinforcing of the quality and ethical standards that the coach should be maintaining in their practice. This raises the issue of who is taking responsibility for the quality of work carried out, as the purely person-centred approach would rule out the possibility of the supervisor taking any of this responsibility. However, there may be situations where the supervisor is contracted to ensure that the quality of coaching offered meets certain standards and that the coach and coachees are suitably protected. In these cases, the person-centred approach would place more emphasis on the coach and supervisor jointly exploring any external frameworks of standards and values.

From this brief review of how a person-centred approach fits with the tasks of coaching supervision, we have immediately run into some challenges around the interpretation of Rogers' theory in a context that is different from the one for which it was intended. Should we adopt a fundamentalist approach and stick to the literal definitions of Rogers' conditions, or are we advocating some interpretation where the underlying beliefs may inform a variety of methods? Can the person-centred approach sit alongside other approaches that are underpinned by different theoretical models? Indeed, these points are frequently debated within the community that comprises person-centred practitioners.

Interpretation of the person-centred theory

Hitchings (2004) outlines some of the disputes between the 'tribes' of the person-centred community, principally between the 'literalists' and the 'experimentalists'. While the literalists maintain that Rogers' six conditions and the non-directive attitude of the therapist are non-negotiable, the experimentalists claim to remain true to the core theory but view it as permissible to be more directive about the emerging processes within and between the therapist and client. For Hitchings, this raises the issue of where the expertise is located or whose perception of reality is most valid. It could be argued that the psychoanalytic school would place the expertise with the therapist while the literalist person-centred school would view it as residing solely with the client. By contrast, the experimentalists would take an 'inter-subjective' perspective, seeing the client's reality as something that is co-created between the two. Worsley (2002), in support of this inter-subjective stance, acknowledges that the therapists can never be the experts on their clients but questions the notion that the clients can always be experts on themselves!

So how would the process of supervision look different between a literalist and an experimentalist person-centred supervisor? The devout literalist would see their role purely as facilitating the coach's awareness of their relationship with their client. Expertise would be viewed as residing only with the supervisee and the six conditions should be strictly adhered to. By contrast, the experimentalist may take a more flexible approach, depending upon the personalities of the two people involved, the needs of the coach and issues arising from the session. A model of supervision outlined by Merry (1999), for example, regards the process as 'collaborative inquiry', where both people are self-directed and can contribute equally to the process. The experimentalists may also question as to whether the six conditions need to be so strictly adhered to. For example, Tudor and Worrall (2004) argue that the first two conditions are not completely necessary for the process of supervision. Supervision that is carried out through the exchange of emails, for example, where the sender may be engaged in a completely different activity when the receiver is reading the message, means that the kind of psychological contact that Rogers described cannot be achieved. If we accept this as a form of supervision, then we cannot assert that such psychological contact is a *necessary* condition. Furthermore, the supervisee may not need to feel incongruent in some way to benefit from a supervision session should they simply want to share and explore their case work.

Supervision may, therefore, look different between these two schools of practitioner groups. This would certainly underline the importance for both supervisor and coach to be clear in their contracting about what it is they offer and need. Part of this process could be an exchange of the principles and theories that underpin their respective practices and an exploration of how these might complement or conflict with one another. Having agreed their positions on what constitutes a person-centred approach and established a framework for their ongoing collaboration, they might also ask how other theories might be integrated into the supervision. For the supervisor, questions could also arise as to how the various models of supervision might fit with the person-centred theory.

The seven-eyed model of supervision (Hawkins and Smith 2006), for example, poses some challenges for the person-centred supervisor. For instance, in mode 2, the focus is on the *interventions* that the supervisee has made with their client. Is this encouraging the coach to adopt a mindset of *doing things to* their client, as opposed to facilitating a resourceful client to find their own approach? In mode 3, the focus is on the relationship between the coach and client, including the way that the client may experience the supervisee. This discussion may include possible transference by the client towards the supervisee, of attitudes developed from earlier relationships. In mode 4, countertransference is explored, that is, possible unconscious reactions by the supervisee towards the client, and in mode 5 the supervisor focuses on their own unconscious reactions and potential parallel processes occurring in the supervisory relationship. In Rogers' views, dealing with transference was a 'grave mistake' (Rogers 1990) that could lead to dependency and lengthen the therapeutic process. To him, the creation of the therapeutic relationship using unconditional positive regard, empathy and congruence was all that was required and far more important than specific therapeutic techniques. While the use of psychodynamic theory in supervision is not a problem per se, as seen from a person-centred perspective it may place too much emphasis on the technique of the supervisor, at the expense of the relationship between supervisor and supervisee.

These challenges of interpretation of the necessary conditions and compatibility with supervision models are not, however, impediments that prevent the beneficial application of the person-centred approach in practice, as the following example will illustrate.

Box 10.1 Case illustration

Liz was an experienced coaching psychologist who I (Bernard) was supervising during a time when she was experiencing some significant doubts and questions about her own effectiveness as a coach. She described how, with certain clients, her confidence in her own ability as a coach seemed to dissipate and her skills and knowledge felt 'like a jigsaw that had broken into 3000 pieces. I don't know where I am – I can't get a sense of whether my coaching is working or not!' Having worked with Liz as a colleague in the past, I knew her well and had a high degree of respect for her professional capabilities. She had approached me for supervision support at a time when she was undergoing a formal accreditation process and managing a demanding caseload of coaching. As a supervisor who integrates the person-centred with other approaches and models, in line with the 'experimentalist' school described above, Liz and I shared a common set of philosophies and practices in coaching. Our previous sessions had focused on issues related to specific clients, but now I was being presented with a generalized and overwhelming sense of anxiety – what was going on?

Liz described her anxiety in terms of her apparent inability to find and utilize the 'appropriate coaching technique' when working with a client. I was curious about this reference to 'technique', partly because it was unusual for her to focus on this but also because Liz had always impressed me with the degree of empathy that she appeared to show towards her clients and the focus she placed upon the relationship that she held with them. Using the Hawkins seven-eyed model as a framework, I encouraged Liz to talk more about the client, her impressions of him and the interventions that she had made (modes 1 and 2). Liz described how this particular client had, at one point, 'appeared quite manic and confused about his own identity and place within the organization'. This had appeared to trigger a reaction in Liz that made her feel that her coaching was 'not working' and that she ought to have some technique available to put it right! In describing her relationship with this client, Liz said that she found it difficult to show him unconditional positive regard. I was struck that Liz, who would usually describe her approach as person-centred, was seeking supervision on a breakdown in this methodology. So what is the person-centred supervisor supposed to do?

Initially, I picked up on Liz's jigsaw metaphor, reflecting that '3000 pieces is an awful lot! I'm wondering how you ever kept all of them together?' Liz smiled in response, perhaps recognizing that she had been expecting quite a lot of herself. At this stage I was unclear about where Liz wanted to take our session and I allowed her space to reflect. She soon began to talk about her feelings on her relationship with this client and I asked her about what she believed that she was providing for him, even if she felt that she wasn't coaching effectively. As Liz spoke about this, she visibly relaxed, became more energized and talked more positively about instances where she had felt empathy and positive regard for the client. Feeling that I was being re-acquainted with an old friend, I shared this with Liz and she acknowledged that something different was emerging for her. The discussion then opened up new insights for Liz on what might be happening in their coaching relationship and some areas that she was curious about exploring further. Her concern for finding the 'right technique' for this situation subsided, as did her anxiety about her efficacy as a coach.

Although this short vignette of a supervision session is not intended as a complete demonstration of the person-centred approach, it provides sufficient material to review the application of the theory. First of all, we might ask whether the six conditions considered necessary were present in this scenario. The psychological contact between Liz and her coach was present, although it would be presumptuous to assume so, simply on the basis of familiarity with each other, as there could be many forms of interference preventing such contact. Liz was in a state of incongruence – experiencing a feeling of anxiety about meeting expectations as a coach and confusion about her relationship with this client. With regard to the supervisor's state of congruence, the supervisor felt empathy for Liz, as he could recognize the anxiety that arises when one questions one's own abilities. Equally, the supervisor did not have any 'answers' to Liz's dilemma but felt a calmness and belief that something positive would emerge from the session. The positive regard that the supervisor held for Liz was not compromised in any way by expectations that he held of her as a person or professional and he hoped that his empathy for her situation was perceived by her, to at least the 'minimal degree' that Rogers described.

In person-centred fashion the supervisor placed his trust in Liz to find some resolution to her manifest anxiety, without trying to impose models or frameworks. He felt that the presence of the trusting relationship between Liz and himself allowed Liz's focus to be drawn towards her own relationship with her client and then for new insights to emerge. Rogers' initial term for his approach was, in fact, 'relationship therapy' and it is this that is key to the process. Liz's initial presentation of a concern for techniques and capabilities could so easily have prompted, on the supervisor's part, a guided tour of tools and techniques and some discussion on what might be 'missing'. In one sense the supervisor was being invited to re-build Liz, arming her with the appropriate equipment, but in another he was simply being invited to listen and provide some of the positive regard for herself that she had lost. As a result, Liz began to view her own challenge of finding positive regard for her client as a relationship issue, rather than one of technical competence.

Naturally, there are alternative approaches that could have taken us to a similar or different place. The interference that Liz was experiencing, which prevented her experiencing positive regard for her client, could have been explored from a

Gestalt or psychodynamic perspective. Perhaps this was a case of 'parallel processing', where Liz's fragmented sense of identity had been a reflection of her client's 'manic behaviour'. Perhaps this client had triggered some association in Liz with some anxiety-provoking situation or individual. Perhaps a systems perspective of Liz and her client would yield some insights on the emerging processes. These are all reasonable possibilities that could have formed the basis of an equally valid and effective supervisory session. The choices presented to a supervisor are not necessarily on *whether* to adopt a person-centred approach or not, but *how* to apply the principles of the theory and how they might integrate with other dimensions of their practice. The reward of such integration is the deepening of the working relationship between the supervisor and their client.

Applying a person-centred approach to supervision

Having examined the interpretation of person-centred theory to supervision and illustrated this with a practical application, we will consider 'when' and 'how' to apply a person-centred approach and when it is less appropriate. When would the person-centred approach to supervision be of most benefit? The short case illustration provided an example of the coach feeling some anxiety, in this case about her own performance and the relationship with her client. Intense moments and anxieties in the coaching relationship are both relevant and commonly occurring supervision topics, as found in the research of De Haan et al. (2010) who asked experienced coaches to identify 'critical moments' that they encounter when coaching that could be seen as turning points in their work. Examples of the coach's anxieties included: the boundaries of coaching; satisfying client outcomes and the coach's own role – what did the client want from them; what were they getting into and were they doing enough? Many of the coaches took these experiences to supervision in order to make sense of their reactions and to gain reassurance that they had handled the moment competently. The person-centred supervisor is well suited to responding to these types of issues which occur frequently in coaching. When a coach is presenting with anxiety and emotion, a supervisor working with congruence, empathy and positive regard is very likely to be perceived as supportive and restorative.

In practice, the conditions of supervision, in particular, uneven power dynamics can create anxiety in the supervisee too. Sheppard (2016) researched the supervisee perspective in coaching supervision, looking at what supervisees experience during supervision and what they do to help and hinder themselves. She found that three factors affecting human nature – fear, power relations and our natural desire for learning and growth – were underlying supervisees' experiences of supervision. All three mechanisms appeared to be fundamental in driving supervisee behaviour. The study revealed how the majority of supervisees learnt to enhance their coaching supervision over time by developing ways of countering these mechanisms of fear and power relations and were motivated to do so by their natural tendency to learn. She advocates that supervisors offer supervisee-led supervision and that supervisees 'drive the bus of their supervision' by becoming active participants rather than passive recipients through increased

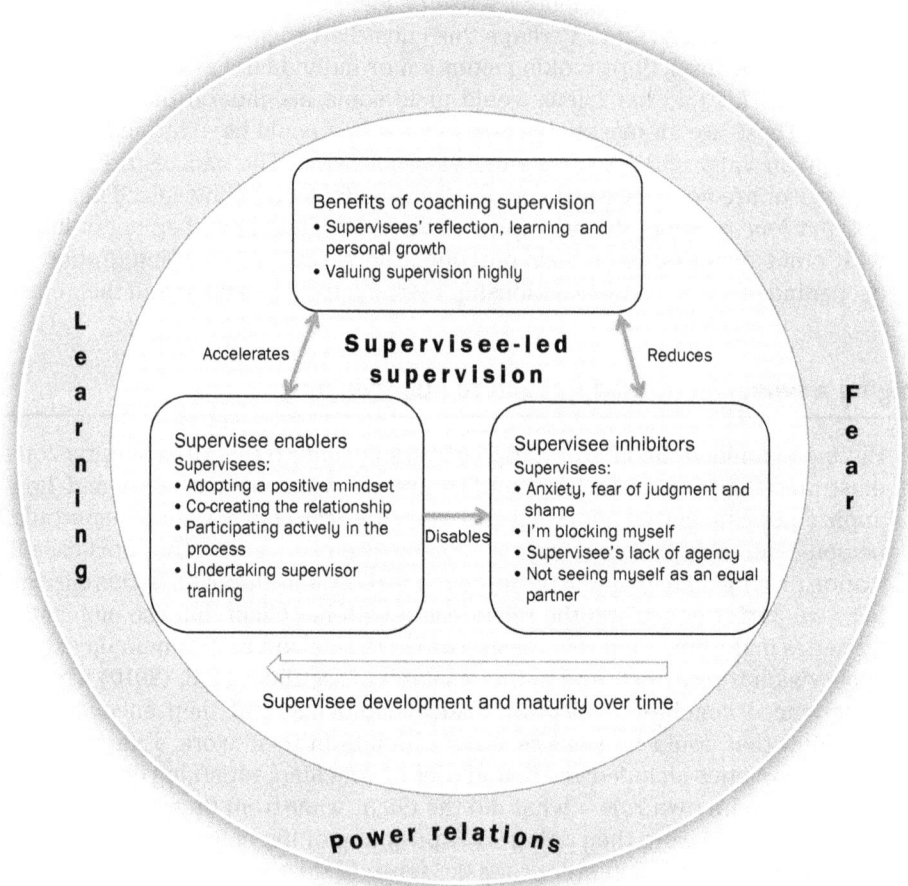

Figure 10.1 Framework for supervisee-led supervision (Sheppard 2016)

awareness of what can help and hinder them in the process. This supports the use of a person-centred approach to equalize the power between the supervisor and supervisee and to give agency to supervisees. A framework for supervisee-led supervision is shown in Figure 10.1.

We consider that a supervisor offering person-centred supervision would clearly be enabling supervisees to 'drive the bus of their supervision' with the supervisor's role being to facilitate the coach's reflective practice. Some supervisor guidelines for adopting a supervisee-led approach in practice are summarized in Box 10.2 below.

Another useful way of giving supervisees control of the content of the supervision session is by using a non-directive technique called Interpersonal Process Recall (IPR). IPR is a technique to help a supervisee to look back at a session

---

Box 10.2 Supervisor guidelines for adopting a supervisee-led approach to supervision

This is intended as a checklist for adopting a supervisee-led approach.

1. When preparing to work with a supervisee, ask yourself:
   - How can you minimize the impact of anxiety and fear in coaching supervision?
   - How can you acknowledge power relations and create an equal partnership with the supervisee?
   - What unhelpful assumptions and beliefs are you holding about the responsibilities of a supervisor and supervisee?
2. Establish the supervisory relationship together by exploring:
   - The supervisee's supervision needs in relation to their development as a coach.
   - Supervisee and supervisor responsibilities.
   - Your wish to create an equal partnership and what might help and hinder this.
   - How you will review the relationship and effectiveness of supervision.
3. During supervision, support the supervisee by:
   - Asking the supervisee what they wish to focus upon and what desirable outcomes would be.
   - Inviting the supervisee to choose what they wish to explore first.
   - Creating a safe space and normalizing any anxiety present.
   - Being transparent about any power dynamics that you notice and not being an 'expert'.
   - Respecting the supervisee's coaching framework and building their confidence.
   - Disclosing your thoughts and sharing your challenging experiences where relevant.
   - Asking the supervisee about their learning from the session.
   - Reviewing how the supervisee experienced the session – what was helpful and what could be improved going forward.
4. Regularly review your supervisory relationship and process with the supervisee by:
   - Discussing how the supervisee's supervision needs are developing over time.
   - Assessing if the supervisee has outgrown you and/or would benefit from an alternative perspective.
   - Supporting the supervisee to obtain closure when the supervisory relationship ends.

with a client in order to recall what was going on for him at various points in the conversation, recognize the interpersonal dynamics of the relationship and what he might have said but chose not to. The technique was originally developed in the 1960s by Kagan (1980) who had a client-centred perspective. It involves the supervisee recording a client session, bringing the recording to supervision and being in charge of the pause button during supervision. The role of the supervisor within an IPR session is to offer a safe, supportive relationship that leaves the coach free to reflect and thereby to become less fearful and more skilled in his practice (Thomson 2011).

When might using the person-centred approach not be appropriate? A person-centred approach will be less appropriate in certain situations, for example if the supervisor is concerned about the mental health of the supervisee or client or when a novice supervisee is asking for and requiring more direction and guidance – something that the purist person-centred coach may feel compromises their principles. When the supervision contract is part of a large coaching initiative with a sponsoring organization, the supervisor may have some explicit obligation to review standards of coaching and to oversee the quality of service provided. This situation may require the supervisor to show flexibility of style and responsiveness to multiple clients and stakeholders and may compromise the principles of person-centred coaching supervision. This approach would not be appropriate if the supervisor does not believe in the key principles of the theory and cannot provide supervisee-led supervision. In our view, the selection of a person-centred approach is not necessarily at the expense of other methodologies, such as cognitive-behavioural, existential, Gestalt, solutions-focused and positive psychology. For Joseph (2014) the person-centred approach does not prescribe techniques of practice but allows a multidisciplinary approach that is grounded in the principles of the theory. Joseph believes that it is not what the supervisor *does* that is important, but how they *think* about their relationship with the coach and how their actions relate to the underlying assumption that they are there to facilitate the coach to self-actualize. This thinking about the relationship and consciously attending to Rogers' conditions is what distinguishes the person-centred approach. Incorporating other methodologies into this framework without compromising these principles is possible, as long as they are congruent with the person-centred approach and not casually imported.

Guidance for further learning and research

The person-centred approach to coaching supervision is something that few would argue against in principle. In practice, what is offered in the name of a person-centred methodology may look very different from one supervisor to another. The underlying principles of a non-directive style, empathy and positive regard appear so deceptively simple that many coaches and supervisors espouse them as guiding values. However, these principles may become challenged when applied in coaching supervision where the differing functions of supervision and the multi-faceted needs of the supervisee and organizational system may demand compromises and flexibility on the part of the supervisor. We need to ensure that we do not passively assume that the necessary conditions are in place and instead, actively review our supervision to ensure that we are truly providing supervisee-led supervision and supporting supervisees in their development.

Questions for reflection

- To what extent do I see the six necessary conditions evident in my own supervision practice?
- Where do I stand on the 'literalist' versus 'experimentalist' school of person-centred coaching?
- What other approaches do I use and how compatible are they with person-centred theory?
- To what extent is my coaching supervision supervisee-led?

Further sources

Rogers' own writing gives a very human insight into the motivation and values underlying his development of the person-centred approach. *On Becoming a Person* (2004, originally published in 1961) is a collection of Rogers' papers, some of them lectures, which provide an accessible insight into his reflections on his own experience. Other useful texts are:

For the application of the person-centred theory to coaching, see the chapter entitled 'The person-centred approach to coaching' (2014) by Stephen Joseph in *The Complete Handbook of Coaching*.

For useful texts on the use of person-centred theory in supervision, see *Freedom to Practise – Person-centred Approaches to Supervision* (Tudor and Worrall 2004).

References

Bachkirova, T. and Borrington, S. (2018) The limits and possibilities of a person-centred approach in coaching through the lens of adult development theories, *Philosophy of Coaching: An International Journal*, 3(1): 6–22.

De Haan, E., Bertie, C., Day, A. and Sills, C. (2010) Critical moments of clients and coaches: a direct-comparison study, *International Coaching Psychology Review*, 5(2): 109–128.

Hawkins, P. and Smith, N. (2006) *Coaching, Mentoring and Organizational Consultancy: Supervision and Development*. Maidenhead: Open University Press.

Hitchings, P. (2004) On supervision across theoretical orientations, in K. Tudor and M. Worrall (eds) *Freedom to Practise: Person-centred Approaches to Supervision*. Ross-on-Wye: PCCS Books.

Joseph, S. (2014) The person-centred approach to coaching, in E. Cox, T. Bachkirova and D. Clutterbuck (eds) *The Complete Handbook of Coaching*. London: Sage.

Kagan, N. (1980) Influencing human interaction: eighteen years with IPR, in A. Hes (ed.) *Psychotherapy Supervision: Theory, Research and Practice*. New York: Wiley.

Merry, T. (1999) *Learning and Being in Person-centred Counselling*. Ross-on-Wye: PCCS Books.

Rogers, C. (1961) *On Becoming a Person*. Boston, MA: Houghton Mifflin.

Rogers, C. (1990) *The Carl Rogers Reader*. London: Constable.

Rogers, C. (2004) *On Becoming a Person: A Therapist's View of Psychotherapy*. London: Constable.

Sheppard, L. (2016) *How Coaching Supervisees Help and Hinder Their Supervision: A Grounded Theory Study*, PhD thesis, Oxford Brookes University. Available from: https://radar.brookes.ac.uk/radar/items/b622add5-7b08-44a1-be82-87a1ebbcf4be/1/.

Thomson, B. (2011) Non-directive supervision of coaching, in J. Passmore (ed.) *Supervision in Coaching*. London: Kogan Page.

Tudor, K. and Worrall, M. (2004) *Freedom to Practise: Person-centred Approaches to Supervision*. Ross-on-Wye: PCCS Books.

Worsley, R. (2002) *Process Work in Person-centred Therapy*. Basingstoke: Palgrave.

11 Supervising according to transactional analysis principles

Julie Hay

Introduction

Transactional analysis (TA) is an approach to understanding why people behave as they do, and to helping them achieve more autonomy. It is also an established psychotherapy modality, practised worldwide and with internationally agreed professional qualifications, with university accreditation of masters programmes in several countries and registration for graduates with the UK Council for Psychotherapy. Developmental TA (DTA) is when the original psychotherapeutic focus on cure shifts to an emphasis on development and growth, as when the practitioner is working within an organizational, educational or coaching context.

This chapter aims to serve as an introduction to some key elements of TA, mainly with a DTA perspective, and how these can enhance in particular the formative function (Proctor 1986) of the supervisory process. It prompts the style of supervision that I label *super-vision* (Hay 2007) to emphasize the objective of facilitating the supervisee's super-vision, or meta-perspective, of their practice.

Some questions you might ask yourself while reading:

- How might a TA perspective enhance my understanding of the processes of supervision?
- How might I incorporate the ideas in this chapter within my current approach to supervision?
- How might I incorporate these alongside other ideas described elsewhere in this book?

TA originated in the 1960s (Berne 1961), and has become a robust and comprehensive approach, with varying schools that focus on elements such as: regression – the cathexis school (Schiff 1975); TA combined with Gestalt (Goulding and Goulding 1979); constructivist (Allen and Allen 1991); developmental (Hay 1992/2009); co-creativity (Summers and Tudor 2000); and relational (Hargaden and Sills 2002).

The classical school initiated by Berne has been likened to cognitive behavioural therapy (English 2007). Constructivist TA aligns with neuroscience and how we mentally construct our worlds, whereas co-creativity emphasizes how we impact on each other's constructions. Relational TA returns to a focus on the role of the unconscious within the therapeutic relationship, and like most TA, is just as relevant in any relationship. Within the German TA literature, there has been more of a focus on systemic considerations and roles (Schmid 2008). Developmental TA has arisen since I began in the 1990s to adapt many of the therapeutically aligned TA constructs so that the emphasis shifted from pathology to health. I also introduced apparent simplifications, which allow us to share complex ideas in ways that coaches can readily understand and apply for themselves.

Each of the TA schools has contributed theoretical constructs of particular value in the coaching process, and hence for supervision also. My selection here, to fit the constraints of one chapter, covers the following:

- An overview of some *typical TA concepts* and (briefly) how these relate to supervision
- *Unconscious processes* (relational school) – Using an understanding of transference and countertransference according to TA principles
- *Contracting* (classical school) – Difficulties in coaching supervision can often be tracked back to inadequate contracts
- *Discounting* (cathexis school) – Why we need supervision, others often perceive what we cannot, we do not know what we do not know
- *TA-based supervision in practice* (developmental and constructivist schools).

Typical TA concepts related to coaching supervision

The term transactional analysis originally referred to analysing the transactions, or interactions, between people, using Berne's (1961) concept of ego states. This analytical process is now referred to as 'TA proper' because TA has come to represent a wide-ranging set of interlinking concepts, many introduced by Berne. We develop *ego states* that interact with others to get our needs met; these interactions can also be thought of as exchanges of *strokes*, which are the units of human recognition we all need to survive; we interact in *time structuring* clusters of increasing intensity in order to form relationships; we engage in unhelpful *psychological games* when we fail to achieve the closeness, or *intimacy*, we seek; and all of this often serves to reinforce a life *script* we adopted when we were too little to interpret our circumstances as a grown-up would. Internally, we may view the world through distorting *windows* (Hay 2009) that allocate *OK/not OK life positions* to us and others, we may *discount* (Mellor and Schiff 1975) evidence that conflicts with our preconceptions, run *racket systems* (self-fulfilling prophecies) (Erskine and Zalcman 1979) that influence how others react to us, and have *miniscripts* (internal processes) (Kahler 1974) that repeat our script patterns in micro format. As if all that were not enough, we also operate within patterns that reinforce our *drivers* (Kahler 1975) or compulsive ways of behaving that are linked to our *process scripts* (Kahler 1978), although when these patterns are under conscious choice they are seen as *working styles* (Hay 2009) and hence as strengths.

Any of the wide range of interlocking TA constructs can shed light on the supervision process and many are relatively easy to apply. For instance, we can analyse ego states to identify, and avoid, potential parent–child co-dependent relationships between supervisor and supervisee. We can review stroking patterns to take account of the risks of supervisees with inadequate support networks relying on these units of recognition from clients or their supervisor – or the same problem for supervisors who need 'admiration strokes' from supervisees. We can analyse how matching or contrasting working styles impact on coaching or supervision processes, and how they begin to 'drive' us under stress.

A common psychological game played in supervision is 'Why don't you . . . Yes, but . . . '. The supervisee behaves like a Victim on the drama triangle (Karpman 1968) – they talk about the problem they have, sigh, maybe claim to be confused, and generally act as if they are helpless. An unaware supervisor wants to be helpful, takes on the Rescuer role, and begins to offer suggestions for what the supervisee might do, i.e. 'Why don't you . . . '. To each suggestion, the supervisee responds, 'Yes, but . . .' and says why the suggestion will not work. Eventually, one of them feels so frustrated that they switch role to Persecutor. Either the supervisor criticizes the supervisee for being so negative, or the supervisee complains that the supervisor is not competent enough. Sometimes this game is played over a longer time period, and possibly involving others: the supervisee acts on the advice given by the supervisor, only to return later and complain about the bad result that has come from doing so. The supervisee may tell others about this as well, while the supervisor is left wondering how being helpful has backfired – again! (a clue to identifying game playing is that feeling of déjà vu when the game punchline comes).

Unconscious processes

Berne (1961) identified the psychological level, or ulterior transaction, as where the real power of any interaction resides. It hardly needs saying that there will be unconscious processes within the supervisory dynamic. This is where the contrast between classical and relational TA can be so helpful. The principles of classical TA are that: we all have *physis* (Berne 1957), which is the urge to develop to our potential (like plants growing from under concrete to be in the sun); we all made decisions when small and can therefore change these now we know more about the world; and we are all OK and need to function in ways that allow us to connect genuinely with others. These principles lead to a supervisory style that is focused on developing the awareness and decision-making abilities of the supervisee.

At the same time, relational TA prompts us to keep in mind that much of significance will be occurring at the unspoken psychological level of the interaction. Non-TA author Stark (2000) identifies one-, one-and-a-half, and two-person forms of therapy, meaning respectively that the therapist: facilitates the client to do the work; or provides a reparative experience for the client; or uses their countertransference to shed light on the dynamics of said client. If we apply this to supervision, we may opt to facilitate the supervisee in applying TA concepts, we may act like a reassuring or challenging parent they lacked in childhood, or we may invite the supervisee to pay conscious attention to hitherto unconscious processes between us and consider how these may illuminate their processes with clients.

There are various categorizations of types of transference within the TA literature but these can be simplified into four (Figure 11.1) based on two axes: whether we are transferring onto the other person elements of ourselves or of a third party, and whether it leads us to positive or negative relationships. It is usually seen as problematic when transference occurs, but it may also be used when it means that the supervisee can be prompted, through a paradoxical intervention from an assumed parental figure, to become more autonomous.

Project self

	Competitive	Concordant	
	We project elements of our own Child or Parent ego state onto the other person and then get into a competitive symbiosis about whose Child or Parent will take precedence	We project elements of our own Child or Parent ego state onto the other person and then believe they are just like us and we are empathising with each other	
Have problem in relating	**Conflictual**	**Co-dependent**	**Appear to get on well together**
	We project elements of 'a third party' onto the other person and then feel we must 'fight' in a Parent–Child or Child–Parent interaction	We project elements of 'a third party' onto the other person and then seek a Parent–Child or Child–Parent symbiosis	

Project someone else

Figure 11.1 Transference formats (Hay 2007: 16)

Concordant transference – There is a risk that those of us engaged within the coaching community may assume that we are all very similar because we have a shared set of principles. We may even choose our supervisor because of perceived similarities, and hence lose the opportunity of the learning that might come from interacting with someone different.

Competitive transference – A very experienced practitioner may unconsciously compete with the supervisor, particularly if they feel they are being told what to do with the client rather than helped to reflect and analyse. Alternatively, the coach may feel competitive about proving that the kind of clients they are working with are much more challenging than the clients the supervisor may be used to.

Conflictual transference – Within a professional context, the supervisor is in a position of authority because they have a responsibility to ensure the supervisee is complying with professional norms. This may lead to an attempt at rebellion (supervisee's Child against supervisor's Parent). An experienced practitioner may instead attempt to occupy the Parent position if they think that the supervisor has had less relevant experience.

Co-dependent transference – This is probably the most common transference to occur within supervision. The supervisor is likely to be more experienced, have passed more professional exams, may be older, and may know more people within the community than the supervisee. It is easy to project onto them the face of nurturing parental figure and expect them to take care of the supervisee.

Contracting

Having considered the unconscious processes, we need to take these into account when we are contracting. Contracting has been regarded as a key element of TA since Berne (1961) emphasized its importance. It is how we invite the supervisee to be autonomous. Autonomy is another key TA concept, being the notion that each of us can function in the here-and-now; being aware of who we and other people are right now instead of engaging in regression, projection and/or transference; being open so no ulterior transactions occur; being aware that we have options for how to behave instead of being stuck in familiar unhelpful patterns; and knowing that we and others are OK even when our behaviour sometimes is not.

Contracting needs to be achieved on three levels: in addition to the unconscious, or psychological, level described above, we need to have clear agreements with all relevant parties about the procedural and professional aspects. When, where, for how long will sessions last; what happens about cancellations; what are the fees and how and when will they be paid; what documentation needs to be kept and who is allowed to see this; what actions by a client would justify breaching confidentiality? Professionally, what are we here to do; what coaching style is expected; is the practitioner appropriately qualified; where are the boundaries of coaching versus therapy or consulting; how is the coaching linked to the client's professional role?

The above are just sample questions to show what a supervisor might ask a supervisee. Often, exploring the coaching contract will result in a coach realizing what was missed that led to any current problems. Contracting needs similar rigour between supervisor and supervisee, especially when there are other parties involved. English (1975) introduced three-cornered contracting, based on noticing that training programme participants often arrived with negative fantasies about what the presenter might intend to 'do to them' on behalf of the wicked organization. Similar dynamics may occur when clients are sent for coaching. Micholt (1992) added the notion of how the psychological distances might vary, with the practitioner too close psychologically to either participant or organization.

Imagining a triangle can illustrate the dynamics and prompt the supervisee to consider whether all sides are equal – or does the supervisee feel closer to the client than to the supervisor, or vice versa, or might the supervisee feel the supervisor is psychologically aligning with the client? Imagine also these triangles stacked up for the three levels. If any level is not balanced, the stack will be insecure. For example, an organization that consistently delays paying for supervision (procedural level) may lead to a frustrated supervisor feeling resentful towards a supervisee (psychological level). A supervisee may unconsciously assume the supervisor will give advice (psychological level) instead of the non-directive role the supervisor plans to adopt (professional level).

There are sometimes more than three parties – the triangles may need to be imagined in multidimensional space! Maybe there is a professional body that supervisor and/or supervisee subscribe to, whose norms must also be taken into account. Perhaps this turns the supervisor into a 'police officer' in the view of the supervisee. There may be an organization paying for the supervision; if so, we may need to take into account what expectations they have of the supervisory process, and how these may impact on aspects such as confidentiality and the openness of the supervisee.

Discounting

Discounting within TA is defined as minimizing or ignoring some aspects of ourselves, others or the situation (Mellor and Schiff 1975). We do this to stay sane, as when we tune out background noise to pay attention to something important or fall asleep in front of the television. Unfortunately, we also discount to maintain our frame of reference, or the script we adopted when a young child and that we have now forgotten exists. By discounting we can maintain our limiting beliefs, continue to interact with others in familiar ways, and justify our failure to deal with problems.

Discounting is the key to why we need supervision. We need someone else who can spot what we are not allowing ourselves to notice. Mellor and Schiff (1975) identified several levels and types of discounting and matched these to six therapeutic treatment levels. I convert these levels into *Steps to Success* (Figure 11.2),

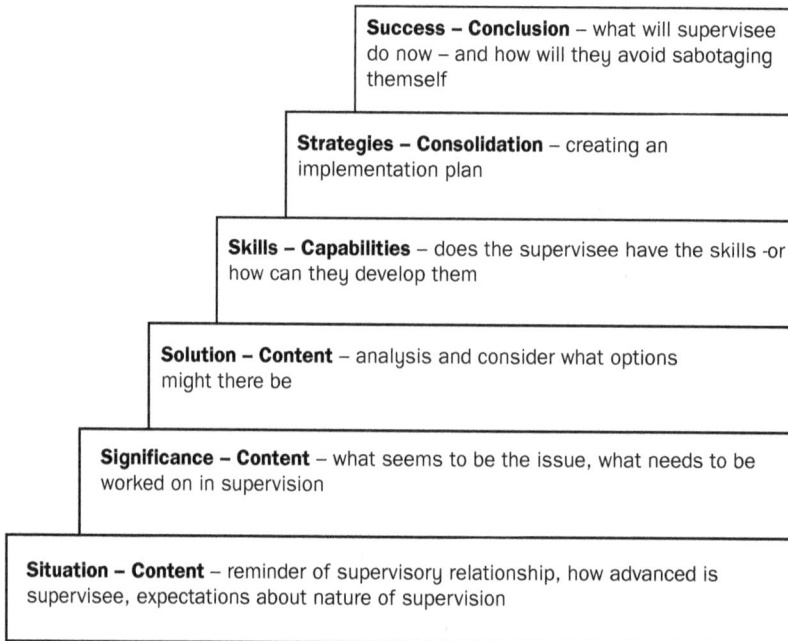

Success – Conclusion – what will supervisee do now – and how will they avoid sabotaging themself

Strategies – Consolidation – creating an implementation plan

Skills – Capabilities – does the supervisee have the skills -or how can they develop them

Solution – Content – analysis and consider what options might there be

Significance – Content – what seems to be the issue, what needs to be worked on in supervision

Situation – Content – reminder of supervisory relationship, how advanced is supervisee, expectations about nature of supervision

Figure 11.2 Stages of supervision and steps to success (Hay 2018: 69)

linked to stages of supervision (Hay 2018). The labels for most steps are self-explanatory in that we discount some aspect of the situation, significance (problem), solutions available, skills available, strategies available, or the possibility of success. We can imagine the supervisor and supervisee standing on the steps, with the supervisor (hopefully) on a higher step – maybe at the top – because they are not discounting what the supervisee is unaware of. The supervisor metaphorically needs to go down the steps to the supervisee's level and then 'coax' them back up the steps (see Box 11.1 for an example). It is usually worth going all the way back to the situation step to ensure that the significance of the issue has been correctly identified and the supervisee is not trying to solve someone else's problem.

Box 11.1 Case illustration

Saroj brought a 'difficult' client to supervision. Saroj had identified that the client was discounting at the solutions level, by insisting there were no options that would resolve the problem of needing to work with a colleague the client disliked. It was clear to me, but not to Saroj of course, that there was a parallel process (Searles 1955) in effect: Saroj disliked this client. I therefore set out to help Saroj climb the steps. We began by reviewing the situation, which in this case meant the contract with the client, the coaching plan and what had happened so far within the coaching.

When we moved up a step to significance, I was able to question Saroj about why this client was difficult whereas other clients who got stuck were not. This prompted Saroj to realize that a personal dynamic was getting in the way; the client reminded Saroj of a former colleague with whom Saroj had struggled unsuccessfully to work. This insight enabled Saroj to identify some solutions that could have been used with that colleague; this in turn prompted solutions from Saroj for working with the client. One solution involved Saroj walking the client up the client's own steps, another option was to have the client explore the Persecutor, Rescuer and Victim roles of the psychological game being played (with Saroj and with the colleague), and yet another was to help the client identify how the ego state they typically adopted with this colleague was leading to crossed transactions.

Saroj did not need more supervision about the steps for skills, strategies and success because once the discounting at a lower level had been dealt with, Saroj was able to think clearly about how to coach the client in new skills, how to prompt the client to develop a strategy for changing their behaviour towards the colleague and how to have the client check for potential self-sabotage of a successful resolution of the issue.

TA-based supervision in practice

Like the other theoretical approaches in this book, TA is a psychological framework and will therefore be useful for understanding the psychological processes of supervision and coaching. It will be used differently depending on the degree of exposure to TA concepts of the supervisee but in some ways will be even more productive for supervisees with little TA knowledge than for those who have already gleaned significant insights from prior exposure to TA.

Box 11.2 Case illustration

Lesley – new to TA

Lesley did not know much TA but was interested to learn. We therefore contracted that I would use TA when supervising and would explain my thinking as necessary so Lesley would increasingly be able to undertake the analysis unaided. This involved me in some mini-teaches and also meant we frequently focused on building awareness of how personal issues affected Lesley's competence as a practitioner.

For example, I needed to explain contracting and especially the significance of the psychological level and psychological distances. A short input enabled Lesley to identify what was not being said with a couple of coaching clients: in one case this was the client's expectation that the coach would do the problem-solving; in another it was that the organization expected the coaching to fail so they could dismiss the coachee with an apparently clear conscience. In both cases, Lesley was able to raise these issues in a non-threatening way and agree more realistic outcomes with the organizational contact: that the coach would facilitate the client's identification of options; and that the threat of dismissal would be made overt and not linked to the coaching per se.

Robin – very experienced

We can compare Lesley with Robin, a very experienced coach who had attended ongoing TA training and supervision workshops for about two years and used it extensively within coaching. Robin therefore tended to arrive for supervision with excerpts of recorded sessions plus transcripts, already analysed using several TA concepts. My supervisory role was for more than listening out for accuracy of analysis – my key purpose was to be the 'discount identifier' who alerted Robin to those elements that had been outside awareness.

These instances of discounting tended to be linked to Robin's personal issues that were as yet unresolved. Because Robin was generally self-aware and analytical, such issues could often be addressed during supervision rather than having to be ringfenced as therapy issues. Thus, Robin's familiarity with his/her own working styles and script meant that Robin readily saw the connection when I pointed out sentence patterns that Robin had missed. Robin thus volunteered the connection between the Please People pattern with an After process script of things feeling good to start but then going wrong – and how coaching with that client had indeed seemed to be going well until the client complained that no real progress was being made and challenged Robin's professional status.

A less self-aware supervisee might have needed careful questioning to reach this awareness, and might have needed to take the issue to therapy in order to work on their script dynamics. Robin, on the other hand, was able to recognize this as a replay of an old pattern, and to use the rest of the supervision session to figure out how and why this client had triggered this reaction at this time – and what to do about it now.

A key consideration is maintaining the boundary between supervision and therapy when applying an approach like TA that has its roots in psychotherapy. If this distinction is not understood, unprofessional practice may be the result. A supervisor and supervisee who both come from a therapeutic background may share expectations about coaching and supervision that blur the boundaries. They may spend supervisory time engaged in personal therapy for the supervisee instead of focusing on the development of the supervisee's practice. This in turn heightens the risk that the coach works inappropriately with clients, encouraging clients to regress and offering a reparative experience by acting as a parent figure. This may mean that clients become increasingly dependent on their coach, perhaps with tearfulness during sessions and much talking about childhood events. There may be little focus on the original aims of the coaching, so that an organization buying coaching to work on the client's leadership skills may find that client exhibiting even less leadership competence in the workplace because of the constant reinforcement by the coach of the client's regressed Child ego state.

Transactional analysis is not the only approach where this applies of course, but the availability of developmental TA is significant in avoiding such problems. Unlike some forms of therapeutic supervision, it is regarded as a key element of DTA supervision that we facilitate the supervisee to stay in the here-and-now. They may regress momentarily, as we all do sometimes, but need to identify they have done this and maintain a conversation about what just happened, what it means and how they need to factor it into their professional work. They may dip into script but need to be able to move back to autonomous functioning; they may recognize a driver pattern and need to let go of the belief that this is the only route to OKness; or perhaps they identify they have played a psychological game with their client (or their supervisor) and instead of berating themself or others, they need to be prompted to become engaged with analysing the dynamics and working out what to do differently in future. The supervisor needs to be clear about boundaries of supervision, which will often have therapeutic impact but should not be using psychotherapeutic methods.

I believe there are significant similarities between coaching and supervision, and other helping professions. Constructivist TA provides the explanation that we are helping others change how they construct their worlds. We are facilitating others to make meaning in different ways, and particularly in different ways to those that parent figures and society expect and may even have imposed. For me, therefore, the supervisor helps the supervisee to take a meta-position in the same way that the coach helps the client to take a meta-position.

There are advantages regardless of the relative levels of TA knowledge of supervisor and supervisee. If the supervisee has studied TA and the supervisor knows little or none, the supervisor may see this as an opportunity to encourage the supervisee to take the lead within the supervision process. This can be a powerful permission (Crossman 1966) and great role modelling for how to maintain your potency without having to be the expert. If the supervisor has TA experience and the supervisee knows none, the supervisor may use their TA knowledge to guide their own thinking, to form hypotheses such as what script is in effect, or to use TA concepts to analyse behaviour patterns. These can be checked out tentatively without using TA jargon and may well provide the supervisee with valuable insights. Another option, as I described above with Lesley, is to provide mini-teaches, with a focus on a specific aspect of the supervisee's or client's activity. If supervisor and supervisee each know only a little TA, the danger of misinterpretation is slight provided the relationship is free of co-dependency and the joint discovery process will contribute to the working alliance. If both know considerable TA, they can save time by talking in professional jargon; being able to label patterns of behaviour in consistent ways eliminates the need for lengthy descriptions of who said and did what.

Guidance for further learning and research

Before suggesting how to learn more, I want to respond to typical criticisms of TA tradition. It is fairly clear that in some ways Berne appeared to be racist, sexist, and homophobic. Although we might argue that could be said of anyone writing in the 1960s, many TA authors continue to use original TA terminology in a similar way. Calling a psychological game Rapo [I renamed it Rebuff years ago] is an obvious example, as is accusing genuine victims such as refugees of playing psychological games. 'Paralysis by analysis' is another common complaint and is true insofar as the psychoanalytic tradition is allowed to creep in but does not apply when clear contracts are established for client change or coach development. Another criticism has been about the apparent lack of research into the effectiveness of TA. However, the *International Journal of Transactional Analysis Research & Practice* (www.ijtarp.org – open access) was launched in summer 2010, with an extensive list in the first issue of research already done, and the *Transactional Analysis Journal* had a special issue on research in 2017.

A good place to start learning some TA is through attendance at a TA introductory course, known as a TA 101 after the way universities in the USA refer to beginners' programmes. These courses cover the major TA concepts, albeit rather rapidly because they typically last only two or three days. Certifications are offered in stages, such as those developed by the International Centre for TA Qualifications (www.ictaq.org). Some universities accredit TA training programmes at master's level, some TA training institutes award their own certificates or diplomas, and some link to ICF or EMCC. However, the International and European TA associations (ITAA and EATA) operate only qualifications that take an average of five years to attain practitioner status followed by another seven years on average to supervisor; they have no specific qualifications related to coaching.

Questions for reflection

Suggested questions for reflection can be adapted to specific individuals, such as a relatively inexperienced practitioner, a very experienced practitioner, a practitioner who has had very little supervision so far, a practitioner who has more experience of receiving supervision than you have of giving it:

- How might the ideas in this chapter help me understand the practitioner/client dynamics?
- How might the ideas in this chapter help me understand the supervisor/supervisee dynamics?
- How might I appropriately share some of the ideas with my supervisees?
- How might I incorporate the ideas into my current theoretical framework of the supervision process?

Further sources

There are many TA books available, but few relate the theories directly to coaching or supervision. One exception is *Reflective Practice and Supervision for Coaches* (Hay 2007). This is written for coaches and their supervisors and the content includes more than can be provided here on: discounting and the steps to success; contracting, boundaries, multi-party contracting, ethics; suggested ground rules for supervision groups; and some material related specifically to supervision about games, strokes and working styles; change and the competence curve.

A publication that addresses supervision and coaching with some TA underpinning is *Supervision for Coaches: A Guide to Thoughtful Work* (Cochrane and Newton 2011). In this, various TA concepts are explored in relation to supervision, interspersed with non-TA ideas and activities.

There are many introductory texts about TA, but where these address supervision they tend to use non-TA approaches. A generally targeted book about applying TA in a working environment, written for the layperson and subtitled *Understanding Attitudes and Building Relationships*, is *Working it Out at Work* by Hay (2009).

References

Allen, J. and Allen, B. (1991) Towards a constructivist TA, in B. Loria (ed.) *The Stamford Papers: Selections from the 29th Annual ITAA Conference*. Madison, WI: Omnipress.

Berne, E. (1957) *A Layman's Guide to Psychiatry and Psychoanalysis*. New York: Simon and Schuster.

Berne, E. (1961) *Transactional Analysis in Psychotherapy*. New York: Grove Press.

Cochrane, H. and Newton, T. (2011) *Supervision for Coaches*. Ipswich: Supervision for Coaches Publishing.

Crossman, P. (1966) Permission and protection, *Transactional Analysis Bulletin*, 5(19): 152–154.

English, F. (1975) The three cornered contract, *Transactional Analysis Journal*, 5(4): 383–384.

English, F. (2007) I'm now a cognitive transactional analyst, are you?, *The Script*, 37: 5 July.

Erskine, R. and Zalcman, M. (1979) The racket system: a model for racket analysis, *Transactional Analysis Journal*, 9(1): 51–59.

Goulding, R.L. and Goulding, M.M. (1979) *Changing Lives through Redecision Therapy*. New York: Grove Press.

Hargaden, H. and Sills, C. (2002) *Transactional Analysis: A Relational Perspective*. Hove: Brunner-Routledge.

Hay, J. (1992/2007) *Reflective Practice and Supervision for Coaches*. Maidenhead: Open University Press.

Hay, J. (1992/2009) *Transactional Analysis for Trainers*, 2nd edn. Hertford: Sherwood Publishing.

Hay, J. (1993/2009) *Working it Out at Work*, 2nd edn. Hertford: Sherwood Publishing.

Hay, J. (1996) Steps to success, *INTAND Newsletter*, 4: 3 September.

Hay, J. (2011) *Transactional Analysis for Coaches and Mentors*. Hertford: Sherwood Publishing.

Hay, J. (2018) Psychological boundaries and psychological bridges: a categorisation and the application of transactional analysis concepts, *International Journal of Transactional Analysis Research & Practice*, 9(1): 52–81.

Kahler, T. (1974) The miniscript, *Transactional Analysis Journal*, 4(1): 26–42.

Kahler, T. (1975) Drivers: the key to the process of scripts, *Transactional Analysis Journal*, 5(3): 280–284.

Kahler, T. (1978) *Transactional Analysis Revisited*. Little Rock, AR: Human Development Publications.

Karpman, S. (1968) Fairy tales and script drama analysis, *Transactional Analysis Bulletin*, 7: 39–43.

Mellor, K. and Schiff, E. (1975) Discounting, *Transactional Analysis Journal*, 5(3): 295–302.

Micholt, N. (1992) The concept of psychological distance, *Transactional Analysis Journal*, 22(4): 228–233.

Proctor, B. (1986) Supervision: a co-operative exercise in accountability, in A. Marken and M. Payne (eds) *Enabling and Ensuring: Supervision in Practice*. Leicester: National Youth Bureau/Council for Education and Training in Youth and Community Work.

Schiff, J.L. (1975) *Cathexis Reader*. New York: Harper & Row.

Schmid, B. (2008) The role concept of transactional analysis and other approaches to personality, encounter, and cocreativity for all professional fields, *Transactional Analysis Journal*, 38(1): 17–30.

Searles, H.F. (1955) The informational value of the supervisor's emotional experiences, *Psychiatry*, 18: 135–146.

Stark, M. (2000) *Modes of Therapeutic Action*. Northvale, NJ: Jason Aronson.

Summers, G. and Tudor, K. (2000) Cocreative transactional analysis, *Transactional Analysis Journal*, 30(1): 23–40.

12 Supervising according to theories of organizational psychology

Carmelina Lawton Smith

Introduction

Organizational psychology is a diverse field that seeks to understand how organizations and the people within them function. It draws on a multidisciplinary approach to provide alternative perspectives and multiple frames of analysis. Coaches come from diverse backgrounds and often bring a wealth of experience with a clear understanding of organizations and the wider context in which they operate. However, with that knowledge and experience can come a frame of reference that limits the scope of view. For example, someone with a career in finance who is now offering coaching to specialist financial institutions is likely to gain entry to this market because they bring credibility and experience, but in so doing may fail to value alternative ways in which an organization can be viewed. Even if they appreciate that some organizations have different cultures, e.g. public sector, they may still view an organization through a 'performance and profitability' lens. The coach essentially brings their existing perspectives about how organizations operate into their coaching role. While this means the coach may understand the context, people and culture, it can limit their thinking and reduce the degree of challenge they use with clients. They can become blinkered by their own past experience and expectation. Using organizational psychology models is one way that the supervisor can expand a coach's frame of reference, influencing what they see, or fail to see.

This recognition of the greater complexity of the coaching context has been a significant trend in recent years. There has been increased interest in working 'systemically' (Lawrence 2015) and an expectation that supervision needs to appreciate the complex interrelationships that the organizational context brings to coaching. Coaching is no longer provided solely by independent executive coaches who hold monthly meetings with senior executives in private offices. Coaching has become a mainstream development mechanism often delivered by managers, peers or HR. It can be on-demand, form part of leadership programmes and be promoted as an important lever in driving organizational culture change. This brings with it the necessity that supervisors have a good appreciation of the organizational context and the many types of supervisee they may encounter.

Using these additional organizational perspectives enables the supervisor to fulfil each of the supervisory functions (Hawkins and Smith 2006). These fresh perspectives can highlight new ways of working, thus facilitating development and greater understanding. Highlighting alternative standpoints can also contribute to the qualitative function, by minimizing blind spots and personal bias, thus maximizing the chances of a successful coaching engagement. In addition, appreciating the multiple perspectives of an organization communicates to supervisees that the supervisor understands the complex organizational contexts in which they work, which can help the supervisee feel supported. Once the supervisee has the language of organizational psychology, they may be better equipped to share concerns and doubts that they may be feeling, but struggle to express due to the complexity.

Organizational psychology, by virtue of its diversity and multidisciplinary nature, brings a rich set of perspectives that can be of value to the supervisor working with this potentially broad audience. Using the multiple views that organizational psychology offers, the supervisor can help the supervisee gain new insights to situations and their practice. In this chapter, the aim is to focus on the macro level and how the ideas, concepts and perspectives offered by organizational psychology can be valuable in supervision. I will review two major approaches to understanding organizations. The first is the 'open systems' model that highlights the inherent dependencies that result from interactions both inside and outside the organization. The second provides alternative perspectives that can be taken within the organization by using different 'frames'. As you read the various examples and descriptions consider which resonate with you, and which you are more likely to gravitate to as a way of seeing organizations. But I will start by bounding the term 'organizational psychology'.

Defining organizational psychology

'Organizational psychology' does not exist as a discrete set of topics that can be listed, 'it is rather a meeting place for various sub-disciplinary interests' (Nicholson and Wall 1982: 4) and may encompass industrial psychology, work psychology, business psychology and organizational behaviour. This chapter will consider ideas that may fall under any of these terms, but that share a focus on psychology within the organizational context. The use of the word 'organization' reflects the relevance to private, public and third sector organizations. The term 'psychology' will refer to 'the study of human behaviour and experience' (Nicholson and Wall 1982), which here we locate in an organizational context. Some question if in the modern fluid working world we can bound 'organizational behaviour', arguing that we need to widen how we think of 'work' and that we must also focus on life outside of the organization to make sense of individual behaviours within organizations (Wilson 2004). This is a valid perspective for the supervisor to bear in mind but for simplicity this chapter will maintain a focus on psychology of the organization.

All individuals that work within organizations are psychological beings. Each individual creates for themselves a personal identity that may be subject to issues of confidence or self-image. These are aspects of the individual's psychology that would be present whether or not the individual was in an organizational context and are necessarily affected by activities outside work. There is always psychology '*in*' an organization, but here we consider more broadly the psychology '*of*' the organization: those aspects of psychology that are affected specifically because they operate within the context of the organization.

This focus means that the *individual* may not be the only unit of analysis. When considering performance, for example, it is possible to review individual learning plans or personal performance targets. But organizational psychology draws attention to other potential units of analysis. We might consider a *task* unit of analysis looking at schedules and priorities or how work is structured and assigned. The unit of analysis may be the *group* and how team working can be enhanced to meet performance goals, while the *organizational* unit of analysis might examine how recognition and reward systems affect performance across departments. Even the organizational *environment* where competition and external concerns are affecting and driving performance requirements may be relevant (Drenth et al. 1998). From each unique unit of analysis, we gain a different perspective and potential solution to enhancing 'performance'.

Throughout its evolution, organizational psychology has never had one single underlying theory (Drenth et al. 1998) but has retained multiple levels of analysis focused on the effective utilization of people in the workplace (Schein 1980). This might include individuals who are stakeholders in the organization, the groups within the organization or the organization as a holistic entity. Organizations are effectively more than the sum of their parts so require multiple levels of analysis to understand them. The field therefore includes topics like personality, stress, learning and skills enhancement, most relevant at the *individual level* of analysis. Group processes, team working, recruitment and training practices, and leadership which have an impact at the *management level* (Schein 1980). At the *organizational level*, culture, power and change become relevant. Each topic can reveal important features from the respective point of view. Motivation, for example, can be analysed from multiple standpoints. From the *individual* perspective we might assess how a person can be motivated. However, different approaches emerge when we consider the team structure; motivating five individuals may not create a motivated team of five and co-dependent goals may be required from the *management* level. At the *organizational* level the policies and procedures also need to create a motivating climate for employees. We may need all aspects to make sense of the situation.

Organizations as 'open systems'

Organizations are never self-contained units. They are complex evolving entities that respond and react to the environment and context within which they operate. Theorists have long tried to define the ideal organizational structure, but this has proved elusive as many situational variables affect organizational success. For example, as an organization grows it needs more bureaucracy and systems that were not required with fewer employees. Technological advances influence how organizations are structured and the advent of reliable remote communication technologies allows for cross-global teams and reporting lines, which impact relationships between people. These dependencies are highlighted in the open systems model which identifies the organization as being open to, and in continual interaction with, external environmental factors. Mullins (2016) summarizes the importance of this: 'In order to be effective and maintain survival and growth, the organization must respond to the opportunities and challenges, and the risks and limitations, presented by the external environment of which it is part' (Mullins 2016: 75–76).

Since all organizational coaching relationships take place within this organizational system, understanding the implications of that system can be valuable in supervision. Hawkins and Smith (2006) draw attention to this in the supervision context explaining that what might first appear as an individual client issue could originate in the larger dynamics of the organization. An example might be a coach who reports difficulties with a senior executive suddenly unable to delegate. They may attribute this to issues of personal trust, yet a review of the wider external environment reveals a recent legal case that culminated in a director being sued for corporate manslaughter. While this may, or may not, be relevant in this case, the wider environmental system is worthy of consideration in the coaching space and one role of the supervisor is to encourage this wider view. While a supervisor and supervisee may not be able to fully appreciate the individual complexities of every specific industry or organization, it is valuable to comprehend the potential dependencies and interrelationships and adopt a systemic perspective. As suggested by Lawrence and Moore (2018), 'The systemic coach seeks to understand the coachee's interpretation of the organisational story, and to locate his/her own role within that system' and the supervisor may be able to support them in this.

The open systems model also provides frameworks by which to consider potential variables within the organization, usually identified as *subsystems*. Authors vary in the 'subsystems' they draw attention to, but one example is to consider the *task*, the *technology*, the *structures*, the *people* and the *management* (Mullins 2016). A coach may come to supervision reporting a client who is having difficulty with team communication wanting to assess options for working on their interpersonal style. Using the open system model could broaden the conversation to discuss each 'subsystem' and to consider how areas may interact. Possible areas for inquiry and solutions may lie as much in new systems or structures as with interpersonal skills.

Giving the coach these wider systems and interrelationships to consider can help them work with clients in a more comprehensive and holistic way. It allows the supervisor to encourage a broader context for enquiry which can also clarify for the coach where they themselves are within the organizational system. The arrival of a coach into an open system can itself affect dynamics. Take, for example, a CEO who employs a coach for one of the directors who has recently returned from long-term sick leave. While the coach may believe this to be a neutral and helpful intervention, it can introduce tension because the coachee feels they are under scrutiny; meanwhile, the CEO confides information to the coach that should be addressed directly to the coachee. The supervisor can draw attention to the fluidity and dynamics that characterize an open system, assessing perhaps the 'ripples' created by the coach within the system (Cavanagh 2006).

At a macro level, organizations and the employees within them are also having to continuously adapt to external pressures in a context described as volatile, uncertain, complex and ambiguous (Bennett and Lemoine 2014). This has led organizations to move towards 'agile' work practices that prioritize adaptability in both people and processes. Organizational structures and processes need to remain responsive to prevailing pressures; environmental concerns, corporate social responsibility and diversity are all current themes that affect organizations and to remain a 'closed system' without adaptation can be damaging. Such issues may well come up in coaching so an appreciation of the implications can be a supervisory asset.

For example, imagine a coach bringing a case regarding a coachee who mentioned that they have been accused of 'inappropriate comments' to female staff. The coach is told that their manager was not overly concerned and that such things were to be expected in a 'male' industry, yet it is clear that HR have taken a different view. The coach might want to examine not only their own feelings about tackling this issue, but also consider a much wider social perspective and the expectations of senior managers in the current cultural climate. There may also be a wider debate about whether coaching the individual alone is likely to bring about the required changes. Such a situation could easily bring far greater interest from HR in the coaching outcomes and as a supervisor there may be merit in directing the coach to this wider systemic perspective. The coach may benefit from considering if they need to engage with the organization in a more holistic way in order to address what might be more than an individual's poor choice of words.

The 'open systems' model could provide a framework for the discussion of issues or facilitate a dialogue around the supervisee's own experiences and assumptions. This might relate to things like organizational culture and communication, power structures or even organizational discourses. It may be a useful way for the supervisee to evaluate and assess how their own assumptions about 'how organizations work or should work' might influence their approach to a client issue. Viewing the organization as an open system is one model from organizational psychology that can enable the supervisee to question existing views of the organization and their personal perspectives.

Alternative views of the organization

A 'paradigm' can be thought of as the philosophical and theoretical lens through which an organization is viewed and will impact what can be seen through that particular 'lens'.

The concept of paradigms is often poorly understood but at a simple level 'paradigms tell us what information to consider important and how to use that information . . . they illuminate some information while leaving other information in the dark' (Weaver and Farrell 1997: 45). For many, what is seen is an automatic function of their meaning-making process and outside conscious awareness, often heavily influenced by the 'schema' that people hold.

Cognitive schemas (Piaget 1957) are effectively mental shortcuts that we all use to navigate and make meaning of the world. However, these schemas can lead us to exclude pertinent information and focus instead only on aspects that confirm our pre-existing beliefs and ideas. Schemas held by the coach could therefore contribute to narrow thinking and make it difficult to investigate new perspectives that may not conform to their established ideas about how the world works. Because such schemas can be difficult to change, the supervisor may be able to highlight the operation of such thinking patterns.

Organizational psychology advances numerous models of organizations but one that focuses specifically on paradigms may be a useful tool for the supervisor by highlighting 'individual schema'. Bolman and Deal (2017) identify four ways that it is possible to frame an organization.

1. The structural frame – 'factories'
2. The human resources frame – 'families'
3. The political frame – 'jungles'
4. The symbolic frame – 'temples and carnivals'.

Each frame reveals a different perspective that can help the supervisee see alternative ways to conceive of an organization and a situation. This can help free coaches from the shackles of past experience and the historical route through which they arrived in coaching. Both coaches and clients can be trapped within an existing frame, and knowledge of alternative perspectives can help move thinking into new more fruitful areas. For example, looking at a set of financial figures can reveal how much an organization spends on employee entertainment and this can be evaluated against corporate standards. But this fails to uncover how that expenditure is received by staff; whether it is seen as worthwhile and motivating, or as a cynical abuse of expenses by the company elite. The financial perspective gives one standpoint but if we focus on the people, we may form a different view. When coaches use only past schema or a single paradigm in their coaching it may limit what they are able to see and as a result restrict areas of inquiry. Using discrete 'frames' to structure the supervisory enquiry can be a helpful way to highlight alternative paradigms.

The structural frame

In this frame, efficiency and effectiveness are dependent on the structures, policies and procedures put in place. Co-ordination and control are essential to achieve organizational goals. The aim is to measure, quantify and define as much as possible to reduce variability and unpredictability. Within the structural frame we consider how authority and the chain of command operates vertically and how lateral co-ordination between teams and working groups can be achieved. This results in rules, policies and procedures with strong planning and control mechanisms. In defining the ideal structure and work flow we need to consider aspects such as the size of the organization, what technologies are in place and the external environment. Therefore, an organization in a volatile or uncertain environment must structure for adaptability and flexibility, perhaps at the expense of economy and simplicity. The organizational goals and strategy will ultimately drive many of these decisions. For example, a large-scale commodity supplier of milk will require a very different structure to that of an elite fashion product.

The human resources frame

The human resources frame addresses the needs of the people involved in the organization and considers the feelings and prejudices that arise. In this frame the activities of management can lead to alienation and hostility, or to engagement and motivation. As a result, managers seek to create participative management and focus on job enrichment and autonomy to build high performance. Within this frame the focus is primarily on people. How to recruit the right people, how to motivate, train and reward key performers. There is debate about how to empower employees and encourage engagement. There is a strong focus on interpersonal dynamics and the ideal make up of teams. People are seen as social animals that bring other issues to the working context. Therefore, organizational success depends on managing the emotions and interactions between these social beings.

The political frame

The political frame highlights the concept of power dynamics and conflict in the organization. The focus is on how decisions are made and the impact that the internal coalitions have on the ability of the organization to reach its goals. This is not to say that conflict is always bad, because it can drive development and growth. However, how conflict is addressed, and power brokered, has a significant impact on organizational outcomes. This frame looks at alternative sources of power and how this power is distributed and used. Power structures can be mapped to gain understanding of situations. Networking, negotiation and bargaining are vital components of a successful enterprise.

The symbolic frame

The symbolic frame addresses the meaning making and cultural norms that exist within the organization. It focuses on what rituals and actions define the values and prevailing culture, how stories are transmitted and what meaning is made of past events and actions taken. Stories encompass the values of the organization and the core ideology permeates through rituals and history. Culture encompasses a set of shared beliefs, values and customs that communicate the 'way we do things round here'. Impressions are managed to fuel common understanding and cultural fit that creates an insider/outsider mentality.

This brief summary highlights four potential frames that can be applied in organizations, and these do not relate to job roles. An HR director in a highly competitive financial sector may well operate with a structural frame; by contrast the financial director of a charity could work with a human resources frame. But often coaches and their clients have a bias towards one or more of these frames. This means they see issues and therefore potential solutions primarily through the lens they currently adopt. Many use a habitual paradigm, which may be the impact of long held values and beliefs. A coach who values structure and organization may tend towards a structural frame. If their client wishes to address issues of micro-management and delegation and is prone to a similar frame, the focus may be on authority, co-ordination and control systems, perhaps looking at how the client needs to restructure responsibilities and tasks to achieve department goals more effectively. However, a coach and client locked in a human resources frame might spend time discussing the interpersonal group dynamics that could result from increased delegation, or the impact on motivation and what training or development might be required. While neither approach is either right or wrong, either individual approach alone presents limitations. It may be possible to enable delegation purely though creating self-managed working teams and training. But if the problems are the result of expanded responsibilities, a change in structure may be required so a human resources frame alone might not resolve the issue. The supervisor can therefore help the supervisee build an awareness of what frames are in place for themselves and the client. This can avoid the potential limitations created by collusion in the same frame and highlight how potential differences of frame may impact the relationship and interaction between coach and client.

As a supervisor, these paradigms can be used in a number of ways. First, when working with organizations, understanding each frame can support effective working relationships, ensuring supervision meets the needs of the sponsor. Second, these frames can enable the supervision process by creating a language and model for discussion with supervisees. They provide a clear framework for debate that is non-judgemental in terms of relative merits of each approach. Lastly the model can be used to extend the perspective of supervisees using each of the 'seven eyes' as a mode of working (Hawkins and Smith 2006):

- In mode 1 the supervisor can help the coach become aware of how the client frame may impact their descriptions and reactions expressed in coaching. It can help the coach gain understanding of the client perspective.
  Is the client locked in one particular frame? What frame is communicated by the client's descriptions?
- In mode 2 the supervisor can draw attention to interventions that the coach can use that may help the client broaden their perspective. This may also highlight if the coach is in danger of using interventions that are only supporting not widening the client perspective.
  What interventions will broaden the frames in view? What frames are implicit in the interventions currently used?
- In mode 3 the supervisor can draw attention to potential similarities or differences of paradigm. If the coach is having difficulty with a client, this may represent an alternative framing of the organization and the potential actions available.
  What frames currently inform the client and coach view? What aspects of the relationship indicate a similar or divergent view?
- In mode 4 the focus is on the coach and may highlight beliefs within the coach tend to drive them consistently into one frame.
  How does the coach usually work? What experiences and beliefs inform their current view of organizations and the people within them?
- In modes 5 and 6 the supervisor starts to look at their own beliefs and frames to ensure they model and use all the frames within their own practice.
  As a supervisor, do I lean towards one frame? How can I hold each frame equally?
- In mode 7 we can place each of these frames in the wider open system and environment.
- How would each frame interact with the wider environment? What can each frame contribute?

The supervisor is in a unique position to identify particular schema consistently applied by the coach to interpret situations and to encourage the development of alternative frames of reference. The case illustration below gives an example of how this model was used by a supervisor with a supervisee to enhance development that ultimately provided improved quality of service for the client.

Box 12.1 Case illustration

The following case study is based on a real situation brought to supervision. The names and context have been changed to protect anonymity, but an expression of gratitude goes to the coach who consented to publication.

Robert was a business coach and came to supervision wanting ideas on how to approach future meetings with a client. He had been working with Carl for some time but felt he was no longer enabling Carl to generate new ideas or to move forward. This is the situation as he described it to his supervisor.

The background

Robert: I am coaching a man called Carl who was recruited two years ago as the Business Development Director of an engineering company. The company has a long traditional history but has been struggling to develop into emerging markets so Carl was recruited to develop new business opportunities. Carl was expected to take at least a year to become familiar with the products and markets but after two years Carl is still struggling to meet the strategic targets set by the MD, Michael. Michael has been with the company for six years and is keen to show growth to the parent company but is worried about Carl. I was brought in by Michael because he feels Carl has potential. I have had a few meetings with Carl and he feels there is a major problem with the sales director, Simon. So, the three key players are: Carl my client, Michael the MD and Simon the sales director.

Carl says that Simon is stopping him achieving his targets as he is obstructive, fails to follow up leads he is given and undermines his suggestions in board meetings. Carl says that he has tried everything to get Simon on side and since they are the same level should not be facing this sort of behaviour.

We talked a lot about Simon who has been with the company over 30 years and rose from the manufacturing floor to sales director. I have talked to Carl a great deal about his relationship with Simon and how he might win him round. We have discussed his communication style with Simon. But everything we have discussed Carl seems to be doing, yet it is clear that despite all our work Carl is still not achieving and I am not sure how to help him.

I can't seem to bring anything new to this situation and do not know what to focus on now.

From the interventions described by Robert he appeared to have approached Carl and his situation from a human resources frame, trying to get Carl to consider the interpersonal relationship to establish how to motivate Simon into a more co-operative stance. However, despite this work no progress was being made. In fact, Robert even felt that Carl had good communication skills and seemed to be doing everything they discussed in coaching meetings.

The supervisor decided to ask Robert questions from alternative frames in an effort to generate new approaches. The aim was to bring new perspectives to the situation.

Supervisor: You said that both Carl and Simon are of the same level but that your client feels he is not treated in that way. Where does Carl believe Simon gets his power from?

Robert stopped and thought about this question as he realized he had not discussed this aspect with Carl at all. This generated a very useful discussion about the power structures that were in place and gave Robert ideas about how he might widen the discussion with Carl. After this the supervisor raised the issue of the culture in the company and the symbols and meaning that might be attached to actions. This also gave Robert some ideas for future discussions with Carl based on the symbolic frame. It was clear that the traditional nature of the organization brought numerous cultural norms that needed to be discussed.

They discussed each frame in turn and Robert came to realize that both he and Carl held a human resources frame so both were approaching the situation in a similar way. Robert and his supervisor discussed how each of the alternative frames could be used to widen the client's perspective

The end of the story

At the next client meeting Robert got Carl to map the current situation and the preferred situation resulting in the emergence of two potential tactics. The eventual solution arose from the political frame, to reduce Simon's power through increased involvement of the MD. Carl decided to speak to the MD and gain his backing to a new development, which gave him enough knowledge to support Carl when required and effectively diminish Simon's level of control. His new project was presented by the MD at the next board meeting and Carl was surprised to see Simon agree with the new proposal.

Review

We can see here that discussing alternative frames with the supervisee ultimately provided new ideas on how to approach the situation. The coach was able to break out of the human resources frame to generate solutions that were grounded in the political frame and how to manage dynamics.

Frames may, of course, overlap. It could be that to reduce Simon's involvement in new projects may require a change to the structures and reporting lines. Effectively, a political frame analysis may generate an idea which needs to be implemented through a structural change. However, using each frame with the supervisee can help generate new ideas and insights on how to work.

Guidance for further learning and research

Organizational psychology covers a huge range of topics that provide a diverse tapestry of concepts and approaches in relation to organizations. Individual topics may prove useful but one of the major benefits of the field is the variety of perspectives it provides.

This chapter has presented a number of alternative perspectives that a supervisor can use to broaden the field of view when working with a supervisee who presents issues based in an organizational context. It highlights various paradigms that can facilitate new thinking about situations to support and develop effective practice.

Over recent years we have seen coaching emerge as a common organizational intervention and it will help supervisors to consider and evaluate how alternative frames may influence the supervision they engage in. Supervisors, as well as supervisees, may hold favoured 'frames' or schema, but as the contexts within which they work expands, it is important to be aware of limiting frames of reference. Increasing supervisory knowledge and experience of organizational topics and concerns remains an important focus for any supervisor working in this domain to enhance credibility and to support coaches in their development.

Questions for reflection

- Are you able to identify your own preferred frames of interpretation in relation to organizations?
- Can you identify the preferences of key coaching or supervision clients?
- Which frame would it be most useful for your practice to develop further?
- If we think of an organization as an 'open system' how might the arrival of a coach affect that organization?

Further sources

Bolman, L.G. and Deal, T.E. (2017) *Reframing Organizations: Artistry, Choice, and Leadership*, 6th edn. San Francisco: Jossey-Bass Publishers. This is a classic text covering the four frames in much more detail and gives relevant organizational examples to illustrate points.

Lawrence, P. and Moore, A. (2018) *Coaching in Three Dimensions*. New York: Routledge. This is an insightful yet easy to read book about coaching in the organizational systemic landscape.

Mullins, L.J. (2016) *Management and Organisational Behaviour*, 11th edn. London: Pearson. This is a general textbook that comprehensively covers most of the key theoretical ideas from organizational psychology.

References

Bennett, N. and Lemoine, J. (2014) What VUCA really means for you, *Harvard Business Review*, Jan–Feb.

Bolman, L.G. and Deal, T.E. (2017) *Reframing Organizations: Artistry, Choice, and Leadership*, 6th edn. San Francisco: Jossey-Bass Publishers.

Cavanagh, M. (2006) Coaching from a systemic perspective: a complex adaptive approach, in D.R. Stober and A.M. Grant (eds) *Evidence-based Coaching Handbook*. New York: Wiley.

Drenth, J.D., Thierry, H. and de Wolff, D. (eds) (1998) *Introduction to Work and Organizational Psychology*, 2nd edn. Hove: Psychology Press.

Hawkins, P. and Shohet, R. (1989) *Supervision in the Helping Professions*. Maidenhead: Open University Press.

Hawkins, P. and Smith, N. (2006) *Coaching, Mentoring and Organizational Consultancy*. Maidenhead: Open University Press.

Lawrence, P. (2015) *Leading Change*. London: Kogan Page.

Lawrence, P. and Moore, A. (2018) *Coaching in Three Dimensions*. New York: Routledge.

Piaget, J. (1957) *Construction of Reality in the Child*. London: Routledge and Kegan Paul.

Mullins, L.J. (2016) *Management and Organisational Behaviour*, 11th edn. London: Pearson.

Nicholson, N. and Wall, T. (1982) *The Theory and Practice of Organizational Psychology*. London: Academic Press.

Schein, E.H. (1980) *Organizational Psychology*, 3rd edn. London: Prentice Hall.

Weaver, R. and Farrell, J. (1997) *Managers as Facilitators*. San Francisco: Berrett-Koehler Publishers.

Wilson, F.M. (2004) *Organisational Behaviour and Work: A Critical Introduction*, 2nd ed. Oxford: Oxford University Press.

Section 3

Models and methods of supervision

13 The seven-eyed model of coaching supervision

Peter Hawkins and Gil Schwenk

Introduction

The purpose of this chapter is to introduce the seven-eyed model of coaching supervision, which is probably the longest established and most widely used coaching supervision model. We will describe the history of the model, consider the key elements and provide a case illustration of the model in action. We will continue by defining the roles and responsibilities of the supervisor and potential pitfalls when this model is used.

The model was first created by Peter Hawkins in 1985 as a systemic and integrative model of supervision (Hawkins 1985), which he later further developed with his colleagues at the Centre for Supervision and Team Development and became known as the seven-eyed supervision model (Hawkins and Shohet 1989). This has been used across many different people professions in many countries (Hawkins and Shohet 2012; Hawkins and McMahon 2020). Since 1995, with other colleagues, he has further developed the model for the world of coaching, mentoring, team coaching and organizational consultancy (Hawkins and Smith 2013; Hawkins 2017). The model has been developed and used by many other coach supervisors, teachers and writers around the world such as Michel Moral in France (Moral and Angel 2019) and Damian Goldvarg in South America and Asia (Goldvarg 2017)

The model was developed to include all the different aspects that can be focused on in supervision and the range of supervisory styles and skills needed for each area of focus. It is based on a systemic understanding of the ways things connect, interrelate and drive behaviour. It integrates insights and aspects of inter-subjective psychotherapy (Stolorow and Atwood 1992; Hawkins and Ryde 2020) focusing on the interrelationship between the internal and relational life of individuals.

The model points out the way in which the systemic context of the coachee can be mirrored in the coaching relationship and how the dynamics of the coaching relationship can be mirrored in the supervisory relationship. These seven areas of potential focus can be useful to both supervisor and supervisee in reviewing the supervision that they give and receive and can help them discover ways they can expand their supervision practice. The seven foci, which are commonly referred to as seven eyes or seven modes, are numbered 1–7 for the ease of reference and learning and are not meant to be applied sequentially.

The seven-eyed model of supervision

Before exploring the seven modes in a supervision session, it is critically important to develop a mutual contract for both the supervisory relationship in general
as well as each specific session. At the beginning of each supervisory conversation it is essential to explore collaboratively the supervisory work that most
needs to be attended to, and the outcomes required for the coach, the clients, the
wider stakeholders and the profession. This helps the supervisor anchor the session in both supervisor and supervise being in partnership, both facing the key
challenges that life is presenting. Typical questions include:

- We will be thinking about your coaching situation in detail in a few minutes. As
  we get started, what is it about this coachee/coaching relationship that is motivating you to bring him/her to supervision today?
- What is the outcome needed for all parties from focusing on this client–client
  relationship?
- What would be the benefit of this outcome for you, the coachee, their organization, and their wider systemic contexts?

It is important to summarize your understanding and get confirmation of the purpose and desired outcomes prior to progressing with the seven modes. This is far
more than just agreeing the logistic details of the session. From our experience of
supervising and training hundreds of supervisors, the supervision starts from the
moment that the coach and supervisor come together. It is important to listen
carefully to the contracting since it will illuminate the coachee's perspective and
aspects of the coach–client relationship. It is especially important to listen for the
verbal and non-verbal expressions and metaphors that the coach uses since they
are all important clues to guide the supervisory conversation. The contracting can
also clarify which modes might be most important for this particular supervision.

Seven modes of supervision

The seven-eyed model is built on two complementary systems. As indicated in
Figure 13.1, the first relationship is the coach–client system and the second, the
coach–supervisor system. Each of these relational systems are nested in a wider
organizational and systemic context, including the organizations that all three
parties work for, the stakeholders of those organizations and the professional
and/or training bodies that the coach and supervisor may belong to.

Mode 1: The coachee and their context

In order to work in service to the coaching client and their organizational context, we refer to mode 1 as 'getting the client(s) into the room'. For us there is
always a minimum of four clients – namely the coachee, their organization, the
wider stakeholders' systems and the relationship between the three. All of these
need to be attended to in mode 1.

The objective of mode 1 is to refresh the coach's awareness of the clients so
that we are able to metaphorically create a 'hologram' of the coachee and their

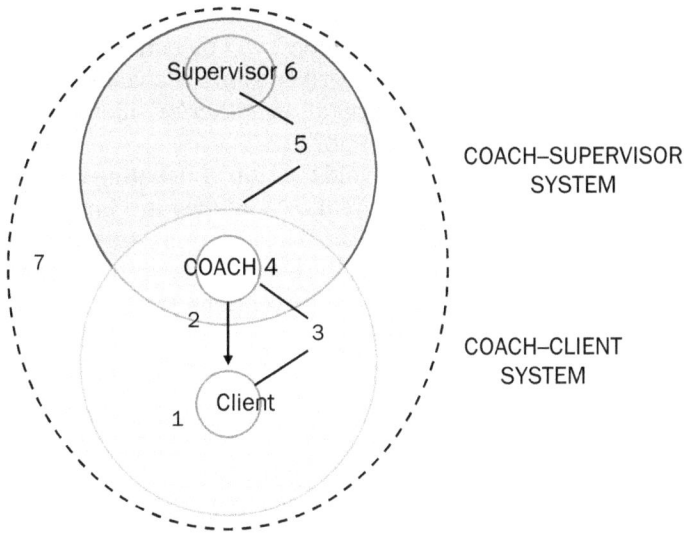

Figure 13.1 Seven modes of supervision

organizational context in the supervisory room. We want to develop a 'felt' understanding of the coachee and the client organization and how they are presenting and framing the issues.

The supervisor's skill in this mode is to help the coach accurately return to what actually happened in the session with the coachee – what they saw, what they heard and what they felt – and to try and separate this actual data from their preconceptions, assumptions and interpretations. It is also useful for the coach to be helped to attend to what happened at the boundaries of their time with the coachee, their arrival and exit, for it is often at the boundaries that the richest unconscious material is most apparent. Typical mode 1 interventions include:

- Think back to the last session with this client and revisit what happened just before the session fully got underway.
- What did the client look and sound like as they came into the session? How did the session start?
- Describe this client. What comes to mind when you think of him/her? How did the coachee present him/herself during the session? Become the client and show me how they were.
- What did you see, hear and feel during the session?
- What is the coaching contract with this client? What are they and their organization needing to achieve, develop and learn from the coaching?

Mode 2: The coach's interventions

Mode 2 looks at how the coach is working with the coachee, how they attend to each stage of the coaching process and the interventions the coach makes, including alternative choices that might have been used. It might also focus on a future situation in which the coach is about to intervene, exploring the possible options and the likely impact of each. Often, mode 2 will be initiated by the coach raising a dilemma or impasse that they have arrived at in the coaching process. They will often present this impasse in the form of an 'either/or' dilemma such as: 'Should I confront the issue, or should I let it go?'

The skill of the supervisor is to avoid the trap of debating the either/or options, and instead to enable the coach to realize how they are limiting their choice to two polarized possibilities and facilitate a shared brainstorming that frees up the energy and creates new options. Then the benefits and difficulties of these options can be explored and some possible interventions tried out in a 'fast forward rehearsal' (Hawkins and Smith 2018).

Mode 2 interventions by the supervisor might include:

- You seem to have a dilemma here! You are wondering whether to do x or y.
- What is the interest or intent behind both parts of the dilemma? What could you do that would enable both interests/intents to be honoured?
- What is the wildest intervention you could use?
- Who else do you know who would handle this well? What would they do?

Mode 3: The relationship between the coach and the coachee

The focus of mode 3 is the relationship that the coach and the coachee are co-creating together. It is here that the relational aspect of supervision first comes to the fore by moving the focus from (1) the coachee and their world, and (2) the activity of the coach, to attending to both the conscious and unconscious relational field co-created in the coaching.

The supervisor has to facilitate the coach in standing outside the relationship that they are part of so that they can see and experience it afresh, from a new angle. The Chinese have a proverb that the last one to know about the sea is the fish, because they are constantly immersed within it. In this mode the supervisor is helping the coach to be a flying fish, so they can see the 'relational water' in which they are normally swimming.

In mode 3, we want to have the coach reflect on the relationship with the coachee. This can be both logical descriptors and more spontaneous descriptors that tap into the unconscious. We might ask:

- If you were a fly on the wall, how would you describe the relationship between you and this client?
- What other relationship does this remind you of?
- If you and this client were marooned alone together on a desert island, what would happen?
- If this relationship were a colour, a piece of music, a type of weather, a country, etc., what would it be?

To a great extent, the answer to these questions is an indicator of what is probably already happening in the relationship. If a coach answers the question about being marooned on an island by saying they would set up separate camps at either end, there may be distancing and unexpressed opposition in the relationship that can now be opened up and explored. If, on the other hand, the coach says that they would enjoy sitting around the fire talking until all hours, there may be a cosiness and a lack of action that can be inquired into.

Mode 3 can parallel the relationships that key stakeholders have with the coachee. For example, one coach recently answered the question about the nature of the dance between her and the coachee by saying, 'I (the coach) am standing on the side applauding the coachee while feeling a bit useless.' As we subsequently explored the coachee context a bit further, it was evident that she was a very competent individual performer who was appreciated for her ability to get things done in the organization. However, there were concerns about how she worked largely independently and there were some concerns about her ability to work effectively with others. Her contact with other colleagues often resulted in conflict situations. In this way, we often want to observe the pattern that the coach has become part of, as an indicator of how others might be relating to the coachee. It is important to pay attention to this easily overlooked aspect of mode 3.

These mode 3 questions can also be used to achieve a better understanding of the coachee's relationships. The supervisor could use similar questions to understand the relationships with key individuals in the coachee's relational web. If the focus of the coaching is about the relationship of the coachee and their manager, the supervisor could ask:

- From what you have heard and understand from the client, what does their relationship with their manager remind you of?
- From what you have heard and understand from the client, if the coachee and their manager were marooned on a desert island, what would happen?

Mode 4: The coach's awareness

In mode 4, the focus is on the coach's own processes. We want to enable the coach to notice what is being re-stimulated in them by the coachee's material, and to use themselves as a resonance chamber for registering what is happening beneath the surface of the coaching system.

In this mode, the supervisor helps the coach to work through any re-stimulation of their own feelings that have been triggered by the work with this client. Having done this, the coach can be helped to explore how these feelings may relate to what the coachee is experiencing but is unable to articulate directly. The coach also explores how their own blocks may be preventing them from facilitating the coachee and their system to change.

Questions in this mode could be:

- What are you experiencing in your body as we discuss this client?
- What emotions or thoughts do you have when you are with them?
- Who do they remind you of?
- When have you been in a similar relationship dynamic? What did you need to say in that situation, which may give you a clue to what needs expressing here?

Mode 5: The supervisory relationship

In mode 5, we focus on what is happening in the relational field between the coach and the supervisor. In this mode, we notice the 'us-ness' of the supervisory relationship in general as well as what has emerged into our relationship as we discuss this coaching scenario.

We can use similar questions to the ones that we use in mode 3. Alternatively, we can simply ask, 'what do we notice is going on in how we work together?' This may lead on to recognizing some parallels with the coaching relationship being discussed which can then be explored. We can also pick up on a specific characteristic of any dynamic that has come into awareness. For example, if we had noticed that the coachee was responding to his manager or colleagues as a compliant-resistant child, we could explore how this is being played out in the ego states of parent, adult or child transaction of the supervisor–coach relationship (Berne 1964).

Frequently, this will highlight similarities between the supervisor–coach relationship that replicate (or sometimes replicate by opposing) the relationship between the coach and the client. This 'parallel process' includes both the conscious aspects (which include the feelings) of how they are relating as well as the unconscious feelings and ways of relating that have been absorbed from the coachee system (Hawkins and Shohet 2006; Hawkins and Smith 2006). The coach can therefore unwarily treat the supervisor in the same way that their coachee treated them or, indeed, demonstrate the way in which the coachee engaged them, by engaging the supervisor in the same way.

Having acquired this skill, the supervisor can then, at times, offer their tentative reflections on the impact of the presented material on the supervisory relationship to illuminate the coaching dynamic. When done skilfully, this process can help the coach bridge the gap between their conscious understanding of the coaching relationship and the emotional impact it has had upon them.

In mode 5, a supervisor would initiate a co-inquiry, rather than ask a direct question that implies the coach would have a ready-made answer. They might say:

- I notice that when you discuss this client we become very argumentative and both our voices speed up and get louder – and I wonder whether this reflects something about the coaching relationship.
- I am wondering how 'that dynamic' (whatever has been noticed) is happening between us. How are we 'xing' in this relationship here?', e.g. 'So, we've noticed that the coachee constantly defers to you, the manager and others. I'm wondering how we are deferring in this relationship here and now and what deference is occurring here'.

Mode 6: The supervisor in self-reflection

The focus for mode 6 is the supervisor's 'here-and-now' experience while with the coach and what can be learned about the coach–coachee relationship from the supervisor's response to the coach and the material they present.

In this mode the supervisor has to attend not only to presented material and its impact on the 'here-and-now' relationship, but also their own internal process. The supervisor can discover the presence of unconscious material related to the coaching relationship by attending to their own feelings, thoughts and fantasies while listening to the presentation of the coaching situation.

It is important for the supervisor to learn to avoid self-censorship but to speak their 'here-and-now' awareness out loud in a non-judgemental and non-interpretative way. If the supervisor can muse and tentatively speak their awareness out loud, it may help the coach to reflect upon and spark further inquiry and dialogue. For example, the supervisor might say:

- I am aware that my heart is beating faster as I hear you telling this and I am feeling quite agitated by the situation.
- I feel sad and empty as I listen to this.

Peter was supervising a coach and every time they talked about a specific client, found it very difficult to keep his eyes open and stay awake. He writes:

At first I felt guilty and embarrassed by this phenomenon and even tried changing the time of these supervision sessions in the hope that not having them straight after lunch would improve their capacity to be attentive! After several sessions and exploring this in my own supervision, I plucked up the courage to mention that every time this client was mentioned I could not keep my eyes open and wondered why this was. The coach replied with: 'It is funny you should say that, but that is exactly what happens to me when I am with this client but I was too embarrassed to mention it!' Not only had the sleepiness been somatically transferred, but the embarrassment, self-blame and feeling guilty had also been paralleled. Following this, the coach was able to confront what was happening in the coaching relationship, unearth deep patterns of passive aggression and help the coachee express their issues far more directly.

Mode 7: The wider context

The focus of mode 7 is on the organizational, social, cultural, ethical and contractual context in which the coaching and supervision is taking place. This includes being aware of the wider context of the client organization and its stakeholders, the coach's organization and its stakeholders, and the supervisor and their organizational and professional context. It also includes the power and cultural dynamics that lie within the various relationships. One of the purposes of mode 7 is to develop the coach's understanding of the coachee's organizational context in order to illuminate the shift that the coachee may need to make a sustainable impact on their wider system.

Mode 7 also includes attention to the wider systemic contexts of the supervisory relationship, which includes the organizations that both the supervisee and supervisor work for and their ambitions and expectations, as well as the professional context. The developmental context of the supervisee is also an important aspect of the context that needs attention. They may still be in professional training or seeking accreditation or a thought leader in the field.

The supervisor has to be able to bring a whole system's perspective to understand how the systemic context of the work being presented is affecting not only the behaviour, mindsets, emotional ground and motivations of the coach and coachee but also themselves. The skill is to attend appropriately to the needs of the critical stakeholders in the wider systems, and also to understand how the culture of the systemic context might be creating illusions, delusions and collusions in the coach and in oneself. Attention to mode 7 also requires a high level of transcultural competence (Hawkins and McMahon 2020; Hawkins and Smith 2013) and awareness of one's own cultural assumptions and prejudices (Ryde 2009).

Some mode 7 inquiries might include:

- What have you learned from the client about the values and assumptions operating in the organization? How is this demonstrated in the relationship between coachee and the manager/peer/customer, etc.?
- How is conflict handled in the organization and by this particular coachee?
- Who are the main stakeholders that you heard about in the sessions? How would you describe the coachee's relationship with each?
- How would the stakeholders view the work you are doing? If we imagine that stakeholder in that empty chair can you go and speak from their perspective?
- How are wider political, economic and social pressures being enacted in the relationships you are working with?
- What is the shift needed in the wider system for it to fulfil its purpose, and what shift needs to happen in the coachee to better serve that purpose?

Box 13.1 Case illustration

Each mode of supervision can be carried out in a skilful and elegant manner or ineffectively, but no matter how skilful one is, a single mode will prove inadequate without the skill to move from one to another. A typical supervision session does not normally follow a chronological path from mode 1 to mode 7. Rather, the conversation progresses from mode to mode based on what the work requires.

Table 13.1 indicates the most common way of moving through the modes with some example questions and interventions that could be used for each mode.

Table 13.1 Examples of moving through different modes

Mode	Typical questions or interventions
Contracting for the session	• What is important about this client situation that motivates you to focus on it today? • What do you want to leave this supervision having achieved, discovered, developed?
Mode 1: Get the client into the room	• In your mind's eye, replay the first five minutes of the first time that you met this client. What do you notice? • What comes to mind as you think of this client?
Often this will lead to mode 3: The coach–client relationship.	• How would you describe the dance that is happening between the two of you? • If you and this client were going to a fancy dress party in some way that symbolizes the coaching relationship, what/who would you both be? How would you both appear?

Mode	Typical questions or interventions
This may be a good time to check how this lands with the coach using mode 4.	• Invite the coach to notice what is happening for them right now. What is the body reaction, how are they feeling, what metaphors or comparators are used?
Now the conversation could move into several modes. It might stimulate some awareness in you as the supervisor – mode 6.	• I feel overwhelmed as I hear how much this client is facing right now. • I'm struck by the relative levels of confidence. It sounds like you are 'adoring' the client.
Often mode 6 is a door into mode 5: the supervisor–coach relationship.	• I wonder if 'adoring' is happening between us? How is this similar or different than the coaching relationship? • What insights does this give about the coaching relationship?
At any point, the conversation may highlight a challenge, impasse, dilemma that the coach is facing. This flags mode 2: the coach's interventions.	• What are the choices or options going through your head regarding this challenge or dilemma? • I notice you are stuck in an either/or dilemma. What could you do that would enable to transcend that frame?
At any point, the conversation may flag some aspect of the wider system or stakeholders that is an opportunity to explore mode 7: the wider system.	• What do you know about the client's stakeholders? How might they view this situation? • Can we put them on different chairs and you speak about the coaching from their perspective? • From what you know about the way things get done in this organization, what would be a culturally acceptable approach? What would be a shift that the culture would tolerate?
Typically, a supervision session finishes by returning to mode 2 to clarify and anchor the coach's next interventions with the coaching client.	• Given our exploration today, what is the shift that your client needs to make that will positively impact their wider system? • What is the shift that you need to make in working with this client? • Typically, this is an opportunity for the coach to do two or more fast-forward rehearsals of how they might respond differently and getting direct feedback from the supervisor.
Review the contract for the session.	• If your clients and their stakeholders were in the room, what would they appreciate about the work we have done together and what would their challenge be to us? • What does that tell us about improving our supervision together?

While this is a 'typical' flow, supervision, like coaching, is co-created by the participants in the conversation. The conversation will go 'where it needs to' and where either the supervisor (or coach) subtly facilitate movement from mode to mode.

To be a competent practitioner of the seven-eyed model, it is important to develop a deep understanding of it through reading and experiential learning. However, practice with specific and detailed feedback is the most important aspect to develop competence and confidence. In training coaching supervisors in the seven-eyed model it is useful to practise in trios, working first with just one mode in the practice sessions and then practising integrating them together. This enables the trainee supervisor to get feedback from both the supervisee and the observer. We also find that video is an excellent tool to enable the supervisor to see how they are working and make adjustments in style and approach.

Guidance for further learning and research

Having worked with this model for over 35 years, we find that it stands the test of time because it is more about a *way* of looking than *what* to understand about the work. New models have been developed, but they all seem compatible with this model. In the same way, we find that people from many very different theoretical approaches can relate to this model and therefore coaches from different schools of coaching can learn together in training using the seven modes. The dialogue between them can be instructive as well and decreases rigid and limiting mind-sets. The philosophy behind it is inquiring and dialogic and encourages this attitude between individuals from very different schools and approaches. Although it would be easy to place this approach within systems theory, we have found that it also is understood well within other, quite disparate, approaches such as humanistic, psychoanalytic and cognitive behavioural.

We find that many supervisors vastly improve their practice if they extend their capability to include all seven of the modes. We have discovered that different supervisors are often stuck in the groove of predominantly using one of the seven modes of working. Some focus entirely on the situation 'out there' with the coachee and adopt a pose of pseudo-objectivity (mode 1). Others see their job as to come up with better interventions than the coach managed to produce (mode 2). This can often leave the coach feeling inadequate or determined to show that these suggested interventions are as useless as the ones they had previously tried. Other coaches have reported taking a problem with a coachee and having left supervision feeling that the problem was entirely their pathology (mode 4).

'Single-eyed vision', which focuses only on one aspect of the process, will always lead to partial and limited perspectives. This model suggests a way of engaging in an exploration that looks at the same situation from many different perspectives and can thus create a critical subjectivity, where subjective awareness from one perspective is tested against subjective data from other perspectives or modes.

As the model encourages an open, inquiring attitude, it is very effective in empowering the coach, who is, after all, our customer as supervisors. Through the use of the model they are better able to give feedback on the help they are being given and request a change of focus. An openness to hearing this feedback can model a similar openness in the coach with their coachee. It can thus be used as a framework for a joint review of the supervision process in which the coach and supervisor reflect together on which modes they have most focused on and to which they might need to pay more attention. (For information on research done using the seven-eyed model, see Hawkins and McMahon 2020, chapter 15.)

It is important that supervision is not seen as an activity carried out by a supervisor, supposedly with 'super-vision'! Supervision is a collaborative inquiry, between a coach, a supervisor and the challenges that life, work and clients are presenting the coach, which ensures that the quality of practice and the capacity and capability of the coach constantly develop, and makes sure they are adequately resourcing themselves for the work they undertake. So far, most research on supervision has been on the work done by the supervisor, or self-reported benefits by the supervisee. More research needs to be done on the benefits of supervision for changes in the supervisee's practice and value creation for all supervisee stakeholders (see Hawkins and Turner 2020, chapter 12).

Questions for reflection

- In the supervision you give and receive, which of the seven modes do you currently most focus on?
- Which of the seven modes do you ignore or least use?
- Which of the seven modes do you think you need to use more to improve your supervision?
- How could you attend more to the wider systemic levels in your supervision?

Further resources

Hawkins, P. and McMahon, A. (2020) *Supervision in the Helping Professions*, 5th edn. Maidenhead: Open University Press. This latest edition gives a major overview of the practice and research on supervision across all the helping professions.

Hawkins, P. and Smith, N. (2013) *Coaching, Mentoring and Organizational Consultancy: Supervision and Development*, 2nd edn. Maidenhead: Open University Press. This book provides additional information about the seven-eyed model and is a major textbook on coaching supervision.

Hawkins, P., Turner, E. and Passmore, J. (2019) *Coaching Supervision Manifesto*. Henley: Centre for Coaching, Henley Business School. This provides a major review of the field of coaching supervision globally and what is needed for the future.

References

Berne, E. (1964) *Games People Play*. New York: Grove.

Goldvarg, D. (2017) *Supervision De Coaching*. Buenos Aries: Grantica.

Hawkins, P. (1985) Humanistic psychotherapy supervision. A conceptual framework: self and society, *European Journal of Humanistic Psychology*, 13(2): 69–77.

Hawkins, P. (1995) *Shadow Consultancy*. Working paper. Bath: Bath Consultancy Group.

Hawkins, P. (2006) Coaching supervision, in J. Passmore (ed.) *Excellence in Coaching*. London: Kogan Page.

Hawkins, P. (2017) Coaching supervision, in E. Cox, T. Bachkirova and D. Clutterbuck (eds) *The Complete Handbook of Coaching*. London: Sage.

Hawkins, P. and McMahon, A. (2020) *Supervision in the Helping Professions*, 5th edn. Maidenhead: Open University Press.

Hawkins, P. and Ryde, J. (2020) *Integrative Psychotherapy in Theory and Practice: A Relational, Systemic and Ecological Approach*. London: Jessica Kingsley.

Hawkins, P. and Shohet, R. (2012) *Supervision in the Helping Professions*, 4th edn. Maidenhead: Open University Press.

Hawkins, P. and Smith, N. (2013) *Coaching, Mentoring and Organizational Consultancy: Supervision and Development*, 2nd edn. Maidenhead: Open University Press.

Hawkins, P. and Smith, N. (2018) Transformational coaching, in E. Cox, T. Bachkirova and D. Clutterbuck (eds) *The Complete Handbook of Coaching*, 3rd edn. London: Sage.

Hawkins, P. and Turner, E. (2020) *Systemic Coaching Delivering Value Beyond the Individual*. London: Routledge.

Hawkins, P., Turner, E. and Passmore, J. (2019) *Coaching Supervision Manifesto*. Henley: Centre for Coaching, Henley Business School.

Moral, M. and Angel, P. (2019) *Le coaching et sa supervision*. Paris: InterEditions.

Ryde, J. (2009) *Being White in the Helping Professions*. London: Jessica Kingsley.

Stolorow, R.D. and Atwood, G.E. (1992) *The Context of Being – The Intersubjective Foundations of Psychological Life*. Hillsdale, NJ: The Analytical Press.

14 The three worlds four territories model of supervision

Mike Munro Turner

Introduction

Awareness of the self and other is at the heart of all coaching supervision, for both supervisor and coach, just as it is at the heart of all coaching. But what do we need to be aware of in ourselves and in the other?

The seven-eyed model (Hawkins and Smith 2013; see also preceding chapter) provides one map of what we can attend to. In developing this model Hawkins and Smith took a research-based approach, reviewing different models of and approaches to supervision to develop a map of where people in the different approaches put their attention. I have found this model very helpful in directing my attention across the broad landscape of the supervision domain.

However, after using the model for some time, I found that it had some limitations and so started to modify it. I found it helpful to split mode 4 (the coach's experience) into what the coach was experiencing in the coaching session itself, and their experience in the here-and-now of the supervision session. Similarly, I found it helpful to distinguish what the coachee was experiencing in the coaching session, and what was going on back in their life outside the coaching session (together represented in the seven-eyed model as mode 1, the coachee system).

Also, the more experienced I became as a supervisor, the more I found myself needing to make finer distinctions about the individual players' experiences. I already had developed a model (the four territories model) that provided exactly these distinctions, which I increasingly incorporated into my supervision practice. I first wrote about this model in 1996 (Turner 1996). Since then, it has been further developed (Munro Turner and Wilson 2008; Newell and Munro Turner 2008).

This chapter describes the resultant coaching supervision model. It aims to help the supervisor bring the coaching session live into the supervision session, raise the coach's awareness, and so enable the coach to have new options in their coaching.

Function of the model

Coaching supervision is generally seen to have three functions (Hawkins and Smith 2013):

1. *Resourcing* – Helping the coach manage the emotions of coachees that they pick up when working with them

2. *Development* – Developing the skills, understanding and capacities of the coach
3. *Qualitative* – Ensuring the quality of the coach's work.

The model presented here focuses on the third of these areas – and in particular on improving the quality and effectiveness of specific coaching relationships and interventions by helping the coach have new choices in their client work. However, in focusing on the qualitative aspects, the model also leads the coach into exploring and engaging with the resourcing and development issues they face.

This model is based on the belief that, by getting the whole system live in the room, the supervisor can tune into the wider system and use the thoughts, feelings and other experiences that arise to provide insight into the coaching, the coach and the coachee. The system here is considered to consist of the supervision session itself, the coaching, the coachee and their workplace, as well as the supervisor and the coach. Getting the system into the room refers to evoking and bringing into awareness all these aspects either directly because they are happening in the moment or indirectly because they have been evoked through the memory, imagination and intuition of the supervisee and supervisor. The model provides a map of this system to help the supervisor direct their attention and that of the supervisee to all the relevant elements of the system.

The three worlds four territories (3W4T) model

The 3W4T model describes the three 'worlds' the supervisor can attend to – the coachee's world, the coaching session and the supervision session. Within each of these worlds, the supervisor can attend to four territories of experience for each of the players involved (themselves, the coach and the coachee). The four territories are Insight, Readiness, Authentic Vision and Skilful Action.

The three worlds

Effective supervisors ensure that they attend to what is happening across the whole supervisory system. To do this they pay attention to three subsystems or 'worlds' (see Figure 14.1):

1. The Work World – Which consists of the coachee in their workplace and wider life.
2. The Coaching World – Which consists of the coach and coachee in the coaching session. Like the Work World, the supervisor has only indirect experience of the Coaching World, either through what the coach tells the supervisor overtly or through what is unconsciously evoked in the supervisor.
3. The Supervision World – Which consists of the supervisor and the coach in the supervision session, and which the supervisor has direct experience of (because of course they are part of it!).

These worlds are linked together in two principal ways:

- By the coach, who is present in the Coaching World and the Supervision World: it is they who bring the Coaching World into the supervision session (and so provide the content for the supervisor to work with). It is they who then take the shifts they make and the insights they have back into the coaching session.

Three Worlds

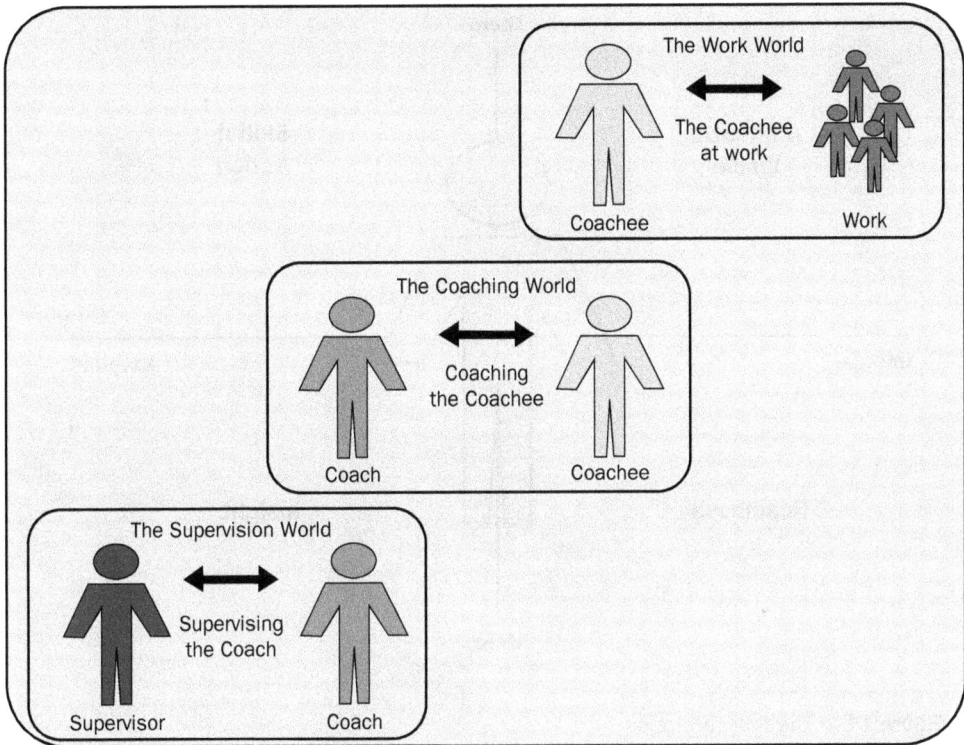

Figure 14.1 The supervisory system

- By the coachee, who is present in the Work World and the Coaching World: they bring their experience of the Work World into the coaching session in order to explore the challenges they face (and so provide the content for the coach to work with). They then take the shifts they make and the insights they have back into the workplace.

These linkages create resonances between the worlds that lead to aspects of the Coaching and Work Worlds being present within the supervision session. So, when the coach enters the supervision session, they bring with them a whole network of conscious and unconscious knowledge, feelings, imaginings, perceptions, needs, desires and intuitions about what happened in the coaching and back in the coachee's world. By encouraging and amplifying these resonances, particularly those that the coach is unaware of, and by developing sensitivity to them, the supervisor is able to access information about, and generate insight into, what is occurring in the coaching session and the coachee's world. This information and insight can then be used to help the coach gain insight and develop new choices in their coaching work.

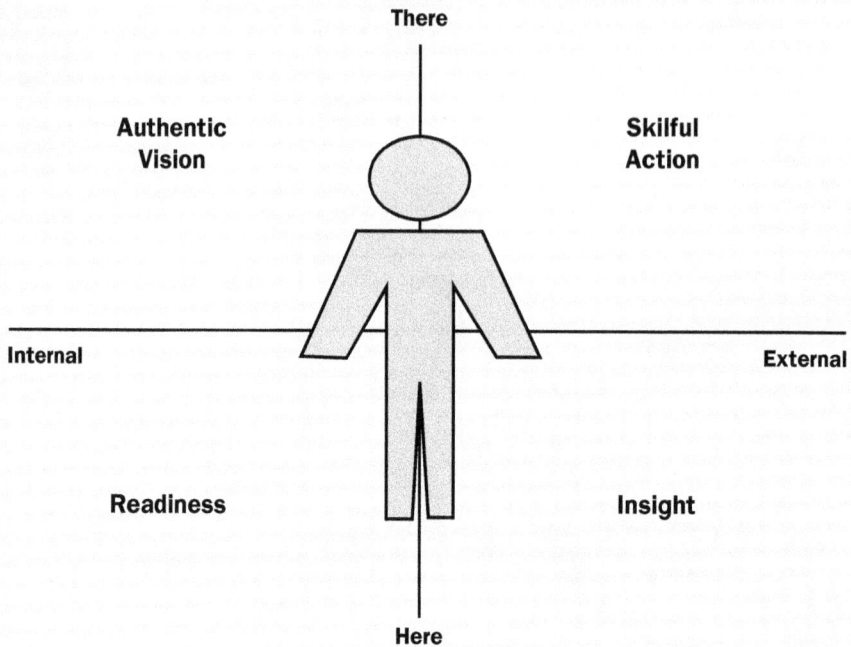

Figure 14.2 The four territories

From Newell, D. and Munro Turner, M.H. (2008) A model of coaching for renewal, *International Journal of Mentoring and Coaching*, VI(1): 94–100.

A model of the person

The experience of each of the individuals involved (supervisor, coach and coachee) can be represented using the four territories model (also known variously as the Renewal Model and the Jericho Model), which maps the four territories of experience: Insight, Readiness, Authentic Vision and Skilful Action (Newell and Munro Turner 2008; see Figure 14.2). It is derived from a right relations model developed by Danielle Roux (private communications 1989–1992).

Table 14.1 shows the perspective each of the four territories offers and what we can focus on in each.

Three worlds and four territories (3W4T)

Combining the four territories model with the three worlds model allows the perspectives the supervisor can attend to in the supervision session to be mapped. There are eight different perspectives. These are illustrated below with examples of the kinds of questions that might bring that aspect of the supervisory system into the supervision session.

Table 14.1 Focus and the four territories

Territory	Aspect of the self	Focus
Insight: seeing what is and what could be in my world	Sensing, perceiving	What I sense and perceive as having happened, as filtered and moulded by my preconceptions, prejudices, projections and assumptions
Readiness: attending to what constrains or enables me in my response to my world; developing my flexibility and resilience	Feelings and concrete mind	My inner experience as evoked by my perception of what has happened, my meaning systems, personal history, habitual thoughts, etc.
Authentic Vision: clarifying the difference that I want to make; my desired way of being; my intent	Creative mind	My imagined ideas about how things could be otherwise, my ability to think differently and explore possibilities
Skilful Action: transforming vision into action	Body	My behaviours – what I did, or might do – guided by my vision of how things could be different

1. The supervisor can ask the coach questions about the coachee:
   - *Insight* – 360-degree data, challenges they face, their life balance, the results they are creating
   - *Readiness* – Psychometrics, ego strength, development stage, personal story and themes
   - *Vision* – Coachee's purpose, the difference/change they want to make, the legacy they seek to leave, their work ambitions
   - *Action* – Habitual behaviours, what have they tried already, what they focus on.

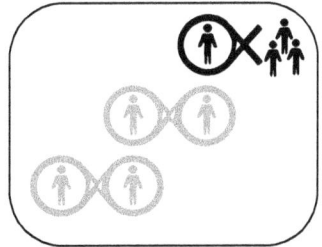

Depending on the particular issue the coachee is exploring in the coaching, it may also be relevant to ask about:

   - The coachee's key relationships (using variants of the questions in perspective 4 below) and about the experiences of other players in the coachee's world
   - *The wider organizational context* – Structure, vision, mission and values
   - *The larger context* – Political, economic, social, technological, legal and environmental factors (which can be recalled using the PESTLE mnemonic).

2. The supervisor can ask the coach questions about the coachee in the coaching session:
   - *Insight* – How does the coachee perceive the coach?
   - *Readiness* – What was the coachee thinking and feeling?
   - *Vision* – What does the coachee want to get from the coaching?
   - *Action* – How did the coachee behave, what did they say, how did they say it?

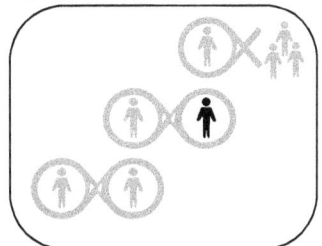

3. The supervisor can ask the coach questions to help them reflect on what they experienced and did in the session, and what they might do differently in future sessions:
   - *Insight* – What did you notice about the coachee, what themes and patterns did you notice in their story?
   - *Readiness* – What were you thinking and feeling, what were you not able to say to or ask the coachee?
   - *Vision* – What was your intent in the session, what was the difference you were trying to make?
   - *Action* – What was your approach in the session, what did you do, what interventions did you make?

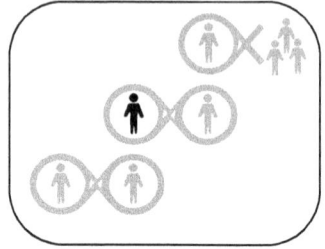

4. The supervisor can help the coach reflect on the coaching relationship and world:
   - What kind of relationship do you and the coachee have?
   - What is happening in the space between you and the coachee?
   - If you were observing yourself with your coachee, what would you notice?
   - If you and your coachee were cast away on a desert island, what would happen?

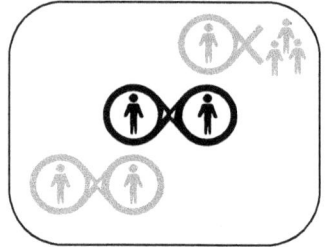

5. The supervisor can focus on the coach as they are in the supervision session:
   - *Insight* – What are you noticing about what is happening in the session, how do you see me and my role, what is the context you are sitting in at this moment?
   - *Readiness* – What are you thinking and feeling, what are you keeping out of awareness, what is trapping you, what is the shift you need to make?
   - *Vision* – What is your desired outcome from the supervision session, what are you feeling your way towards?
   - *Action* – What do you notice about how you are acting in the session?

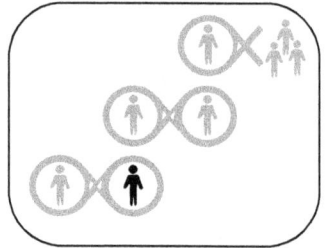

6. The supervisor can use their own experience in the moment to be aware of what is going on for them:
   - *Insight* – What is really happening here, how do I see the coach behaving, am I addressing Resourcing, Developmental and Qualitative areas, what do I see playing out, do I see a shift in the coach?
   - *Readiness* – How free am I to be the best supervisor I can be (free from my own history, from what the coach evokes in me, from what the issues they bring evoke in me), what do I need to let go of, what am I thinking and feeling,

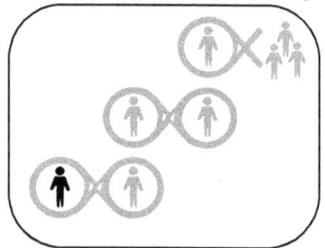

what impulses and needs am I experiencing, what is being evoked in me, how can I use the resources I have to deal with what is being presented?

- *Vision* – What do I aspire to, what meaning and purpose do I need to embrace or allow in helping me create a shift in the coach?
- *Action* – How can I act to create a shift in the room?

7. The supervisor can notice what is happening in their relationship with the coach, and in the Supervision World as a whole:
   - What kind of relationship do we have?
   - When I connect to my own experience, that of the coach, and the space between us, what do I notice?
   - Is there a parallel process in operation?
   - What's worked well in our session today, and what might we have done differently?

8. The supervisor can notice and work with the relationship between the different systems, helping the coach make the shift in the supervision session that will lead them to being able to shift the coachee and so cause a shift back at work:
   - Can I bring into my awareness all three systems simultaneously?
   - How does what is happening in each relationship shed light on what is happening in the other ones (e.g. how does what is playing out in the supervision session shed light on what happens in the coaching session – the parallel process)?
   - What is the shift I need to make to enable the coach to shift to enable the coachee to shift and so create a shift back in the workplace?

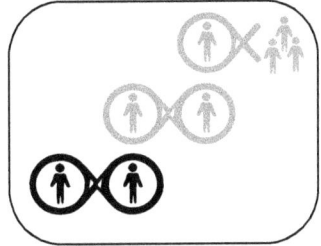

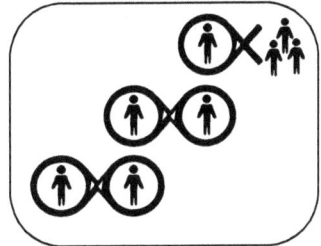

Practising supervision – how to use the model

The four territory model introduced earlier can also be used to guide the supervisor in structuring the supervision conversation. In this context it takes the form shown in Figure 14.3. Having contracted with the coach, and identified a coachee to work with and the reason for bringing them to supervision, the supervision conversation can then cover the following:

1. **Bringing the whole system into the room.** Gather information on the whole supervisor–coach–coachee–work system by enquiring about or noticing across the three worlds and four territories. Generally, attention will focus initially on the Work World, then the Coaching World and then the Supervision World. The supervisor has access to information within themselves about the Coaching and Work Worlds, as well as about the here-and-now of the supervision session itself, which they can contribute.

2. **Connecting what needs to connect.** Having got the system into the room, the coach can begin to see the gaps, contradictions, conflicts, blind-spots, either/ors, etc. in what is present, either directly themselves or through interventions by the supervisor. Seeing these gaps may shift how the coach sees what is going on in

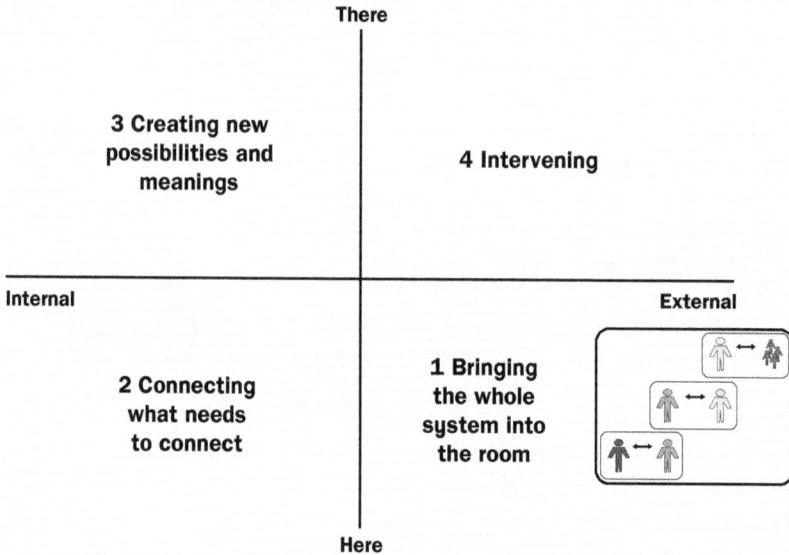

Figure 14.3 Supervision process

their coaching and so free them up to have new choices – and sometimes they will need the help of the supervisor in making connections and filling in the gaps.

3. **Creating new possibilities and meanings.** A shift in seeing what needs to connect may be all that the coach needs to be able to return to their coaching with new options. Or they may need new ways of looking at the situation. This may involve reframing the situation so that new options appear. The supervisor seeks to discern and enable the shift the coachee needs to make to have new choices in their work.

4. **Intervening.** The final step is to help the coach ground the insights they have gained from the supervision and be clear about what they will do differently or how they will be differently in the next coaching session. If the coach has made a clear shift during the supervision session, then this stage may be less about designing specific interventions and more about helping the coach maintain their shifted state.

While the above order reflects the broad flow of the supervision conversation, in practice the conversation will move back and forth between the various areas. The session can conclude with a review, exploring what worked and what could be improved.

The skills necessary to apply this model successfully are implied by the elements of the supervision conversation outlined above. Key among these are:

- Bringing the system fully into the room – like spinning plates at the circus, the supervisor seeks to energize all elements of the system simultaneously so that a synthesis can emerge and the whole be seen.

- Creating a space in which the coach can be aware of as much of this system as possible so that they are able to connect what needs to be connected.
- Being sensitive to as much of the system that has been brought into the room as possible so that the supervisor is also able to become aware of what needs to connect and so, if necessary, help the coach make the connections themselves.

Box 14.1 Case illustration

One of the most interesting, and potentially powerful, phenomena that can arise in supervision sessions is that of parallel process. A parallel process is occurring when 'the pattern of relationship in one area is enacted in another, with no conscious awareness of what is going on' (Hawkins and Smith 2013: 167). It can therefore provide a rich source of information in the supervision session about what is happening in the coaching and back in the coachee's wider life. This illustration includes parallel processes operating between the worlds within the three worlds four territories model.

Work World

Having contracted with the coach (Thomas), I start by asking about the coachee.

Thomas tells me he has had an initial session with the coachee (Jane). He describes her as being a well-regarded programme manager in the public sector. Jane feels she lacks the potential to progress further because of her lack of confidence, particularly around difficult personalities. Questioning by Thomas has established that 'difficult personalities' are people who are more senior than her and people she perceives as being stronger than her. As well as this being a problem at work, Jane mentions that this is an issue with her husband, a senior policeman with a powerful personality. She also says she thinks too much about what other people think of her, that she needs praise, and that she is afraid of being 'found out'. She wants the coaching to help her be more assertive with these senior, stronger people. Realizing I haven't heard about the Action quadrant of Jane's work life, I ask how specifically she acts in the presence of 'difficult' people. Thomas says that she's cautious and careful, and tries hard not to do anything controversial that might upset them.

Coaching World

Thomas has brought Jane to supervision saying, 'How do I get into this with her? Where should I go with this? I feel stuck.' Focusing on Thomas's inner dynamics (Readiness) I am curious as to why he's feeling stuck as I know him to be a competent coach who would typically not be stumped by a situation like this. It is likely therefore that there is something else going on here that is interfering with his normal competence. I make a mental note to return to this. To give Thomas a different perspective, I move his attention onto a different territory of experience, Vision, using the 'If you were marooned on a desert island together what would happen?' question. This shift in perspective frees him up to think differently and he immediately replies, 'I'd be the one making the suggestions and leading, and Jane would be very co-operative – she'd want things to work.'

I point out this apparent contradiction to Thomas. On the one hand, he doesn't know where to go in the coaching, and yet on the imagined desert island he sees himself as the leader. So Thomas finds himself in the bind of feeling he has to provide leadership – but not knowing what to do.

Thomas reflects on this – 'Yes, I'm taking the responsibility myself. I'm taking on being the stronger, more senior person where I know the answers and where Jane is co-operative, but not assertive.' It seems Jane has recreated in the session the reality she deals with in her day-to-day life by unconsciously coaching Thomas to play the role of a stronger, more senior person and he has unconsciously accepted this role, a clear example of a parallel process linking the coach's and coachee's Readiness territories.

However, this insight has not freed Thomas up as his next response is, 'But I still need to know what questions to ask her.' While this sounds like an Action issue, it seems likely that it is rooted in the opposite quadrant, Readiness, where some out-of-awareness process may be interfering with Thomas's ability to know where to go with Jane.

Supervision World

Wondering whether my 'here-and-now' experience may shed some light on Thomas's dilemma, I turn my attention to the Supervision World. Focusing inwards on my own Readiness territory, I notice that I, too, am feeling a pressure to come up with some answers and uncertain as to where to go next. Thomas's feeling of stuckness and uncertainty about how best to coach Jane has communicated itself to me where it has emerged as a felt pressure to fix Thomas – a second parallel process.

Recognizing these linkages gives me the opportunity to use them to inform the supervision. I now have a direct experience of what may be going on, not just for Thomas in his coaching session, but also for the people around Jane back in her place of work, and at home. I turn my attention to my creative mind (Vision) and start to wonder what is the shift I need to make in this supervision session which might defuse the second parallel process and in turn defuse the first?

The parallel process between Jane and Thomas is a complementary one in which Jane's compliance has evoked Thomas's directing stance. But both are in a bind – Jane because she knows being compliant won't deliver what she wants at work, and Thomas because he doesn't know what direction to give!

By contrast, in the parallel process between Thomas and me, our experience is similar – we are both feeling a pressure to come up with answers. And then I realize (more clearly now with the benefit of hindsight) that this is true for Jane as well – it's just that her way of avoiding the discomfort of feeling incompetent is to be compliant and let others take the lead. If this hypothesis is right, then I need to step out from the parallel process and then enable Thomas to do the same so that he is freed up to, in turn, free up Jane. I hypothesize that this will involve each of us making a shift in our Readiness of being willing to not know, to feel uncertain and to feel incompetent.

I realize that my focusing on coming up with solutions (Vision) for Thomas for him to use (Action) on Jane has been maintaining the parallel process. Parallel processes are usually rooted in the Readiness quadrant and, as I focus on my inner experience, I realize my need to appear to be the 'expert supervisor' has been driving my interventions. To break it, I need to stop searching for solutions within myself, drop my 'expert supervisor' persona and switch my attention to clarifying my intent (Vision) – which I realize needs to be to focus on helping Thomas access his own insight. Turning my attention to my externally facing quadrants I realize that this will involve making interventions that keep pushing the thinking back to Thomas (Action), and that seeing that Thomas, rather than me, is working hard is what will tell me I'm being successful (Insight).

By seeing the chain of causality from the Work World, through the Coaching World to the Supervision World I have been able to free myself up. I now need to help Thomas free himself up, so I turn our attention to the Coaching World.

Coaching World

Recognizing that Thomas is stuck in a fixed pattern of thought with regard to Jane, I try focusing his attention outside this coachee system by asking, 'What would you do with a typical coachee?' Thomas gives an immediate and confident answer listing the questions he would ask and the approach he would take. 'So what's stopping you do that here?' He immediately replies, 'She expects me to have the answers.' Thomas laughs as he sees the pattern and then says, 'I don't feel confident to not know' (his Readiness quadrant). He pauses, reflecting on what he's said, and then commenting that this is what Jane also experiences (her Readiness quadrant). There is a palpable change in his energy, which suggests his Readiness has shifted.

I ask him what has shifted for him. Thomas says that he's realized that wanting to feel confident is interfering with his ability to coach well. Further exploration of this shift in Readiness helps him recognize that, by allowing the feeling of not being confident, he can extend his range as a coach (since he can now coach Jane both when he is feeling confident – and when he's not). He recognizes that he needs to be willing to not feel confident (Readiness) – partly so that he can ask the questions that need asking, and partly to demonstrate to Jane that one can be confident despite not knowing (Action). Focusing on his Readiness, I wonder aloud if his feelings of 'unconfidence' can become an ally in his coaching, allowing him to use his own feelings of 'unconfidence' in the next session as an indicator that he's doing real work with Jane and enabling her shift back in the workplace.

I ask Thomas to imagine himself in his next session with Jane. I ask about what his experience will be in each of the four territories to ensure that there is coherency between his territories. He says:

- Readiness – I feel comfortable about being 'unconfident' – and I can even see myself welcoming it as an indication that I'm really engaging with Jane.
- Vision – my intent is to help Jane engage with her unconfidence as a way of increasing her confidence in dealing with difficult people. I am holding a vision of myself, and of her, as people who are comfortable and even energized by feeling uncomfortable.

- Action – I will ensure that I don't intervene to offer Jane solutions but will hold back to create the space for her to be more assertive. I may even make a paradoxical intervention along the lines of 'Jane, you're a powerful woman – you can even get others to be assertive over you!', to help her reframe how she sees herself.
- Insight – I will be looking out for Jane's discomfort around not knowing so that I can help her get more used to being with this feeling.

Guidance for further learning and research

It is important to keep in mind that the principal purpose of this model is to provide a map of what a supervisor can attend to so as to ensure that the whole system is brought into the room. It can be useful in a number of ways:

- For novice supervisors, it provides a framework to guide our interventions, enabling us to ensure that we cover the necessary ground. As we become more familiar with the model, so using it to guide our attention will become increasingly second nature.
- For coaches working in peer group supervision sessions, it provides a structure to our conversation, helping us to cover the territories effectively.
- For experienced supervisors, it provides an anchor point to which we can return when we feel lost or cast adrift in our supervision sessions. It also shows us where we prefer to focus as supervisors, and where our gaze does not fall.
- For all supervisors, after a supervision session it provides a framework for reflecting on the session and analysing what happened, and a structure for writing it up. After the session in the case illustration above had finished, I reflected using the 3W4T model on what had happened. Some of the movement described above only became apparent in this post-session sense-making process. And more became apparent only in writing this case illustration.
- For coaches using a two world (Work and Coaching Worlds) four territory model, it enables self-supervision and reflection after coaching sessions. The output from this can then be a useful input to our supervision sessions.

This framework separates out and makes explicit the variety of places the supervisor can direct their attention. This exhaustiveness is a strength – but it also means that the model is more complex to learn and apply than, for example, Hawkins and Smith's seven-eyed model. Indeed, when first developing this approach, I used the map for note taking but then found that I got distracted from the supervision process by trying to work out where to place particular notes on the map. Rather, the model is at its most powerful when it has been internalized and can be referred to live inside one's head during a supervision session, or is being used to learn about supervision either in post-session reflections or while observing supervision sessions. These considerations can help to enrich your use of this model and your self-supervision and, at the same time, become interesting research questions that can be investigated for further understanding of the supervision practice.

Questions for reflection

In applying the 3W4T model to your own supervision practice you could consider:

- How does your existing approach to supervision fit within the 3W4T model? Are there areas your approach doesn't cover, or areas it covers which the 3W4T model doesn't?
- Which of the eight perspectives do you most readily focus on when supervising; and which are you most likely to ignore?
- Applying the model involves holding as much of the supervision system in awareness as possible – a kind of multi-focal vision. To what extent are you able to do this, and how might you develop this capacity further?
- How might you use this model for self-supervision?

Further reading

For more information on the seven-eyed model, see Hawkins and Smith (2013) and the preceding chapter in this book.

For a more detailed understanding of the four territories model, see Newell and Munro Turner (2008), Munro Turner and Wilson (2008), and various articles at https://www.mikethementor.co.uk.

For an introduction to connecting to centre from where you can then direct your awareness onto the various elements of the model, see Munro Turner (2020).

References

Hawkins, P. and Smith, N. (2013) *Coaching, Mentoring and Organizational Consultancy: Supervision, Skills and Development.* Maidenhead: Open University Press.

Munro Turner, M.H. (2020) *Freeing the Self.* [online] Mike the Mentor. Available at: https://www.mikethementor.co.uk/freeing-the-self (accessed 15 July 2020).

Munro Turner, M.H. and Wilson, S. (2008) Developing leaders: coaching for renewal, *International Journal of Coaching and Mentoring*, 1(2): 39–48.

Newell, D. and Munro Turner, M.H. (2008) A model of coaching for renewal, *International Journal of Coaching and Mentoring*, 1(1): 94–100.

Turner, M.H.M. (1996) Executive mentoring, *Counseling at Work*, Spring: 5–6.

15 The seven conversations model of supervision

David Clutterbuck

Introduction

This chapter outlines and discusses a practical framework for contextualizing the coach–client interaction as it takes place before, during and after the coaching conversation. This breadth of perspective enables the coach to explore the relationship as a whole, rather than just within the confines of the coaching session.

While most textbooks refer to the coaching conversation as if it were a single, discrete dialogue, in practice both coach and client carry out reflective dialogues in their minds before, during and after the spoken conversation. Each of these additional dialogues has an important role to play in the nature and the effectiveness of the coaching conversation. Within supervision, the seven conversations provide a practical method for bringing different perspectives to bear on how both coach and client approach the learning dialogue and the learning relationship. They also focus attention on the thoughts and behaviours of both parties in the coaching relationship.

The seven conversations of coaching (Megginson and Clutterbuck 2009) were originally conceived as a means of deconstructing the coaching dialogue, with the aims of identifying where the dialogue was most and least effective and helping coaches raise their awareness of what was going on in both their own minds and those of their clients (and to a lesser extent what was occurring in the space between). The stimulus for development of this approach was that coaches frequently became 'stuck' somewhere between having a general sense that a coaching relationship was not working properly or that they were not delivering sufficient value to the client, and having a clear understanding of what was going wrong. Very often, for example, they assumed that the problem lay with how they were engaging with the client within the coaching session, when the real issues related to unconscious conversations either they or the client were having internally before the formal coaching session. Expanding the coach's perspective of where the coaching conversations were taking place offered an alternative and arguably faster method of exploring the relationship and conversational dynamics.

The seven conversations have proved to be a practical and flexible tool within the supervisor's toolbox. Among the reported benefits reported by supervisees are the following:

- It provides a structure, against which to explore elements of the coaching conversation.
- It helps coach and supervisor identify issues for reflection between supervisory sessions.
- It provides a framework on which to hang a wide variety of techniques and approaches.

Observations show that it also shifts the emphasis of reflection and analyses away from what the coach said or did, and towards the dialogue between the coach and the client – and hence permits more of a systems approach to understanding the conversational dynamics. It therefore provides a practical framework, around which the supervisor can help the coach both identify development needs and resolve issues with current clients. This chapter first describes the model, then discusses its application within the context of supervision.

Description of the model

The seven conversations have been presented at EMCC and Conference Board conferences and published in *People Management*. They are:

1. The coach's reflection before the dialogue (their preparatory thinking before the coaching conversation)
2. The client's reflection/preparatory thinking before the dialogue
3. The coach's internal, unspoken reflections during the dialogue
4. The spoken dialogue
5. The client's internal, unspoken reflections during the dialogue
6. The coach's reflections after the dialogue
7. The client's reflections after the dialogue.

Most coach development and support focuses on the middle of these – the spoken dialogue. Yet the effectiveness of the spoken dialogue depends heavily on the other six conversations. Building our competence in each of the conversations is essential in mastering the coaching role. Below, I explore each conversation in more detail and provide some pointers for the supervisor in attending to it.

The coach's reflection before the dialogue

The purpose of this dialogue is to ensure that the coach is mentally prepared for the coaching conversation. The quality of the conversation is dependent, to a significant extent, on the quality of thinking both coach and client put into their preparation. In this dialogue, the coach considers how they have helped so far and in what ways. Inevitably, this leads them to reflect upon their own emotions and motivations (e.g. Are they trying too hard to help?; Do they care too much?). Other issues they reflect upon might include the following:

- Context – What is the 'big picture' for this client? What metaphors might I use to describe the client's situation? What metaphors does the client use? Do I understand what drives the client and why? Who else is present in our conversations and in what ways?
- Avoidance – What issues or emotions is this client avoiding? What issues is the coach avoiding? What collusion may be happening between them?
- Attitude – How the coach feels generally about this relationship can have a major impact on the subsequent conversations. Useful questions to ask include: Am I looking forward to this meeting? (If not, what's the issue and what should I be doing about it?) and What are my responsibilities in this relationship?

Of course, there are many other powerful questions coaches can ask themselves. But considering this kind of question in advance of the coaching session seems to help free up intuition, by raising awareness of the conversational and relational dynamics. It also helps prevent distracting thoughts such as 'I need to articulate this in order to file it away' from intruding into the main coaching conversation. And it gives the coach ammunition with which to address concerns about the relationship and the client's authenticity. This ammunition might otherwise have been lost in the ebb and flow of the main conversation around the issue the client brings to the table.

The supervisor's role is fundamentally to direct the coach's attention to this conversation and support them in reflecting on it.

The client's reflection before the dialogue

Preparation by the client is equally important and can be equally demanding. At least an hour's quality reflective space is typically required to prepare for an intensive coaching session. Particularly useful themes include:

- *What they have learned since the previous session, by conscious or unconscious consideration of questions raised by the coach, or by letting insights they gained within the session percolate.*
  Useful questions here include:
  - What has happened to me and my thinking since our last meeting?
  - How have I and my perceptions changed?
  - How have I made use of the insights I gained?
- *What issues they would like help with in the next session and why.*
  - What issues have been resolved and what new issues have arisen?
  - What's the relationship between these issues and my overall goals?
  - What thinking have I already done around these issues?
- *Their own attitudes and motivations towards the coaching conversation and coaching relationship.*
  - Do I really want to resolve this issue? What are my motivations for introducing it *now*?
  - How prepared am I to be challenged on this issue?
  - What more could I do to help the coach help me?

Having this dialogue – even if they address only one or two of these questions – helps the client accept their responsibilities in the relationship. It also helps them to structure their thinking, so that they are better able to articulate the issue and how it affects them. And it reinforces what might be called 'conversational honesty' – the openness that underpins mutual positive regard.

As a supervisor, I find that many coaches are so concentrated on what they need to do for the client that they forget that a dialogue needs active participation by both parties. A frequent outcome of analysing this discussion is that the coach feels less guilt about lack of progress on the part of the client and becomes more courageous about confronting the client's lack of preparation.

The coach's reflection during the dialogue

This inner dialogue takes place in parallel with the process of listening and asking questions. Sometimes called 'reflection-in-action' (Schön 1983), it requires both coach and client to participate fully in the conversation and observe it as dispassionately as possible. The focus of this inner conversation shifts intuitively, in response to verbal, physiological and other triggers. At times the focus will be inner directed; at others outer directed. Inner-directed conversations relate to 'How am I helping?' and might address questions, such as:

- What is the quality of my listening?
- What am I observing/hearing? What am I missing?
- Is my intuition turned on?
- What assumptions am I making? How might these be acting as a filter on my listening and my understanding?
- Am I spending too much attention on crafting the next question?

Outer-directed conversations, in contrast, raise awareness of issues, such as:

- What is the client not saying?
- What is the quality of the client's thinking?
- How am I feeling in the moment? If I feel uncomfortable, what is making me so?

The role of the supervisor here is to help the coach verbalize their observations, so that they can begin the process of including them in their intuitive repertoire. On occasion, I have helped the coach design exercises aimed at making them more 'attentive to their attentiveness' – simple exercises they can apply within or outside the coaching context.

The spoken dialogue

This is the part that attracts the most attention. It's also the easiest conversation and therefore highly beguiling. Inexperienced or inexpert coaches frequently are aware only of this conversation, and oblivious to the inner conversations going on simultaneously in themselves and the client (if they have an inner conversation at all!). I would argue that effective coaches maintain awareness of all three, while instinctively reviewing the dynamics of the spoken conversation, asking themselves questions such as:

- Is there consonance between what is said and our body language?
- Is there a logical pattern of development to the conversation?
- Are we exploring issues from multiple perspectives?
- Are we exploring issues in sufficient depth?

From observation of coaches in assessment centres, it seems that inexperienced coaches often tend to feel they have to keep the conversation going, which puts them in the driving seat. More experienced coaches allow the conversation to find its own path and help the client make choices about which direction to follow, when there are forks in the road. An analogy is an orchestra, where the players decide what the tune will be and the conductor merely holds them together. Allowing the conversation to happen in this way enables the coach to notice so much more – the choice of words and phrases, the tone and energy of the conversation, non-verbal communication, particularly at the level of micro-expression, and the structure of the client's reasoning.

One of the biggest barriers to attending to this conversation can be the need by some coaches to constrain the conversation within a predetermined model or process – for example, GROW (Whitmore 2002), clean language (Sullivan and Rees 2008) or solutions focus (Jackson and McKergow 2007). If the constant, unspoken question is 'Am I keeping this conversation on track?' or 'Am I doing the process right?', then the coach's focus tends to be on the process, not on the client.

Part of the supervisor's role here is to help the coach feel less anxious about *controlling* the spoken conversation, which allows the coach to be more fully attentive to the client.

The client's reflection during the dialogue

The client can contribute more to the learning dialogue if they are also process aware. The management of the conversation and its direction then become a shared activity.

It is unlikely, however, that many clients will be aware of their own inner conversations. Yet at some level they will be making choices about what they say, how honest they will be with the coach and how much attention they are paying to their own words and emotions. Part of the coach's role is to act as a mirror on this inner conversation, helping to surface unspoken thoughts and to heighten the client's self-awareness. Using approaches such as Gestalt can be very powerful in this context.

However, there is another aspect that I find few coaches have considered – the coach's responsibility to help the client develop their own skills of self-observation. It may be more difficult for the client to reflect on their inner conversation in the full flow of the spoken conversation, but frequent pauses for reflection provide opportunities for them to consider questions, such as:

- What assumptions or filters am I applying in answering the coach's questions?
- How am I helping the coach understand my issues?

As in the second conversation above, the supervisor's role here includes helping the coach examine both their own and their client's responsibilities. On several occasions, for example, an outcome of analysis of this conversation is that the coach determines to confront the client, as with 'Why do you think I feel you are not being honest with me?'

The coach's reflection after the dialogue

'Reflection-on-action' (Schön 1983) is also a critical part of the coach's continuous improvement and personal growth. While the meeting is still fresh in their memory, the coach should review the five antecedent conversations, asking themselves questions about:

How I helped

- What did I do to enhance the quality of the client's thinking?
- Was I appropriately directive/non-directive?
- Did we create a 'bias for action'?

What choices did I make?

- What questions did I withhold and why?
- Was I sufficiently challenging?
- Did I give the coachee sufficient time to think?

What did I learn?

- What patterns can I discern from this and previous conversations with this client?
- What would I do differently another time?

What concerns do I have?

- Where did I struggle?
- What negative emotions am I aware of?

The client's reflections after the dialogue

One of the advantages of holding coaching sessions where the client has to travel subsequently is that it gives them space for reflection in the immediate aftermath of the coaching conversation. This post-meeting reflection is vital in terms of translating good thoughts into practical action. Failure here is often, in my experience, associated with coaching relationships where the client talks endlessly about their issues during the session, but makes little progress between sessions.

The coach's responsibility extends, in my view, to helping the client develop the skills, ability and motivation to reflect purposefully and hence gain full value from the session. This may mean discussing with them how and when they will reflect and contracting with them that they will do so.

Critical areas, on which this conversation can usefully focus, include:

Learning

- What new ideas and insights have I gained?
- What do I need to think about more deeply?

Intention

- How am I going to put this learning into practice?
- What do I want to explore with other people?
- What changed expectations do I now have of myself?

Process and behaviour

- Was I sufficiently open and honest?
- What could I have done to extract more value from the conversation?
- What will I do differently in preparing for the next coaching session?

The supervisory conversation here often centres on what the coach might reasonably expect of the client in post-session reflection and follow, up. A frequent conclusion by the coach is that they should be more assertive in making their expectations clear, even though it is up to the client to decide what to do!

Using the seven conversations

The seven conversations are particularly useful:

- When the coach feels in some way inadequate or that they have 'failed' the client
- When the client procrastinates constantly, leaving the coach frustrated
- When the coach feels too close (intimate), or too distant from the client
- When the coach has a sense that there are unidentified others in the room
- When conversations are repeated, with no sense of significant progress in the client's thinking or behaviour
- When the coach simply has the intuition that they are 'missing something important' in the conversation or the relationship
- When the coach feels there is a moment (or longer) of disconnect in the conversation but can't pin down what was occurring (Clutterbuck 2008).

Analysing the conversation helps the coach first to identify the point in the conversation where they first became consciously aware of their concern, then to work back in the conversation(s) to try to identify earlier points, where there are clues to what is coming. These clues may, of course, be other than verbal – a conversation is made up of much more than just words. The discipline of conversation analysis, with an aim to 'reveal the organized reasoning procedures, which inform the production of mutually occurring talk' (Hutchby and Woolfitt 2008: 2), has much to offer here in terms of technique and process, although it is not essential for the supervisor to be highly versed in analytic techniques.

It is also important to keep in mind that conversations are about a lot more than simply imparting information. According to Gee (2005: 2), 'The primary function of human language is . . . to support the performance of social activities and social identities and to support human affiliation with culture, social groups and institutions'. That sounds a bit like a definition of coaching!

There is a challenge for coaches in the potential conflict between attentiveness and reflection-in-action. If the coach is to be fully engaged with the client, can they at the same time allow part of their mind to be analytical and almost observing as a third party? It seems from dialogue with coaches, both within supervision and more generally in group training sessions, that people have widely differing abilities to do this.

The seven conversations process enhances the seven-eyed model (Hawkins and Smith 2006). It examines the conversation from the perspective of the client, the strategies and interventions used by the coach, and the relationship between the coach and the client. It can help contextualize the conversation and the coaching relationship, by revealing and exploring conversations the client is not having, or conversations that are antecedents to those occurring in the coaching session. It can also be used by the supervisor and supervisee to deconstruct their own conversations – for example, when the supervisor reflects back to the coach their feelings and observations about what is being said and how it is being said. I sometimes find myself asking, 'Which bits of the conversation with the client have you transposed to *this* conversation, between us?'

Supervising with the seven conversations

Choosing whether to attend to observations from each of the conversations, and whether to draw the client's attention to them, requires a combination of intuition and judgement. In supervision, I make similar choices. However, most of the dialogue using the seven conversations framework comes from the coach's post hoc recognition of unconscious observations, revealed by reviewing the conversations.

I find myself constantly experimenting with different ways of using the seven conversations to help the coach gain insights. Typically, I might begin by asking the coach questions such as:

- What is it about this particular coaching relationship that gives you a sense of unease or that something is not quite right?
- How clear in your mind is this feeling? How clear is it to you what causes this feeling?
- What is at the edge of your awareness about this relationship?
- Does your concern relate just to the most recent session with the client or does it arise from several sessions?

Having identified the source of concern (which may simply be a general, unfocused feeling at this stage) we work through the seven conversations in whatever order the coach wishes. If I sense that they are avoiding reflecting on one of the conversations, I voice what I'm feeling and invite them to consider what they want to do with that piece of information. Sometimes they acknowledge the avoidance and change the order in which we review each conversation; sometimes we 'park' the observation and agree to review it at a later point in the supervision dialogue. The seven conversations framework gives us a structure with which to prioritize what we focus on and ensure we don't forget elements that we decide to park.

If we feel that an analysis of the verbal content would potentially be useful, an additional set of questions comes into play. These questions include:

- What words or phrases captured your attention then?
- With the attentiveness of recollection, what words or phrases capture your attention now?
- Do these words or phrases echo those from previous coaching conversations with this client? (Or – often even more revealing – with another client?)
- What makes these significant for you?
- What makes them significant for the client?
- Is the client aware of this significance?

Of course, analysis can be seductive and could potentially even be an avoidance tactic – focusing on the detail to avoid larger implications. It's a matter of judgement when the coach has acquired sufficient understanding of the conversational dynamics and their choices – both then and in future conversations – to move from deconstruction to construction.

The seven conversations in the context of the coach–supervisor relationship

Everything said thus far with regard to the coach–client conversation is, of course, relevant to the coach–supervisor conversation. Among obvious considerations here are:

- How are the multiple conversations we are having here reflective of the conversations between you and the client?
- How is the internal conversation you had about this case before coming to supervision playing out right now?
- What internal conversation would each of us recommend to the other after this supervision session?

Box 15.1 Case illustration

In the case below, the coach came to supervision with a specific client in mind. The stimulus for applying the seven conversations was a combination of an intuitive sense by the coach that the coaching relationship was not working as well as it could and a difficulty in pinpointing what the problem was and/or where the source of the problem lay. The initial dialogue explored what the coach's intuition was telling them both at the current time (as they sat in the supervision session) and as they recollected from the session(s) with the client. The decision to use the seven conversations as a framework for exploring this issue was taken jointly – suggested by the supervisor and agreed to by the coach, in the spirit of experimentation.

The coach felt a level of frustration that, while the dialogue with the client was open, energetic and positive, very little of substance emerged at the end. She felt that the client was not taking the relationship seriously enough. The spoken conversation was energetic and enjoyable, but the client seemed reluctant to commit to any firm course of action.

Two conversations gradually emerged as having particular significance. One was the client's reflections before the coaching session. It emerged that gathering information about the issue had been driven by the coach. The client's starting point was a general feeling of unease about his progression in the organization. He felt no urgency – he had brought the issue simply because the coaching session provided an opportunity to explore it.

The other conversation, which the coach and supervisor explored in depth, was the conversation in her mind during the coaching session. She had experienced increasing frustration at his apparent reluctance to engage with ideas about how he could move his career on, for example by being more proactive in managing his reputation.

The coach decided to work on the first of these conversations to begin with. An initial question was whether the client had even had this conversation. The coach had assumed that, because the client had chosen this issue, he had given it some thought already, but the recollected conversation suggested this was not so. A lesson the coach extracted here was the importance of identifying what pre-thinking a client has done, before plunging into the coaching dialogue.

At this point, she expressed the perception that she would feel more confident if she had some approaches in her kitbag to help the client take a step back and have the inner conversation, as a precursor to the main conversation. Various alternatives were discussed, ranging from the simple questions 'What thinking have you done about this already?' or 'What conversation might you usefully have had about this with yourself in preparation for this meeting?', to giving the client a sheet of paper on which to write or draw everything they know and feel about the issue. We also briefly rehearsed a conversation she might have with the client to set expectations about his preparation for the next session.

We then moved on to her inner conversation during the spoken coaching conversation. An analogy emerged of sailing, where the direction of the wind and the angle of the rudder and sail are always partially or fully opposed and making headway is often a matter of moving sideways, rather than directly ahead. Her attempts to steer the conversation were diverted by his unwillingness to commit to a particular course. Reliving some of the points in the conversation, where she had felt this most strongly, a critical question evolved – 'Whose need was it to have an outcome from this conversation?' The coach quickly realized that the urgency to find a solution was hers, driven by her need to feel that she had helped, and that the client's need was to understand his situation and his motives more fully. What the client could do about career progress was less important to him at this point than deciding whether he wanted to progress and, if so, in what direction.

From analysing this specific conversation, the coach was able to explore with the supervisor a much wider range of issues, relating to potential conflict between her needs and those of her clients. In particular, she realized that her strong sense of responsibility for her clients and their welfare had both benefits and downsides and that she needed to manage this aspect of her practice more proactively. The value of the seven conversations approach was that it allowed supervisor and coach to focus their deconstruction of what was happening between the coach and the client and to view the coach–client interaction longitudinally (that is, as a series of recurring pre-session, during, and post-session events over time).

Guidance for further learning and research

Feedback from coach clients has broadly been that the seven conversations are efficacious in helping them think methodically about their coaching practice and to pinpoint when and where in the coaching dialogue issues of concern may be located. Coaches I have supervised also report that they have been able to use the approach in self-analysis, particularly to identify when coaching relationships do not seem to be progressing as expected.

However, as a relatively recent concept, there is neither a wide body of experience, nor any form of empirical review of how it works in practice. It is also difficult to link the approach to empirically researched supervisory practice. I hope that in future there will be opportunities to experiment with and compare use of the seven conversations in combination with more traditional approaches to supervision. The framework has not been used to underpin research into the coach–client or coach–supervisor relationship, yet this would be a logical development. Such research as exists focuses either on the relationship, or on the coaching or supervision conversation. Bringing the antecedents and post-session reflections more clearly into the picture holds promise of significant insights. It would also be interesting to explore whether or how the nature of the various internal, unspoken conversations might differ according to the stage (before, during and after) and the supervisory approach, i.e. to explore each conversation in the context of reflexive practice (e.g. Archer 2009).

Comparison with other frameworks for supervision suggests that this approach addresses some but by no means all of the wide range of tasks associated with the supervisor role. For example, Harris (1983) identifies eight key tasks, which appear to have informed the frameworks created by Hawkins and Smith (2006), Proctor (1988) and Carroll (2004). The seven conversations framework helps the coach master specific skills (listening to the wider conversations), enlarge understanding of the client and of process issues, increase the coach's awareness of self and of their impact on the process, and help overcome personal and intellectual obstacles towards learning and mastery. However, it has relatively little impact in terms of developing understanding of concepts and theory. Nor does it necessarily encompass the ethical dimension of supervision.

If you decide to experiment with the seven conversations, the place to start is with your own practice. I have found it informative to compare the conversations that take place in one or more of my coaching relationships with those that occur in my supervision. It is also recommended that you read more widely in the recent literature on dialogue in coaching (e.g. Steller 2019).

Perhaps the most valuable advice I have given myself in using the seven conversations is not to use it as a process for managing supervision sessions, but as a stimulus, reinforcement and balance for my intuition. 'Apply gently for best results!'

Questions for reflection

- How aware am I of how my and my supervisees' internal conversations before our sessions influence the conduct and outcome of those sessions? What would have to happen to raise my awareness?
- How am I helping my supervisees engage in pre- and post-supervision reflection?

- What changes do I want to make to my internal discourses, to be of greater service to my coach clients?
- How can I raise my ability to attend to both the spoken and my inner conversation during supervision sessions?

Further sources

There are no publications to date that elucidate the seven conversations model other than this chapter. However, there is a rich resource relating to reflective practice in general. The first significant publication in modern times was Donald Schön's *The Reflective Practitioner* (1983), which distinguished between *reflection-on-action* and *reflection-in-action*. Hay (2007) and others incorporated these concepts into their models of the supervision process

Building on the work of Boud and Walker (1998; Boud 2010), Greenaway (undated) explores the concept of *reflection before action*, offering a menu of practical approaches for developing this ability.

Kovacs and Corrie (2017) also provide a very practical overview of reflection in coaching that challenges common assumptions.

References

Archer, M.S. (ed.) (2009) *Conversations about Reflexivity*. London: Routledge.

Boud, D. (2010) Relocating reflection in the context of practice, in H. Bradbury, N. Frost, S. Kilminster and M. Zukas (eds) *Beyond Reflective Practice: New Approaches to Professional Lifelong Learning*, pp. 25–36. Abingdon: Routledge.

Boud, D. and Walker, D. (1998) Promoting reflection in professional courses: the challenge of context, *Studies in Higher Education*, 23(2): 191–206.

Carroll, M. (2004) *Counselling Supervision: Theory, Skills and Practice*. London: Sage.

Clutterbuck, D. (2008) Moments of disconnect, unpublished essay, Oxford Brookes Business School.

Gee, J.P. (2005) *An Introduction to Discourse Analysis: Theory and Method*. London: Routledge.

Greenaway, R. (undated) *Investigating the Value of Reflection Before Action*. Available from: https://reviewing.co.uk/articles/Reflection-Before-Action.pdf.

Harris, E. (1983) A working-alliance based model of supervision, *Coaching Psychologist*, 11(1): 35–45.

Hay, J. (2007) *Reflective Practice and Supervision for Coaches*. Maidenhead: Open University Press.

Hawkins, P. and Smith, N. (2006) *Coaching, Mentoring and Organizational Consultancy*. Maidenhead: Open University Press.

Hutchby, I. and Woolfitt, P. (2008) *Conversational Analysis*. Cambridge: Polity.

Jackson, P. and McKergow, M. (2007) *The Solutions Focus: Making Coaching and Change SIMPLE*. London: Nicholas Brealey.

Kovacs, L. and Corrie, S. (2017) Building reflective capability to enhance coaching practice, *Coaching Psychologist*, 13(1): 4–12.

Megginson, D. and Clutterbuck, D. (2009) *Further Techniques for Coaching and Mentoring*. Oxford: Butterworth Heinemann.

Proctor, B. (1988) *Supervision: A Working Alliance* (videotaped training manual). St Leonards on Sea: Alexia Publications.

Schön, D.A. (1983) *The Reflective Practitioner: How Professionals Think in Action.* London: Temple Smith.

Steller, R. (2019) *The Art of Dialogue in Coaching: Towards Transformative Change.* New York: Routledge.

Sullivan, W. and Rees, J. (2008) *Clean Language: Revealing Metaphors and Opening Minds.* Carmarthen: Crown House.

Whitmore, J. (2002) *Coaching for Performance: Growing People, Performance and Purpose.* London: Nicholas Brealey.

16 Tapping into implicit processes in supervision

Michael Soth

Introduction

Implicit processes – in coaching itself as well as in coaching supervision – have become more significant in twenty-first-century practice, which is in contrast to their traditional neglect throughout the last century of psychological disciplines and the history of the talking therapies. In this chapter I focus on four areas of implicit processes that have been traditionally neglected:

- *Implicit non-verbal processes* – Across a full multi-dimensional spectrum of bodymind (whole organism) processes
- *Implicit unconscious processes* – By integrating humanistic and psychodynamic notions of 'unconscious'
- *An extended notion of implicit parallel processes* – By adding three additional matrices of parallel process to the established two matrices of coaching and coaching supervision
- *Implicit tensions inherent in the supervisory position* – By recognizing the supervisor's role and tasks as necessarily conflicted in the triangle between client and coach, and other implicit roles.

I will aim to integrate humanistic experiential ways of working on the one hand with psychodynamic principles of accessing unconscious processes on the other. This framework allows the supervisor to access implicit processes in their own awareness to begin with, and then also explicitly in interaction with their supervisee. This can be done by using different embodied and creative techniques and methods of tapping into implicit processes, to bring more awareness to them, directly enhancing the usefulness of supervision and the learning which the supervisee derives from it.

Defining 'implicit processes'

The term 'implicit process' is modern terminology, derived from cognitive neuroscience, for what in the psychodynamic tradition used to be called unconscious processes. Whatever terms we use, the concept refers to a vast and diverse field of human experience and awareness outside of (self-)reflective consciousness (McGilchrist 2009). Rational, reflective, deliberate, explicit reasoning is the tip of an iceberg, sitting largely unwittingly atop a mountain of diverse and complex non-conscious processes, of which it tends to have quite an undifferentiated appreciation. For therapeutic and coaching purposes, the neuroscientific distinction between explicit, narrative and declarative memory on the one hand, and implicit, procedural memory (which is recognized as foundational to emotional and behavioural habits) on the other, is of crucial importance. However, we need to be wary of 'dual process theories', which, while they acknowledge the significance of implicit processes, set up an unhelpful duality, subsuming multiple levels of embodied consciousness into a catch-all notion of implicit processes. This essentially reduces a rainbow of multiple dimensions of consciousness not only to greyscale, but just black and white.

Out of that dualistic conception and categorization then, various researchers and practitioners derive notions and approaches that recognize, appreciate and validate the power and significance of implicit processes (e.g. 'implicit relational knowing'). Across diverse communities of practitioners, implicit processes are recognized as hugely significant in how we organize ourselves in the world and relate to other people, and therefore as central to any kind of change process or helping relationship. In recognizing that traditional practices, with their emphasis on left-brain, verbal and explicit deliberate change efforts, often neglect implicit processes, new techniques and approaches are being created that reverse the traditional emphasis and promise more efficient, deeper and more lasting change. However, as indicated above, such reversals can end up jumping from the frying pan into the fire and are often no less dogmatic than the traditional practices they critique and aim to replace.

In the rest of this chapter I will try to rescue the diverse multitude of implicit processes from its undifferentiated fate within this dualistic, polarized conception

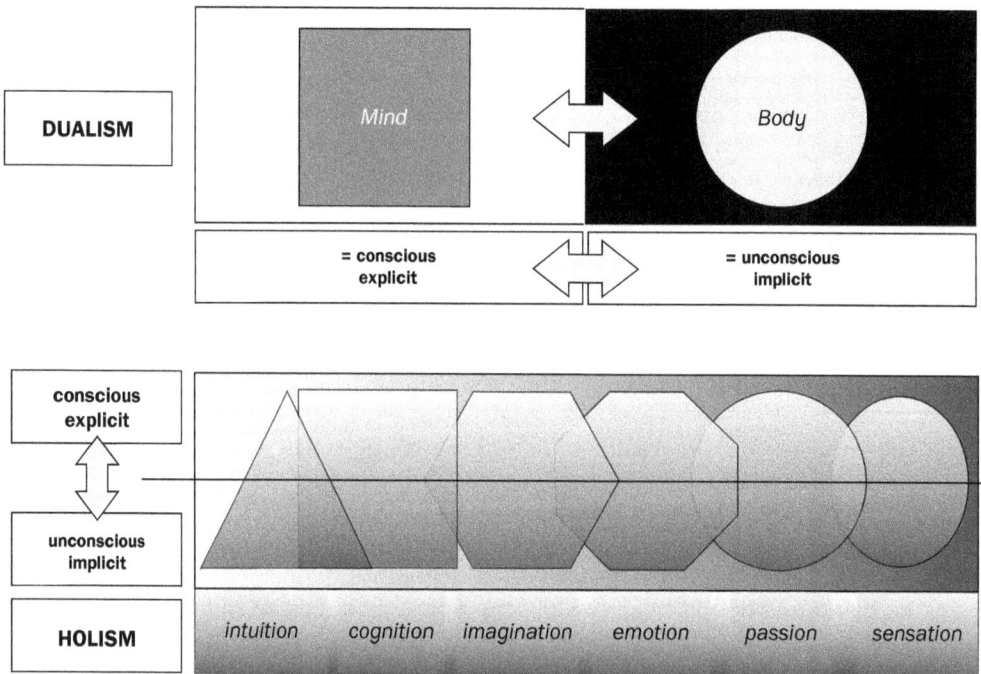

Figure 16.1 Beyond bodymind dualism: a multi-dimensional spectrum of consciousness

and propose a shift to a holistic spectrum of different dimensions of consciousness, each of which has explicit and implicit components. This will provide us with a much more comprehensive and practically helpful framework for working towards the integration of implicit and explicit processes on each and every level of consciousness. This should allow the practitioner to take a more nuanced and less biased and less polarized relational stance.

Rather than locating explicit processes exclusively in left-brain, reflective rational consciousness, and relegating implicit process to everything else, we can conceive a different view (see Figure 16.1). This view recognizes that the different levels of our bodymind awareness – sensations, excitations, passions, emotions, imaginations, cognitions and intuitions – each have areas accessible to our awareness as well as implicit and unconscious territories. The integration of these different levels of awareness, and their fluid intercommunication with each other, generates a subjective sense of wholeness. This heuristic bodymind formulation of a vision and intuition of wholeness arguably might be seen to inspire the coaching and therapeutic process. Whether I have awareness, access and influence on each of these levels of consciousness determines whether I experience them as resources or as obstacles; as wellsprings of the self that I identify with or as alien forces and foes that are at odds with my ego identity and opposing my best-laid plans.

The coherence between these different aspects of my being constitutes my sense of agency and identity in the world. Unlike Freud's dualistic formulation, which aimed at making the unconscious conscious, I do not need to make every implicit faculty and function of my being explicit in order to experience it as a resource. However, for coherence to become subjectively possible and experienced, I *do* need to attend to the conflicts and fragmentations of my inner world. I need to engage with the structure of my *psyche* and its splits and habits of repression and disassociation, which block access to these resources and exclude them from the wholeness of my being.

An overview of approaches working with implicit processes

A key principle of *all* approaches working with implicit process, whichever realm of the bodymind spectrum they access, is to encourage and entice the reflective left-brain to surrender its dominance: to pause thinking, talking and mental meaning-making, and to pay attention to the phenomenological exploration of 'here-and-now' bodymind experience. The essence of that invitation is into a kind of mindfulness that *attends* with open curiosity to the detail of moment-to-moment emergent sensory, somatic, emotional and imaginal experience and *follows* it. This involves staying with a sensation, following a movement impulse, watching an image unfold, breathing into 'felt sense' or an intuition, attentively staying with and following what emerges, mindfully following the flow, the stream of data provided by implicit processes. This is both a crucial skill in our self-awareness but also in our toolbox of helping others do the same, whether that is in coaching or in supervision.

Working with and across the holistic spectrum means recognizing that a significant proportion of implicit processes manifest in the realm of spontaneous physical emotional somatic processes, that is, through the 'body'. At the same time, implicit processes also manifest across a whole spectrum of what is usually termed 'mental' processes, including everything Freud (1912) called the pre-conscious and unconscious 'mind'.

We can identify different traditions that have developed special expertise – both in terms of theory and technique – in working with certain portions of the full bodymind spectrum, some focusing on the somatic, others on the imaginal end of the spectrum.

Somatic implicit processes

The tradition of the body-oriented therapies and somatic psychology was quite marginal in the field until the 1980s. It has since then gained validation and credibility through the revolution in neuroscience confirming many of its intuitions and ways of working, which focus on sensations, movements and emotions spontaneously arising in felt experience. Over the last 50 years this field has matured into a pluralistic discipline offering a comprehensive framework of theories and techniques, many of which have grown out of Wilhelm Reich's work in the 1930s, and has developed special expertise in accessing primarily the spectrum of *somatic* implicit processes (physiological, visceral, muscular including breathing), recognizing how the habits of body structure constitute and reflect the emotional, psychological and mental habits. The non-dualistic, holistic and psychosomatic understanding of this tradition (Marlock et al. 2015) offers a way beyond the limitations of the talking therapies, and how these have been imported into coaching, which is also reflected in many of its practices including supervision. The particular approach probably most established among the coaching community is Focusing (Gendlin 2003).

Imaginal implicit processes

Jungian approaches (1967), Assagioli's Psychosynthesis (1993), Mindell's Process-oriented Psychology (1985) and a wide variety of creative and arts-based approaches, all have developed special expertise in working with implicit processes of the imagination, such as images, fantasies and dreams.

It is through the combination of working with both somatic and imaginal implicit processes, and how they interlink and influence each other, that we gain access to the full bodymind spectrum. However, as soon as we attempt to help another person become aware of implicit processes that we think we can perceive occurring in their bodymind (of which they are, by definition, unaware), we are stepping into relationally delicate territory. Implicitly, we are challenging the limitations of their subjective identity and sense of self. This is not possible without the risk of also undermining their agency and autonomy. From our perspective we may be doing this with all the best intentions and for benign reasons, but that is not necessarily how it will be received: we may be falling into the trap of becoming just another authority who tells them who they are and what they do not know. All techniques for helping others that access their implicit processes operate within a relational asymmetry and derive historically from one-person psychology (Stark 1999).

Implicit in the habitual position which a coach takes in relation to their clients is a variety of factors. These factors include their own characterological habits and identity, their own process of expanding self-awareness through therapy and coaching, as well as biases and fixed assumptions absorbed through their training. Whether and how a coach accesses their clients' unconscious is predicated on how they manifest the perennial paradigm clash between the humanistic and psychoanalytic traditions and their respective conceptions of the unconscious. It also depends to what extent the coach has managed to integrate this tension. This significant and often implicit element of any coaching and supervisory relationship will be addressed next.

The paradigm clash between humanistic and psychodynamic traditions of supervision

Traditionally, the field of the psychological therapies (and to some extent, coaching) has been divided between humanistic, behavioural and psychoanalytic traditions. The last 25 years have seen attempts, partly inspired through the integration of traditional approaches (e.g. Clarkson 2003), to bring together humanistic and psychoanalytic traditions. These traditions have their own underlying meta-psychologies, theories and techniques, which on many levels and in many respects are fundamentally in opposition. The contradictions, arguments and splits between these traditions can also be seen as manifesting in different – historically divisive yet ultimately complementary – conceptions of implicit and unconscious processes, and how these notions also percolate into supervision.

Oversimplifying the distinctions and contradictions for the sake of brevity, we could say:

- The humanistic tradition emphasizes unconsciousness as a lack of embodied, experiential awareness in the present moment, on the assumption that full human potential and peak states of wholeness can be actualized through positive intention and practice. The self-actualizing tendency drives a growth process towards a more embracing sense of self, greater awareness and complexity, and thus a comprehensive integration of implicit processes through expanded consciousness. This meta-psychological perspective is also close to the Jungian and transpersonal conception.
- The psychodynamic tradition emphasizes unconsciousness in more pessimistic terms as developmentally entrenched habits of feeling, thought and behaviour, which constitute a self-replicating, self-reinforcing relational universe both internally and in relation to others. A central assumption of this tradition is Freud's formulation of the 'repetition compulsion', especially as it manifests in the transference in relation to the analyst. The unconscious is not seen as a function of inattention or lack of experience (or a wholeness that just has not happened yet, but is potentially achievable). Rather, it is maintained through fixed characterological, defensive structures in the *psyche*, which keep at bay internal conflicts internalized a long time ago and now constituting the structure of our mind. Consequently, on this view, becoming aware of implicit processes is much harder. In the classical version, the best developmental

outcome we can hope for is an achievement of Klein's depressive position: by making our unconscious woundedness conscious and 'working it through' to the point of learning to live with it, a mature acceptance of our fundamentally conflicted and limited reality becomes possible.

In summary, there is a profound clash in how these traditions conceive of unconsciousness. Hence, these traditions come to quite contradictory conclusions as to what kind of relational stances, theories and techniques are most effective and – in blunt terms – best value for time and money in coaching, and thus in coaching supervision.

One of the main philosophical differences concerns the power differential between client and coach, and supervisee and supervisor. As Gomez (2004) has suggested regarding the essential differences between these traditions, humanistic practitioners predominantly work through an empathic, supportive and reparative 'alongside' stance intended to empower the client and facilitate their growth, *emphasizing equality within the human encounter*. In contrast, Gomez locates the essence of the psychodynamic tradition in taking an 'opposite' stance. This stance appreciates the profound transformative power of the transference by inviting and allowing implicit processes to 'construct the therapist as an object'. This happens according to the logic of the client's conflicted relational universe, which thus becomes available for here-and-now investigation and change. Implicitly, this recognizes that most developmental wounding originates in the profound inequality and power differential between children and their caregivers on whom they are comprehensively dependent. The psychodynamic tradition prioritizes the working-through of 'negative' relational patterns rooted in developmental trauma over humanistic 'positive' adult collaboration, by *fostering a relational space open to profound inequality*.

The psychodynamic critique of humanistic practice is that it fails to address the deep unconscious roots of the client's problems in life by engaging as an apparent equal with the superficial defences of the pseudo-adult, thus failing to address the most crucial and critical implicit process of all: *the unconscious dynamic between client and coach*. The humanistic critique, in turn, accuses the psychodynamic tradition of replicating and reinforcing patterns of detrimental power differential by requiring *implicit subjugation to its paternalistic doctrine*, with nineteenth-century dualistic assumptions pervading its whole edifice of meta-psychology, theory and technique, ultimately blocking the client's potential and self-actualization.

The polarization and lack of integration across the field is reflected and embedded in the mindset and practice of the individual practitioner and remains one of the most pervasively entrenched implicit difficulties. It can manifest in various ways: mostly, the supervisee's habitual position tends to implicitly take for granted the echo chamber of their own partial tradition and training, with most coaches operating predominantly in the humanistic paradigm; a significant number of coaches integrate some psychodynamic theories and ways of working, but tend to oscillate between humanistic and psychodynamic stances in a way that is ultimately confusing to their client (a danger that is the main point of Gomez's warning).

The supervisor then can notice how the cult-like preconceptions and dogmas of the traditions are present implicitly as habitual positions and restrictive ways of working. These are taken for granted by supervisees, manifesting especially in terms of the relational space and atmosphere that their presence generates through the implicit stance they take. Helping them become aware of how they, as an individual practitioner, manifest the historical splits across the field is a question both of explicit teaching and experiential modelling in supervision.

Working with implicit processes in supervision

These paradigm clashes inevitably lead to very different conceptions of supervision, its priorities, and the role of implicit processes within it, especially when it comes to power differential, authority and containment, but also in terms of different ways of working, tools and techniques.

From within the polarization we can caricature the humanistic supervisor's stance as a *benign older sibling* who shares their greater experience by facilitating the continuing development of their supervisee towards eventual collegial equality, using the whole creative toolbox of experiential techniques. In contrast, the psychodynamic supervisor continues to focus on patterns of unconscious constructions rooted in the inequalities of early development; their stance as a supervisor – as an extension of their stance as a practitioner – focuses on transference and countertransference processes. Here the supervisee benefits from the sense of containment they can derive from the supervisor's embracing awareness of their whole being, including all their unconscious processes; however, the traditional non-experiential left-brain verbal focus of much psychodynamic supervision easily acquires the deferential atmosphere of reporting to headmaster.

When we recognize the limitations and shadow aspects of these contradictory, segregated and polarized traditions, the development of an integrative form of supervision promises a synergy between them, by which their diverse gifts and wisdoms actually come to complement each other, without minimizing the paradigm clashes between them. One of the main tools I use for this, in both individual and group supervision, is experiential exploration of what I call 'charged moments' in the client–coach interaction through embodied role-play. The technique clearly is based upon two-chair work derived from Gestalt, doing justice to a humanistic emphasis on experiential and phenomenological process. It aims at bringing together the various parts of the *psyche* and the various aspects of the bodymind into an integrated whole, a procedure that I call 'gathering the fragments'. Unlike its humanistic origins, one of my main aims in using these role-plays in supervision is to help the supervisee catch glimpses of the transference–countertransference dynamic, the enactments and parallel processes generated by unconscious forces. I want to help the supervisee access the unconscious relational dynamic they are caught in with the client *based on minimal conscious information*. This averts the need for lengthy left-brain reporting by the supervisee (which can easily take up to half a session per client in traditional supervision) and *maximizes shared attention to implicit and non-verbal processes*. Any more detailed facts and information that were initially missing, but are helpful and needed, can emerge *through* the role-play rather than through 'dry' reporting.

To summarize, the importance of accessing implicit processes in supervision is largely about making the actual bodymind experience of the coaching session come alive again in the supervision session, so we are not left with merely 'talking about' it in fairly abstracted left-brain fashion as our only option. We want to bring the atmosphere and relational dynamic between coachee and coach into the lived experience between coach and supervisor.

Working with the implicit through an extended notion of parallel processes

The established model of parallel process (Hawkins and Shohet 2006) demonstrates that a discernible portion of the vast territory of implicit processes is constituted by parallel process between the coaching matrix and the supervision matrix. This model can be extended and enriched by adding a further three matrices (Soth 2007) that expand the framework for noticing and working with the multi-dimensional manifestations of parallel process. I have claimed that this extension provides us not just with helpful insights for supervisory practice, but constitutes an organizing principle for all disciplines across the helping professions. In fact, it can be argued that the principle of parallel process applies far beyond that, in all complex multi-dimensional systems, as the way in which information is passed between the subsystems various levels, parts and subsystems of the whole system (or 'holon').

For practical purposes in coaching supervision, we can extend the notion of parallel process as replicating the very broadly and loosely conceptualized 'relational dynamic' between client and coach in the linked and related subsystem of the supervision matrix. Following psychodynamic principles, and specifically object relations, we can trace the way a client relates to their coach back into the client's inner relational universe and its origin in childhood development. We can then combine the object relations view of the inner world of the mind as being populated by mental representations of internalized significant others with Reich's bodymind notion of character as the frozen landscape of developmental trauma.

By adding the internal relational matrix, the internal bodymind matrix and the 'primary scenario' matrix (Figure 16.2), the extended model has several advantages:

- It traces the transference–countertransference process in coaching back to its origins in the client's inner world.
- It integrates a fine-grained developmental understanding of that inner world and its parts including their biographical and early developmental history.
- It offers a holistic conception of how that inner world becomes a relational bodymind process between client and coach in the here and now.
- It explains how the multi-dimensional complexity of all these matrices is linked together into a meaningful whole via parallel processes throughout the whole system which can become transformative through becoming explicit.

The example below illustrates how the systemic manifestations of a corporate culture can be absorbed and communicated from coachee to coach to supervisor via parallel process, with collective and individual psychology triggering and reinforcing each other.

Extending & expanding our notion of 'parallel process'

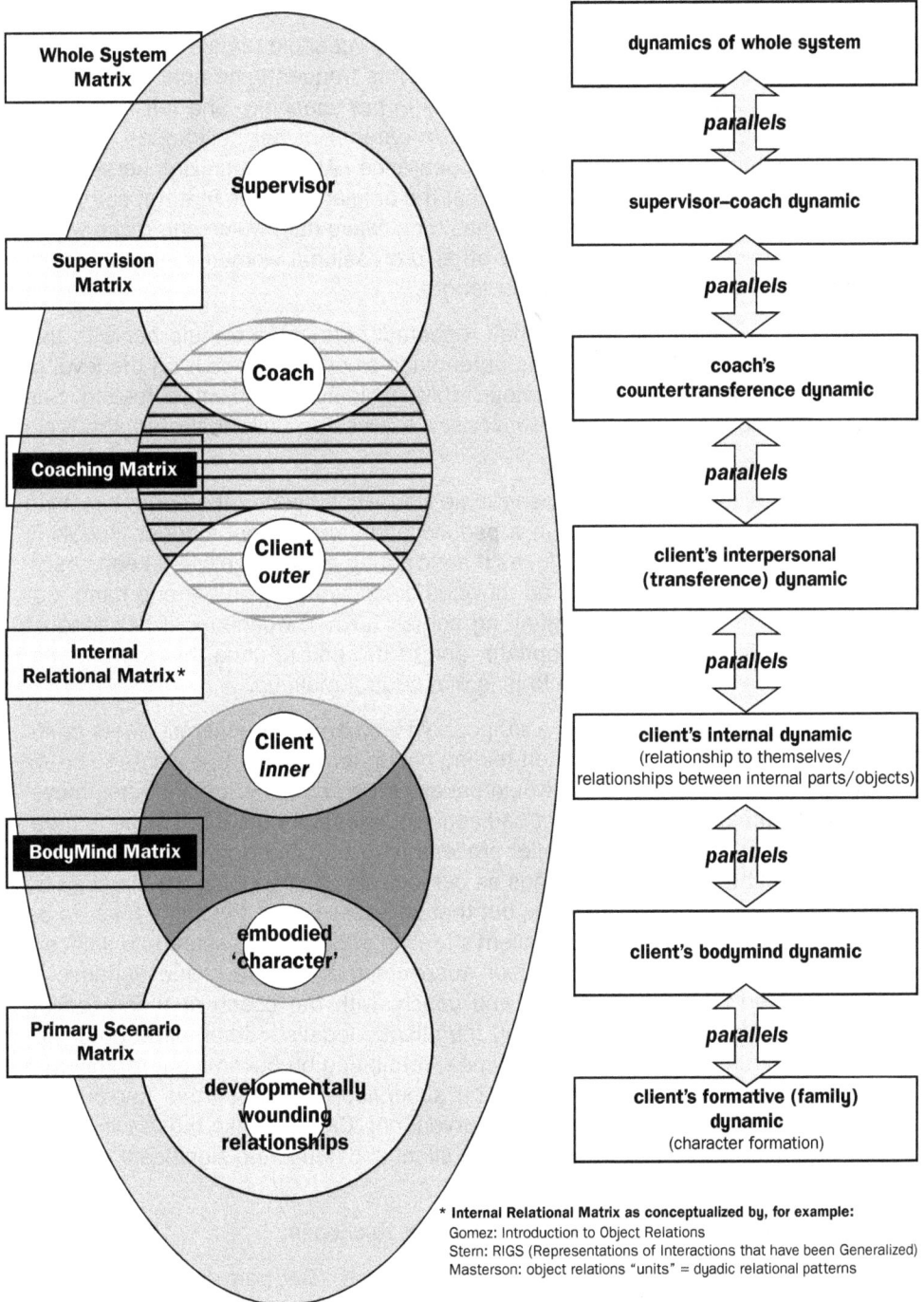

	parallels	
Whole System Matrix		dynamics of whole system
	parallels	
Supervision Matrix	Supervisor	supervisor–coach dynamic
	parallels	
Coaching Matrix	Coach	coach's countertransference dynamic
	parallels	
Internal Relational Matrix*	Client *outer*	client's interpersonal (transference) dynamic
	parallels	
BodyMind Matrix	Client *Inner*	client's internal dynamic (relationship to themselves/ relationships between internal parts/objects)
	parallels	
Primary Scenario Matrix	embodied 'character'	client's bodymind dynamic
	parallels	
	developmentally wounding relationships	client's formative (family) dynamic (character formation)

* **Internal Relational Matrix as conceptualized by, for example:**
Gomez: Introduction to Object Relations
Stern: RIGS (Representations of Interactions that have been Generalized)
Masterson: object relations "units" = dyadic relational patterns

Figure 16.2 Extending and expanding the notion of parallel process

---

Box 16.1 Case illustration

The coaching client brought to supervision is a 29-year-old female lawyer working for a large, male-dominated corporation, who has frequently brought the issue of her status as a woman within the company to her coaching. She felt humiliated when her employer recently commented in earshot of her colleagues that she should maintain a 'more professional appearance'. After scrutinizing herself systematically, she eventually concluded that the only anomalous feature, compared to her female colleagues, is that she has long, wavy hair, which she often wears down. She has noticed that the few other professional women in the company have all cut their hair above shoulder length.

Her coach, a 35-year-old woman, has repeatedly struggled to help her with this ongoing issue, as her client seems determined to only address it on the level of legal principle and strategic behaviour, while avoiding all subjective feeling. She keeps bringing this client to her supervisor, expressing how frustrated she feels while listening:

> She just talks at me in an impenetrable way – she spends the entire coaching session debating the issue, in a pseudo-legal, impersonal manner, speaking rapidly and breathing shallowly, as if anticipating attack. The client keeps oscillating between referring to it as 'obvious discrimination' on the one hand, but then, on the other hand, scrutinizing herself further, wondering if her conduct has been in any way inappropriate, and in the end refuting this, defensively insisting on her nondescript clothing and neutral makeup.

While listening, her supervisor, a 40-year-old woman, who generally feels confident in her femininity, finds herself feeling hot under her hair. She wants to brush it away from her face, but what would usually be a spontaneous and easy movement now comes with unpleasant self-consciousness. As the experience is unfamiliar, she surmises that a parallel process may be occurring, recognizing that the coach, in her frustration, sounds as persecutory in describing the client as do the client's male superiors at work, but that she seemed, at the same time, to be identifying for a moment with the client's feeling of painful exposure and self-conscious awkwardness. The supervisor suspects that the traumatic dynamic is being enacted between the client and coach, with the coach at times feeling oppressed in her role and agency by the client's legalistic internalization of her company culture, but then, at other times, retaliating by becoming a representation of the male observers herself. The supervisor translates this hunch, in a series of invitations, into a role-play intervention: 'Can you take these two chairs and show me the interaction between the client and you in the significant charged moment from the last session?'

The coach is immediately clear which moment to choose:

Coach: When I asked her for the second time, 'But how did you feel when you overheard that comment, emotionally, and in your body?', she accused me of invalidating her, by making the issue about her 'irrational' feelings rather than about the fact of discrimination.

Supervisor: So then how did you respond?

Coach: I just kept looking at her, hoping she would stay with the feeling atmosphere that had entered the room between us, because she seemed deeply hurt, but she hurriedly looked away, changed the subject and then made a non-credulous excuse for leaving the session early.

The supervisor then invited the coach into her embodied countertransference experience, at the point where she had insistently and repeatedly asked the client about her feelings. The coach could access a sense of impatient, dismissive frustration, and recognized that she was caught in enacting the client's experience of being in her office, surrounded by impatient, judgemental male gazes and attitudes.

By using the experiential tool of role-play, the supervisor had successfully helped the coach gain awareness and connect with previously implicit processes: both sides of the feeling atmosphere and dynamic in the client's work environment (the male dismissiveness and the female humiliation). It helped her, eventually, to understand more fully how the client's family background had precipitated her into a vocation that replicated the dynamic between her parents, with her identifying with her mother's position and projecting the father's stance onto her male superiors. This, in turn, helped the coach hold the client's internal conflict between her legalistic father-mind and her subdued mother-body in her own awareness; the coach consequently stopped taking polarizing positions in relation to the client, which had been implicitly perpetuating the dynamic throughout the coaching relationship. From this non-polarizing stance, she was then able to facilitate the client's awareness of her internal conflict and how it was being enacted in her workplace. The client eventually became able to challenge her male colleagues in productive and creative ways, which also helped them in becoming more effective in their use of 'soft' people skills, essential to their work.

Implicit conflict within the supervisory position: five conflicting roles

So far, we have only drawn upon the classical 'one-person psychology' origins of the psychoanalytic tradition (Stark 1999), where the client's transference is the one and only source of the coach's countertransference and the parallel processes arising from it. However, the coach, as well as the supervisor, are inhabiting their professional stance *through* their own subjectivity, and are bringing their own issues, their own habitual conflicts, and their areas of unconscious and dissociated experience into the professional relationship. The humanistic tradition, including most coaching, has always been conceiving of the process as an authentic human encounter between two people, that is, two 'psychologies' and their corresponding shadow aspects and woundedness are involved.

Supervision that integrates these traditions also needs to integrate one-person and two-person perspectives. Supervisors' idiosyncratic and subjective inhabiting of their professional role with its inherent conflicts is a significant aspect of the implicit processes occurring across the two-person psychology field in coaching, and deserves specific attention.

The supervisory role inevitably contains two conflicting aspects which are in constant tension with each other (Figure 16.3):

- As an elder, it is the supervisor's task to maintain '*client advocacy*' and make sure that the supervisee practises within the responsibilities, competencies, ethics and frames that the general public can expect from a proficient qualified reflective practitioner; this involves an essential *assessment function* which is in line with the colloquial meaning of the term 'super-vising'.
- As an elder, it is also the supervisor's task to *champion the supervisee's development* towards their full potential, watching over them and protecting as well as facilitating their evolving competency, by *mentoring* them.

So, the supervisor needs to champion the interests and welfare of *both* the client and the supervisee, maintaining an awareness of that triangle. In situations where there is conflict between client and supervisee, the supervisor cannot be expected to be exclusively on the supervisee's side. In that moment, the supervisor becomes like a *guardian of the profession*, monitoring and potentially challenging the supervisee's lack of professional competency. If there is a complaint by the client against the coach, it is precisely because of client advocacy that the supervisor is seen as co-responsible for the supervisee's work. At the far end, that may need to include the unpleasant possibility that the supervisor feels unable to ethically support the supervisee's work. These two conflicting roles, *client advocate versus mentor*, are necessarily inherent in the supervisor role.

There are other roles that the supervisee may expect from or project onto the supervisor, which are not, strictly speaking, part of the tasks and role of the supervisor. However, there are certain aspects of the therapist, the assessor, the tutor and the colleague/peer that inevitably do come into the supervision process and overlap with it (Figure 16.3). All of these, to some extent, can inform/complement and enhance the tasks of supervision or conflict/interfere and detract from them.

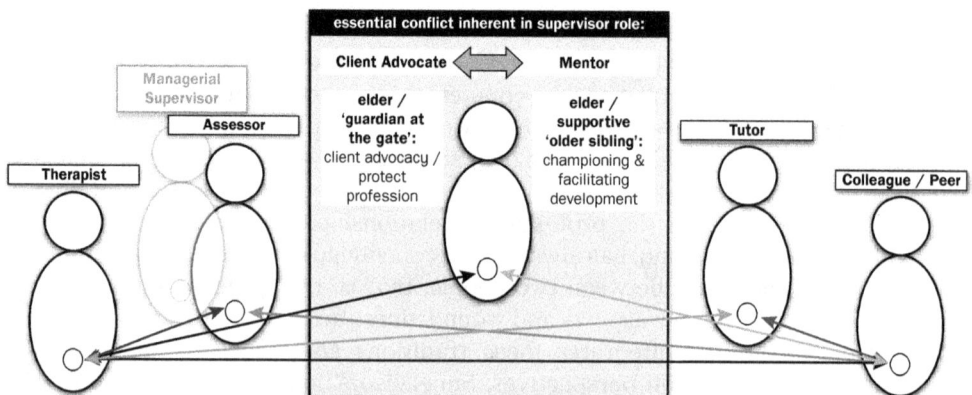

Figure 16.3 Conflicting roles within the supervisory position

Unless the supervisor can remain continuously aware of the tensions between these diverse roles, and of the advantages and disadvantages of engaging in them in relation to a particular supervisee, they may oversimplify the supervisory task in their mind. This can lead not only to missing many of the implicit processes, but more importantly to missing the way the supervisor themselves may be contributing to enactments. This can jeopardize the working alliance. Much of the time the way we experience these conflicting roles as supervisors contains parallel process information about the supervisee's dilemmas. In reality, supervisors constantly operate in the force field between these roles, making decisions about including and excluding, prioritizing or backgrounding some of them in favour or at the expense of others. When ignored or avoided, any of these roles can subterraneously drain energy, blocking or interfering with the tasks of supervision. It is therefore important that the supervisor maintain their sense of tension and conflict between them rather than simplifying and reducing their role to a more straightforward and linear task.

Guidance for further learning and research

The topic of working with implicit processes has been attracting more attention among coaching supervisors recently. There is an awareness of the knowledge and experience required to tap into these processes. It goes without saying that increasing the capacity for such work would benefit from supervisors attending to their own personal history and significant influences in their life that may affect their work. Their development work might usefully include engaging with traditions that are discussed in this chapter.

It is important, however, to recognize that translation of many traditions of working with the implicit processes needs dedicated research in the context of coaching and coaching supervision. By definition, the implicit is not easy to study and it is hoped that with recent interest in this level of work in supervision more researchers will be inspired to explore how many interesting propositions manifest themselves in practice.

Questions for reflection

- How can I expand my awareness within the supervision session to include the full range of multiple bodymind levels of consciousness, to tap fully into my embodied 'implicit relational knowing'?
- Where does my understanding of and work with unconscious processes sit within the paradigm clash between humanistic and psychodynamic traditions, and how could I broaden and deepen my integrative reach across the split?
- How am I positioned and positioning myself relationally within the force field of the implicit tensions between the five roles inherent in the supervisory position, and how does this serve the supervision?
- How can I use my awareness of the extended notion of parallel process to deepen and enhance the supervision, by focusing it more effectively on the 'charged moments', the significant dynamics and the crucial issues?

Further sources

Clarkson, P. (2003) *The Therapeutic Relationship*. London: Whurr Publishers. This book describes with relevance to practice the most interesting interplay between humanistic and psychoanalytic tradition.

Gendlin, E. (2003) *Focusing*. London: Rider. In this book Gendlin describes a unique approach of working with the implicit with the focus on the body.

Hawkins, P. and Shohet, R. (2006) *Supervision in the Helping* Professions, 3rd edn. Maidenhead: Open University Press. This book explains well how to spot parallel processes in supervision that are relevant to coaching context.

References

Assagioli, R. (1993) *Psychosynthesis: A Manual of Principles and Techniques*, 3rd edn. London: Aquarian/Thorsons.

Clarkson, P. (2003) *The Therapeutic Relationship*. London: Whurr Publishers.

Freud, S. (1912/1958) Recommendations to physicians practising psychoanalysis, in J. Strachey (ed. and trans.) *The Standard Edition of the Complete Psychological Works of Sigmund Freud*, Vol. 12. London: Hogarth Press.

Gendlin, E. (2003) *Focusing*. London: Rider.

Gomez, L. (2004) Humanistic or psychodynamic – what is the difference, and do we have to make a choice?, *Self & Society: An International Journal for Humanistic Psychology*, 31(6): 5–19.

Hawkins, P. and Shohet, R. (2006) *Supervision in the Helping Professions*, 3rd edn. Maidenhead: Open University Press

Jung, C. (1967) *Symbols of Transformation*. Princeton, NJ: Princeton University Press.

Marlock, G., Weiss, H., Yong, C. and Soth, M. (2015) *Handbook of Body Psychotherapy and Somatic Psychology*. Berkeley, CA: North Atlantic Books.

McGilchrist, I. (2009) *The Master and His Emissary: The Divided Brain and the Making of the Western World*. London: Yale University Press.

Mindell, A. (1985) *Working with the Dreambody*. London: Routledge and Kegan Paul.

Soth, M. (2007) *Extending and Expanding Our Notion of Parallel Process*. Presentation to 1st UKCP Conference on Supervision, 2007.

Stark, M. (1999) *Modes of Therapeutic Action*. Northvale, NJ: Jason Aronson.

17 Using constellations in supervision

Ty Francis

Introduction

Over the last ten years, there has been a surge of interest by organizational coaches in the practice of 'Constellations': a systemic philosophy and methodology that is a development of Bert Hellinger's (1998) family systems psychotherapy. Its diagnostic and solutions-focused possibilities are making an invaluable contribution to the fields of systemic organizational coaching and supervision, not least because of the novelty of its methodology for uncovering and working with 'hidden dynamics' in relationship systems.

At its simplest, a constellation is a way of spatially mapping the elements of a system so that the entangling undercurrents of an issue are revealed. The methodology is as useful in one-to-one supervision as in group supervision; as powerful in a workshop with people who represent the various aspects of a client's issue, as in individual consultations using objects on a desktop (and increasingly, by using avatars or symbols on specialist software, when working online).

Where the Constellations approach can claim uniqueness is in its combination of four factors: its particular focus on embodiment through the apparatus of the constellation; in the theory of systemic principles known as 'The Orders of Love' (Hellinger 1991) that represent the epistemological basis of this work; and in the philosophical stance in relation to 'love' that distinguishes the work of an experienced constellations practitioner. Also, of particular relevance to supervisors and coaches are the related 'systemic ordering principles' known as 'The Orders of Helping' (Hellinger 2003) that characterize the ethical basis of this form of systemic supervision.

In this chapter, I shall address how Constellations can help supervisors to explore and illuminate issues that coaches bring for enquiry. These issues might belong to the client system and wider stakeholder network that the coach is engaged with; to the coach's patterns of working with different clients over time; and within the supervisor–coach relationship. I hope to illuminate how the Constellations methodology continuously shapes and informs supervisory guidance relating to the coach's choices about how and where to intervene in the client system. Importantly, I shall highlight key precepts of the underpinning theory of Constellations work and the *stance* of a Constellations practitioner.

When engaging with this chapter, it might help the reader to keep in mind the related questions of how this description of Constellations supervision challenges their own theory of practice, what its contributions might be and what a creative synthesis of this approach with the reader's own coaching supervision practice might look like.

Overview of supervision practice with Constellations

Constellations is a deeply relational approach, distinguished by an interplay of systemic, embodied and dialogic perspectives and practices. While the approach is rapidly gaining in popularity, it is relatively new. Consequently, there is a narrow (but expanding) theory base for the work; attention is often lavished on the mechanics of constellating – leading to an over-emphasis on the often dramatic technique of the constellation to the detriment of a critical and integrated understanding of the theory, and a more nuanced contextual awareness of its place in systemic practice. Nevertheless, Constellations remains a powerful and practical way of exploring hidden dynamics at play in the client system and wider relational field, including the coach–supervisor relationship.

So, what does supervision from a Constellations perspective look like? As Urschel (2020) notes, systemic supervision is predicated on an understanding that there are multiple ways of knowing and of accessing information in a system, many of which go beyond the conscious mind. With a constellation, we explore the *implicit,* rather than the *explicit* domain of knowing, and use a dynamic form of embodied process to surface unconscious patterns. It is the unusual nature of this embodied exploration that distinguishes the Constellations approach.

For readers who are unfamiliar with Constellations, it might be useful to get an overview of the mechanics of the process first, before understanding more about this particular systemic theory, which I shall describe later in this chapter.

In a process articulated and illustrated by Whittington (2016), the supervisor might ask the coach to identify aspects of the issue under consideration – both people in their roles (for example, the CEO who brought the coach in and is the commissioning client for the work; or the marketing team; or the coach) as well as more abstract elements (such as the Stock Exchange, or the profit motive, or the values of the organization). In group supervision, we would invite group members to represent these systemic elements, but in individual supervision we would use floor markers or objects on a desktop to represent the systemic elements. In online supervision, the supervisor could make use of specialist Constellations software or invite the coach to find objects in their room to lay out on the floor or on their desktop.

The coach positions each element intuitively, using only the relative direction and proximity to the other elements as a guide. Together with the supervisor, the coach considers the whole arrangement. As they co-enquire, the supervisor draws on his/her knowledge of the systemic ordering principles (described below) and suggests moving some representatives or objects and offering brief sentences to the coach based upon these principles. A configuration might be presenting itself that looks like the one represented in Figure 17.1.

The supervisor offers a 'reading' of the constellation and explores what resonates with the coach. This reading is not an interpretation, as much as a phenomenological description of what presents itself. For example, in the constellation illustrated in Figure 17.1, we can see that the CEO, Stock Exchange and Profit Motive are all facing roughly the same direction; the Marketing Team is looking at the Stock Exchange; the Values of the organization are close to the CEO but moving in the opposite direction; and the Coach – who is very close to the CEO – is

Figure 17.1 An example of a coach's initial configuration of elements in a constellation

looking at the Values but obstructing the CEO's view of the Marketing Team. The supervisor 'stays close' to the phenomenology of the constellation and resists interpretation, while sharing these observations with the coach.

This reading and what the unique configuration suggests are then explored together by the supervisor and coach. The supervisor's knowledge of The Orders of Love (to be described later in the chapter) informs the coach's meaning-making through a process of dialogue (Isaacs 1999). The systemic ordering principles also inform 'embodied experiments' such as the supervisor repositioning one element at a time (moving the coach back, for example), or offering sentences (such as inviting the coach to say to the CEO, 'I'm more interested in your values than in your profit motive'). The resonance and 'felt sense' (Gendlin 2003) of these some-times-provocative statements is weighed by the coach, and in this way insights and different action possibilities emerge that might not have been so obvious before.

This spatial mapping is itself immensely useful, as it affords the supervisor and coach a meta-perspective. Furthermore, it enables the supervisor to discuss with the coach, patterns in the system that have been revealed, and to explore a variety of interventions: for example, what the effect on the whole is, if the coach changes position, or if a representative is removed, or if someone who might have been forgotten about is added to the constellation, or if something could be said that might relax the representatives and restore more ease . . .

From this description we can see that there are two main uses of Constellations. First, the supervisor and coach team can use the constellations 'map' to better scan the systemic environment diagnostically, gather and make sense of data, and structure an approach that provides the client with insight and new action options. Second, the physicality of the constellation and the dynamic way it affords the coach different vantage points on the client's issue helps to continuously shape and inform the coach's choices about how and where to intervene in the actual client system. The constellation functions rather like a spreadsheet – changes in one area create a ripple effect throughout the whole, so the process of supervision proceeds hermeneutically.

However, the value of Constellations work in supervision is not limited to this mapping technique. Supervision may *or may not* make explicit use of the constellation to map systemic dynamics. With experience, supervisors' integration of the technique and informing theory enables them to constellate without setting up a constellation (Stam and Schreider 2016). Either way, the focal points of supervision – the fundamental roles and responsibilities of the supervisor from a Constellations perspective are:

- *Supporting the coach in finding the optimal systemic place from which to intervene.* Perhaps one of the greatest contributions of Constellations to supervision is its ability to chart the topography of the client's situation, and hence to enable the coach to see how s/he is positioned within this systemic landscape. For example, is the coach too close to the client, or facing away, or standing between the client and the issue so that the client cannot see what is going on? Is the coach supporting the client's boss more than the client, or collapsing under the weight of systemic pressure? These and other possibilities are dramatically visible when we set up a constellation: being able to walk around the issue (quite literally) can be of enormous value to coaches, to reorient themselves in their client work.
- *Enabling the coach to surface and make meaning of the hidden dynamics at play in the client relationship and broader situation.* A constellation is not needed to work with the *explicit* knowledge of the situation and system, but with the *implicit* knowledge – with what is tacit, unrecognized, unacknowledged, marginalized or excluded in some way. Very often, the best use of a constellation is when problems recur over time, no matter how much attention or resource is expended on them; or when we are working with 'wicked problems' (Grint 2010) of great complexity, and no way forward seems clear or viable. By setting up the unique elements of a situation in supervision and noting the 'pinch-points' and aspects of flow between them, we have an enriching opportunity for co-enquiry and dialogue.
- *Facilitating the coach to discover a new narrative that reshapes their work and liberates client potential.* One of the most powerful contributions of Constellations work is to offer experiential reframes of the stories we tell ourselves about the world. Hawkins and Turner (2020) suggest that this is the most transformational level of engagement and can lead to the longest-lasting shifts of perception and practice. It necessitates care on behalf of the supervisor, as we are working with the underlying assumptions that shape not only our coaches' perceiving, thinking and relating but their deepest ways of being.
- *Assisting the coach to understand their personal dynamics and patterns – which usually relate to their own families of origin.* What the coach brings

from his or her own systemic legacy in the way of both resources and limitations, forms a part of the supervisory picture. Noting our own systemic loyalties and biases, frees us to value the different perspectives of others and also to move to a humbler place of 'not knowing' in the face of systemic complexity – a hallmark of effective relational practice, according to Critchley et al. (2007). Illuminating blindspots and charting examples of parallel process is central to this approach.

- *Educating the coach to 'see systemically'*. We live in a culture that privileges individualism – a paradigm that is extremely pervasive, and so for many coaches it takes time to integrate a holistic paradigm to the point where seeing patterns of connection, interaction and inter-relationships over time, becomes second nature. The Constellations supervisor can be of profound service in catalysing a more systemic way of considering client issues. This also includes a radical openness to working with family systems issues occasionally: after all, our deepest relational patterns were formed in and by our families of origin. Working systemically with Constellations requires a willingness from the supervisor to work across the range of nested systems: behaviours that arise in the workplace might be located in family systems, community systems, economic, cultural or ecosystems, and more.

The supervisor's stance

The supervisor's skill is in working phenomenologically – not giving analysis, interpretation or opinion, but providing an impartial and non-judgemental presence that describes what is presenting itself. Hellinger (1998: 249) defines his phenomenological method as working without fear and without intention. This is quite an exacting orientation to master, as it necessitates the supervisor suspending any wish to help, or to come up with a solution, and requires an impeccability about naming uncomfortable 'truths' clearly. As Horn and Brick (2005: 51) state,

> The critical system dynamics operate unseen and become visible only when one is able to put aside all intention and allow the effects of the constellation to penetrate.

The aim is two-fold. First, by setting up a physical representation of some presenting elements in a system, the supervisor enables the coach to pay attention to their felt sense of their current place in the system and what presents itself from within this topography – for example, what the coach can see or not see. This leads to discussion of the possible benefits and concealed costs to remaining in this place; how the coach might have been unwittingly recruited into this place by the client system; and what loyalties might be operating out of awareness. Second, the physical representation of the system provided by the constellation enables the coach to move around, 'stand in other people's shoes', and gain glimpses from different vantage points and perspectives. This often confounds the coach's initial framing and narrative, widens the possibility space and returns autonomy to the client. In this way, the coach is encouraged to step outside of the content they have been immersed in and see patterns across the whole system, over time.

At the heart of this orientation is the willingness of both supervisor and coach to enter the unknown together, through the medium of the constellation, and work with not knowing. In part, this is achieved by the supervisor asking as few questions as possible and keeping the questions factual. This way, we are not so likely to get drawn into the coach's narrative. It is also helped by the supervisor working without having an agenda, goals, or fixed outcomes, and not rushing into premature sense-making, but instead exploring interconnections and patterns. This intentionlessness adds difficulty but also rigour to the supervision process and supports emergent and often unimaginable solutions.

In a very particular sense, this stance can be described as 'loving'. What we mean by 'love' in this context is suggested by Maturana, who writes eloquently of love as something that expands intelligent behaviour: 'Most problems in companies are not solved through competition, not through fighting, not through authority. They are solved through the only emotion that expands intelligent behaviour . . . This emotion is love' (Maturana and Bunnell 1999: 1).

Like Hellinger, he is referring to love as the force that serves life – the essential energy that enables flourishing, that is expansive, generative, creative, and that supports growth, peace, fulfilment, 'success' . . . The psychoanalyst Eric Fromm once described love in a similar way: 'Love is not primarily a relationship to a specific person; it is an attitude, an orientation of character which determines the relatedness of a person to the world as a whole, not towards one object of love' (Fromm 1995: 36).

Hellinger was far more phenomenological in his definition of love. He described it in a practical formula, as *Seeing + Distance – Judgement*. To love in this way requires certain things of us as supervisors: a separation from individual concerns and personal loyalties (including to our clients) so that we can gain a bigger-picture perspective that is enriched by contextual relevance; a willingness to resist over-investment in solutions and even in the helping relationship itself; and to let go of blame or praise, disgust or approval, and other reactions, so that we can remain compassionately neutral.

The informing Theory of Systemic Constellations

As I have suggested, the constellation itself has limited value as a systemic map, without an understanding of this particular systemic theory. It is this theoretical scaffolding that enables us as supervisors to diagnose and deal with presenting issues brought by the coach; and that directs the process work we do as Constellations practitioners using movements, sentences and ritualized gestures. The three main concepts of this theory are the Orders of Love, Conscience and the Orders of Helping.

The Orders of Love

'Orders of Love' are natural forces in human relationships, first articulated by Bert Hellinger (1991, 1998). Akin to heuristics, they describe what enable healthy and fulsome relationships to flourish, and they also identify what impedes such relationships. They are 'orders' not in the sense of commands but in the sense of being systemic principles that restore order. The five Orders of Love that guide Constellations supervision and wider practice, are:

- *Acknowledgement* – which is fundamental to all of the other systemic principles and suggests that all aspects of organizational reality need recognizing, and that nothing should be covered up.
- The ordering principle of *Time* draws our attention to the importance of precedence – that who or what went before, profoundly influences what happens now. This sounds axiomatic, yet most change programmes in organizations take as their initial assumption that the past has little importance and can be ignored and that what matters most, is to drive towards a desired future.
- In addition, our *Place* needs consideration within the structure of the organization. If it is clear where someone's place is within the system (for example, respecting leadership, functional contribution, expertise, experience and so on), then people can concentrate on their work and not interfere in others' responsibilities.
- Issues that support *Belonging* also need consideration for the client or organization to thrive. In family systems, members of the family have an inalienable right to belong; in organizations, everyone has the right to belong according to the quality of their contribution. When people are devalued, ignored or forgotten about (even previous employees who have been dismissed unfairly), there are consequences for others in the system.
- Systems thrive on an equitable balance of *Exchange* between members, so in any exchange – for example, in pricing with customers, or reward and recognition packages for employees – there needs to be a balance of give and take. From this systemic perspective, over-giving can be as weakening as under-giving.

Conscience

Hellinger uses the term 'conscience' to refer to the nature of our affiliations, loyalties, bonds and belonging. So, conscience in this sense protects our membership of groups through our adherence to those groups' unspoken rules, norms and culture.

Which groups we owe loyalty to has profound systemic implications – for example, being promoted requires us to be disloyal to some extent, to the norms of the group we belonged to previously, and to embrace the norms of the level of system we are moved to. Because we are inevitably a part of many co-existing systems (for example, a family, a community, a culture, a faith group, an organization) we experience multiple loyalty-conflicts, which create a drag factor as we try to make progress towards goals.

Sometimes we are aware of where our loyalties lie, but often conscience operates at an unconscious level. We simply feel stuck. Stuckness is always related to conscience as it invites us to make an uncomfortable choice to move beyond the comfort zone of feelings that keep us loyal to one group. Therefore, growth and development are only possible if we risk being unfaithful or disloyal to the norms and mores of groups we identify with.

The Orders of Helping

The 'Orders of Helping' is a subset of Constellations theory that provides an ethical framework for supervision as well as coaching – both are forms of helping. Seen systemically, helping can strengthen, but it can also weaken: in part, because of the possibility of establishing dependency; and also, because the inner movement of wanting to help can inadvertently put us above our clients, and therefore subtly infantilize them. The resentment and resistance this might generate can subvert our heartfelt intention to be of service and can entangle us as supervisors in our clients' systems and/or reactivate unprocessed issues from our own family of origin.

Hellinger argues that the basis of all helping is the parent–child relationship. As children, we take so much from our parents that the impulse to give also develops. So, helping originates from a need to balance exchange. In personal relationships between equals such as life-partners, each gives a little bit more than they received and so happiness deepens over time through such 'give and take'. However, Hellinger (2003: 47) asserts that in professional relationships, this model of exchange is dangerous:

> [When] someone presents himself or herself as needy, then they develop a transference towards the helper, like a child towards a parent . . . Then the therapist, by behaving like a better parent, becomes an enemy of the client because a client deep down in his heart is always loyal to his parents. (Hellinger 2003: 47)

To propagate the harmony of giving and taking in professional relationships, Hellinger enumerates five heuristics that can help prevent our entanglement as supervisors and coaches, in the client situation.

- *First Order: Acknowledging our limitations*
  Sometimes we might feel compelled to give what we don't have. However, we can only give to clients what we have and only expect to receive what we really need. For example, we cannot give false promises of security or success in a journey of personal or strategic change. Giving out of our own unmet needs is rarely effective.
- *Second Order: Acknowledging the 'givens' of a situation*
  We may intervene only to the extent that the circumstances allow. Our helping gains strength when we confront and accept the limitations of the situation with our client. We lose strength when we try to do too much.
- *Third Order: Acknowledging our place as helpers*
  Helping elicits a powerful transference of parent/child. As supervisors, we need to reject being seduced into the role of parent-substitute. We fall into this 'parenting' trap, for example, when we try to over-protect our clients or fail to name a difficult truth.
- *Fourth Order: Acknowledging our clients' systemic embeddedness*
  The one who needs help is always part of a wider system and of all that has happened previously in that system. What truly helps is therefore always in service of the greater whole. We ignore this Order of Helping when we define too narrowly who needs to be considered to help resolve client difficulties.

- *Fifth Order: Acknowledging our clients just as they are*
  The basis of supervision is a respectful relationship with our client just as they are, as well as with those our client dismisses or judges. This Order of Helping therefore implies acceptance of every person just as they are. For our helping to be truly effective, therefore, we need to master two paradoxical inner movements: first, of focusing on the person we are helping while drawing back and freeing ourselves from our personal feelings and reactions to the client's story; and second, offering ourselves as supports without wanting to achieve anything specific – so we let go of our own intentions, wishes and hopes and remain unassuming.

Evaluating this approach

While Constellations is growing in popularity among coaches and supervisors, this is a controversial methodology with a meagre, critically evaluated evidence base of efficacy. All reputable practitioners would agree that the use of Constellations in supervision and coaching warrants more research. Yet the same has also been said of systemic coaching and systemic team coaching (Hawkins 2011). Some of the criticisms levelled at the approach include claims that it is too directive, too influenced by family therapy, and that the growing field of practitioners is unregulated with no objective standards of what constitutes quality.

The critical question is: what meaning and validity can be ascribed to the information brought to light by a constellation? From within the Action Research tradition (Denzin and Lincoln 2005; Etherington 2004; Reason 1998) we acknowledge that there is no 'best' way to evaluate quality when it comes to dealing with subjective accounts of experience. The supervisor as Action Researcher works *with*, not *on* the coach, and in Denzin's words (1998: 315) 'fashions meaning and interpretation out of ongoing experience'. Therefore, to ensure quality outcomes, supervisors have to immerse themselves in the lived experience of our coaches; work with information inductively and reflexively; and assemble a montage of impressions from across aspects of the system under exploration.

I am attracted to Denzin's view of evaluation as the art and craft of 'bricolage' – of constructing quality from a diversity of sources or impressions. In its ability to offer perspectives from multiple points of a system, the constellation form offers us just such diversity. In addition, the supervisor's (and coach's) commitment to work on their own patterns from their families of origin, as well as their own organizational and community systems, is essential to working cleanly with clients and assuring high-quality outcomes. Etherington (2004: 31–32) describes this form of critical reflexivity as: 'The capacity of the (supervisor) to acknowledge how their own experiences and contexts (which may be fluid and changing) inform the process and outcomes of inquiry.'

We need to ensure quality through avoiding interpretations and instead offer phenomenologically referenced observations as well as systemic hypotheses and experiments. Working without intention does not imply a casualness to the goals of the coaching contract with the client: it is rather about respectfully including and transcending them as we open solution-spaces through this work.

Ultimately, I believe this approach is best evaluated pragmatically. Broussine (2008) ascribes weight to questions such as, whether the supervision is, 'giving insight into the authentic lived experience in the social system being investigated'. I also believe in the value of aesthetic criteria – the degree to which Constellations supervision can provide a vividness of experience that shifts perceptions and actions; the degree to which coaches and their clients feel enlivened or settled by the work; the felt degree of clarity, focus, goodness of fit and sense of being more connected, that can come through this way of working.

Guidance for further learning and research

What does the supervisor and coach need to learn to practise Constellations, and what research directions might move this approach forwards? As with other approaches, training in the underlying principles and theory base of Constellations is important, as well as gaining experience of constellating. It is also helpful to look beyond our usual ways of considering skills as learned capabilities, to the more demanding orientation of stilling the mind, taking in the whole situation and letting connections and possibilities emerge from a stance of 'creative indifference' (Friedlaender 1918) and not knowing. This is perhaps the greatest challenge to those new to this way of working. The process of putting our experience and skills aside and emptying ourselves so that we are guided by the constellation takes time.

Related to this, another of the more demanding aspects of this approach is for the supervisor or coach to work with his or her whole self – their powers of cognition, emotion, sensation and intuition. Gestalt coaches such as Siminovitch (2017) and Bluckert (2016) talk about the development of 'presence' and the use of 'self as instrument', referring to the need of the coach (and I would add, supervisor) to be authentic, open, grounded, mindful and present, and to use all of the personal resources available to them through their life experience. This is a particularly demanding orientation as it calls for both strategic and intimate forms of relating, as well as skills in working phenomenologically and an acuity to holding the vagaries of the client situation.

There has not yet been any comparative or critical evaluation of coaching or supervision outcomes derived from Constellations work. There is therefore a great need for research into which aspects of the work add value and at what levels of the system. I believe it is important to track not only 'individual' client outcomes, but as Hawkins and Turner (2020) note, outcomes all along the systemic value-chain. Does Constellations improve the health and well-being of people and relationships, and if so how, are crucial questions.

Questions for reflection

- What added value to you as a coach or supervisor, might be the inclusion of the constellations mapping methodology?
- What is it like for you to be intentionless in your supervision or coaching practice?

- In terms of diagnosis and intervention, how much of a resource to you in your coaching work do you think the five systemic ordering principles could be?
- How might the 'Orders of Helping' enable you to develop your stance when working with clients?

Further sources

Horn, K.P. and Brick, R. (2005) *Invisible Dynamics*. Heidelberg: Carl-Auer. This is one of the first books that sketched the application of Constellations at work. The focus of this book is not specifically on coaching, but on wider business consultancy and the application of the Constellations methodology to management and teams.

Stam, J.J. and Schreider, B. (2016) *Systemic Coaching*. Amsterdam: Systemic Books. This is a practical guide to applying this systemic coaching approach without setting up a constellation. The book is helpful in discussing the stance of the constellating coach and includes useful sections on organizational trauma and systemic symptoms.

Whittington, J. (2016) *Systemic Coaching & Constellations*. London: Kogan Page. This is a very accessible and comprehensive primer for understanding Constellations theory, method and practice, specifically as it relates to coaching. Helpful in identifying how to work with 'tabletop' and 'workshop' forms of constellating.

References

Bluckert, P. (2016) Presence and the intentional use of self as an instrument of change, in *Courage and Spark*. Available at: https://courageandspark.com/presence-and-the-intentional-use-of-self-as-instrument-of-change/ (accessed 20 July 2020).

Broussine, M. (2008) The seductive qualities of critical awareness, in M. Broussine (ed.) *Creative Methods in Organisational Research*. London: Sage.

Critchley, B., King, K. and Higgins, J. (2007) *Organisational Consulting: A Relational Perspective*. London: Middlesex University Press.

Denzin, N.K. (1998) The art and politics of interpretation, in N.K. Denzin and Y.S. Lincoln (eds) *Collecting and Interpreting Qualitative Materials*. London: Sage.

Denzin, N.K. and Lincoln, Y.S. (2005) *The Sage Handbook of Qualitative Research*. Thousand Oaks, CA: Sage.

Etherington, K. (2004) *Becoming a Reflexive Researcher – Using Our Selves in Research*. London: Jessica Kingsley.

Friedlaender, S. (1918) Schöpferische Indifferenz. Vol. 10 of *Gesammelte Schriften*, Geerken, H. and Thiel, D. Originally published in 1918 with a second, revised edition in 1926. Munich: Ernst Reinhardt Verlag.

Fromm, E. (1995) *The Art of Loving*. New York: Thorsens.

Gendlin, E. (2003) *Focusing. How to Gain Direct Access to Your Body's Knowledge*. London: Rider.

Grint, K. (2010) Wicked problems and clumsy solutions: the role of leadership, in S. Brooks and K. Grint (eds) *The New Public Leadership Challenge*. London: Palgrave Macmillan.

Hawkins, P. (2011) Systemic approaches to supervision, in T. Bachkirova, P. Jackson and D. Clutterbuck (eds) *Coaching & Mentoring in Supervision: Theory and Practice*. London: Open University Press.

Hawkins, P. and Turner, E. (2020) *Systemic Coaching: Delivering Value Beyond the Individual*. London: Routledge.

Hellinger, B. (1991) *For Love to Flourish: The Systemic Preconditions for Love*. A lecture by Bert Hellinger. Munich. Translated by Beaumont, H. Spring, 1994.

Hellinger, B. (1998) *Love's Hidden Symmetry: What Makes Love Work in Relationships*. Phoenix, AZ: Zeig, Tucker & Co.

Hellinger, B. (2003) The art of helping, *Systemic Solutions Bulletin*, 4: 47–50.

Horn, K.P. and Brick, R. (2005) *Invisible Dynamics: Systemic Constellations in Organisations and in Business*. Heidelberg: Carl-Auer.

Isaacs, W. (1999) *Dialogue and the Art of Thinking Together*. New York: Currency Doubleday.

Maturana, H. and Bunnell, P. (1999) The biology of business: love expands intelligence, *Reflections*, 1: 2.

Reason, P. (1998) *Human Inquiry in Action: Developments in New Paradigm Research*. London: Sage.

Siminovitch, D. (2017) *A Gestalt Coaching Primer: The Path Towards Awareness IQ*. Boston, MA: Gestalt Coaching Works.

Stam, J.J. and Schreider, B. (2016) *Systemic Coaching Without the Constellation*. Amsterdam: Systemic Books.

Urschel, M.D. (2020) A systemic approach to supervision, in M. Lucas (ed.) *101 Coaching Supervision Techniques, Approaches, Enquiries and Experiments*. London: Routledge.

Whittington, J. (2016) *Systemic Coaching and Constellations*. London: Kogan Page.

18 Choosing our supervision interventions

Michelle Lucas

Introduction

As the practice of coaching supervision has developed, it has been subject to many influences. Initially borrowing approaches from helping professions, coaching supervision is now a distinct and recognized field of practice. The book *101 Coaching Supervision Techniques, Enquiries, Approaches and Experiments* (Lucas 2020) is organized into 10 philosophies clarifying how they are applied in coaching supervision. Some coaching supervisors describe their approach as eclectic, drawing from a range of existing philosophies, approaches and models. Some position themselves as subject matter experts offering a deep understanding of one particular discipline or school of thought. Others develop their own bespoke approach to supervision. No matter what theoretical base or framework informs a coaching supervisor's work, they must somehow decide what will best serve their supervisee in the moment. That is the question that this chapter seeks to address.

In a comprehensive review of the coaching supervision literature (Bachkirova et al. 2020), only two of the 114 items reviewed explored the supervisor's challenge of selecting the most appropriate supervision intervention. Moral and Lamy (2016: 168) implied that this selection is 'often an intuitive decision'. Later, Lamy and Moral (2017) identified numerous methodologies to analyse the ethical dilemmas brought to supervision. They concluded that 'the work to select the best method for a given type of dilemma has not been done yet and is an open area of research' (2017: 7).

Throughout this chapter I use the notion of an 'intervention' as the focus for the supervisor's decision. This term comes from the second eye of Hawkins and Smith's (2006) seven-eyed model. The intervention relates to the technique, model or question the practitioner makes in the moment with their client. In the context of this systemic model, the coach's intervention influences, and is influenced by, the other six perspectives in a constantly evolving manner. Here, applying similar thinking to supervision, I consider what the supervisor attends to as they decide how to intervene.

The decision on how to intervene is complex. The supervisor role has many facets (mentor, sounding board, critical friend, coaching the coach, ethical guide) and the presenting issue may not fit neatly into the recognized formative, normative, restorative purpose of supervision (Proctor 1986). The structure proposed here simplifies what is, essentially, fluid and uncertain. Applicable to both individual and group supervision, this mental map can be used in the moment of a supervision session or at least upon reflection. The structure is influenced by the three Cs proposed by Faire (2013): Contract, Competence and Client's best interest.

The context for her model is to help the coach decide if the work sits in the territory of coaching or somewhere else. These same three elements are useful in the context of coaching supervision as the supervisor considers what intervention will serve their supervisee in the moment.

1. What have we Contracted for?
2. What do we have the Competence to deliver?
3. What is in the Client's best interest?

The body of this chapter is therefore organized into these three sections, plus an additional one;

4. What is possible given our particular working environment?

In each section, I weave in real examples to illustrate how these questions may manifest and how they can be resolved in the supervision work.

What do we contract for?

Contracting is much more than a formal contract outlining the practicalities of the supervision arrangement. When establishing the contract, some supervisees explicitly seek a supervisor who works in a manner consistent with their own coach training, others deliberately select a supervisor from a different theoretical base to provide challenge and new thinking. The contract may also be implicit. How the supervisor expresses their work on their website, or the style or methods they used in a sample session may have contributed to the selection decision.

Our working style is therefore a critical part of the supervision contract. How and where the supervisor trained, their role models, and whether the supervisor is accredited with a professional coaching body, will influence how they articulate their style of working. Regardless of any formal requirement, describing our work clearly enables supervisees to understand what range of interventions the supervisor might make and how they are likely to experience supervision.

As the supervisor grows their repertoire, additional approaches might shift the supervisee's experience of the work. Where an intervention could be experienced as different to our default supervision style, re-contracting will be necessary. An example of this occurred when delivering group supervision to internal coaches. Typically, the supervision dialogue had mirrored the cognitive bias in the organizational culture. However, I noticed that the current issue might benefit from a broader and more emotional exploration. So, I prepared the group for how this might be experienced and re-contracted to gain their permission for a different kind of work.

Coaching supervision is often described as a collaborative relationship. Yet, in practice, the dynamic can be unbalanced. The supervisee typically holds some vulnerability, bringing something that lies outside of their awareness. Conversely, the supervisor's role comes imbued with positional power. Many supervisees implicitly trust the supervisor to propose a way of working. However, if we slide into a way of working without involving the supervisee, this is inconsistent with empowering the supervisee to be the architect of their own reflection. As we contract, it is helpful to identify exactly how we will generate a co-created exploration. Supervision may have an educative component, and so in my own practice, I contract to offering my insight transparently, I offer choice in what interventions we might use, and explore their sense of where each might take them. Enquiring how we might work together tends to have a liberating effect; once started, the supervisee typically creates their own avenues of enquiry. Over time this approach deepens the supervisee's understanding of what they need/don't need from their supervisor.

Engaging in this level of re-contracting can have an impact on the flow of the session. However, slowing down, explaining alternative ways of working is essential if we value our supervisee's informed consent. As Faire (2013: 14) says, 'if we haven't contracted for it, we have no business going there'.

What do we have the Competence to deliver?

The notion of Competence as outlined by Faire (2013) contains three elements:

- *Competency* – Having the underpinning knowledge and skill to deliver supervision
- *Capability* – The cumulative experience generated from applying our supervision knowledge / skills
- *Capacity* – Having a level of energetic presence that enables us to notice, hold and contain the complexities / paradoxes that emerge from the supervision process.

Competence is typically gained through training. Each practitioner has their own sense of what territory they are equipped to travel with their supervisee and when referral will be necessary. The challenge of clarifying competence is perhaps greater for eclectic supervisors, whose breadth of expertise could be mistaken as specialism in multiple domains. For example, my background in psychology does not make me a psychodynamic practitioner. Clarifying our areas of competence is an ethical issue and, with a new supervisee, is perhaps our first opportunity to show vulnerability and build trust. An absence of transparency would cause confusion and undermine the integrity of both our coaching supervision community and the specialist area which we are ill-equipped to represent.

While it may be true that most coaching supervisors are experienced coaches, some supervisees make generous assumptions about the extent of our knowledge. Many times, a supervisee has asked me for specific advice on how to improve the use of a technique that I have not used. The lack of specific technical expertise is almost inevitable when working with a large portfolio of supervisees, the range of their individual practices is likely to be far broader than that of the supervisor. As Moral and Lamy (2016: 178) identify, 'the supervisor needs to be able to help supervisees who use reference frameworks that he (the supervisor) does not know well'. However, there are also times when the supervisor will know the technique. While sharing technical expertise can be a legitimate use of our developmental role, the supervisor must be mindful of their motivation for the intervention. Responding from an expert position is likely to encourage dependence, reducing the supervisee's resourcefulness and creativity. Rather than showcasing our technical mastery, the supervisor's value is to enquire what might have been happening relationally and systemically, in those critical moments which are brought for supervision.

Capability requires more than the acquisition of information and knowledge, it requires practice. For example, when trying a new recipe, we learn through experience that we to need to adjust our oven temperature and season according to taste. The delivery of coaching and coaching supervision is no different. To maintain credibility, we need to have practised and experienced an approach. Only then can we know how to articulate an intervention comfortably and sense how our supervisee(s) might respond. The challenge is finding an environment in which we can first practise this extended repertoire.

If we choose to do this directly with our own clients, then it becomes a matter for the contract. For example, in my own practice, there are a few supervisees where we have developed a level of trust and have contracted that I may introduce an approach that I have not used before. Perhaps, paradoxically, their permission makes me more vigilant. I am conscious that any one individual's openness and readiness might shift from session to session. I am alert to hesitations in response to these yet untested approaches. I offer flexibility and variations, which allows individuals to stay in their stretch, rather than their panic zone. It is not prudent to rely solely on the quality and longevity of the supervision relationship. The underpinning trust could easily be broken should experimentation dent the sense of psychological safety. Essentially, the supervisor must weigh up the ethical appropriateness of prioritizing their own developmental needs.

Capacity considers how effectively the practitioner will hold the space for clients. The supervisor considers whether given everything that they are managing, they can maintain an appropriate level of presence for their supervisee(s). Broussine (2000) describes capacity as 'being able to hold complexity, ambiguity and paradox in order to be effective'. His focus was local authority chief executives and yet this also describes the role of coaching supervisors. As supervisors we are working with multiple systems, our clients may be projecting their own or their clients' unfinished business onto us, we may need to work with resistance and/or defence mechanisms in our clients, their clients, and simultaneously in ourselves. A fundamental ingredient of supervision is the potential to work with the parallel process. However, if we are not fully present, the supervisor is more likely to be drawn into the parallel process, and less likely to notice it. The bar is high in supervision; we need to be selfish about our self-care. It may be appropriate to start the session or take a moment within a session, to ground ourselves as well as our supervisee(s) before we move on.

Supervising a group requires multiple streams of attention. We need to consider the supervision content, the process, the group dynamics and our own here-and-now experiences. There is a lot to hold and work with. As my group supervision practice grew, I started to question whether I was genuinely giving each stream equal attention. At the same time, I noticed that the more established the group became the more able they were to manage the content of the supervision enquiry for themselves. For longstanding groups, we now contract specifically for them to manage the content and process. That frees up my capacity to work at a meta-level; offering targeted personal developmental feedback and having the bandwidth to fully notice group dynamics and parallel process. Working with these groups has taught me that while a supervisor's capacity may be limited, the capacity for supervision can be multiplied when we acknowledge that capacity is not just held in the supervisor, it is held in the group.

What is in the clients' best interest?

The supervisor has a duty of care to two clients – one directly (the supervisee) and one indirectly (the supervisee's client). Indeed, the normative role of the supervisor reminds us that it is our indirect client that is the ultimate beneficiary of the supervision work.

With our direct client (the supervisee), the interventions that we make take into consideration the developmental stage of the practitioner, both as a coach and as a supervisee. As a seasoned practitioner, it is easy to forget what it was like in our early days of coaching practice, consumed by performance anxiety and eager to fill our coaching toolbox. When I work with MA Coaching and Mentoring students, they contract with their clients that they are in training. This context gives me permission to hold my normative role lightly and instead to package my interventions appropriate to their developmental stage.

As a supervisor, we are aware that the parallel process affects the efficacy of a practitioner. For example, they come to supervision stuck with a stuck client. Of all the avenues of enquiry that we could travel, the supervisor considers what the supervisee is ready for. While the practitioner's stuckness may be the result of parallel process, unless we are working with an experienced coach, this is unlikely to be the best point of entry. With a novice practitioner we might first need to work at a restorative and relational level, reassuring them that they have made some good choices. We might then work with a more developmental intervention, considering how they might leverage past experience, and harnessing what they know in hindsight. Working at a more basic level often reveals a lack of rigour in their coaching practice, which once highlighted serves to generate a more thoughtful and ultimately more ethical practitioner. My sense is that if I meet the supervisee where they are developmentally, it serves to enhance their experience of supervision as a collaborative endeavour. As they continue with supervision, I feel sure that there will be plenty more opportunities for us to notice and work with the parallel process.

The reverse is also true, as when a practitioner is lacking resourcefulness, it is common for their thinking to slip back to earlier developmental levels. A coach who might ordinarily work at Hawkins and Smith's (2006) Level 4 ('Process-in-context-centred') may present their supervision enquiry at an earlier stage . . . asking 'Did I do OK?' (Level 1 – 'Self-centred'), or 'How might this impact on the client relationship?' (Level 3 – 'Process-centred'). While a restorative intervention might be needed to begin the work, we would not be serving our supervisee or their client well if we don't also test whether they have the capacity, with support, to engage in a wider or deeper enquiry.

Being an experienced coach is not the same as being an experienced supervisee. While some practitioners have deep client experience and are mature thinkers, without substantive engagement in supervision, they may lack maturity in their use of the supervision space. Research by Sheppard (2017) highlighted that as supervisees deepen their experience of the supervision process, they are more able to co-create the supervision relationship, there is a reduction in fear and shame and they are more able to welcome their vulnerability and learning.

Supervisors who position themselves as client-centred will give the supervisee the respect to determine how they use the supervision time. Sheppard (2017) describes this as 'supervisee-led supervision'. My respect deepens when I believe the supervisee is choosing from an informed position. For example, I will invite supervisees to describe the case they are bringing, and then ask, 'And what do you need from me?' or 'And how would you like to use the group?'. Their response to this question provides me with data as to where they are in their supervision expertise and informs how I might intervene appropriately.

First experiences of supervision can be seen as an opportunity to gather new tools and extend the use of familiar ones. These supervisees respond by suggesting that I (or the group) share experiences of managing similar situations. This generates a CPD quality to the supervision. To help broaden supervisees' choices I provide a handout offering a variety of possible techniques to work with. Over time supervisees start to notice how those different techniques shape the supervision dialogue, enabling them to select an approach which will illuminate their enquiry.

On occasion a supervisee's choice of approach feels at odds with their maturity. The supervisor can help raise awareness of the likely extent and impact of the supervision discussion. Effectively, this prompts a level of challenge, questioning whether their choice is legitimate or an easy option. It also prompts curiosity around why a safer kind of exploration is appearing. Perhaps it is a signal that the supervisee is avoiding the real work and that there is some restorative work to do, or it may indicate a difficulty with the supervision relationship or the contract.

In established relationships, the supervisor helps the supervisee consider their motivation for their question and/or chosen approach. For example, when the supervisee recognizes that their request to share experiences reflected a need to normalize their reaction, the exploration can focus on this underpinning need, rather than the content of the case. This provokes a richer supervision discussion and culminates in value for all their clients, not just the one they brought to supervision.

Eventually, the mature supervisee becomes focused and assertive in what they need. Typically, they have already subjected their question to considerable independent reflection, and they can almost anticipate their supervisor's or peers' reply. For example, a supervisee at an advanced group said, 'I'm not looking for reassurance, I want your thoughts and insights why even though I know it was good enough, I did not feel this at the time.'

The supervisor's duty of care for the supervisee's client reflects our professional assurance responsibilities. It is a conundrum because, as Spinelli (2020: 125) points out, 'the client who is the primary focus of the over-seeing supervision encounter is not actually present'. The supervisor is working with the coach's memory of the session; we might check what the coach recalls of their client's response, but the supervisor is working with partial information. However, I have come to notice (and trust) my visceral reaction when something feels incongruent. The challenge is, how to bring that to the supervisee's attention in a way that protects the coaching client, demonstrates my respect for my supervisee's choices, while both trusting my own reaction and staying open to the possibility that I am mistaken. Before making an intervention, I assume that the supervisee was working with good intent. This sparks my curiosity where I can work from a position of neutrality. Second, I work transparently with my reaction and invite the supervisee to help me understand things more fully. Almost always this type of double-sided exploration generates new insight and a joint clarity about appropriate next steps.

What is possible given our particular working environment?

This section encourages the supervisor to consider whether they have an environment that fully enables the work. Factors under consideration are time, space and the impact of working remotely.

There are two distinctly different supervisor styles in managing time. In the first, time is divided equally among those present or between agenda items. Essentially, the time dictates how far the supervision dialogue unfolds. Alternatively, it is the unfolding of the supervision issue that dictates the time taken. Regardless of the supervisor's preference for time management, a sense of whether the chosen intervention will fit the time available is needed. Hawkins and Smith's (2006) seven-eyed model offers a useful illustration – it is a complex model that can shift the supervisor towards an expert role. So, the supervisor needs to consider both the time required to generate understanding of the model, and the time needed to work with the issue.

The supervisor will be cognisant of whether, in the time available, they can let an intervention unfold at its own pace. Where a technique would need to be truncated it may be prudent not to continue. One example is a perceptual positions exercise, like the two chairs experiment. Here, one needs to set it up fully, close it out appropriately, and include a learning review where the supervisee processes their experience. So, even if there were sufficient time to execute the core of the technique, some additional time is needed in case unresolved issues are surfaced.

The supervisor may also consider whether the mood evoked by the space is congruent with the work ahead of them. For example, when internal coaches enter a room with a circle of chairs, the sense of anticipation is palpable. The layout seems to signal that they are entering a more therapeutic territory. Depending on the group concerned, the supervisor might leverage or counterbalance this ambience. For example, with an existing group working in the context of significant organizational change, I embraced the therapeutic impact of the chair circle, and chose an embodied and systemic approach for the arrival activity. This facilitated the voicing of their frustration and disorientation; it quickly created a readiness and a shared vulnerability, and the work began at a deep level. Conversely, working with a new group in an imposing space, I started with a skoosh-ball activity, inviting everyone to share something practical and recording answers on a flipchart. Intentionally, this set the scene for a more familiar training environment and drew them gently towards the supervision work.

In organizations, appropriate meeting spaces can be hard to find, requiring the supervisor to adapt their approach. For example, in a room with fixed furniture, constellation work may require the use of smaller scale objects. In a space that feels restrictive, it can be a good idea to take a walk. Easier with individual supervision, but even in a group, supervisees can pair up and reflect on a question while getting air or coffee. This can freshen up both the energy and the group dynamics. Additionally, choosing a different chair upon return encourages a different perspective and disrupts any implied positional dynamics. Where the room is small and/or the supervision experience is feeling overly intense, the energy can be shifted by offering a short individual exercise. A free-writing or journaling activity like those outlined by Holder (2019: 130–138) can have the effect of reconnecting with oneself in what is otherwise a crowded (intellectual or physical) space.

Remote working is commonplace; nonetheless, consideration needs to be given to how to replicate work typically delivered on a face-to-face basis. Where an intervention relies on physical resources, additional preparation may be needed. For example, I send supervisees a resource pack, items like Lego, picture cards and dice, which cannot be shared digitally. I use a flipchart marker when sharing drawings so that they are visible via webcam. I have also created shared folders on Dropbox and prepared digital whiteboards, giving quick access to key models and images. The choice of virtual platform and the level of functionality available continues to expand; however, we need to be mindful that a highly technical intervention could be a distraction. For example, when using a sophisticated digital whiteboard with a group, difficulties in accessing and navigating the board prompted anxiety, overshadowing what was intended as a reflective activity.

Practical adaptations aside, the most important adaptation we can make is re-examining the paradigm of how we add value. A common assumption is that it is necessary to see what the supervisee is creating as they create it. This is so easily achieved when working in person, that we hardly notice it. However, what we see may lead us to intervene with questions that are for our understanding. When working remotely, this assumption quickly surfaces, as we cannot witness the supervisee's work as it unfolds. Rather than an impediment, this is an invitation to intervene differently. Our questions will become cleaner, provoking the supervisee to notice more for themselves. Further we are better positioned to pay attention to the supervisee's process. For example, when the supervisee is drawing, not seeing their creation means I am free to observe how they engage with the work prompting enquiry at a meta-level. In turn this invites the supervisee to move away from content and to notice how they are experiencing the work.

Working with and without the framework

At the outset of the chapter we positioned the three Cs structure as a simplification. Indeed, the work might lie outside our contract; we might not be the best person or in the best space (both literally and metaphorically) to help. However, sometimes the supervisor needs to do something because the supervisee is in distress. Re-contracting in those moments is both essential and difficult as often the supervisee is not well resourced. Maintaining our ethical responsibility to do no harm, our minimum intervention will serve to mobilize sufficient personal capacity such that they can access the support they need.

As we journey towards mastery, many of us seek to work easefully and intuitively. However, an aspiration to work constantly in this state requires caution. Unless we are working with 'Conscious Competence' (Burch 1970), how can we consider what is truly right for our client? The chapter's four-fold structure intends to provide a framework for reflection. Initially, it is useful to facilitate a practice review ('reflection-on-action') (Schön 1983). Once familiarized, it can become integrated into a supervisor's in-the-moment considerations, in a consciously competent way ('reflection-in-action') (Schön 1983). Through deepening our reflective practice, the wisdom of our external supervisor gradually develops the voice of our own 'internal supervisor' (Casement 1985). As we contemplate our interventions, this voice acts as our compass, navigating a route that helps us serve our direct and indirect clients well.

Guidance for further learning and research

As stated earlier there is minimal existing research on this element of the supervisory encounter. Future research might treat group and individual supervision separately. Moral and Lamy (2016) make connections between participative group supervision and leveraging collective intelligence. Their methodology highlights the level of complexity involved when studying group processes. Phenomenological research, particularly case studies, may embrace rather than reduce the complexity. Individual supervision research would have less variables to manage. Given supervision's developmental nature, longitudinal studies mapping significant moments in a coach's development to critical moments in individual supervision would seem appropriate. However, any research needs to consider why it is helpful to understand more about the supervisor's choice of intervention. I do not see this as a means of reassuring supervisors that they have chosen the 'best' intervention, or to offer supervisors a formula for improved supervisee satisfaction. I would be interested in:

- How does a supervisor balance quality assurance for the coaching client, while working in a supervisee-led way?
- What do supervisees notice about how the supervisor articulates their work and how the supervisor practices?
- What ethical issues arise when supervisors experiment with a new technique on a live client issue?
- What difference do virtual platforms make to the quality of supervision work?

Answers to these research questions might serve to illustrate greater complexity and dynamism in the supervisor's selected intervention. I hope it would reveal more variables that will serve to confuse us and, in doing so, keep us at our learning edge.

> **Questions for reflection**
>
> - How explicitly do I seek permission for the interventions I make?
> - How can I share my wisdom in a way that empowers the supervisee to uncover their own?
> - What might I notice that no one else is positioned to see?
> - How would I intervene if I knew my own supervisor was watching?

Further resources

Clutterbuck, D., Whitaker, C. and Lucas, M. (2016) *Coaching Supervision: A Practical Guide for Supervisees*. Abingdon: Routledge. A principle of the current chapter is the co-created nature of the supervision partnership. Chapter 5 of this text supports supervisees to play a pro-active role in their supervision relationship.

Lucas, M. (2020) *101 Coaching Supervision Techniques, Approaches, Enquiries and Experiments*. Abingdon: Routledge. Aimed primarily at the supervisor, this book encourages the practitioner to build their repertoire through both respecting the underpinning philosophy and adapting techniques for their own style.

Turner, T., Lucas, M. and Whitaker, C. (2018) *Peer Supervision in Coaching and Mentoring*. Abingdon: Routledge. While the context of this book is peer supervision, Chapter 2 takes a look at reflective practice. There is more detail of Broussine's three Cs on pp. 27–29.

References

Bachkirova, T., Jackson, P., Hennig, C. and Moral, M. (2020) Supervision in coaching: systematic literature review, *International Coaching Psychology Review*, 15(2): 31–53.

Broussine, M. (2000) The capacities needed by local authority chief executives, *International Journal of Public Sector Management*, 13(6): 498–507.

Burch, N. (1970) *The Four Stages of Learning Any New Skill*. Solana Beach, CA: Gordon Training Institute.

Casement, P. (1985) *On Learning from the Patient*. Abingdon: Routledge.

Faire, M. (2013) The three Cs of professional practice, *AICTP Journal*, November, Issue 6: 13–15.

Hawkins, P. and Smith, N. (2006) *Coaching, Mentoring and Organisational Consultancy: Supervision and Development*. Maidenhead: Open University Press.

Holder, J. (2019) Creative forms of reflective and expressive writing in coaching supervision, in E. Turner and S. Palmer (eds) *The Heart of Coaching Supervision: Working with Reflection and Self-Care*. Routledge: Abingdon.

Lamy, F. and Moral, M. (2017) *Stretching Ethical Dilemmas: A Creative Tool for Supervisors*. Presented at the 7th International Coaching Supervision Conference, Oxford Brookes University, 13 May 2017.

Lucas, M. (ed.) (2020) *101 Coaching Supervision Techniques, Approaches, Enquiries and Experiments*. Abingdon: Routledge.

Moral, M. and Lamy, F. (2016) *Selecting a Supervision Process in Collective Supervision*. In Proceedings of the 6th Mentoring & Coaching Research Conference, Eotvos Lorand University, Budapest, Hungary, 6–7 July 2016.

Proctor, B. (1986) Supervision: a co-operative exercise in accountability, in A. Marken and M. Payne (eds) *Enabling & Ensuring*. Leicester: Leicester National Youth Bureau/Council for Education and Training in Youth and Community Work.

Schön, D. (1983) *The Reflective Practitioner: How Professionals Think in Action*. London: Temple Smith.

Sheppard, L. (2017) How coaching supervisees help and hinder their supervision, *International Journal of Evidence Based Coaching & Mentoring*, 15: 111–122.

Spinelli, E. (2020) An existential approach to coaching supervision, in M. Lucas (ed.) *101 Coaching Supervision Techniques, Approaches, Enquiries and Experiments*. Maidenhead: Routledge.

Section 4

Contexts and practical modalities of supervision

19

Supervising in groups

Eliat Aram and Coreene Archer

Introduction

This chapter is called 'supervising in groups' to refer mainly to the space offered to consider each supervisee's client system and their dynamics. Importantly, it also refers to supervising groups, which is where the group itself, as a whole, provides a useful lens to study the dynamics between clients and coaches/consultants within their systemic context.

The Tavistock model, which we will describe in this chapter, lends itself well to supervision in groups for two main reasons: the basic premise is that all individuals exist only in context and that their context comprises different types and compositions of groups. The concept of the 'group-as-a-whole', which is different to conceptualizing the group as comprising a certain number of individuals, means that through the power, authority and leadership relationships within the group, the group develops its own unique identity. The group's identity is different, although not separate from, the individuals who make it up. In supervision, therefore, there will be merit in exploring the dynamics of the group as a tool to understand the dynamics that may occur in the supervisees' own contexts. Relevant to understanding the concept of the group-as-a-whole are the concept from Gestalt theory that the whole is more than the sum of its parts; the notion of 'parallel process'; and the concept of 'fractal' from complexity theory.

In this chapter we first look at the theory of groups and the underpinning principles that help us understand the nature of groups and how they function. We draw on several perspectives and summarize with the Tavistock understanding of groups. We then follow with application to practice, with particular attention to exploring the dynamics of difference. Increasingly, supervisors are called to work with diverse groups and to help them explore the different aspects of their identity and the difficult emotions that they can evoke. This can range from obvious differences, such as ethnicity, a disability or gender, to hidden differences including sexuality or belief systems, or differences that can manifest in more subtle ways, such as a difference in discipline or expertise. In this chapter we seek to explore how to work with these dynamics and emotions such as envy, anger, hatred or desire, which can lead to what is often experienced as difficult conversations. We close the chapter with recommendations for further learning and research.

Understanding the relatedness between the individual and the group from psychoanalytic, group analytic, Gestalt and complexity lenses

In psychoanalytic thinking, groups are interpersonal relationships, which are influenced by complex emotional forces and unconscious wishes. In translating his individual psychology into mass psychology, Freud held that members of a group shared an emotional experience, which was different to the experiences of the individuals in isolation (Gabriel 1999). Freud argued that the mental processes of individuals changed significantly when they became part of a crowd in that the emotional and unconscious processes within crowds predominated over any forces of reason. It was the leaders who held the group together mainly through their role in the unconscious life of the group. He viewed groups as a regressive state of child-like dependency of group members on their leader, which could only be moderated by organization and task (Le Bon 1960).

For Klein (1948, 1975) and Bion (1961), the individual's attitude towards group membership was fundamentally ambivalent, based on a fantasy of the group as an overwhelming entity like the mother. There is a basic conflict between the individual and the group. On the one hand, there is an individual's commitment to themselves in the form of their aspirations, needs, beliefs and all that makes them unique. On the other hand, there is an individual's yearning to belong, to be part of, to dissolve into, and to become anonymous in a group, that is, to be the opposite of what makes them unique and different (Gibbard et al. 1974; Rice 1965; Slater 1966).

In his exploration of group dynamics, Bion (1961) refers to a process whereby individuals, conversing in their attempts to do the work, are influencing and changing the character of the group-as-a-whole, which in turn is shaping the individuals' assumptions and beliefs in relation to the group and to other groups. According to Bion, the group is part of what we, as individuals, are.

The central notion in Foulkes' theory of Group Analysis is that of the matrix. 'By matrix is meant a common communication ground which is shared' (Foulkes 1990: 291). 'The social matrix can be thought of as a network in quite the same way as the brain is a network of fibres and cells which together form a complex unit . . .' (Foulkes and Anthony 1957: 258). Foulkes emphasized the creative forces in groups and communication in therapy as the route to health. In addition to his psychoanalytic training, Foulkes was highly influenced by the work of the sociologist Norbert Elias, particularly Elias' move away from the split between nature and nurture. He saw the social as a form of nature and selves or personalities as emerging in social interaction.

In some of his writing, Foulkes prioritized the group over the individual, the social over the biological, and the whole over the part. He said that there was no 'self' outside of relationships and, therefore, no individual without the group. The group was there prior to the individual and the individual was social through and through to the core (Foulkes 1964). However, he repeatedly made it clear that this in no way denied the existence of individuals, saying that it is individuals who are treated in group therapy. In essence, he saw the individual and the group as inseparable, but he often moved between the two. Dalal (1998), in his analysis of Foulkes' thought, described him as having two strands, which he called the orthodox Foulkes and the radical Foulkes.

Gestalt contributions to thinking about groups come from the notion of the 'field'. The 'unified field' (Parlett 1997) represents the 'web of interconnection between person and situation, self and others, organism and environment, the individual and the communal' (p. 16). Groups are therefore viewed as processes of figure-ground formation and destruction within the context of a field. The field is, therefore, the context within which people interact.

The concept of 'the group-as-a-whole' and its contribution to the practice of supervision

The Tavistock Institute's approach to understanding and working with groups originated with the work of Bion, who was convinced of the importance of considering, not only the individual, but also the group of which the individual is a member. In the 1940s, Bion conducted a series of small study groups at the Tavistock Institute of Human Relations, reporting his experiences in a series of articles for the journal *Human Relations* and later, in a book entitled *Experiences in Groups* (Bion 1961).

Viewing the group as a collective entity evolved into a method. In a series of conferences from 1957 the focus of study shifted from the roles that individuals assume in groups to the dynamics of leadership and authority relations in groups. It was accepted that individuals cannot be understood or changed, outside the context of the groups of which they are members. This idea shaped the design of the group relations conference as a teaching modality. Under the influence of Ken Rice, Tavistock groupwork in the 1960s focused on group relations and moved away from attempts at personal growth and the study of interpersonal dynamics.

The basic principle: a cluster of people becomes a group when (i) interaction between members occurs, (ii) members' awareness of their common relationship develops, and (iii) a common group task emerges.

Various (hidden or unconscious) forces can operate to produce a group: an external threat, collective threat, collective regressive behaviour, or attempts to satisfy needs for security, safety, dependency and affection. A more deliberate force is the conscious choice of individuals to band together to perform a task.

The group-as-a-whole requires a perceptual shift on the part of the observer, a blurring of the individuals' separateness, and seeing the collective interactions generated by group members. We focus on the group as foreground and individuals become background.

The group-as-a-whole approach can be summarized as follows:

- The primary task of any group is what it must do to survive.
- The group has a life of its own only as a consequence of the fantasies and projections of its members.
- The group 'uses' its members in the service of its primary task.

The behaviour of any group member at any moment is the expression of his or her own needs, history and behavioural patterns, and the needs, history and behavioural patterns of the group.

Whatever the group is doing or talking about, the group is always talking about itself, reflecting itself. Understanding the process of the group provides group members with heightened awareness and the ability to make previously unavailable choices about their identities and functions in a group setting.

This fits well with the idea of the group as a fractal of its wider context. The concept of a fractal comes from the complexity theories and defines a fractal as a self-similar pattern, so that it is simultaneously expressing itself as both unique and similar (Prigogine and Allen 1982; Goodwin 1994). The idea here is that at any level of the system that one is engaged in – in an organization it could be the board, a department, a unit – one will see a behavioural pattern, a conscious or possibly hidden or unconscious dynamic which is self-similar yet also unique. There is an example of fractal reproduction in Box 19.1.

Box 19.1

A large R&D technology company, with which we were involved as consultants, has structured itself with two presidents – one was the CEO and one was the Chief Technology Officer. Over time it has become apparent that the CEO is also the outward face of the company, the diplomatic one, the one with public relations awareness, whereas the CTO is the technological brain, clumsy in words and perhaps even aggressive, a 'genius' in the words of his colleagues and hence forgiven for his big mouth. So the pair developed a pattern of behaviour whereby the CTO would be kept away as much as possible from the public eye and every now and again as he put his foot in it, the CEO would step in to limit the potential damage to reputation or relationships both externally and with colleagues. Over time, it has become apparent that the dynamic of the pair has expanded itself to other parts of the organization. In one instance, the R&D department and the systems engineering department developed an ever-increasing conflict that showed up predominantly between the heads of those department, one accusing the other of being arrogant and budget spending and maverick and the other accusing in return the engineer of being too linear and conservative in his thinking, hindering creativity. When we looked around we discovered many pockets of similar paired conflicts, which cascaded down into and across the various parts of the organization. We have understood that until we dealt with the dynamic of the pairs, the rest of the organization will not shift- fractal behaviour means that when you change one part of the system it has ripple effect on other parts of the system, so it almost doesn't matter where you start although starting at the top, in typical organizations, usually is likely to have a more powerful and immediate effect.

A supervision group offers a unique opportunity to examine those fractals because we are in a contained thinking space, away from the daily hamster-wheel, and can reflect and explore, through discussing the clients of our supervisees, the power dynamics and our political selves in a way that pays attention to the details of our engagement and involvement in a context. What is important from the supervisor is to attend to movement: the flow from one client case to another; the space between, the pauses, the actions and the rhythmical relationship between them.

The supervisor's stance from this perspective

Supervision in groups from this perspective is not a process that is about reaching some objective learning targets or unfolding 'best practice'. It is about deepening practice, insight and learning. The supervisor's stance is one of 'creative indifference' in Gestalt terms, which is not about being indifferent in the everyday sense – that is, not caring what happens to the client – but holding open the numerous possibilities for the client's next steps without prioritizing one possibility over another on their behalf, not even the client's well-being. It is based in phenomenological philosophy and hence requires the coach/supervisor to suspend judgement and hold open their curiosity to the phenomenon in front of them as it unfolds in the 'here-and-now' of the interaction.

Bion in his book *Attention and Interpretation* (1993) expresses this same stance of 'spirit of inquiry': 'the "act of faith" (*F*) depends on disciplined denial of memory and desire' (p. 41). For Bion, the act of faith is based on an acceptance of the unknown, since nobody knows what will happen. It is essentially a spiritual approach to the self but from his point of view, the act of faith derives from a scientific state of mind and should be freed from its usual religious connotations.

In that same book, Bion (1993) draws on letters of the poet Keats, who wrote about 'negative capability', which has since become a very influential idea in our work. He quotes from Keats' (1817) 'Letters to George and Thomas Keats':

> . . . several things dove-tailed in my mind, and at once it struck me what quality went to form a Man of Achievement, especially in Literature, and which Shakespeare possessed so enormously – I mean Negative Capability, that is, when a man is capable of being in uncertainties, mysteries, doubts, without any irritable reaching after fact and reason. (pp. 128–129)

Bion quotes from Keats in order to reinforce his idea that the analyst is more able to analyse when they free themselves from the need to understand and make sense. He suggests that the more disciplined the analyst is to release themselves from having any possession of memory, desire, understanding or sense, the more possible it would become for them to work best with what the patient needs.

This fits well with the concept of the 'edge of chaos' from chaos and complexity theories. Life at the edge of chaos is paradoxical (that is, patterns are both stable and unstable simultaneously), self-organizing and adaptive (that is, emergent and having a capacity to learn from experience), and complex (that is, agents interact locally and can produce global patterns that are intrinsically unpredictable and can evolve into an undetermined future).

The supervisor of a group that operates at the edge of chaos (i.e. has the potential to learn from and through experience) is an anthropologist. They will be participating as another agent of change in the process of creating – without assuming a capacity to know more or beyond or outside of the human interaction – but with the competence to endure uncertainty and doubt with a touch of humility as to one's individual capability. It means we are dependent upon each other in the task of creating change, learning and developing; but there is no blueprint, not one who is in control – yet a collaborative effort that can yield, also, negative, destructive, outcomes. So, in groups, each moment cannot be anything but fresh and unique yet paradoxically familiar enough to be recognized as related to our base, our history, our context, our ground. It is ordinary and extraordinary, possible and impossible at the same time.

Because learning is a paradoxical process of continuity and transformation, because it is not about reaching homeostasis or a resolution but about holding together in creative tension contradictory concepts, it will always involve the processes of panic, shame and rejection at the same time as feelings of growth, change and transformation (Aram 2001). This is because the process of supervision challenges one's meaning-making processes and addresses the questions of 'Who am I?' – the existential sense of being-in-the-world, and 'How am I?' – the sense of becoming-in-the world. It is potentially creative and destructive at the same time.

This supervision is about significant shifts in a person's life, yet at the same time it is ordinary. In the 'helping professions' we are expected to be in supervision – and it becomes part of our ethical practice. As such, it is a process that involves the reproduction of 'existing' knowledge, yet its effects are to a large extent unknown, perhaps inherently unknowable. The teaching in the learning process is 'done' by ordinary people who themselves undergo transformations during the process of supervising. The poignant moments of transformation can happen in the most ordinary conversations. The type of supervision that we are advocating here is not transactional, it is emergent, non-linear in nature and iterative. A key factor in this type of supervision is attention to and capacity to deal with challenges and work with difference, hence we turn our attention to these aspects now.

Challenges of supervising in groups

Group supervision most often takes two forms. The first is peer supervision where all members of the group are hierarchically at the same level. This format allows the group to function with greater informality. Each member of the group takes turns to share challenges, issues and critical incidents to which the other members share their thoughts, insights and suggestions. This type of feedback allows all the participants to learn from the thoughts shared with the freedom to incorporate them into their professional repertoires – or not. The disadvantage of working as a peer group is that it makes it more difficult to explore the dynamics of the group. Difficult emotions such as competition or envy within the group can be left unaddressed.

There are clear benefits to working with a supervisor who holds and leads the group (the second form). The need for containment is often overlooked in the developmental space whether working with an established group of coaches or those in training. Anxiety is usually found in the learning space because it requires a psychic shift from a position of professional competence to a learning position where doubt, exposure and failure are also present. When the boundary of professional identity becomes semi-permeable for the purposes of learning, other emotions and dynamics are also exposed.

For a supervisor, and for those being supervised in this form, there might be a temptation to change group supervision to individual supervision with observers. The temptation is to return to our earliest group experience, the family group where the dynamics of competition, frustration, suppression and many others are at play. When a group supervision session is structured and delivered well, it expands the space for learning through interaction, whether at a peer level or with a primary supervisor, and allows for fluid movement between mentoring, modelling and reflection.

Working with difference in group supervision

Groups are spaces where issues of power, competition, race, gender and other aspects of a diverse identity often emerge and can be considered and explored. These can be difficult conversations. Turner (2016) suggests 'a possible beginning in our understanding of difference – that we identify our self not just by who we are but also by who we are not' (p. 20). In group supervision, this is a vital element that helps coaches examine those aspects of themselves or more importantly of their clients that are hidden from view. Turner reminds us that although these are not new ideas and stretch as far back as Hegel, the examination of ourselves through the lens of the other and states 'the other needs the subject as much as vice versa and that they identify each other by what they believe they are not' (p. 20).

In the following two short case studies, work with two different groups illustrates how difference at an unconscious or conscious level can affect the roles each member takes up.

Box 19.2 Case illustration

While working on a European project to improve the employment of unemployed and low-skilled young people who have been failed by education, it was possible to see the unconscious enactment of dependence in the system, through the dynamics in the team, which highlighted their differences.

At the start of the (virtual) meeting, the oldest and most established member (an older white man) of the group was already present when I, the group's supervisor, joined the meeting. I had worked with this group in various formations so was known to them. As it is usual for the supervisor to start the group, whether virtual or face to face, I wondered from his early arrival if he had taken up the role of containment. We spent a little time reconnecting before the second member of the group joined us. Her position in the group is complex in that she (a younger white woman) is new to the coaching/consultancy role, although she had been in the sector for a long time. We continued polite and general conversation until the final (and youngest) member of the group joined us (a black woman) who was new to the role as well as the project and the organization. The older man seemed impatient with the reconnection chatter and tried to start the supervision conversation. I wondered if he was concerned about time management, about the loss of focus on the primary task or unconsciously asserting his dominance as the only man in the group and the most experienced person in the room. In my role as supervisor, I was aware that it was my responsibility to contain the group and to lead the session, so I gently took the role back and started the group. As the group progressed, it was clear that the dominant role had been taken by the older man throughout the project. When I pointed out his behaviours, I attributed this to his role in the project as project director. The two women easily deferred to him and had taken up a student position. As the two women described how they were taking up their roles in the project, stepping out of the student position seemed to be a pervasive problem. The invitation to group for supervision was offered to them as peers. Through the process of group supervising, it was possible to notice the dominating/deference dynamic. This is an example of a 'parallel process', or fractal: the supervision group dynamic reflecting the dynamic outside of the group supervision, in the project itself.

In this team, the key difference was their experience in role and this manifest in the unconscious attempt of dominance by the only man in the group. The interplay of role, experience, gender, race and power – or lack of – can affect the way we make ourselves present with our clients or colleagues. It is essential to pay attention to these subtle behaviours as they affect, and could distort, the group dynamic.

This case also illustrates how group supervision offers a forum for feedback and the development or honing of new skills, in ways that cannot be accomplished as effectively through individual supervision because the supervisor is unable to observe interactions between colleagues, whereas in this case the project group comes together as a whole to supervision and its project dynamics manifest in the 'here-and-now' of supervision.

Working with the dynamics of racial difference from the role of supervisor can be difficult for both coach and supervisor as they are usually multi-layered, fluid and complex. In a human rights speech following hurricane Katrina, Angela Davis (2006) said of racism: 'we used to be able to understand it. We could say exactly what was racism, what wasn't. And now it's not that easy. And that is because racism itself changes. It moves, it travels, it migrates, it transmutes itself.' Davis' description of racism at the group macro level can also be applied to groups of all sizes. A psychoanalytic perspective allows us to

> recognise that there is a detrimental psychological impact on the other from not being witnessed by the subject. Also, this lens then logically recognises the selfishness of the subject as it forms its own identity: it has no responsibility for the other, doesn't need to recognise the other, and will even go to great lengths to undermine the humanity of the other in order to maintain its dominance.

Regardless of context for supervision when working in a group, there is an intrinsic value to the occupant of the client role if there is freedom to work with the dynamics of racial difference because there aren't many spaces where it is possible to have a safe discussion.

The context of the case study in Box 19.3 is the development of business coaches. The members of the group had each been matched with a business to offer support and work with any emergent challenges. The relationships were not always easy, and the purpose of supervision was to help process the complex feelings that were evoked.

Box 19.3 Case illustration

In a mixed group supervision setting, one member, a white man, explained his case: he was working with a client who had not selected him on the basis of chemistry, but had been allocated to him as part of a wider group process. Both the client and the coach had basic information about the other. He was keen to work with his client, a black man, and tried to arrange a meeting. Initially, the working relationship was conceptualized as a face-to-face relationship. However, the client refused to meet the coach. They had a telephone conversation and the next session was arranged, but an hour before they were due to meet, the client cancelled. The coach persisted with the case and continued to try to meet with his client, without success. Disappointed by this outcome, the coach asked his supervisor and the group, 'How do I work with issues of resistance that seem based in discrimination and remain professional?'

Part of the difficulty with this case is that there is no clear evidence that race was the underlying reason for this resistance, except the discomfort and rejection that was experienced by the coach as he repeatedly tried to arrange sessions. As he described the situation and his feeling about it, the fact that his supervisor and other group members were able to acknowledge that there may be a racial dynamic created a sense of safety for him and allowed him to explore next steps from the space of curiosity rather than rejection and pain.

Guidance for further learning and research

Like individuals, groups have a separate life and identity that can affect the behaviour of its members. It is important to hold in mind that the group space has to be co-created to feel safe and confidential, the possibility for revelation of struggle or weakness can be permitted and therefore lead to growth. Without the full use of this space as experiential, development can be diminished.

For supervisors interested in exploring issues related to difference, there has been a growth in research in the area. A starting point would be to explore and understand in what way the groups in each study are different – either from the team they are part of or the groups they work with. On the subject of difference, there is now extensive reading material available. *White Fragility* by Robin di Angelo explores white identity in relation to the complex mixed identities that exist in the USA. Reni Eddo-Lodge's *Why I'm No Longer Talking to White People about Race*, is a thorough analysis of issues of race, politics and power in the UK.

Finally, Brené Brown explores vulnerability in her book *Daring Greatly*, which is a key to change in the area of difference as it requires risk-taking.

Questions for reflection

- What are the implications of the notion of 'the group-as-a-whole to my practice?
- How can I hold a stance of inquiry and paradox in the supervision process?
- How do I work with the power dynamics that emerge in supervision sessions?
- Can I work with hidden difference and what does difference mean to me?

Further sources

Dalal, F. (2010) *Race, Colour and the Processes of Racialization: New Perspectives from Group Analysis, Psychoanalysis and Sociology*. Hove: Routledge. Dalal explores how people differentiate between races in order to make a distinction between the 'haves' and 'must-not-haves', arguing that this process is cognitive, emotional and political rather than biological.

Obholzer, A. and Roberts, V.Z. (eds) (2019) *The Unconscious at Work. A Tavistock Approach to Making Sense of Organisational Life*, 2nd edn. Abingdon: Routledge. This edition draws on a body of thinking and practice that has developed over the past 70 years, often referred to as 'the Tavistock approach' or 'systems-psychodynamics'. It explores the complexities of organizational life in which the group is central.

Stacey, R.D. (2003) *Complexity and Group Processes: A Radically Social Understanding of Individuals*. Hove: Routledge. This brings together the author's decade of work on developing the complexity theories and their applications to organizations. His views on the key questions about the nature of human relating provide a helpful framework to a supervisor grappling with these questions, particularly in a group supervision context.

References

Aram, E. (2001) *The Experience of Complexity: Learning as the Potential Transformation of Identity*. PhD dissertation, University of Hertfordshire, UK.

Bion, W.R. (1961) *Experiences in Groups*. London: Tavistock.

Bion, W.R. (1993) *Attention and Interpretation*. London: Routledge.

Brown, B. (2015) *Daring Greatly*. London: Penguin.

Dalal, F. (1998) *Taking the Group Seriously*, International Library of Group Analysis 5. London: Jessica Kingsley.

Davis, A. (2006) Angela Davis speaks out on prisons and human rights abuses in the aftermath of Hurricane Katrine, *Democracy Now*. Available from: https://www.democracynow.org/2006/12/28/angela_davis_speaks_out_on_prisons (accessed June 2020).

Di Angelo, R. (2018) *White Fragility*. London: Penguin.

Foulkes, S.H. (1964/1984) *Therapeutic Group Analysis*. London: George Allen and Unwin.

Foulkes, S.H. (1990) *Selected Papers* [edited by Elizabeth Foulkes]. London: Karnac.

Foulkes, S.H. and Anthony, E.J. (1957) *Group Psychotherapy*. London: Penguin.

Gabriel, Y. (1999) *Organisations in Depth*. London: Sage.

Gibbard, G.S., Hartman, J.J. and Mann, R. (eds.) (1974) *Analysis of Groups*. San Francisco, CA: Jossey-Bass.

Goodwin, B. (1994) *How the Leopard Changed its Spots*. London: Phoenix Books.

Klein, M. (1948) *Contributions to Psychoanalysis 1921–1945*. London: Hogarth Press.

Klein, M. (1975) *Envy and Gratitude and Other Works (1946–63)*. New York: Free Press.

Le Bon, G. (1895/1960) *The Crowd: A Study of the Popular Mind*. New York: Viking Press.

Obholzer, A. and Roberts, Z. (eds) (2019) *The Unconscious at Work: A Tavistock Approach to Making Sense of Organisational Life*. London: Routledge.

Parlett, M. (1997) The unified field in practice, *Gestalt Review*, 1(1): 16–33.

Prigogine, I. and Allen, P.M (1982) The challenge of complexity, in W.C. Schieve and P.M. Allen (eds) *Self-organisation and Dissipative Structures: Applications in the Physical and Social Sciences*. Austin, TX: University of Texas Press.

Prigogine, I. and Stengers, I. (1984) *Order out of Chaos*. New York: Bantam Books

Rice, A.K. (1965) Individual, group and intergroup processes, *Human Relations*, 22: 565–584.

Slater, P.E. (1966) *Microcosm: Structural, Psychological and Religious Evolution in Groups*. New York: John Wiley.

Turner, D. (2016) We are all of us Other, *Therapy Today*, 27(5): 18–21.

20

Peer supervision

*Tammy Turner, Michelle Lucas
and Carol Whitaker*

Introduction

The road to coaching mastery is paved with reflective practice. Reflective practice is 'the ability to step away from your work and identify patterns, habits, strengths and limitations in your work and/or within the system you work in' (Turner et al. 2018: 25). The extent to which our 100th hour of coaching delivery is better than our first, is intimately linked to whether we have subjected our work to evaluation by ourselves and others. Reflective practice comes in many forms – individual reflection, peer supervision and professional supervision – and is the solid foundation of quality coaching. Its purpose is to extend the coach's awareness of themselves, of their client(s) and other elements in the wider system, to enhance their way of being, their way of working and the overall impact in the coaching relationship. We hold that it is this kind of reflective practice that provides the substance of all forms of supervision.

In this chapter, we clarify two characteristics specific to peer supervision: namely, that it is reciprocal and that peers are not trained supervisors. It is these characteristics that bring both benefits and challenges to this form of reflective practice. Those challenges can be managed through the development of three coaching skills. Where peer supervision has its limitations, accessing professional supervision alongside peer supervision is an integrative approach. How this approach works in practice is illustrated using four international case studies. This integrated approach may impact professional supervisors and in turn the wider coaching industry. We conclude by offering a set of criteria that could be used by professional bodies and professional supervisors to enhance and contain the work done in peer supervision relationships.

What do we mean by 'supervision'?

Definitions of supervision have been provided elsewhere in this book and have been created in the context of professional supervision. Most definitions point to a collaborative quality in the relationship, for example: a 'working alliance between two professionals' (Inskipp and Proctor 1993: 184); a 'collaborative process facilitating coaches (and coach supervisors) to grow their reflective practice' (Clutterbuck et al. 2016: 18).

Yet it would be misleading to suggest that its collaborative nature alone makes supervision, 'supervision'. Ultimately, it is the application of a specific skill set that makes the encounter a supervisory one. Typically, a professional supervisor will have undergone specific training, equipping them with the necessary competencies.

Bachkirova and Jackson (2011: 233) consider it essential that supervisors have an understanding of the following:

1. Contracting ethically in multiple contexts
2. Models and theories of supervision
3. Understanding intrapersonal and interpersonal dynamics, particularly in relation to power in coaching and supervision
4. Models and theories of individual development and in particular of coach development
5. Assessment and evaluation of coaching effectiveness appropriate to the context and nature of coaching
6. Supervision of complex coaching situations, particularly referral and ethical dilemmas.

Given the increased complexity and interconnectivity of our world, we add two more qualities.

7. Systemic understanding (see Turner et al. 2018: 13)
8. Experience of group facilitation and awareness of common group dynamics that enable or impede the work.

What is distinctive about peer supervision?

The *Oxford Dictionary* definition of *peer* is as follows: 'A person of the same age, status, or ability as another specified person'. This is rather narrow in the coaching context. We believe that the synonyms 'equal', 'fellow' and 'co-worker' have greater resonance, and this is the frame for our definition.

When professional supervisors are working together in either paired or group supervision, this may also constitute peer supervision. However, our definition focuses on *coaches* (or mentors) working together as peers: 'Peer supervision is a collaborative learning environment created between fellow coaches, mentors or other professionals (practitioners). It is of mutual benefit to the practitioners involved as well as being of service to their clients and the wider system' (Turner et al. 2018: 7).

The first distinction is that peers 'are without supervision training' (Turner et al. 2018: 7). Most coaches who set up peer supervision relationships will not come equipped with the foundational supervisor competencies identified by Bachkirova and Jackson (2011). While some coaches may have received professional supervision and/or have read about the process, they are, nonetheless, untrained.

The second distinction is that the relationship 'is reciprocal, generates the power to reflect on practice together, and peers share vulnerability and support in equal measures' (Turner et al. 2018: 7). The reciprocal nature of the peer relationship creates a sense of parity and equity. This sense of mutuality is an integral element of peer supervision. Mutuality differentiates peer from professional supervision, a uni-directional relationship where the professional supervisor role comes with imbued power.

Although peers often have comparable levels of expertise, the apparent simplicity of this statement needs to be treated with caution. In practice, peer groups often have different levels of experience/expertise. What is paramount is the sense of equality among those engaging as peers. As soon as one peer feels 'better than' or 'less than' another peer, the perception of mutual benefit in the relationship is jeopardized.

Given these distinctions, 'supervision' between peers could perhaps more accurately be described as an extended form of reflective practice. This is not to imply that it is better or worse than professional supervision. Due to the absence of specific supervision training and a reduction in power dynamics, 'peer supervision' and supervision are different activities and therefore produce different results.

What are its benefits and its challenges?

When a peer relationship works well, there is a sense of co-created space, shared power, and generative learning between them. However, just as the professional supervisor cannot avoid their role power, their peers cannot avoid their implicit connectivity. In any supervisory context, the complexity of individual experiences and the constant possibility of power-play, requires careful navigation. Achieving genuine mutuality requires a dedicated and proactive approach to ensure that peer supervision is not just a chat between colleagues.

Seeking to understand its benefits, our research identified seven reasons why practitioners choose peer supervision (Turner et al. 2018: 20–21):

1. Cost – often the exchange between peers is one of time rather than financial.
2. Confidence – the label 'supervision' comes loaded with the perception of a managerial energy, therefore those practitioners who lack confidence may feel more comfortable working with someone who is at a similar level of experience.
3. Shame – supervision is often seen as a place to bring our difficult moments. It is perhaps easier to be vulnerable with someone when they too bring their struggles.
4. Convenience – historically, there has been a shortage of coaching supervisors available, certainly in geographies outside of Europe; for those who have preferred in person work, connecting with local peers has been logistically simpler.
5. Confidentiality – in some emerging markets coaching and supervision are niche businesses in competition for the same clients. Supervision therefore needs to be contained within the practitioner's organization in order to protect client information and competitive advantage.
6. Sense-checking – sometimes a practitioner has a minor concern and wants a second opinion. These kinds of conversations are easily engineered with a peer, but more difficult to do so outside of a scheduled session with a professional supervisor.
7. Study and/or skills enhancement – often formed between alumni following a training programme, this can feel like a natural place to continue to develop skills.

Despite all these benefits, working together as peers also brings challenges. Often the nature of the challenges that emerge is connected to the practitioner's motivation for seeking out peer supervision. Table 20.1 lists the challenges that can arise depending on the practitioner's motivation:

Table 20.1 Challenges arising in peer supervision work and links to practitioner motivation

Challenge	Underlying practitioner motivation
1. Collusion and confirmation bias	Feeling safe and needing to belong
2. Disorientation/confusion	Exploring difference and diversity of thinking
3. Discounting your own experience	Believing that you will learn and benefit from others' experience
4. Developmental stagnation	Continuing a formative relationship from a development programme
5. Minimizing your own supervision needs	Feeling flattered when the other(s) invite you to work with them
6. Breeding competitiveness	Comparing yourself to your contemporaries
7. Dual relationships/conflicts of interest	Working with a colleague out of convenience and investing in their needs
8. Dependency	Believing that you don't have other choices in who you work with and staying with the status quo
9. Lack of ownership	Avoiding personal responsibility, likely to have been allocated to work with the other(s)
10. Overinvesting in the relationship	Prioritizing the sustainability of the relationship over the quality of the work

Table 20.2 Four specific pitfalls and indicative group behaviours

Group pitfalls	Indicative group behaviours
Group think	An over-investment in the group's ideas
Different levels of experience	Less experienced peers look for reassurance from the more 'experienced'
Different pace of communication and/or working through a topic	Discussion stays at a surface level. Different degrees of tolerance in relation to silence and thinking style.
Power dynamics	Individual assumes an authority 'role' or position rather than collectively engaging the group

These 10 challenges (see Table 20.1) may arise in both individual and group work. Examples of behaviours that peers might notice and which indicate these issues are arising are discussed in greater detail in Turner et al. (2018).

In groups, four additional challenges may arise (see Table 20.1). These are more complex to manage as peers are not necessarily trained to notice blind spots. Examples of behaviours that peers might notice, and which could indicate these issues are present are detailed in Turner et al. (2018).

How can peers manage these challenges?

With this list of challenges, it is reasonable to see why some authors (e.g. Bachkirova and Jackson 2011) would argue that practitioners who work together in peer supervision need to equip themselves with specific supervisory compe-tences. Coaches might consider supervision training as requiring a significant investment of both money and time. Instead, they may choose enhancing their reflective practice with others in peer supervision due to availability and afford-ability. This additional training would be inappropriate for those developing prac-titioners who do not yet have the capacity to learn supervision skills. Perhaps, paradoxically, if peers became trained supervisors, then the work would move out of the domain of peer supervision into professional supervision – as the peers would be professional supervisors themselves, even if no money changed hands.

Doing peer supervision well is not about creating 'mini-supervisors'. It is about developing three things that are already a legitimate part of a practitioner's skill set:

Co-creating a contract and developing contracting skills

Just like establishing a coaching agreement, a peer supervision relationship is more successful when those involved co-create a contract which clarifies their working agreement. The work of Hawkins and Smith (2006) suggests the super-vision contract should consider five areas: Practicalities, Boundaries, Working Alliance, Meeting Format, and the Organizational and Professional Context. The work of Hay (2007) invites us to consider three overarching components when working with peers: Procedural, Professional and Psychological. We have added a fourth consideration, Political (Turner et al. 2018: 107), recognizing the sys-temic influences when our work has an organizational context. The specific top-ics that fall within these headings are expanded upon elsewhere (see Turner et al. 2018) and will be familiar to many practising coaches.

The outcome is an agreed contract, written or verbal, that all parties agree will be honoured in the relationship. However, as soon as the peer supervision work begins, the complexity of the client work and individual differences become apparent. No matter how thoroughly the contract was formed, it becomes out-dated and needs re-contracting. Nuances arise that were not covered in the con-tract; things that seemed important are in reality held more lightly, and, conversely, things that were thought to be unimportant cause significant dents in the working relationship.

Often overlooked, an essential skill for the sustainability of peer supervision relationships is contracting, which we describe as 'a critical set of skills that are used throughout the relationship, which enables all parties to voice and explore issues when things become unclear or difficult' (Turner et al. 2018: 106). Contract-ing is a dialogical activity that provides a solid place from which to build the operational peer-to-peer relationship.

We recommend that all peer supervision partnerships proactively and regu-larly hold reviews to consider what of the contract is working well and what might need to change. Turner's Shared Outcome Model (2014) highlights that to have a fully shared outcome, there needs to be shared understanding and accep-tance of accountabilities and responsibilities (Figure 20.1).

Once these contracting skills become embedded, the peers can use them in the moment, voicing disquiet as it occurs and engaging in 'spot contracting' to agree

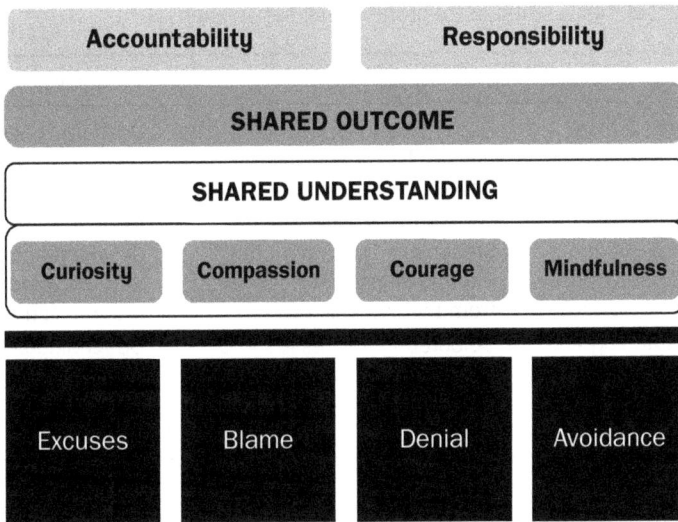

Figure 20.1 Shared outcome model (Turner 2014)

how to determine a shared outcome. However, before these contracting skills can be employed, practitioners need to notice there is a need to re-contract. This is only possible if peers have a good level of awareness of both self and others.

Raising awareness of self and others

Deepening one's self-awareness is an ongoing journey for all helping practitioners. The more the practitioner works to understand their own processes, the lower the risk of contaminating their client work with their own unfinished business. The same is true for managing oneself in a peer supervision relationship. The shared outcome model offers a useful framework in which to consider how the practitioner's reactions and behaviours can either support or inhibit striking a contract and constructive way of working with others.

Above the line behaviours include curiosity, compassion, courage and mindfulness. All of these are enabling forces in relationships, and each practitioner can develop their understanding of how these behaviours manifest in themselves when they are at their best.

Below the line behaviours include excuses, blame, denial and avoidance, and each practitioner develops an awareness of how these manifest when they are at their worst. This level of awareness enables the practitioner to evaluate how they are being, ideally in the moment, but at least upon reflection. Noticing variations (either personally or through feedback from peers) prompts the practitioner to consider what has made this shift. Once identified, it is possible to explore if the cause of the behaviour is connected to the peer relationship (and therefore re-contracting would be helpful) or from the practitioner's wider life (in which case some personal development work may be needed).

Table 20.3 Example topics suitable for professional supervision

Normative	Restorative	Formative
Clarifying personal ethical position and/or unique coaching approach/style	Regenerating – especially when taking on emotions that may have been sparked by clients	Building coaching repertoire to avoid feeling stale or habitual
Feeling unsure about complex elements in the work (tri-parties, systemic influences, team coaching)	Developing a solid coaching presence – quietening the internal chatter that distracts from the client work	Exploring root causes of development areas/skills that are resistant to progression
Checking understanding and seeking feedback on coaching competencies	Celebrating successes and being free to be self-centred	Deepening self-awareness to generate a better understanding of relational dynamics

Boundary management

In coaching or mentoring, it is commonplace for the client to bring issues that are on the cusp of suitability for this type of work. The coach or mentor will have a sense of the extent of their competence and will have the skills to refer to an alternative practitioner. In peer relationships this will also occur. Each person will have a sense of how well equipped they are (individually or collectively) to manage what is being brought to peer supervision. When a peer starts to feel out of their depth and unable to truly be in service of another peer, it is a signal that any further discussion will require a dialogue with a professional supervisor. A practitioner may leave peer supervision feeling they haven't quite managed to resolve the matter, again a signal that dialogue with a professional supervisor might be helpful. Table 20.3 highlights some common topics that indicate that professional supervision would be a useful addition to peer supervision. We have organized them according to Proctor's three functions of supervision (1986).

The argument for an integrated approach

Below are four case studies that illustrate how peer supervision and professional supervision can co-exist. As proposed, peer supervision is not an alternative to professional supervision, it is both different and complementary. The cases illustrate how the use of a trained supervisor is not an either/or choice, rather a distinct element, which, when combined, adds value. The integrated approach brings external inquiry and contributes to extending the peers' repertoire of supervisory techniques guarding against developmental stagnation (challenge identified above in Table 20.1). Correspondingly, these integrated approaches have a generative effect – peer supervision becomes stronger and professional supervision becomes deeper.

Peer groups case studies using integrated approaches to reflective practice and supervision

Peer supervision group of coaches within professional bodies

- **Context:** Since 2015, over 180 members formed multiple peer supervision groups and pairs organized through either an International Coaching Federation (ICF) chapter or through the University of Sydney Coaching and Mentoring Alumni (USCMA), for an annual fee. The fee covers the administration of members, a copy of Turner et al. (2018), plus training from Tammy Turner. The training follows important topics (see Tables 20.1 and 20.2) covered in the book and sets the groups up for success, dealing with topics such as contracting to set up group agreements, developing a shared contract, what to bring to peer supervision, running the session, when to engage a professional supervisor, ethics and dilemmas; and a significant emphasis on reflective practice for peer members to notice themselves in their work.
- **Purpose:** To provide a safe space to enhance professional coaching development, embed learning from training and/or to extend community between coaches in remote areas.
- **Format:** Each peer supervision group or pair organizes their schedule, though it is suggested 10 × 90-minute sessions over a year. Established groups may meet for a full day to practise coaching techniques, share industry research, methodologies, trends or for social events. Some groups hire a professional supervisor to facilitate a group process review or when particular supervision expertise is deemed helpful.
- **Benefits:** Strong group psychological safety creates profound learning and increased coaching capability. In the USCMA peer supervision group, a member noticed that applying learning from the peer supervision training enhanced their own reflective practice. The strength of peer supervision and its longevity can be attributed to commitment of the individual members to reflective practice, taking time to prepare and to practise using the lessons in the book, rather than just having a chat.
- **Limitations:** Peers may 'compete' in a small marketplace, making confidentiality, managing boundaries, adhering to group process and commitment to each other sacrosanct. In a longstanding group there is a need to avoid complacency, for example, in ICF NZN they brought in a professional supervisor to help the mature group stay at their learning edge.

Developmental learning sets among leaders at Element Six (part of the DeBeers Group)

- **Context:** Specialist, high-tech manufacturing global organization. Talent function looking to increase manager-as-coach competency and shift organization from alpha leadership towards servant leadership culture.
- **Purpose:** To enable a different leadership style in the 'Innovation' function; create the shift by sharing knowledge and experience of 'how to' and 'how not to' develop coaching skills. Support resolution of individual issues encountered during the change, by using a process congruent with the emerging culture.

- **Format:** Formal opportunities organized by 'Talent' function established local developmental learning sets. Methodology of dialogue like action learning sets using two rounds of dialogue. In the first round, peers offer coaching questions to extend, stretch and deepen thinking. In the second, sharing opinions, ideas and suggestions.
- **Benefits:** Leaders learned by doing; developing skills through real practice and observation. Knowledge was exchanged more memorably than through formal training; the process invited individuals to leverage other people's experience, adapting it to their context.
- **Limitations:** Without repeated formal intervention from the Talent function, the initiative waned, and numbers dropped. Importantly, those that continued have become champions of the new culture within the 'Innovation' function.

Peer supervision group of coaches who trained together

- **Context:** Four coaches who met on a Coaching Masters' programme in 2013 formed a peer supervision group as part of the training. It is still going strong. A diverse range of coaching practices span UK government internal coaching, blue chip global law firms, board coaching and SMEs. Several are now trained coaching supervisors and/or run coach trainings themselves.
- **Purpose:** To support group members' development as coaches; a resourcing space sharing Continuous Professional Development (CPD) learning and fostering community.
- **Format:** Meets quarterly in London for 3 hours; occasional longer sessions for deeper dives. The time is shared equally with everyone choosing how they want to be supervised, without a chair. Time is allocated for sharing learning and wider CPD. Periodically, the group contracts an external supervisor to add fresh perspectives, bringing additional approaches to the group's supervision toolkit and to support them in evaluating group processes.
- **Benefits:** Camaraderie and mutual support – group frequently shares ideas outside of formal sessions. Strong mutual trust generates the safety necessary for vulnerability and deep learning in sessions. Regular peer supervision helps members enhance their own 'internal supervisor'.
- **Limitations:** Risk of comfort zone – need to regularly focus on group process to maintain healthy dynamics. Individuals may want to explore an issue at greater depth or welcome specialist insight, for example trauma-informed coaching or a modality (e.g. Constellations), and, in these instances, they will reach out to an independent professional supervisor.

Peer supervision groups among internal coaches (supported by an external professional supervisor)

- **Context:** A network of organizations in the public sector with pools of internal coaches coaching both within their organization and other organizations in the network. Coaches work with one to two clients at a time, in addition to their formal responsibilities. Initially, there were no qualified internal supervisors available to support the community.

- **Purpose:** To develop a sense of community, share knowledge and continue the development of internal coaches.
- **Format:** Quarterly 3-hour sessions at a variety of locations, inviting the whole pool of coaches. Two of the sessions are facilitated by an external professional supervisor (introducing some supervision facilitation techniques). Two sessions are facilitated internally using the techniques provided.
- **Benefits:** A 'train the trainer' approach increased facilitation skills in the coaching community, encouraging them to 'self-serve' with a view to increasing independence over time. Structured approaches offered predictability about how supervision would work. Coaches reported increased levels of confidence, welcomed the additional support and attendance improved from previous attempts at group supervision. Following two sessions with the external supervisor, 40 per cent of participants felt able to facilitate smaller sessions of four to six coaches independently.
- **Limitations:** An external supervisor required budget that could not be guaranteed year on year. In this context, the level of external involvement anticipated at the start of the initiative was felt superfluous given the internal coaches felt confident enough to facilitate the sessions independently using the techniques demonstrated.

Implications for professional supervisors and training organizations

As professional supervisors writing in support of peer supervision in 2018, there were concerns that there might be some backlash from the professional supervision community. What if those engaging in peer supervision no longer needed the services of professional supervisors? To date, this concern has not surfaced. As the case studies illustrate, those who work together as peers almost always reach out and involve independent professional supervision as well. Another risk of publishing *Peer Supervision in Coaching and Mentoring* was that it might have been perceived as a training manual, short cutting the need for professional coach supervision training. However, the professionalism of supervisors is quickening; 36 per cent of members of the Association of Coaching Supervisors (established in 2010) joined in the last 2 years, and 45 per cent of these are newly qualified supervisors.

Nonetheless, these concerns have some legitimacy. Professional supervisors need to rise to the challenge of potential dilution and to increasing industry complexity. Here we identify three areas where a practitioner's skill set can be deepened and/or expanded.

Psychological mindedness

What is noticeable is that when coaches come to professional supervision having had some peer supervision already, we are then working with material that has already been subjected to considerable reflection. The work with peers allows the practitioner to unpick the first layer of reflection. This raises the bar for the professional supervisor; the issues that are brought are deeper and less easily resolved.

Table 20.4 Comparison of topics taken to peer and professional supervision

	Explored with peers	Explored with supervisor
Normative	Is this discomfort unique to me or common among coaches?	What is causing the discomfort?
Formative	This technique isn't working. What else could I use?	What prompted you to use this technique? What other choices did you have?
Restorative	Feeling supported, getting reassurance	Exploring parallel process, transference, countertransference and ethical issues of self-care

When professional supervisors let go of the provision of transactional support, placing that as the domain of peer supervision, we empower coaches to develop their independent reflective practice and their practice with peers more fully. As a result, the professional supervisor becomes liberated from more basic levels of enquiry, giving them space to explore blind spots, collusion and/or other areas where they can add depth beyond the peer realm. Table 20.4 illustrates how this might operate, indicating the shift in the work between peer and professional supervisor.

Group dynamics and group development

Many professional supervision training programmes focus mainly on developing individual supervision expertise. Either it is assumed that the supervisor understands how to facilitate groups already, or they are encouraged to engage in additional and specific training. However, as the case studies illustrate, an obvious area of specific value a professional supervisor can bring is meta-reflection with a group. Group think, collusion and developmental stagnation are all potential challenges and supporting peer supervision groups to consider how they might be limiting themselves can extend their capability.

An example of using an external professional supervisor to support group process reviews is when a collective of professional supervisors called 'Evolve' formed what is known as a peer supervision chain. Only over time working as a group did they recognize the value of bringing in independent professional supervision (Gilbert et al. 2015). The professional supervisor can help the peers develop processes for monitoring as well as spot it in action and provide real time feedback between each other. Observing peers in action, the supervisor can role model how to offer developmental feedback and then on subsequent occasions offer developmental feedback on the peers' observational and feedback skills.

Team coaching, organizational systemic and future requirements

Historically, professional bodies' competency frameworks for individual coaching place the client's agenda at the centre of the work and the coach seeks to enable their client's resourcefulness. However, as the range of organizational coaching increases to include internal coaches, leaders as coaches and team coaching, the engagement increases in both its complexity and systemic nature. As a result, having an integrated peer and professional supervision can enhance delivery and capacity for the coach, clients and the wider system.

The competencies for team coaches and for those who supervise them go beyond the requirements for individual coaching. Typically, the systemic perspective in professional supervision considers the context in which the client operates. In multi-person and/or team scenarios, issues such as ethics, transference and power dynamics take on more complexity. In team coaching, practitioners often work in pairs (as co-coaches); one is coaching while the other is observing dynamics. The team manages the agreed goal in the session and in their daily interactions; while the coach/es hold both the systemic lens towards greater purpose and offer suggestions to steer them towards their agreed outcomes. Team coaches need to understand working in a system, the implications of their impact on their co-coach, the team, the team leader, and/or the interventions they introduce, and the ripple effect across the organization. To feel equipped in the moment in this complex adaptive system, the most important 'competency' is to have capacity in uncertainty.

Peer supervision can support team coaching pairs' reflective practice and provide the content to bring to professional supervision. Supervisors of team coaches need to understand multiple connections and the wider system beyond the team. For example, supervisors at the Global Team Coaching Institute (GTCI) are required to be a qualified consultant or team coach (currently practising), have specific team coaching training, supervision qualifications and show how they attend to their ongoing development.

As organizations seek to scale up coaching initiatives, contain costs, build capability and adaptability for the future, team coaching will continue to increase. The differences between individual and team coaching create implications for the industry. Training organizations serving coaches and supervisors will need to broaden their existing programmes to encompass these broader and more systemic skill sets. The competency frameworks and accreditation processes of professional bodies will also need to reflect the increasing complexity and specialist knowledge required at each level.

Guidance for further learning and research

Professional supervisors can deliberately support the growth and rigour of peer supervision groups. Integrating peer and professional supervision offers an opportunity for the professional supervisor community to continually stretch themselves. An integrated approach invites professional supervisors to bring cumulative value to client organizations.

Here are the core elements in ensuring peers have longevity and an enriching peer supervision experience:

- Formal set-up, including a commitment to work together for a minimum period, ideally a year
- A written contract that has been co-created collectively, reviewed regularly and re-contracted as required

- A commitment to meet regularly and scheduled in advance
- Mechanisms for ensuring all members participate by bringing quality material for reflection in equal measure
- Reciprocity as the core feature of the working relationship – for example, roles of facilitation and administration are shared equally
- Access to external professional supervision, either individually or collectively.

These should be adopted by the professional bodies (whether or not peer supervision is allowed for accreditation or credentialing purposes). As previously mentioned, enhancing peer supervision typically encourages working with professional supervisors to ensure their engagements have an appropriate amount of rigour.

As the world in which we practise is becoming increasingly interconnected and complex, we recognize the scope of individual reflective practice is too limited. To broaden the scope to encompass both peer and professional supervision better serves the practitioner, the client, the client's system, and the industry as a whole. Only by reflecting with others can we begin to see our blind spots and understand that our contributions are part of the system. As human beings have a need to belong, peer relationships can provide a safe space to stretch learning and help grow communities of practice and support the sustainability of the profession.

Questions for reflection

- What differences do you notice in what is brought to professional supervision when supervisees have subjected their work to reflection with a peer?
- How can you manage your supervision expertise without creating a power dynamic?
- What is the role of coach training organizations and professional bodies to align and include an integrative approach to reflective practice?
- What can a professional supervisor do to encourage supervisees to engage with peer supervision?

Further sources

Many of the concepts in this chapter are elaborated further in Turner, T., Lucas, M. and Whitaker, C. (2018) *Peer Supervision in Coaching and Mentoring: A Versatile Guide for Reflective Practice*. Abingdon: Routledge.

For those familiar with a transactional analysis approach to reflective practice using an integrated approach, we recommend Hay, J. (2007) *Reflective Practice and Supervision for Coaches*. Maidenhead: Open University Press.

A useful introduction to reflective practice, for supervisees is the Association of Coaching (2016) *Developing Your Coaching through Reflective Practice* [pdf]. Available at: https://www.associationforcoaching.com/page/ArticlesGuidesCoach (accessed 27 August 2020)

References

Bachkirova, T. and Jackson, P. (2011) Peer supervision for coaching and mentoring, in T. Bachkirova, P. Jackson and D. Clutterbuck (eds) *Coaching & Mentoring Supervision: Theory and Practice*. Maidenhead: Open University Press.

Clutterbuck, D., Whitaker, C. and Lucas, M. (2016) *Coaching Supervision: A Practical Guide for Supervisees*. Abingdon: Routledge.

Gilbert, S., Lucas, M. and Turner, E. (2015) Chain reaction, *Coaching at Work*, 10(1): 44–49.

Hawkins, P. and Smith, N. (2006) *Coaching, Mentoring and Organizational Consultancy: Supervision and Development*. Maidenhead: Open University Press.

Hay, J. (2007) *Reflective Practice and Supervision for Coaches*. Maidenhead: Open University Press.

Inskipp, F. and Proctor, B. (1993) *The Art, Craft and Tasks of Counselling Supervision, Part 1: Making the Most of Supervision*. Twickenham: Cascade Publications.

Oxford dictionary peer definition: https://www.lexico.com/definition/peer (accessed 27 August 2020)

Proctor, B. (1986) Supervision: a co-operative exercise in accountability, in A. Marken and M. Payne (eds) *Enabling & Ensuring*. Leicester, UK: Leicester National Youth Bureau/Council for Education and Training in Youth and Community Work.

Turner, T. (2014) *The Importance of Contracting: Using the Shared Outcome Model* [pdf]. Available at: https://www.turner.international/resources-1 (accessed 17 August 2020).

Turner, T., Lucas, M. and Whitaker, C. (2018) *Peer Supervision in Coaching and Mentoring: A Versatile Guide for Reflective Practice*. Abingdon: Routledge.

21 Supervising team coaches

Alison Hodge

Introduction

This is a chapter about supervision, not about team coaching. Nonetheless, we need to explore the context of team coaching before turning to the issue of its supervision in order to address the complex question of who supervisors are serving. Once this has been established, we are then able to turn to what supervisors need in order to provide the effective reflective, restorative space that enables the team coach to learn and grow through their work with the supervisor.

In this chapter I want to look at three key areas within the field in which the practice of team coaching supervision is developing, to raise awareness and invite the reader to consider the following significant issues:

- The challenges of supervising in a practice context that is still, as yet, to be fully understood (Jones et al. 2019; Hodge and Clutterbuck 2019a)
- The diverse factors that may arise from the complex territory of team coaching with its interdependent, interconnected elements that the team coach brings to supervision.
- The team coaching supervisor's capacity and capability to create a container for the supervisee (team coach) and what informs the development of team coaching supervisors and their practice.

For the purpose of this chapter, I am working on an assumption that the supervisor who engages in team coaching supervision has reached a stage of awareness and fundamental learning around the purpose, the tasks and core models available in coaching supervision. These are discussed elsewhere in this book and reviewed briefly in relation to the supervision of team coaching by Hodge and Clutterbuck (2019b).

While reading this chapter, it would be useful to hold the following questions in mind:

- What knowledge, skills and capabilities do you require as the team coaching supervisor to support team coaches in a practice that is still as yet to be fully understood?
- How do you as supervisor of team coaching create a container and facilitate the team coach to explore and reflect on themselves and their work in this field?
- How do you as supervisor attend to your capacity to sit in this complexity?

To set the context for this chapter, I refer to recent research (Clutterbuck and Hodge 2017) that identified that there are diverse reasons for organizations to seek team coaching, particularly for their senior teams. Interventions might range from helping a team to achieve its potential, to aligning team members around a common purpose or resolving internal conflicts. At the heart of the work of team coaching, interventions aim to improve relationships both within the team and with other stakeholders. The overall intention is to improve collective performance and results for the wider systems in the which the team is operating. This therefore involves multiple participants and stakeholders with many layers of relationships and motivations and is therefore more complex for all participants including the team coach than the typical individual coaching where the primary focus may be on one person's performance and growth.

Given that the purpose of team coaching allows for multiple intentions and purpose, using diverse methods and intervention approaches, the team coach is likely to need a level of experience and skill that is significantly over and above the core competences of one-to-one coaching (Clutterbuck and Hodge 2017; Hodge and Clutterbuck 2019b). Recognizing this, several of the professional coaching bodies are researching and developing competency and capability frameworks for accrediting team coaching practice. It is hoped that these may bring increasing clarity to the team coach practitioner around their practice and development needs. This may also offer a framework for the team coaching supervisor to explore the work with their supervisee.

Bearing this complex context in mind, I now consider how the current literature may inform the development of team coaching and team coaching supervision.

Current literature that may inform the development of team coaching supervision

At this stage, there is no one seminal model of team coaching (Jones et al. 2019). However, there is a growing body of literature that is differentiating team coaching as a discipline (e.g. Hawkins 2014; Britton 2015; Thornton 2016; Hodge and Clutterbuck 2019a). While *coaching the team* forms the foundation blocks (Clutterbuck 2020; Hawkins 2014), the practice may at times also include elements of team building, team development and team facilitation, applying many of the same skills and capabilities across all these functions or tasks.

As a discipline in its early stages of development, there is a limited specialized literature devoted to team coaching supervision (Hawkins 2014; Thornton 2016; Hodge and Clutterbuck 2019a, 2019b). A high-level review suggests three themes that I now go on to discuss: systemic thinking, relational interactions followed by interdependent, adaptive systems. These themes can be seen to be represented respectively by three key contributions: Hawkins (2014), Lawrence (2019) and Bateson (2018).

With an emphasis on systemic team coaching, Hawkins (2014) has developed the '10-eyed model', which is an extended version of the widely accepted 'seven-eyed model' (Hawkins and Smith 2013). This wider frame invites those involved (either as coach or supervisor) to consider not only the immediate participants in the team coaching, but also to cast the net more widely to consider the 'team ecosystem' with all stakeholders and the relationships between all parties. Hawkins (2014) argues that, in taking this approach, supervisors need to be trained in systemic team coaching and systemic supervision.

The need for the team coach to know that their supervisor has experience of team coaching (Clutterbuck and Hodge 2017) may lie in their need to feel safe and better understood. Perhaps then they can bring more of their own hesitation, doubt and messiness if the supervisor has been 'out in the field'. While they may gain reassurance that they are not alone, and receive perceived empathy from the supervisor, a possible danger lies in the potential for the supervisor to collude, take over or make assumptions that they both really know what the coach is experiencing or needs to do. I would argue here that rather than focusing primarily through the systemic lens, supervisors need to concentrate on creating a container to enable the team coach to explore the complex situations in which they find themselves and the impact this may have on them in their practice.

Lawrence (2019) challenges us to consider that our focus needs to be the relationships and interactions between people and their environment. Rather than focusing on teams and their stakeholders per se, he invites us to consider what level of systems thinking we are engaging with in our environment and with whomever we are working. Taking this approach, he considers what he now describes as 'meta-systems thinking' (Lawrence 2020) and argues that regardless of the client group, at a meta level, the team are a part of a broader context, everyone being impacted by experiences and relationships outside of the room. The team coach thus needs to be flexible enough to notice the interpersonal dynamics while being sensitive to whatever elements may be outside of the room for any one or all of the participants.

While Lawrence acknowledges the relevance for the team coach of paying attention to developing their skills in team coaching, he invites the practitioner not to sacrifice their wisdom and experience from other disciplines and contexts; these inform a framework of team coaching that benefits from the individuality of the practitioner who is up-skilling at many levels. He also argues that there is not one, seminal model that will suit all or cater for the requisite awareness and capability of the practitioner. Lawrence argues that it's the way the team coach thinks about the work and how they bring this awareness that will determine their impact.

This now brings me to the theme of interdependent, adaptive systems and the work of Bateson (2018). With her concept of 'warm data', Bateson (2018) invites the reader to turn away from models that may meet an habitual urge to form mechanistic patterns to make sense in a linear or sequential process. Beyond the norms of systems theory and complexity theory, she argues that practitioners (including team coaches and supervisors) need to attend to interrelationality and interdependency. She advocates building capacity and capability to interact with the complexity of 'evolving living systems' that may not be represented or personified easily in a structured model.

Trans-contextual research offers multiple descriptions of the way in which a 'subject' is nested in many contexts, termed 'warm data', which is defined as 'Trans-contextual information about the interrelationships that integrate a complex system'. Bateson invites us to explore 'how interactions in complex systems interlink. These . . . increase our ability to take into account the integrity of multi-layered living systems, to think about multi-layered 'interactions', and to engage change at a contextual level' (Bateson 2018).

I see a real congruence between this notion of 'warm data' and the complex – and at times unpredictable – practice that is called team coaching. This, in turn, will inform how team coaching supervision develops from existing approaches of one-to-one and group supervision (discussed elsewhere in this book). For instance, in team coaching and supervision we have the 'parts' that we might term knowledge and skills that derived from disciplines such as organizational development, human resources, leadership development, team building, group facilitation, coaching, adult learning, adult development, process consulting or psychology. In practice, therefore, the supervisor needs to be aware of how these 'parts' interconnect and interrelate, learning from each other as open-ended, thus co-creating something new that may not have a clear structure or pathway.

The themes that I have explored in this section would indicate that the team coach, and indeed the supervisor, is likely to need or to develop the capacity and capability across some or all of these 'parts' or disciplines, over and above their core coaching and supervision capabilities and interpersonal skills. From this discussion I would now like to move on to consider the practice of team coaching supervision. Again, informed by earlier research (Clutterbuck and Hodge 2017), what does appear difficult for the supervisor is how they engage in and facilitate reflection on living interrelated phenomena involving so many moving and interconnected elements all of which are learning with and from each other.

Mapping the complex territory of team coaching and supervision

As I have discussed already, team coaching presents challenges that may be significantly more demanding than those that emerge in one-to-one executive coaching. Team coaches readily acknowledge their need for and appreciation of supervision of their practice in this arena (Clutterbuck and Hodge 2017).

Given that, as yet, there is no seminal model or framework of team coaching supervision, my intention here is not to create such a model but rather to explore the territory with its many factors and elements, that the team coach and supervisor needs to be aware of and attend to during an assignment. Figure 21.1 represents this territory.

I invite the reader to imagine the territory and all its factors being like the living system of a forest where plants, trees, animals and insects all cohabit, interact and share the space. The whole system is interconnected, interdependent, in constant motion, and never still – the 'warm data' of Bateson (2018). Imagine then the team coach, or coaches, together with their supervisor, starting to explore this territory with the diverse relationships and dynamics of all the parts of the system, together with the impact they have on each other. Each factor within the overall territory includes a number of elements that may be considered and that I now discuss.

The coach or coaches at the centre

The challenge for team coaches and their supervisors is where to focus attention within one supervision session, or over the period of an assignment. I have deliberately placed the coach/coaches at the centre of the map so that the supervisor

MAPPING THE TERRITORY OF
TEAM COACHING

Figure 21.1 Mapping the territory of team coaching

may avoid the risk or temptation of getting overly involved in the team coaching itself. Increasingly, because of the complexity of the work, coaches are working as a mini team themselves, often in dyads, where they share the task and the process. Questions the coach brings to supervision include: How to manage themselves in this complexity? What is their flexibility and capacity to facilitate and coach in this maelstrom of interactions? What is their own history and their patterns being in groups and how this may impact on their engagement with the leader, the diverse members, with each other if in a dyad, with the wider system? How do they attend to their roles and responsibilities with their own capacity to coach a team and how this may differ from one-to-one coaching?

Individual participants

Here the coach may be sensitive to the individual members of the team, with their preferences, their patterns and their approach to learning. It is also important to notice individuals' personal motivation, preferred aptitude and methods of participating in the team – if indeed they actually want to be a member of the team. Issues around diversity and inclusion may arise here. The Milan Approach to systemic therapy (Campbell et al. 1991) may inform the coach in terms of emphasis on growth and the participants' ability to make choices; using hypotheses as an approach to guide the dialogue within the team and in supervision; acknowledging the art of this process (rather than being mechanistic and following a fixed pathway); allowing curiosity, creativity and irreverence to come to the heart of the relationship; focus on participation and how this informs what might be happening. Here is an opportunity for the coach to integrate their personal skills and orientations into a framework that falls within the definition of team coaching.

Leadership

There is often an ostensible team leader (by title or function) whose effectiveness depends on their experience and understanding of their role and responsibilities. Whether they also hold the psychological leadership of the team is sometimes doubtful and may only show up when everyone comes together.

Contracting, explicit and implicit

There is a perpetual and recurring need for the coaches to contract and re-contract at every stage of the assignment. While practical details may appear straightforward, individual needs, assumptions and expectations are likely to be in constant flux. This, in turn, impacts on the coach's engagement with and commitment to the team coaching. The coach may also attend to how individual members contract with each other and the leader. How the participants will engage, collaborate, etc. may need to be reviewed throughout, depending on what was agreed overall (Carroll 2005; Hay 2007).

Stages of group or team development

What becomes clear in team coaching assignments is that the group, as it evolves into a team – and possibly into a high-performing team (Carr and Peters 2013) – does not flow in a straight trajectory of 'improvement' towards effectiveness. The team members may change, and their individual circumstances and relationships may also change. Team coach/es need to be alert to this evolving and sometimes bumpy progression (e.g. Bion 1968; Lencioni 2002; Kantor 2012).

Psychological phenomena and groups

Each participant comes to the group/team with a history of membership of other groups. Either consciously or unconsciously, they may associate their experience in the team with that of their family of origin, sibling and parental relationships, or former school experiences, and may thus repeat learned behaviours and reactions that are well embedded. Here, too, each participant will bring their personal needs for power or control, and the coach will need to consider the impact authority and competition may be having on how team members engage with each other and with the coach. Contributing to the co-creation of safety and trust that will enable the participants to learn and grow together is an important task for team coaches (Kantor 2012; Thornton 2016).

Relationships

Closely linked with the psychological phenomena that occur, often at an unconscious level, are the multiple relationships not only with and between team members, but also with other stakeholders outside the team, and their relationship with the organization itself (Critchley 2010). It might also be relevant to consider the impact of unconscious transference and countertransference between team members and the coach – is the coach a relief for them, or a threat? What is it in the context of systemic dynamics? What do they project onto each other and the coach? Emotional intelligence (Bharwaney 2015), enabling collaboration, a shift from the 'I' to the 'we'. Here, too, we might consider aspects of diversity and inclusion, especially in cross-cultural teams (Whelan 2005).

Customs and culture of the organization

Team coaches need to be alert to assumptions and patterns around 'this is how we do things around here', which make learning new ways of working as a team challenging. Norms, habits, the way we do things, team structures, mutual responsibility for outcomes, increased collaboration and effectiveness, embracing diversity and dispersed leadership are all elements that may impact on the outcome (Bharwaney et al. 2019).

Collective intelligence

Shared sense-making, emergent collective knowing, when it needs to come out of task focus, predicts a group's performance and correlates with individual group members' ability to reason about the mental states of others (Woolley et al. 2010). Collective intelligence may depend on the composition of the group (average member intelligence), and factors that emerge from the way group members interact when they are assembled (e.g. conversational turn taking behaviour (Woolley et al. 2010) and average social sensitivity of group members, not merely individual intelligence.

Team coaching framework

As we enter the field with emerging models of team coaching, how does the coach offer an approach to their client that demonstrates their understanding of adult learning, adult development, team learning and team development (Lencioni 2002; Clutterbuck 2020 Hawkins 2014; Britton 2015)?

External influences

At any given time during an assignment, the team and the coach cannot predict what may be happening in the wider context in which the work is happening. Political, economic and social conditions are in constant flux, all of which are outside the control of the coach, yet may have a huge impact on the team's capacity to engage in the coaching, their commitment to engage and their overall intentions and thus the progress and outcomes of the work.

Ethical issues and dilemmas

These may arise during any individual or team coaching assignment and team coaches will benefit hugely from taking these to regular supervision, where they can explore what may be arising in the safety of 'not knowing' to gain clarity. For example, questions may arise around whether to coach the individual team members and team leader. Or, does the coach work with the team leader in isolation and engage other coaches to work with individual team members (Carroll 2013)?

Progress reviews

Again, fundamental to a team coaching assignment and integral to the contracting process is determining and agreeing how each stakeholder, and the team as a whole, will review and evaluate the work. In supervision, team coaches often share their fears or frustrations about the rate of progress or an apparent lack of change in the team. They are then able, in supervision, to consider the team's expectations for what change is realistic and resist the urge to take too much responsibility for reaching the team's collective outcomes. What is the direction of travel? What does progress look like? How might this be evaluated and thus adjustments made to the purpose or timeline? What are the team's definitions of success, what is the team moving towards?

In concluding this review of the territory of team coaching (Figure 21.1), it may be used simply as a checklist for the team coach and supervisor to see what may be missing, the blind spots or to choose a direction of focus. I do not want to call this a model because there is the potential for this to be interpreted as static or linear. Equally, we would not expect to work our way methodically through each of the factors in sequence. What is actually going on in practice may be described perhaps more like a pinball machine or a kaleidoscope – when one element in one factor moves, so the whole configuration changes and another element may be foregrounded. However, it is clear that none of these factors is at the forefront all of the time; instead, they inform each other and the process is in constant motion.

With so many possible factors and elements to consider, it is clear that the supervisor needs to create appropriate containment that enables the team coach to reflect on the work and on who they are in this work. What strikes me is how the supervisor's capacity to do this is vital. They need to bring and model equity, respect, non-judgement, parity, fairness, listening equally and trust (Woolley 2010), holding that everyone is doing their best and has an equally valid point of view, perspective or contribution. It strikes me that at the heart of this is a real need for compassion within the complexity.

I believe at this stage that instead of trying to create a model of team coaching supervision, supervisors need to develop their capacity to hold a constantly moving series of interconnected factors and elements without trying to make a simple order or structure out of them. Given this, I now go on to look more closely at the role of the supervisor.

The role of supervisor of team coaching

I believe that the supervisor's role in general is one of resourcing the coach, without rescuing, by providing encouragement that enables the coach to gain clarity around their process and the task. The additional intention in team coaching supervision is to explore the purpose, the multiple layers of complexity and diverse elements that the team and thus the team coach may be working with. Supervision provides the space and containment for the coach to stand back from and reflect on what may be emerging, changing, evolving during the change process that the team is going through. A key task includes enabling the coach to ground themselves and establish what they are and are not really responsible for.

Team coaching and subsequently supervision enables the coach and the supervisor to not only draw on an extensive range of tools and models that they are constantly refreshing and integrating, but also allows them to bring more of themselves, their life experience and wisdom into the space. Thus, in supervision we may explore the coach's unique blend that enables them to be effective as we consider and facilitate their development and capacity to be fully present while also being flexible enough to enable the learning in their client teams.

The supervisor enables the coach to attend to their self-doubt, their not knowing, at the same time staying curious as to whether these feelings of doubt and anxiety are theirs alone or those of the team or part of the team (Thornton 2016). The coach may arrive in supervision concerned with their capacity to add value and make a tangible impact or difference with their client. They can have real fear for their potency, their effectiveness. Within the container that is supervision, the coach is able to sit with the not knowing, being held in this safe space by the supervisor that does make a difference, that does add value but may not appear to be action oriented or goal/achievement focused. The supervisor needs to be able to sit with their client's fear, mistrust, discomfort, fallibility, confusion and doubt without trying to rescue them or offering to help, instead facilitating awareness and learning for the coach.

While it may be tempting to try to co-coach the team with the coach, or take over as consultant, the supervisor may try to fix whatever they believe may be happening with the team (Hodge and Clutterbuck 2019b). Supervisors need to develop their own capacity to recognize and hold the interrelational dynamics, provide the container for deep reflection, be facilitative and hold the space for the coach to explore (Hodge 2016). This is particularly challenging when the processes in and beyond the client and organizational system are very strong.

Guidance for future learning and research

Based on this review of team coaching and supervision, whatever our approach as supervisor, we need to enable the team coach to explore themselves and their work, constantly revisiting the purpose, desired outcomes and expectations of the client. I would add that to enable this level of reflection, it is essential that supervisors have developed their own self-awareness, maturity and interpersonal capacity to be fully in relationship, in support of team coaches and their clients, aptly captured by Murdoch's (2013) assertion that 'who you are is how you supervise'.

I propose that supervisors need many of the personal skills and self-awareness that a team coach needs. They may well also need to develop their knowledge and experience of coaching in organizations, wider systems, organizational change, levels of systemic approaches (Lawrence 2020), as well as an appreciation of stakeholder engagement (Hawkins 2014; Turner and Hawkins 2016). In order to support and enable the team coach to develop, I would also advocate that supervisors would benefit from developing their understanding, capacity and skill to be in and facilitate group learning and development (Thornton 2016). It is vital that the supervisor develops their capacity to be present and stay out of the coach's way when the coach may be distressed, anxious, fearful or when they are finding their own path through the forest (Murdoch 2013; Thornton 2016).

As the practice of team coaching supervision gains clarity and momentum I foresee that some sort of structural supervision framework would provide the supervisor with some further clarity or a degree of reassurance in their purpose. At the same time, I would advocate that this framework seeks to capture or personify the fluid, evolving emergence that allows for the complexity and the learning at an individual, group and organizational level.

As I come to the end of this chapter, I would now like to pose four questions for reflection to inform the team coach and the team coaching supervisor:

Questions for reflection

- What is the value and relevance of the supervisor's own experience and relationship with groups in supervising team coaching?
- What would a team coaching supervision model or framework look like?
- What is the relevance to supervisors of their own experience working in and with teams in organizations or wider, diverse and disparately located systems?
- As team coaches increasingly work in dyads or teams, is group supervision the ideal format for team coach supervision?

Further sources

Clutterbuck, D., Gannon, J., Hayes, S. et al. (eds) (2019) *The Practitioner's Handbook of Team Coaching*. London: Routledge. This handbook provides the team coaching supervisor with a comprehensive selection of perspectives on the many different aspects of team coaching and its development.

Edmondson, A.C. (2019) *The Fearless Organisation: Creating Psychological Safety in the Workplace for Learning, Innovation and Growth*. New York: John Wiley & Sons. Based on research, Edmondson explores the impact of fear as it manifests in organizations, especially with teams.

Heffernan, M. (2019) *Uncharted: How to Map the Future Together*. London: Simon & Schuster. Heffernan invites us to consider what we need to do and who we need to be as we plan and engage with the future.

References

Bateson, N. (2018) Warm data. Available from: https://batesoninstitute.org/announcement/warm-data/ (accessed June 2020).

Bharwaney, G. (2015) *Emotional Resilience*. Harlow: Pearson.

Bharwaney, G., Wolff, S.B. and Druskat, V. (2019) Emotion and team performance, in D. Clutter-buck, J. Gannon and S. Hayes et al. (eds) *The Practitioner's Handbook of Team Coaching*. London: Routledge.

Bion, R. (1968) *Experiences in Groups*. London: Tavistock Publications.

Britton, J. (2015) Expanding the coaching conversation: group and team coaching, *Industrial and Commercial Training*, 47: 116–120.

Campbell, D., Draper, R. and Crutchley, E. (1991) The Milan systemic approach to family therapy, in A.S. Gurman and D. Kniskern (eds) *Handbook of Family Therapy*, Volume 2. Abingdon: Routledge.

Carr, C. and Peters, J. (2013) The experience and impact of team coaching: a dual case study, *International Coaching Psychology Review*, 8(1): 80–98.

Carroll, M. (2005) Psychological contracts with and within organisations, in R. Tribe and J. Morrissey (eds) *Handbook of Professional and Ethical Practice for Psychologists, Counsel-lors and Psychotherapists*. Hove: Brunner-Routledge.

Carroll, M. (2013) *Ethical Maturity in the Helping Professions*. London: Jessica Kingsley.

Clutterbuck, D. (2020) *Coaching the Team at Work*. London: Nicholas Brealey.

Clutterbuck, D. and Hodge, A. (2017) Team coaching supervision survey. Available from: https://alisonhodge.com/wp-content/uploads/2020/03/team-coaching-supervision-survey-2017.pdf (accessed June 2020).

Critchley, W. (2010) Relational coaching: taking the coaching high road, *Journal of Management Development*, 29(10): 851–863.

Gray, D.E. and Jackson, P. (2011) Coaching supervision in the historical context of psychothera-peutic and counseling models: a meta-model, in T. Bachkirova, P. Jackson and D. Clutterbuck (eds) *Coaching and Mentoring Supervision: Theory and Practice*. Maidenhead: Open University Press.

Hawkins, P. (2014) *Leadership Team Coaching*, 2nd edn. London: Kogan Page.

Hawkins, P. and Smith, N. (2013) *Coaching, Mentoring and Organisational Consultancy*, 2nd edn. Maidenhead: Open University Press.

Hay, J. (2007) *Reflective Practice and Supervision for Coaches* Maidenhead: Open University Press.

Hodge, A. (2016) The value of coaching supervision as a development process and its contribu-tion to continued professional and personal wellbeing for executive coaches, *International Journal of Evidence Based Coaching and Mentoring*, 14(2): 87–102.

Hodge, A. and Clutterbuck, D. (2019a) Supervising team coaches: working with complexity at a distance, in D. Clutterbuck, J. Gannon, S. Hayes et al. (eds) *The Practitioner's Handbook of Team Coaching*. London: Routledge.

Hodge, A. and Clutterbuck, D. (2019b) Guidelines for team coaching supervision, in J. Birch and P. Welch (eds) *Coaching Supervision: Advancing Practice, Changing Landscapes*. Abingdon: Routledge.

Jones, R., Napierskey, U. and Lyubovnikova, J. (2019) Conceptualising the distinctiveness of team coaching, *Journal of Managerial Psychology*, 34(2): 62–78.

Kantor, D. (2012) *Reading the Room*. San Francisco: Jossey-Bass.

Lawrence, P. (2019) Defining team coaching, in D. Clutterbuck, J. Gannon, S. Hayes et al. (eds) *The Practitioner's Handbook of Team Coaching*. London: Routledge.

Lawrence, P. (2020) Team coaching revisited. Available from: https://www.ccorgs.com.au/wp-content/uploads/2020/04/White-Paper-Systemic-Team.pdf (accessed 6 August 2020).

Lencioni, P. (2002) *The Five Dysfunctions of a Team*. San Francisco: Jossey-Bass.

Moral, M. (2011) A French model of supervision: supervising a 'several to several' coaching jour-ney, in T. Bachkirova et al. (2011) *Coaching and Mentoring Supervision*. Maidenhead: Open University Press.

Murdoch, E. (2013) Foreword, in E. Murdoch and J. Arnold (eds) *Full Spectrum Supervision*. St Albans: Panoma Press.

Proctor, B. (2000) *Group Supervision.* London: Sage.

Thornton, C. (2016) *Group and Team Coaching: The Secret Life of Groups,* 2nd edn. London: Routledge.

Turner, E. and Hawkins, P. (2016) Multi-stakeholder contracting in executive/business coaching: an analysis of practice and recommendations for gaining maximum value, *International Journal of Evidence Based Coaching and Mentoring,* 14(2): 48–65.

Whelan, S.A. (2005) *Creating Effective Teams.* London: Sage.

Woolley, A., Chabris, C.F., Pentland, A. et al. (2010) Evidence for a collective intelligence factor in the performance of human groups, *Science Magazine,* 330(6004): 686–688.

22 Supervising internal coaches

Christine K. Champion, Alison Maxwell and Kate Pinder

Introduction

While the last decade has seen an expanding literature on coaching and coaching supervision, relatively little has yet been written about the particular challenges of supervising the internal coach. This chapter seeks to explore the key developments in the field of supervision of internal coaches, since the original publication of this chapter (Maxwell 2011). We briefly review internal coach supervision practices in organizations, noting the rise of the internal coach supervisor.

The chapter briefly summarizes the types of ethical dilemmas brought by internal coaches to supervision and outlines some of the practice challenges that we commonly see. These observations are taken from our experience as external supervisors working with internal coaches across a diverse range of organizations over a number of years. Short case studies are included to illustrate some of the key issues.

In addition, the challenges of supervising the internal coach are discussed, highlighting the potential practical, professional, psychological and political issues a coaching supervisor must be aware of and address. An initial comparison of the relative merits of coach supervision provided by internal and external resources is offered. The chapter concludes with reflection questions for practitioners and suggestions for further learning and research.

Organizations have experienced a rapid rise in the use of internal coaches. Coaching surveys (for example, Ridler 2015) note increasing reliance on the internal coach as a means of supporting employee development and performance. While this trend appears to have been primarily driven by cost-saving motives, many organizations have sought to establish 'coaching cultures' (Ridler 2015) and have developed their managers and staff accordingly. The rise of the internal coach has also been accelerated by the provision of 'train to coach' programmes, and it is possible to call oneself a coach after a few days' training. Longer and more rigorous programmes are also now available leading to more meaningful certification and/or qualification, and some universities offer qualifications up to Master's and Professional Doctorate levels. In parallel, the last decade has seen an increasing professionalization of coaching in general and in particular coaching supervision. However, coaching supervision has yet to be mandated and the uptake of supervision globally is highly inconsistent (Turner et al. 2018). Nevertheless, in most coaching markets the use of coaching supervision appears to be on the rise. This has, in part, been driven by professional bodies who now strongly advocate the use of coaching supervision and require evidence of adequate supervision arrangements as an integral part of their accreditation programmes for all coaches. In the UK, for example, the European Mentoring and Coaching Council (EMCC) and Association for Coaching (AC) have both introduced specific competency frameworks for supervision and offer accreditation of supervision practice. The Institute of Leadership and Management (ILM) offers Level 7 qualification in coach supervision.

Perhaps as a result of these developments, organizations now appear to have greater understanding of coaching and the need for coaching supervision, even if this is not necessarily translated into practice. For example, a survey of coaching sponsors in 105 blue chip international organizations found that although 88 per cent agreed that supervision is a fundamental requirement for any professional executive coach, under half reported feeling confident that all their coaches participated in supervision (Ridler 2015). Similarly, the more recent 'Manifesto for Supervision' (Hawkins et al. 2019) notes the paradox of much greater advocacy of coaching supervision yet its continued underuse.

St John-Brooks (2010) reported post-training support for internal coaches as highly inconsistent and little seems to have changed in this regard. Recent years have seen an increase in the numbers of organizations who are active in provision of continuous professional development for their internal coaches. This has taken a variety of formats, including informal 'action learning' and discussion groups, further access to training as well as to external speakers and experts in the field. However, many organizations still appear to feel that on-going development for their coaches is unnecessary, or of low value.

With regards to internal coach supervision, practice can be seen as equally variable. While some organizations provide on-going coach supervision as a matter of course, in others coaches are left to set up their own supervision arrangements, sometimes at their own cost and in their own time. In general, group supervision is seen as a more cost-effective solution than one-to-one supervision, although St John-Brooks (2018, 2019) and Turner et al. (2018) both note the rise of peer or co-supervision within organizations as a means of providing developmental support. While organizations still appear to depend heavily on externals to provide supervision services, the last decade has seen increasing investment by organizations in training of their own supervisors. This has been partly driven by cost considerations, but supervision training also represents a natural career path for seasoned coaches.

Taken together, this evidence would suggest that we are still far from a world in which organizational coaches systematically engage in their on-going professional development and are supported as a matter of course by high-quality coaching supervision. Further, there is a need for improved infrastructure to support internal coaching. The professional infrastructure for internal coaching needs to be put in place at an early stage to support the quality of coaching – not least the provision of high-quality supervision for coaches . . . and an openness to supervision (Ridler 2015).

The case study below gives an example of the infrastructure deployed to support an internal coaching programme, and details how supervision of their coaches and internal supervisors was enabled.

Box 22.1 Case illustration

Coaching and supervision infrastructure in a UK financial organization

A UK financial organization had trained 30 internal coaches, including middle and senior managers. Three internal supervisors, who were all very experienced coaches, were given responsibility for managing the internal cadre of coaches. Supervision was offered monthly to the coaches in a group format and on a one-to-one basis as needs dictated. The three supervisors, one of whom was formally trained as a supervisor, had external supervision quarterly, as well as optional one to one phone calls between sessions. Quarterly face-to-face sessions were held on a one-to-one basis, and also as a group. The group professional development agenda for the sessions was tabled in conjunction with the external supervisor. This covered questions of frequency of supervision for the internal coaches, CPD topics to be explored with their groups, as well as boundary and other ethical issues raised by both coaches and supervisors.

Ethical issues and practice challenges

In this section we explore two aspects of internal coach supervision. First, we briefly examine the types of ethical issues or dilemmas that are typically brought by internal coaches to supervision. Second, we outline a number of practice challenges that we have noted while providing supervision within organizations. These latter points relate to how internal coaches approach the coaching task and engage with the supervision process.

Ethical issues and dilemmas

In our experience many of the ethical issues and dilemmas brought to supervision by internal coaches are similar to those brought by external coaches. However, internal coaches appear particularly prone to issues regarding boundary management, holding confidentiality and dealing with internal power relationships (St John-Brooks 2018; Moral and Angel 2019). We see the following issues repeatedly in our supervision practice:

- *Boundary and confidentiality management* – Internal coaches are not necessarily used to defining and holding defined boundaries around their coaching work. This includes an appreciation of the circumstances in which it is not appropriate to coach and those situations outside their competence. From a confidentiality perspective, internal coaches are also particularly prone to requests for information on their coachees, for example, from line managers or HR professionals.
- *Role conflicts* and *other conflicts of interest* – Many internal coaches hold dual roles in their organizations, for example HR manager and coach, leader and coach. They therefore may be asked to hold competing agendas, and/or hold

confidential information about their coachees and about the organization which the coachee may not be aware of. The case study in Box 22.2 demonstrates one such scenario. Such situations raise issues of role dualities as well as boundary management in supervision (Box 22.2).

Box 22.2 Case illustration

Role dualities

Helen worked in a large multi-national, in which she combined the roles of a senior leader with that of an internal coaching supervisor. During one-to-one supervision with a coach, she learns of a coachee's poor management practices and behaviours. Helen's values are so challenged she is drawn into the content of the situation and neglects to attend to the needs of the coach she is working with. Unconsciously, she is drawn into 'leader-mode', motivated by a desire to take action to fix the problem.

- *Potential for collusion* – Internal coaches are enmeshed in the culture and practices of the organizations they work for and may share, consciously or otherwise, many of the same assumptions and beliefs. Providing an independent and objective perspective to their coachees can therefore prove difficult.
- *Power relationships* – Wrynne (2011: 59) notes that coachees have a tendency to see internal coaches as 'the embodiment of the organisation', resulting in a distortion of the power relationship between them. This can result in coachees being less open to exposing their concerns and vulnerabilities or in coachees trying to influence their coaches for their own ends. Power differentials may also inhibit an internal coach from challenging sufficiently when working with senior leadership (Box 22.3).

Box 22.3 Case illustration

Power and manipulation

A senior manager requested some career coaching from Sara, a mid-level HR manager. He heard from the chief executive that Sara was involved with re-structuring plans that might impact on his position in the organization. The senior manager sought to access information indirectly about his likely career options and guidance from Sara how to best equip himself for such positions. If he were successful, the restructure would result in him managing Sara, albeit indirectly.

Practice challenges

In addition to the above ethical challenges, we note the following patterns in how internal coaches approach coaching and engage with the supervision process.

- *Contracting and contracting rigour* – In our experience, internal coaches tend to pay less attention to contracting with their clients. Contracting is often not a simple matter and finding out 'who is the client' can be challenging. St John-Brooks (2018) also points out that three-way contracting is often avoided inside organizations, particularly when senior management are involved.
- *Task-focused coaching* – Our experience suggests that internal coaches are often primarily concerned with helping their clients to solve their practical workplace problems. Anxiety is therefore provoked when they can't help a client find a solution. The quality of their coaching can become overly judged by outcomes, and there is less reflection on the process of their coaching or the quality of relationship with coachees.
- *Non-systemic coaching* – Internal coaches appear to be more prone to take a non-systemic perspective on their coaching, underplaying both their own influence on the work, and the wider context in which it takes place. There also appears to be a tendency to problematize clients, particularly in remedial coaching relationships (Cavanagh 2006), rather than consider the whole system of influences at play (Box 22.4).

Box 22.4 Case illustration

Making the client a problem

Peter, an internal coach, was asked to work with an employee who had a record of mental health issues, related to past traumatic life events. The coaching assignment was contracted to look at the employee's resilience and coping strategies. However, Peter was unduly influenced by the client's manager's opinion that the employee was a 'problem' and decided the engagement was beyond his skills.

- *Time pressures* – Many internal coaches offer their services as an adjunct to their day job and might not have the full support of their line managers. Finding additional time for coaching supervision may therefore be a luxury for many internal coaches.
- *Inadequate experience* – While availability of coach training has expanded, it would appear that many novice internal coaches do not have sufficient coaching hours to develop proficiency and confidence. While there is little recent data in this area, a survey of practising coaches (St John-Brooks 2010) suggested that 41 per cent of respondents coached for less than 5 hours per month, and that 42 per cent had one or fewer clients. As a consequence, supervision sessions may be forced to revisit the basics of coaching practice, rather than focus on extending capability.

Challenges for the coaching supervisor

While the challenges brought to supervision by internal coaches have been documented to an extent (St John-Brooks 2010, 2018, 2019), less has been written about the challenges faced by the coaching supervisor working with such groups. In this section we explore these issues under four broad headings – procedural/practical, professional, psychological and political issues. An initial comparison of the relative strengths and/or weaknesses of internal and external coaching supervision is made, based on our experiences in the field.

Procedural/practical issues – logistics, protocols, stakeholder management, contracting and how participants engage and work together

The coaching supervisor faces an array of practical and procedural problems, especially when external to the organization. For example, a common language and understanding of coaching cannot be assumed, and stakeholders are likely to hold multiple understandings of 'supervision', how it works and what is required to set it up successfully. In order to operate effectively, the coaching supervisor needs both a practical understanding of the organization and its administrative gatekeepers as well as a strategic sense of its development agenda.

In the course of their work, coaching supervisors are required to manage multiple stakeholders, and to navigate a complex web of internal relationships and competing needs. Answering the question 'Who is my client?' may not be easy and potentially multi-layered. Figure 22.1 represents a typical network of relationships

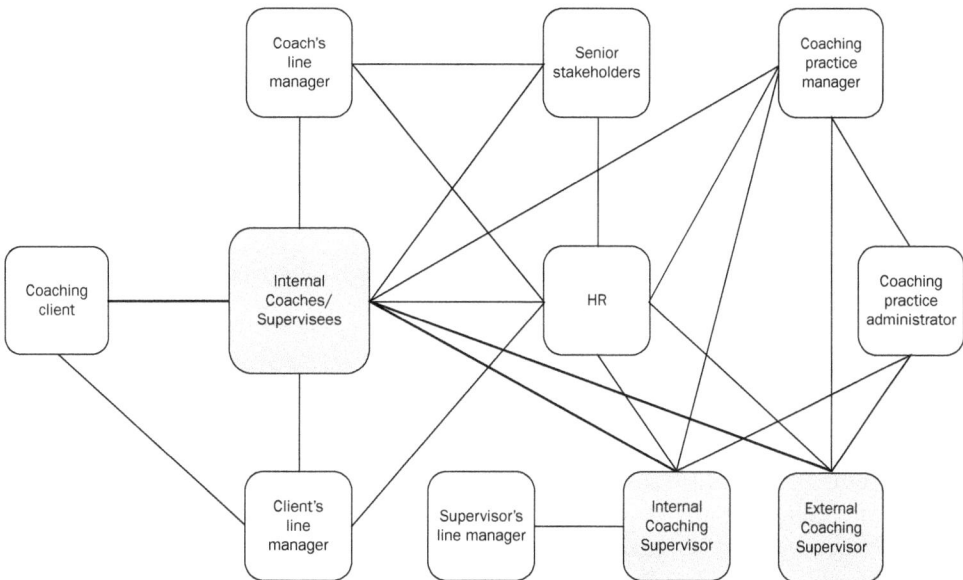

Figure 22.1 The complex system of stakeholders in supervision of internal coaches (adapted from Maxwell 2011)

that a coaching supervisor may be involved with. It demonstrates the potentially complex nature of contracting – with supervisees, commissioning bodies such as HR and those tasked with managing coaching across the organization. Across these many relationships, the supervisor has, in part, the responsibility of ensuring a shared understanding of supervision, to clarify and align expectations with all stakeholders, and to create the conditions in which supervision can flourish.

This multiplicity of stakeholders, while inevitable, can create issues in its own right. For example, coaches may wonder why the organization has chosen a particular supervisor and where that supervisor's allegiances lie. Trust may be undermined if a supervisor is suspected of reporting back to the organization or expressing opinions regarding an individual's capacity to coach. Turner and Passmore (2018) discuss the responsibilities supervisors have in reporting coaches who they believe have acted unethically, unprofessionally or illegally, even when the organization is not paying for their services directly. The confidentiality of the supervision process may therefore be in question, prejudicing the types of issues participants are willing to bring to supervision and their engagement with the process. Clarity of expectations and transparent communication between participants is therefore vital.

Our experience also suggests that one of the biggest practical issues associated with group supervision is ensuring continuity of attendance. All too frequently, attendance can be seen as optional, and/or of lower priority than the 'day job'. Coaches with small caseloads can see time in supervision as disproportionate. Robson's (2016) study of internal coaches found that some coaches' managers questioned the value of supervision and that coaches were asked to demonstrate the value of the time. Internal group sessions can also get hijacked for discussion of administrative and organizational issues, and the actual time devoted to case load may be compromised.

From a procedural and practical perspective, the internal supervisor has many advantages over the external supervisor, not least that of a perceived cost advantage. Internal supervisors are also advantaged in that they are more likely to

Table 22.1 Comparison of internal and external supervisors – procedural issues

Factors	Internal coach supervisor	External coach supervisor
Cost to organization	Proportion of salary plus on-costs	According to fee negotiated
Common language/ coaching philosophy	More likely to share common assumptions and language. Coaching philosophy based on initial training	May have differing language, assumptions and coaching philosophy
Encouraging continuity of attendance	May cancel more frequently when costs are not directly incurred	May be less likely to cancel when costs are incurred with an external supplier
Rigour of contracting	May assume less importance if assumptions are made	May contract more rigorously as assumptions are less likely
Managing stakeholders	Likely to have prior knowledge of key figures and relationships	May be unaware of key figures and relationships

have established working relationships across the organization, and consequently have more insight into how to manage stakeholders. However, this intimate knowledge of the organization may also lead to making assumptions and unwarranted shortcuts. For example, rigorous contracting may be seen as unnecessary or overly procedural, and therefore not be conducted with the same thoroughness as someone coming to the situation with fresh eyes. Our experience also suggests that internal coaches are more likely to attend supervision sessions when an external supervisor is present. There appears to be a greater likelihood of legitimizing other work pressures and prioritizing these when an internal supervision is engaged. More research is necessary to explore the range of factors that may influence attendance.

Professional issues – skills and behaviour of both supervisor and supervisee, expectations of depth and quality of work together

New coaches benefit from group supervision by learning from peers (Passmore and McGoldrick 2009). However, novice coaches, struggling to find sufficient clients, can feel they have little to offer, or indeed gain from, supervision sessions. As internal supervision groups often include coaches of widely differing expertise and confidence, it is important for any group supervisor to be inclusive while catering for all needs. Coaches may also feel they cannot display their vulnerabilities and uncertainties in front of colleagues, especially when those colleagues are more senior. Supervisors working with groups therefore need expertise in group dynamics (Forsyth 2010), as well as an awareness of how organizational power dynamics can intrude into supervision sessions.

From a professional skills perspective, comparisons between internal and external supervisors are difficult to make. It cannot be assumed that internal

Table 22.2 Comparison of internal and external supervisors – professional issues

Factors	Internal coach supervisor	External coach supervisor
Competence of the supervisor	May not have specific training in supervisor skills. May have less experience of supervision	May have external qualifications in coaching supervision and greater experience of supervision
Breadth of work experience	May be limited to experiences within an organization	Likely to operate in multiple organizational settings
Breadth of supervision techniques	May use more limited range. May be limited to those used on initial coach training	Able to offer a broader range of techniques and drawn on a range of approaches
Skills transfer to organization	Adds value by embedding skills and knowledge internally	More limited and indirect contribution to organization
Choice of supervisor	Choice limited to senior coaches/internal supervisors	Access to wider market of coaching supervisors
Development cost	Organization bears cost of training internal supervisors	External supervisor bears the cost of training and CPD

supervisors are less qualified than external supervisors, and indeed some internal supervisors carry equivalent coaching and supervision workloads. Drawing on our experience, we note that internal supervisors are often given this role due to their seniority as coaches rather than as a result of specific supervisory training. A qualified external supervisor is therefore more likely to bring a greater range of skills and perspectives to the role, as well as being able to benchmark practices with other organizations.

Psychological issues – intra- and interpersonal dynamics, conditions of trust and emotional safety

Hodge (2014) speaks of the importance of mutual trust, safety and respect as conditions for openness and effective engagement in coaching supervision. This is particularly important if coaches are to express and explore feelings of inadequacy, self-doubt or shame (de Haan 2012), or to explore areas of self-deception (Bachkirova 2016). Sheppard's research (2018) highlighted four common ways in which coaches might inhibit themselves in supervision. These relate to anxiety, fear of judgement, self-limiting beliefs and perceived lack of agency. These intra- and interpersonal dynamics require careful and empathetic handling by the coaching supervisor as well as attention to the development of appropriate emotional 'holding' and psychological safety (Finlay 2015).

Our experience of group supervision suggests a common tendency for group members to get 'caught up' with others' moods and to get overly engrossed in the content of each other's narratives. Rather than staying curious about the underlying process and dynamics, supervisees can overly identify with others' situations and risk colluding with each other's perspectives. It can also be very hard for supervisees to separate themselves from the systems they work within unless the organization is of sufficient scale to locate them in different parts. Several organizations have solved this particular problem by ensuring coaching relationships are not set up within the same business area where possible, although this may be more difficult for supervisory relationships.

It is in the realm of psychological issues that there is perhaps the most potential for differences between internal and external supervisors. As an organizational

Table 22.3 Comparison of internal and external supervisors – psychological issues

Factors	Internal coach supervisor	External coach supervisor
Cultural alignment	More likely to have knowledge of the organizational context, priorities and values	Likely to be an 'outsider' – may require onboarding to be effective
Potential for collusion	Continuing exposure to organizational norms and assumptions. Risk of 'groupthink' higher	Less likely as operating across many organizations. Counter-balance to 'groupthink'
Depth of work	May be overly task focused. May have lack of skills to work with intrapersonal aspects	Often more qualified and experienced in working intra-personally

insider, the internal supervisor is continually exposed to the norms and expectations of the organization in which they work. The internal supervisor is therefore likely to share some of the same organizational frustrations and narratives as the coaches they supervise. Some authors therefore view collusion as also a particular challenge for internal supervisors (Turner and Passmore 2018) and peer supervisors, and question the extent to which they can be objective and provide effective challenge and exploration of issues. This theme was echoed by participants at the 2020 AOCS virtual conference:

> From my experience, collusion comes up a lot within supervision, particularly as there is a lot of change going on in the business which affects may coaches and supervisors in their day jobs. It's something that needs attention, to help identify what is the supervisee's stuff and what is the supervisor's. (Internal supervisor, personal communication)

There are also potential differences in the 'depth' of working. Coaches may feel more able to discuss personal issues that impact their practice with an external supervisor, where no other relationship exists. Coaches may also see the internal supervisor more as a 'facilitator and process owner', rather than as an expert who has a depth of experience and knowledge in supervisory dynamics and practice.

Political issues – issues of power, influence, loyalty and obligation

Working inside an organization, either as an internal or external supervisor, brings with it a number of 'political' issues. For example, within any supervision group, participants may be of very different seniority in the hierarchy and may have reporting line relationships. Having a heightened awareness of the potential power dynamics at play in a supervisory situation, whether openly acknowledged or not, is therefore essential to any supervisor, if it is to be of value.

From our experience, we would also argue that matters of power and hierarchy potentially influence supervisor–supervisee relationships, leading to dialogue editing or inhibition of the degree of challenge that can take place. Sheppard (2018) comments in her study that most supervisees did not identify as equal partners, with the supervisor being perceived as having expert power. This appears to be an under-explored aspect of coaching supervision, and little is known of how these power dynamics impact on the effectiveness of supervision.

Perceptions of power inequality may be particularly exacerbated for internal supervisors, where expert power can be combined with positional power, and role dualities may impact upon the supervisory relationship. Cullen and Edwards (2015), in their discussion of their supervision work at PWC, also list one of the challenges for internal supervisors as being seen as part of the hierarchy and therefore assumed to be judging and evaluating coach performance. Such situations raise issues of confidentiality in supervision and effective boundary management. They also pose questions about who can challenge the internal supervisor and who helps them to stay within the boundaries of their supervisory role.

Table 22.4 Comparison of internal and external supervisors – power issues

Factors	Internal coach supervisor	External coach supervisor
Role duality/ conflict of interest	Supervisor likely to hold multiple roles. Conflict of interests more likely	Less likely to hold dual roles. Conflict of interests between competing stakeholder needs may exist
Power dynamics	Likely to be more aware of power dynamics but also more subject to them	Less awareness of power dynamics but less likely to be subject to them
Capacity to challenge	May be constrained by power relationships	May be consulted as an external expert

However, from a power perspective, internal supervisors are likely to have far greater awareness for the political landscape in which they operate and so may bring more systemic awareness to their coaching. Furthermore, the status of internal supervisors may lend them the authority to challenge current custom and practice. Supervision, if explicitly agreed as part of contracting, can therefore provide a unique forum to 'harvest' organizational 'intelligence', which can be of benefit more widely. The paucity of literature in this area of harvesting systemic organization themes suggests there is scope for more evidence-based research into how organizations engage in this practice.

Guidance for further learning and research

In the last decade, organizations have invested in coach training for their managers and employees and more people now consider themselves a coach. However, participation in continuous professional development and coaching supervision continues to be patchy, often conflicting with the demands of the coaches' day job. We therefore still have a long way to go before systematic and regular supervision with a qualified supervisor is the norm.

The last decade has also seen the rise of the internal supervisor, and some large organizations now have mature and well-developed infrastructure for supporting the practice of their internal coaches. However, this is far from ubiquitous, and many internal coaches appear to be relatively unsupported by their organizations or depend on other coaches for support in some sort of peer mentoring arrangement. While more experienced coaches may have much to offer others, they often do not have specific qualifications in coaching supervision, or any in-depth training in group work or group dynamics.

This chapter has summarized the types of practical, professional, psychological and political challenges faced by coaching supervisors, presenting an initial comparison between internal and external supervisors on these dimensions. We suggest that internal supervisors may be particularly prone to collusion with organizational patterns and norms of behaviour and may not bring the objectivity or richness of experience that an external supervisor might bring. This too remains a largely under-researched area, even though writers (St John-Brooks 2018; Moral and Lamy 2017; Moral and Angel 2019) are beginning to explore the terrain.

Questions for reflection

- How can the process of reflective practice and inquiry be embedded as a regular internal coaching practice through the process of supervision?
- How can we evaluate the effectiveness and impact of coaching supervision for all stakeholders?
- Can internal supervisors ever be objective – how might loyalty to the organization and loyalty to the individual supervisee conflict?
- How do we raise self and systemic awareness of the additional complexity of the setting where an internal supervisor is engaged in supervising internal coaches?

Further sources

Birch, J. and Welch, P. (eds) (2019) *Coaching Supervision: Advancing Practice, Changing Landscape.* Abingdon: Routledge. This book discusses issues and raises similar questions to this chapter, with an example of internal coaching supervision at the University of Birmingham, and includes a case study example of boundaries, confidentiality and role conflict.

Cochrane, H. and Newton, T. (2018) *Supervision and Coaching.* Abingdon: Routledge. This book uses a transactional analysis approach and explores techniques for group processes in the chapter on supervision in practice.

Lucas, M. (ed.) (2020) *101 Coaching Supervision Techniques, Approaches, Enquiries and Experiments.* Abingdon: Routledge. This text covers a broad range of 101 different practical supervision techniques, from leaders in their fields, presented in 10 chapters, reflecting the philosophical basis of each technique. It is aimed at both novice and more experienced supervisors to broaden their repertoire and develop their practice.

References

Bachkirova, T. (2016) The self of the coach: conceptualization, issues and opportunities for practitioner development, *Consulting Psychology Journal: Practice and Research*, 68(2): 143–156.

Birch, J. and Welch, P. (eds) (2019) *Coaching Supervision: Advancing Practice, Changing Landscape.* Abingdon: Routledge.

Cavanagh, M. (2006) Coaching from a systemic perspective: a complex adaptive conversation, in D.R. Stober and A.M. Grant (eds) *Evidence-based Coaching Handbook: Putting Best Practices to Work for Your Clients.* Hoboken, NJ: Wiley.

Cochrane, H. and Newton, T. (2018) *Supervision and Coaching.* Abingdon: Routledge.

Cullen, D. and Edwards, S. (2015) Testing the reality, *Coaching at Work*, 10 (2): 37–42.

De Haan, E. (2012) *Supervision in Action.* Maidenhead: Open University Press.

Finlay, L. (2015) *Relational Integrative Psychotherapy: Process and Theory in Practice.* Chichester: Wiley.

Forsyth, D.R. (2010) *Group Dynamics.* Belmont, CA: Wadsworth, Cengage Learning.

Hawkins, P., Turner, E. and Passmore, J. (2019) *The Manifesto for Supervision.* Henley on Thames: Association for Coaching and Henley Business School.

Hodge, A. (2014) *An Action Research Inquiry into What Goes on in Coaching Supervision to the End of Enhancing the Coaching Profession.* Doctoral dissertation, Middlesex University.

Lucas, M. (ed.) (2020) *101 Coaching Supervision Techniques, Approaches, Enquiries and Experiments.* Abingdon: Routledge.

Maxwell, A. (2011) Supervising the internal coach, in T. Bachkirova, P. Jackson and D. Clutterbuck (eds) *Coaching & Mentoring Supervision: Theory & Practice.* Maidenhead: Open University Press.

Moral, M. and Angel P. (2019) *Le coaching et sa supervision, outils et pratiques,* Paris: InterEditions

Moral, M. and Lamy, F. (2017) *Stretching Ethical Dilemmas: A Creative Tool for Supervisors.* In 7th International Conference on Coaching Supervision, Oxford Brookes University, Oxford and at the 7th EMCC International Coaching and Mentoring Research Conference, Greenwich University, London.

Passmore, J. and McGoldrick, S. (2009) Super-vision, extra-vision or blind faith? A grounded theory study of the efficacy of coaching supervision, *International Coaching Psychology Review,* 4(2): 143–159.

Ridler and Co. (2015) *Sixth Ridler Report: Strategic Trends in the Use of Executive Coaching.* London: Ridler and Co. Available from: https://www.ridlerandco.com/ridler-report/ (accessed 6 July 2020).

Robson, M. (2016) An ethnographic study of the introduction of internal supervisors to an internal coaching scheme, *International Journal of Evidence Based Coaching and Mentoring,* 14(2): 106–122.

Sheppard, L. (2018) Supervision: help or hindrance?, *Coaching at Work,* 13(1): 34–38 and 13(2): 37–40.

St John-Brooks, K. (2010) What are the ethical challenges involved in being an internal coach, *The International Journal of Mentoring and Coaching,* 8(1).

St John-Brooks, K. (2018) *Internal Coaching: The Inside Story,* 2nd edn. Abingdon: Routledge.

St John-Brooks, K. (2019) Supervision for internal coaches, in J. Birch and P. Welch (eds) *Coaching Supervision: Advancing Practice, Changing Landscape.* Abingdon: Routledge.

Turner, T., Lucas, M. and Whitaker, C. (2018) *Peer Supervision in Coaching and Mentoring: A Versatile Guide to Reflective Practice.* Abingdon: Routledge.

Turner, E. and Passmore, J. (2018) Ethical dilemmas and tricky decisions: a global perspective of coaching supervisors' practices in coach ethical decision making, *International Journal of Evidence Based Coaching and Mentoring,* 16(1): 126–142.

Wrynne, C. (2011) *How Might the Experience of Internal Coaching Differ from the Experience of External Coaching?* Unpublished Masters dissertation, London Southbank University.

23 Supervising organization consultants

David Birch and Erik de Haan

Introduction

If supervision is now regarded as a foundation for sound professional practice among coaches, growing numbers of organizational development (OD) consultants are also benefiting from the supervision of their organization consulting and design work. This applies both to those working as internal practitioners within large organizations and to those working independently or as part of a consultancy. In this chapter we look at the various forms of consulting supervision, and reflect on their pros and cons. We argue that OD supervision is a distinctive field in its own right; however, the issues it faces are also of relevance to coaching supervisors. We end with a few dilemmas that may arise for the OD supervisor.

OD consulting is a broader field than individual coaching, comprising organizational interventions such as process consultation, team and organization development, organization design, strategic conferences and whole-system methodologies (Checkland 1981; Schein 1987; Weisbord and Janoff 1995). The broad reach of these interventions means that consultants are working closely with the organization's strategic agenda and the interplay of fast-moving social and political dynamics. Compared to coaching supervision, which tends to focus on the practice of team or individual coaching, OD supervision deals with the practitioner's active participation in the messiness of complex and multi-layered organizational systems. OD supervision also encompasses wider aspects of the professional's role, such as (1) the way the consultant interacts with other consultants within the context of larger-scale assignments; (2) the dynamics of the consultant's home base or consulting organization, for example around the allocation of assignments; and (3) the potential for the supervisor to hold their supervisees to account, confront unethical behaviour or safely feedback themes from supervision to the organization. In other words, good OD supervision may not necessarily be focused on the content of the supervisee's client work at all but rather on the supervisee's relationships with their colleagues and clients, in service of their learning and effectiveness as a practitioner (De Haan and Regouin 2016).

OD consulting supervisors and supervisees can decide to work together in three different modalities: individual supervision, shadow consultancy or peer supervision. We discuss the merits and limitations of these approaches below.

Modality 1 Supervising the individual consultant

This is supervision that is fully focused on the individual consultant and her practice. Individual consulting supervision works best when the supervisor is external to the organization, allowing them to attend to the interplay of transference and countertransference (Searles 1955; Ledford 1985) in the supervisory relationship. Because the supervisor has not had any direct experience of the consulting environment, their impressions are shaped by the way the supervisee is remembering or describing their work. By playing back to the supervisee what they are observing in them and how they are feeling, the supervisor is able to help the supervisee inquire into the assumptions, prejudices and associations that they make with respect to their clients, their consulting practice and themselves.

Box 23.1 Individual consulting supervision case 1

Roger is a consultant working for a niche consultancy, participating in organizational-development assignments and tailored executive education. The firm has five partners (owners) and 15 senior consultants. Roger is seen as someone who may be able to become a partner over the next five years or so. The firm pays for him to meet with a supervisor at least quarterly. Although they talk about his client work, Roger is preoccupied with the dynamics within the firm, where differences of opinion between the partners are repressed and played out unconsciously by the senior consultants. The partners maintain an impression of always agreeing, but others in the firm do notice that they rigorously meet behind closed doors while for other meetings the door is always open. Roger regularly feels criticized by one of the partners and feels that he is in competition with another senior consultant also aspiring to partnership.

As an outsider to the organization, the supervisor 'holds up the mirror' in a way that helps Roger appreciate his contribution more clearly. He learns how some of his own reactions are understandable in terms of his own family history, and from the fact that he feels quite exposed and vulnerable in the firm while he feels much more impactful and confident when working with his clients. Through his work in supervision, Roger manages not to escalate any of the tensions, and eventually he is invited into the partnership. Only then does he experience the raging power struggles in the partnership and finds it useful to continue working with his supervisor.

Modality 2 Shadow consultancy

This is where the supervisor is working as a 'shadow consultant' (Schroder 1974) to a pair or team of consultants; in other words, supporting a consultancy team in an 'off-line' supervisory role. Like individual supervision, the supervisees' clients do not encounter the supervisor, except perhaps as a name on a contract or invoice. The supervisor works away from the glare of the client engagement, 'in the shadow' of the consulting team, attending to the resonances within the team as it works on the assignment. This distance from the client system and the presence of inter-consultant dynamics enables the supervisor to pick up still more patterns of transference/countertransference, or what is often called parallel processes (Searles 1955).

In this arrangement, the supervisor contracts to work with the consultants working on a specific project, but shadow consulting can also take place in mixed groups of consultants working across a number of different projects.

Box 23.2 Shadow consulting case 1

A shadow consultant started supervising a team of change consultants working at a financial services organization. As the group session progressed, she noticed that whenever the project leader was speaking, her mind wandered. Even forcing herself to listen did not help. When others spoke, she found it easier to concentrate. When the same thing happened during the second session, she decided to share her experience with the group in a way that avoided criticizing the project leader. She asked whether others felt the same way and whether this might be a reflection of their work with the organization. To her astonishment, several team members admitted that they too found it hard to follow their project leader's thought processes. The leader was initially embarrassed, but with the help of the group came to realize that their key client, the CEO, was isolated and remote from his colleagues, who also seemed to only half-understand what he was trying to communicate. The supervisor pointed out that the team's experience of the project leader was, in fact, a classic example of a parallel process; in other words, a replication of what was happening in the client system.

The supervisor then helped the team reflect on how this insight might also be relevant to the CEO, who was similarly defensive when the project leader shared their observations but astonished at their accuracy when he sought feedback from his closest colleague.

This case study illustrates how a shadow consultant can play an important role in helping consultants 'step back' from the immediate drama or conflict and inquire into the assumptions, prejudices and unconscious processes that can interfere with their ability to think clearly about their clients or their own teamwork. The shadow consulting supervisor needs to listen carefully to their clients' narratives, without actually believing them to be the 'whole truth'. As she listens, the supervisor senses the potential relationship between the consultants' narratives and the organizational process that they are immersed in with their clients. Working in the 'rumblings of the collective shadows' (Shohet and Shohet 2020), she hesitates to raise her own felt sense, not entirely sure if this is her own professional 'lapse' or has relevance for her supervisees. Her role is to reflect on herself, use courage to share her difficulties, and invite her supervisees to come alongside her reflections. As they do so, they understand how their participation in the client system has distorted their own capacity to think and respond clearly and appropriately.

Modality 3 Peer supervision

This involves peer-to-peer working among a group of colleagues from a consulting team or organization, with supervisees moving back and forth between consulting and supervising roles. The advantage of this approach is that the peer supervisor has their own direct experience of the team or organization, which means they can test certain hunches and ground them in the reality of their own experience. This may, however, compromise their ability to pick up on parallel processes, or the inevitable tensions between supervision, consultancy and participation in the organization. For these reasons, peer supervision can benefit from the input of an external supervisor to facilitate the process and support peer-to-peer working. An external supervisor can help the peer supervisor to stay sufficiently detached from the content of their colleagues' work in order to notice and inquire into their transference and parallel process. Whether or not an external supervisor is used, peer supervision groups work best when they have contracted on the timing, purpose and roles of supervision.

Box 23.3 Peer supervision case 1

A team of 15 consultants working on a culture change project were grouped into five peer-supervision groups, or 'trios'. Each trio met for an hour once a fortnight, with colleagues taking it in turns to play the role of the supervisor. In one trio, a colleague was concerned about the management style of one of the senior client staff, which they felt was aggressive and bullying. With the help of their trio, they explored their feelings and reactions, including their unacknowledged prejudice associated with the person's educational background. This helped them empathize with the individual and re-evaluate their critical stance. Rather than confront the person, they decided that they would build a closer relationship with the person and influence from a position of support and respect.

Attending to relational and organizational dynamics in OD supervision

As we have seen in the examples above, the distinguishing characteristic of consulting supervision is that the consultant's internal relationships with peers and managers become more prominent and provide unique material to help supervisee and supervisor learn about the relational patterns and dynamics in the OD work. The parallel process is prominent in all supervision, but this ability to carry the *systemic* back into the *system* is distinct and powerful.

The degree to which the patterns are amplified or reduced depends on an aspect of the personality of supervisees and supervisor called personal 'valency' (Bion 1961). A person's valency for picking up unconscious patterns is strongly related to their personality and personal experiences in life. Patterns we are able to pick up consciously are patterns we are able to experience and observe. Patterns we tend to pick up unconsciously are patterns that somehow 'stir' us up, moving us emotionally because they sway us like other earlier patterns that we could not quite (allow ourselves to) experience and which are thus handled less consciously.

In this way, individual supervisors can pick up important determining patterns (blocks to change, opportunities for new change, etc.) that are normally below the level of conscious awareness, but they can only do so within a specific and limited spectrum of valencies. The phenomenon is comparable to the phenomenon of 'resonance' in physics, where an object can only pick up and amplify particular frequencies of, for example, sound waves, and not others.

Each of the different modes of consulting supervision offers a unique potential for picking up organizational patterns. Each supervisee acts as 'lens' for picking up patterns and issues in the organization(s) with the supervisor also spotting issues with the 'lenses' themselves. In the *coaching supervision* process (see Figure 23.1) the situation is most straightforward, because the supervisor has only one lens and no direct access to the supervisee's client organization. This offers a clear-cut window onto the coaching relationship and behind that the organizational dynamics. There is relatively little room for amplification or resonance, and the coach's valency has a modest place in the exploration.

Note that the vertical lines in Figure 23.1 represent other client relationships that the coach and supervisor will have. The horizontal line to the right of the supervisor connects to their supervisor.

In *individual consulting supervision* (Figure 23.2), there is more room for picking up patterns, as the consultant has been directly exposed to organizational dynamics *between* people working for the organization. We can see that the consultant has a broader role in the organization than the coach in Figure 23.1, and will pick up more organization dynamics from direct exposure, and may even become relatively 'native' or 'immersed' within the organization.

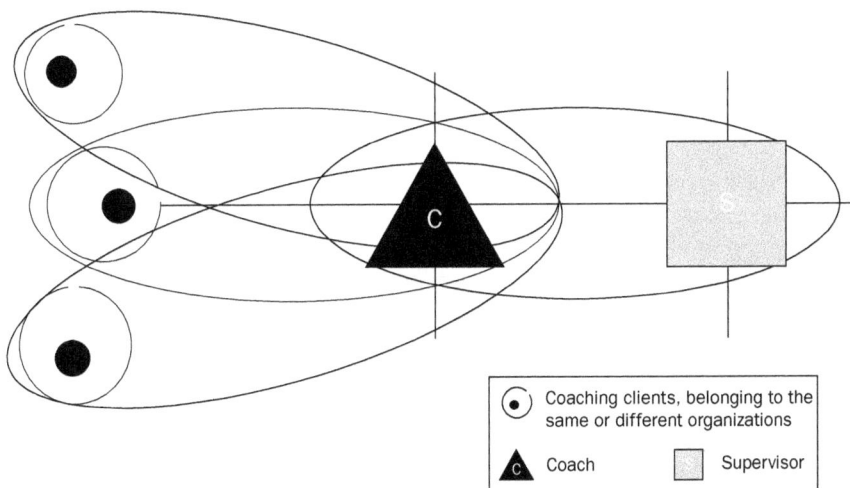

Figure 23.1 Schematic depiction of executive coaching supervision for one individual coach

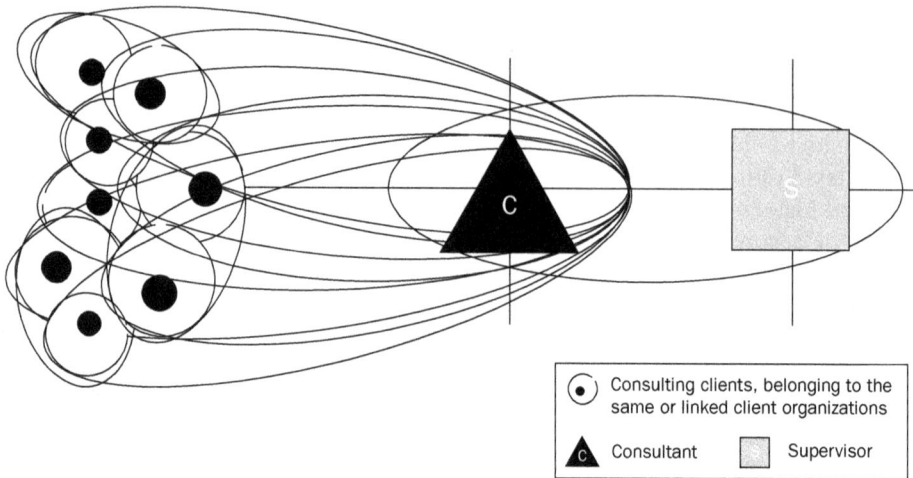

Figure 23.2 Schematic depiction of individual supervision for a consultant working on a single assignment

---

Box 23.4 Individual consulting supervision case 2

Naomi is an internal consultant working on a complex restructuring project. She works part-time and reports to the HR director. Midway through the project, the HR director resigns and is replaced by someone new to the organization. Naomi is taken aback to find that her new boss wants her to refocus her efforts on a different project. Naomi appreciates the importance of this work but feels aggrieved that she has not been consulted over the change and her restructuring project is being overlooked. In her individual supervision, her supervisor suggests using a table-top constellation to explore the political dynamics of her situation. Using the supervisor's collection of buttons, Naomi maps her position in the system. She places her own button far from the new HR director but close to the buttons representing the CEO and Strategy director. Her supervisor encourages her to speak from each of the positions represented. This helps Naomi express her frustration with her new boss and loyalty to the CEO and Strategy director. She comes to appreciate the isolation of the HR director and lack of knowledge about her. She also speculates that he may feel threatened by her proximity to the CEO. Naomi leaves the session with some insights and ideas how to build a more constructive relationship with her new boss.

In *shadow consulting* (Figure 23.3), the supervisor is exposed to a much 'richer' dynamic between consultants, with more 'antennae' towards organizational patterns. In our experience dynamics between consultants working in teams may reflect, or mirror, strong and unconscious organizational dynamics. This is shown

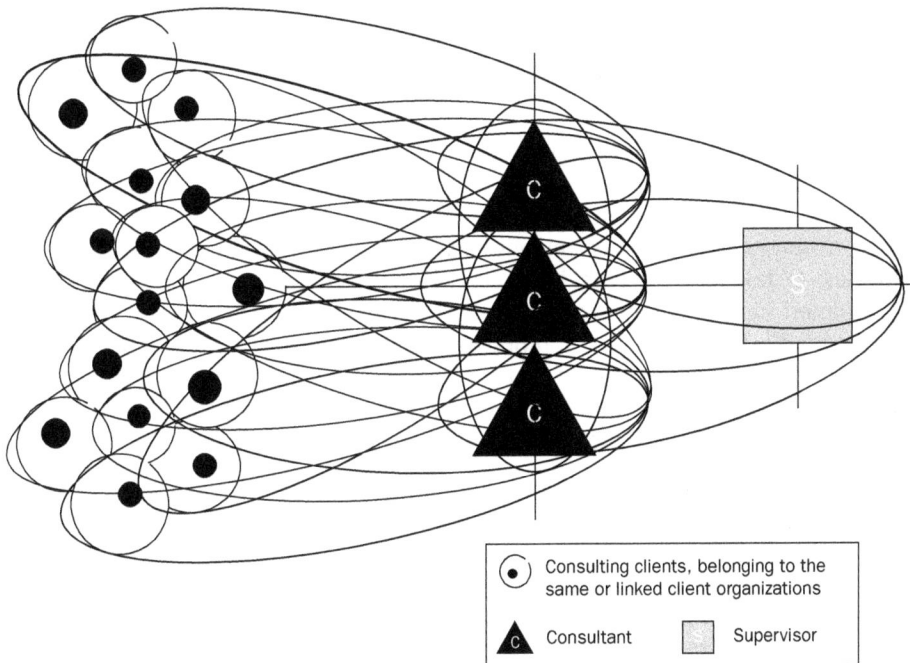

Figure 23.3 Schematic depiction of 'shadow consulting' supervision for a team of OD consultants working on a single assignment

in some of the examples above and in Hirschhorn's example of a deputy director who is under intense pressure and works with a pair of organization consultants who are in turn supervised by the author (Hirschhorn 1988: 40).

Box 23.5 Shadow consulting case 2

Graham was part of a consulting team engaged by a prestigious university to help engage the professoriate in its research strategy. He became aware that he was avoiding another consultant, Helen, which troubled him as they usually worked well together. He felt that Helen was disinterested in his ideas and seemed intent on pursuing her own agenda with the client. This was exacerbated by the close relationship that Helen had established with a successful senior professor.

Graham knew that he ought to raise his concerns with Helen but felt anxious at the prospect of doing so. He was convinced that Helen would ridicule or humiliate him if he brought the subject up, so he chose not to share his resentment with his colleague. He was also aware of a growing anxiety that he was failing in Helen's eyes, and that she was privy to critical feedback from the client about his contribution to the project. Eventually, it was Helen who brought the topic up with Graham, concerned that her colleague had grown so distant recently. Graham agreed that it would be a useful topic to take to the next meeting with the team's shadow consultant.

The shadow consultant supervisor helped Graham and Helen discover how they had come to identify with their respective client contacts in the institution. Helen had a rapport with a highly influential senior professor. Graham, meanwhile, had established a bond with a less prominent academic, who the senior professor often expected to take on the less interesting administrative tasks. Graham became accustomed to hearing their complaints about how the senior professor showed little interest in their ideas and contributions and felt generally used and abused by them. The supervisor suggested that they might be participating in a 'parallel process', where the dynamics present in the relationship between the two clients was being recreated between Helen and Graham.

With the shadow consultant's help, Helen and Graham each role-played the client who they felt closest to, using their intuition to explore their clients' feelings about one another and the strategizing process. To Graham's surprise, Helen was adamant that 'her' professor would have been horrified to know that his colleague was so angry with him, which opened up a discussion about how they could help the two professors become more aware of their unconscious patterns of behaviour. In a facilitated workshop their clients were encouraged to actively listen and inquire into one another's thinking. Following a process review, the professors agreed that this conversational process should become a regular feature of their strategic process.

Graham felt relieved that his relationship with Helen had been restored and he learned how an exploration of his supposedly personal feelings in supervision had provided such a powerful insight into how he might serve his clients in the future.

In this case the consulting supervisor is picking up patterns that are three layers deep. First, organizational patterns are manifest in patterns of individual sponsor behaviour, in this case professional rivalry and failed negotiations on leadership. These then influence the relationship between consultant and sponsors, which is finally experienced in the 'here-and-now' by the shadow consultant.

Finally, in *peer supervision* (Figure 23.4), the supervisor has access to a still wider pattern of dynamics, including their own direct experience. The situation is still richer, but also 'messier', as the supervisor will be less clear about what she is picking up is attributable to. The supervision of the peer supervisor is particularly important as a way of grounding certain ideas and observations, and to become aware of patterns that are now no longer accessible.

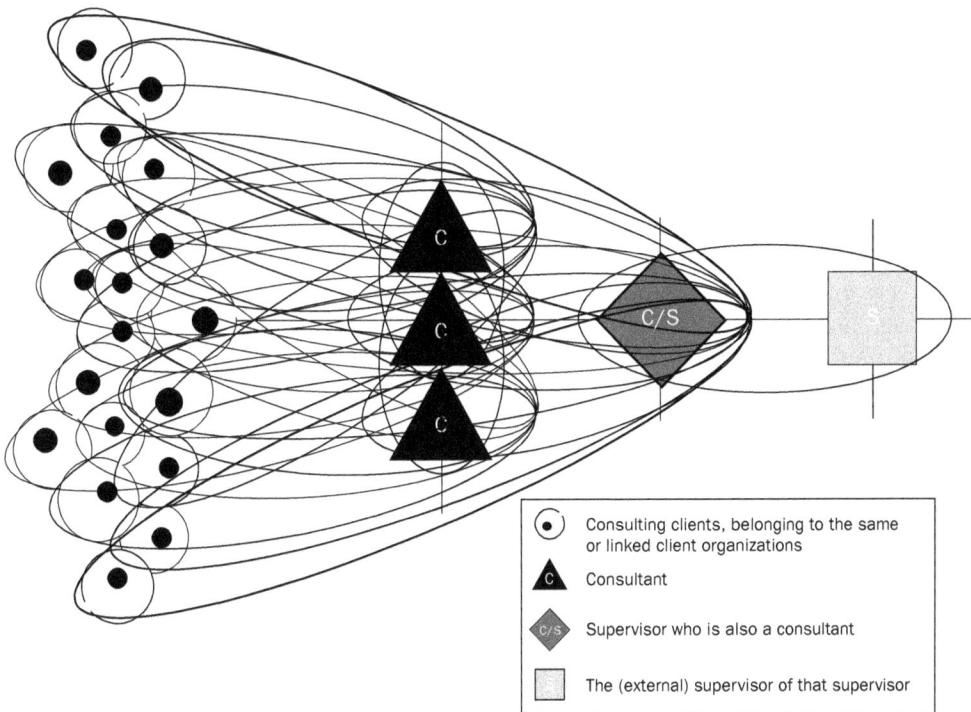

Consulting clients, belonging to the same or linked client organizations

Consultant

Supervisor who is also a consultant

The (external) supervisor of that supervisor

Figure 23.4 Schematic depiction of peer supervision for a team of OD consultants working on a single assignment

Box 23.6 Peer supervision case 2

An internal supervisor was working in a global corporation and had been asked to supervise a pair of OD consultants, who had been tasked with a sensitive internal improvement project. The two consultants had happily worked together before, but their relationship had become strained as this assignment pulled them in different directions. Also, in another piece of work an external client had split up the pair, making one of them respond favourably to 'outrageous' requests and the other becoming increasingly resentful of that. They both felt bruised and aggrieved afterwards, on the brink of a complete breakdown of relationship.

The request for 15 hours of 'supervision' felt like a piece of mediation between the two. They both kept emphasizing how different they were, referring to a personality instrument that they used in the company. The supervisor got somewhat distracted as she had strong feelings about that tool and how literally it was being used in the company. Only gradually could she explore other, more hidden, areas of the consultants' personalities and raise the boundary issue of taking the psychometric data concretely and explanatory for the personalities of the individuals (Metselaar and De Haan 2015).

At one point the supervisor asked for a metaphor as to how they were experiencing themselves in the small team. After some reflection, one of the consultants said, 'I see myself as a hedgehog or porcupine in this relationship, where I often curl up in defence and withdraw within myself if I am feeling attacked. I think porcupines have both spines and quills. I can raise my spikes, I can even shoot my quills, and I probably do both at times.' The other consultant contributed a different image: 'It is as if I am walking in the forest near my house, and then suddenly an alien is dropped in front of me, and I no longer feel safe. Or sometimes it is as if I am on a fast ride in a fairground horror house, where at every corner some object or ghost is hurled at me and I fear for my life.' It was a tremendous breakthrough when they all realized that the two scary metaphors were in fact . . . complementary.

Later in supervision they deepened their realization that not only did they complement each other very well, but they also spanned virtually all the conflicts within the company. They could now translate what they saw as their personality differences into the awareness of different styles and allegiances within the system in which they operated. Based on this insight, their internal consultancy offer went from strength to strength as they built a 'band of sisters and brothers' and fearlessly confronted fears and splits within the organization. Later still, they rediscovered their early, friendly collegiate relationship, which they deepened, with more spontaneity and with the ability to stand up and openly disagree if necessary.

The peer supervisor is picking up patterns that are sometimes four layers deep as in this case. First, organizational patterns that have stirred her up in the past. Then organizational challenges as experienced by the consultants, apparent in patterns of individual client behaviour. These then become topics for consultation and also apparent in the relationship between consultant and client, some of which is also experienced in the 'here-and-now' by the peer supervisor. Only then do these patterns become available for conscious processing. It is precisely because of the inhibitions and emotions enabled by the supervisor's valency, that these patterns can be picked up in the first place. Valuable as they are, they will be biased or coloured by the personal experiences they went through in the same organization, before becoming conscious and available to work with.

Dilemmas for OD consulting supervisors

Although the different modes of supervision are quite distinct from one another, the potential approaches open to the supervisor are broadly similar, whatever the mode or the client context. In particular, supervisors tend to experience a number of dilemmas, which crop up again and again when working with clients. In the following paragraphs, we hope to capture some of those, and to convey something of how it feels to work as an OD consulting supervisor.

In the first place as human beings and as supervisors we feel the limits – and hidden promises – of our valencies quite acutely. We become aware of our own countertransference (Ledford 1985) without necessarily knowing what it is about: we feel unease, discomfort, distraction, displaced anger, boredom or other feelings that feel real but may be a manifestation of the client/consultant dynamics that are experienced by the consultants being supervised. In other words, we feel the sensation in our 'antennas' before we can even begin to make sense of the signal. And if we attend to the sensation, we become aware of the inadequacy of our measuring equipment in this area, which is so strongly entwined with our own unresolved issues and transferential patterns. This dilemma begins as discomfort, then emerges as a choice whether to attend or not, and may become a huge doubt about whether what we feel is of any use to our supervisees.

Second, if we then move closer to reflecting back and communicating some of our observations, we can feel dilemmas about how impactful we should be, or how tentative. Of most benefit to the supervisee is usually to be *both*

1. Impactful: concise, sharp, challenging, new, original, focused; and
2. Tentative: as an invitation to further reflections rather than as the final word on any matter the consultant(s) is bringing.

Furthermore, when addressing or opening up new client material, we will experience dilemmas as to how much to set the tone. Is it more useful to our clients and ultimately to the organization to work in an emergent way (i.e. similar to how an executive coach or OD consultant might work)? Or is it important to be directive and map all aspects of the 'case' more actively, working more like an expert consultant?

Similarly, we may have dilemmas around when to work in conversation (i.e. reflectively), and when to work more in a 'playful' way, for example by recreating the organization's dynamics in role-play, 'two chair' work, psychodrama and organization constellations. Emergent, playful ways of working may provide a stronger lens into unconscious dilemmas within the client organization, because in these interventions the supervisees will be less able to censor their material.

Next, we have experienced dilemmas and concerns in terms of the role we play for the client organization. Ultimately, the client organization should be the main benefactor and the ultimate client of our work, but it is – usually – one step removed from the supervisory relationship. We have noticed that we struggled at times to be aware of our own engagement with the organization. On the one hand, we know we need a certain level of detachment to begin picking up organizational patterns that were not noticed by the consultant. On the other hand, we aim to be impactful in the consultant's client organization. As an organization supervisor one finds oneself in a similar predicament to that of a wildlife documentary filmmaker, where one's observing presence will at some stage, unknown to them, begin to have an impact on the ecosystem observed. The scrutinizing lenses of consultants and supervisors are not just passively observing, they are also present objects in the field of view of the organization's employees, and so they may become a yardstick for measuring progress in the organizational domain. The presence of a coach supervisor is usually much more at a distance to their supervisees' client organizations, such that this dilemma does not occur.

Finally, we have experienced dilemmas about the normative aspect of supervision as well. If a consultant's manager is only interested in revenue or billable days as a 'measure of success', their supervisor is in a much better place to hold meaningful performance conversations with consultants. However, such conversations hold an intrinsic risk of the supervisor becoming a surrogate 'performance manager' for the consultant.

Some consultancy firms have internal 'mentors' working alongside external supervisors, whose task it is to hold those performance conversations that go beyond billable days and who report directly to the consultant's line manager.

Summary and research potential of OD supervision

On the whole, OD consultants have to work within an organization while holding on to their outsider's perspective. They have to apply their knowledge, experience and intuition as they engage with the organization, acquiring, as they do so, an insider's perspective on the organization's issues. Such a stance of being an 'outsider within' is not straightforward at all, and carries with it all sorts of temptations, risks and limitations (De Haan 2006). On the one hand, there is a risk in staying overly analytical and detached, which often results in observations, ideas and solutions that are more relevant for the consultant – or for their previous clients – than for the case in point. On the other hand, consultants risk becoming over-involved if they identify too strongly with the organization's agenda and issues. One could call this the dilemma of 'aloofness versus collusion'.

However, supervision can be of great benefit to organization consultants as it can help to maintain a balance between these opposing risks and temptations. A supervisor stays – as much as possible – outside of the client engagement, and is much freer to comment on what might be going on for the client and within this client–consultant relationship. Supervision can have an immense formative effect on consultants, not to mention the value it has in a normative and restorative sense (Proctor 2008). Organization consultants often experience anxiety and stress as they try to balance a very diverse portfolio with competing obligations to clients and colleagues. Supervision can help to reduce the stress by helping the consultant to reflect on and understand their own reactions and responses. The supervisor is in an ideal position to provide some 'normative' feedback on a consultant's practice, based on a respectful appreciation of the complexities and challenges that they face. The supervisor's understanding is often better than that of the consultant's line manager or even the consultant herself. We are excited by the prospect of further development and professionalism of consulting supervision so that it can take up its rightful place in the support and quality assurance of organization consultants and expert consultants alike.

Supervision can also be a highly appropriate space to research consulting interventions. This is already happening in the form of qualitative 'Action Research', where themes are identified and fed back anonymously to the client organization (see, for example, De Haan 2012: 119). We see a lot of potential for more quantitative process research as well, because of the demarcated, measurable space and time for supervision as a 'laboratory' for researchers that can capture some of the changes brought about by the more diluted, fuzzy and unbounded consulting interventions. For example, coaches' and consultants' experience of 'safety' and 'trust' in supervision has been the subject of quantitative research (De Haan 2017). Also, it should be possible to organize a randomized controlled experiment comparing consultants with and without supervision, or consultants with and without coaching assignments as part of their interventions.

Guidance for further learning

The following activities are to enable further reflection about the rich profession of consulting supervision:

1. Ask two clients or friends who work for the same organization to engage in a short conversation about the challenges that they face over the next couple of weeks. Notice not only which challenges they choose to address but also how they speak about these challenges. Very often, the way in which they conduct their conversation will tell you something about the challenges themselves. After the short conversation you may ask them how their responses were 'typical' for their organization's culture. Then you can share your own observations about how they spoke with each other and how these apparent dynamics between them may relate to the issues that they discussed.
2. Make a timeline of all the employers that you have worked for, including yourself if you have been self-employed. Try to find at least one aspect that all these organizations have in common. Then ask yourself what your choice of employers may tell us about you. What are the themes or patterns that you are likely to pick up quite quickly with clients because of your previous organizational experience?
3. Take some time after your next supervision session to map out the dynamics at play. Describe the interaction at that supervision session on four different levels: within the client organization, between the supervisee(s) and clients in that organization, between the supervisee(s) and you, and between you and you (i.e. in your own mind) when you come out of the session. See if you can find any overlap between these patterns of interaction, and try to understand which of these four levels most ignites this key pattern (i.e. where are its origins?).

Further sources

The following three texts are useful further reading:

Larry Hirschhorn (1988) *The Workplace Within: Psychodynamics of Organizational Life*. Cambridge, MA: MIT Press. This is one of the finest tools available for those wishing to deepen their understanding of what goes on in organizations today and extending their social sensitivity in the workplace.

Marjan Schroder (1974) The shadow consultant, *Journal of Applied Behavioral Science*, 10(4): 579–594. Schroder's short article is one of the earliest recognitions of some of the specifics of the task of the (internal) organization supervisor. With great sensitivity and powerful examples, Schroder demonstrates how even a peer OD consultant can do a good job supervising their consulting colleagues.

Peter Hawkins and Nick Smith (2006) *Coaching, Mentoring and Organizational Consultancy: Supervision and Development.* Maidenhead: Open University Press. This is a practical resource book that examines the values and assumptions that underpin organizational consultancy and explores the vital importance of supervision to maintaining an ethically sound practice.

References

Bion, W.R. (1961) *Experiences in Groups.* London: Tavistock.

Checkland, P.B. (1981) *Systems Thinking, Systems Practice.* Chichester: Wiley.

De Haan, E. (2006) *Fearless Consulting.* Chichester: Wiley.

De Haan, E. (2012) *Supervision in Action: A Relational Approach to Coaching and Organization Supervision.* Maidenhead: Open University Press.

De Haan, E. (2017) Trust and safety in coaching supervision: some evidence that we are doing it right, *International Coaching Psychology Review,* 12(1): 37–48.

De Haan, E. and Regouin, W. (2016) *Being Supervised: A Guide for Supervisees.* London: Karnac Books

Hawkins, P. and Smith, N. (2006) *Coaching, Mentoring and Organizational Consultancy: Supervision and Development.* Maidenhead: Open University Press.

Hirschhorn, L. (1988) *The Workplace Within: Psychodynamics of Organizational Life.* Cambridge, MA: MIT Press.

Ledford, G.E., Jr. (1985) Transference and counter-transference in action research relationships, *Consultation,* 4(1): 36–51.

Metselaar, C. and De Haan, E. (2015) A critique of the use of diagnostic instruments in executive coaching, *Coaching Today,* July: 16–17.

Proctor, B. (2008) *Group Supervision,* 2nd edn. London: Sage.

Schein, E.H. (1987) *Process Consultation.* Reading, MA: Addison-Wesley.

Schroder, M. (1974) The shadow consultant, *Journal of Applied Behavioral Science,* 10(4): 579–594.

Searles, H.F. (1955) The informational value of the supervisor's emotional experience, *Psychiatry,* 18: 135–146.

Shohet, R. and Shohet, J. (2020) *In Love with Supervision: Creating Transformative Conversations.* Monmouth: PCCS Books.

Weisbord, M. and Janoff, S. (1995) *Future Search: An Action Guide to Finding Common Ground in Organizations and Communities.* San Francisco, CA: Berrett-Koehler.

24 Supervising organizational transformation

Michel Moral and Florence Lamy

Introduction

When we step back and take a helicopter view of consultancy, coaching and supervision resources that are employed or hired by an organization, we generally see a coexistence of several subsystems that work quasi-independently (Figure 24.1). These subsystems are:

- A subsystem of coaches that includes external and internal coaches, the latter often headed by a 'head of coaching'. Supervision is rarely organized for the whole subsystem.
- A 'change subsystem', including internal and external consultants. Consultant supervision is a recent activity, which has been explored by De Haan (2012) and Birch and De Haan in this volume, but not widely used.
- A sponsor's subsystem where several functions coexist such as Human Resources, Strategy, Management Development and similar entities that are in charge of fulfilling the corporate mission and keep heading towards the vision. Sometimes some or all of such functions are absent from the main instruments of corporate governance, and they may have a limited audience at the C-level.

Organizational transformation now includes coaching as an approach in addition to organizational development (OD), which has existed since the 1950s. Also, the concept of a 'coaching culture' has developed since its first appearance in the literature (Caplan 2003) and organizational coaching (OC) which emerged around 2010. In this form of coaching, the coachee is the organization as an entity, in the same way as in team coaching the coachee is the team as an entity. Another significant evolution is that the number of internal coaches has significantly increased during the last decade and a large number of managers and executives have been trained in coaching, even if they do not practise it.

The question for supervision, then, is how to supervise this complex system formed of external coaches, internal coaches, manager coaches, internal clients, consultants and possibly internal supervisors who are involved in the process of organizational transformation? In particular, can we anticipate directions that are potentially more effective, and do we need to apply new concepts and techniques? This question was raised by Moral (2011) and Moral and Henrichfreise (2018), and two studies have been conducted to find an answer: Moral et al. (2017) and another one in progress.

In this chapter, we will review the existing approaches for transforming an organization and how we can approach supervision of the whole system. Some attention will be given to internal coaches and supervisors who are now part of the game.

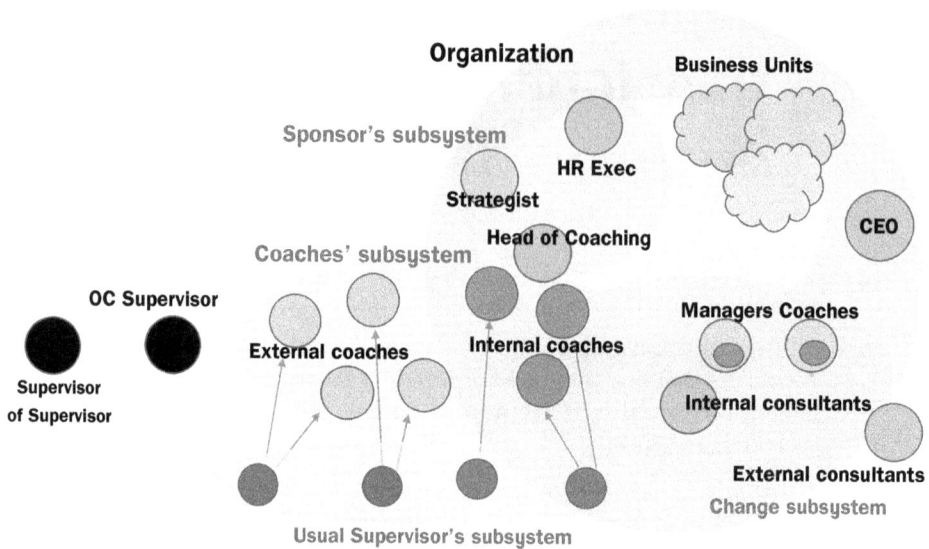

Figure 24.1 Systemic representation of stakeholders and subsystems in an organizational transformation

The concept of organizational transformation

Many books have been written addressing organizational transformation describing different approaches to supervising. Supervision of the whole organizational transformation has not been looked at yet when, at the same time, the landscape is changing rapidly. For example, the number of internal coaches is growing, and this modifies the way supervision will be done. We set out here three different directions for organizational transformation, before looking specifically at the effect of internal coaches as part of the system being supervised.

Consultancy approaches

The first approach was taken by authors who promoted methods relying on either the organizational development paradigm (Lewin 1951; McGregor 1971) or corporate culture change methods (Schein 1985). Such models can be categorized as either 'commitment based', trying to convince employees and middle management by showing positive images of the future, or 'compliance based', changing behaviours by imperatives. We can also mention Argyris (1970) who developed his Intervention Model, Porras and Silvers (1991) who introduced their Involvement Model, Srivastva and Cooperrider (1990) who designed Appreciative Inquiry, and Peterson and Smith (2000) with their Sense Making model. Some other models are related to OD in the sense that they are also deployed in a consultancy approach: Business Process Re-Engineering, and the Psychological Approach with Peterson and Smith (2000) and Warren Burke (2002) who developed the concept of 'change agents'. All these models are frequently deployed by consultants.

Supervision of consultants, internal and external, has been studied by De Haan (2012) who finds a number of similarities and differences with supervision of internal and external coaches. For instance, the amplification of parallel process between the client and the team of consultants looks like what occurs with a team of internal coaches. On the other hand, de Haan pointed out that there is an increased risk of over-identification between a group of consultants and their client. He identifies three different supervision contracts and relationships: 'organization consulting supervision' (focus on the consultant), 'shadow consulting' (the supervisor works away from the client) and 'peer supervision' (supervision within the group of consultants). His main focus is on the relationship between the supervisor and the consultants, and he uses the notion of valency introduced by Bion (1961: 136) who defines it as: 'our individual susceptibility to resonate with various unconscious demands'.

Coaching culture

A second direction for organizational transformation was taken by those authors who promoted the notion of a 'coaching culture', which has significantly developed since it was first introduced by Caplan (2003). Five other books on that topic were subsequently published: Clutterbuck and Megginson (2005), Crane and Nancy-Patrick (2007), Hawkins (2012), Jones and Gorell (2014) and Clutterbuck, Megginson and Bajer (2016).

The number of internal coaches has boomed during this period and a large number of managers and executives have been trained in coaching, even though they do not necessarily practise it. In that context, 'coaching culture' means that all coaches, both external and internal, and managers trained in coaching form an organized system, and contribute to the strategic objectives of the company in question (Figure 24.2).

Different definitions of coaching culture have been proposed, for example:

A Coaching Culture exists in an organization *when a coaching approach is a key aspect of how the leaders, managers, engage* and develop their people and engage their stakeholders, in ways that create increased individual performance and shared value for all stakeholders. (Hawkins 2012: 21)

A Coaching Culture is one *where people are empowered and where coaching happens at every level*. And, not only does it happen at every level, but it adds to bottom line performance. It is the recognized development tool that touches every part of the employee life cycle. (Jones and Gorell 2014: 13)

These examples demonstrate that the concept of culture is used to show that this approach deploys coaching in depth and breadth implying a readiness to allocate supervision resources broadly. Following Caplan, this way of making coaching a prevalent style of management and of working together has become more and more well known in Anglo-Saxon countries and many companies have deployed this concept. The general idea, promoted in existing publications, is that both the employees and the company benefit from coaching practised at every level, which we will call the 'embeddedness (incidence) of coaching' (Figure 24.2). A further development, used for measuring coaching culture penetration, is that the

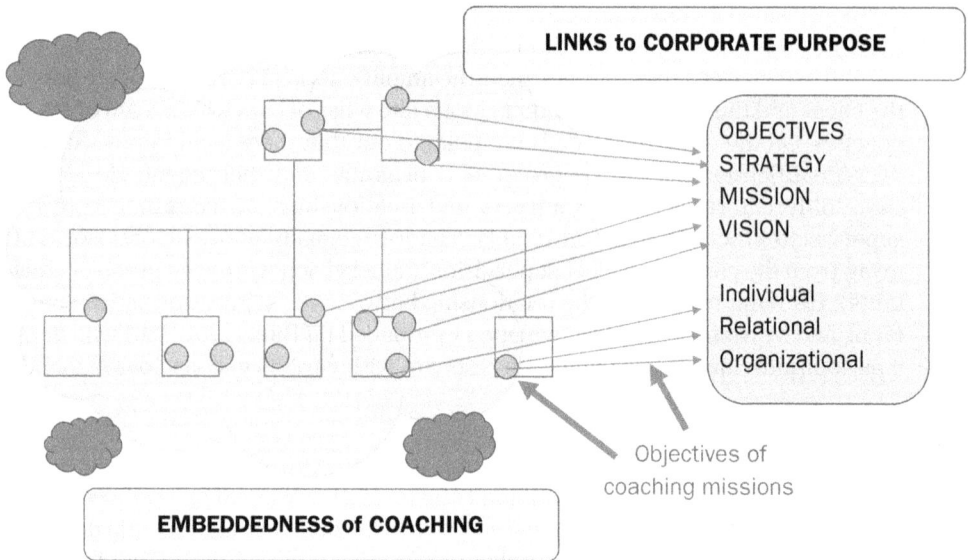

Figure 24.2 Coaching culture

objectives of the coaching missions should be connected to the strategic goals of the organization.

In 2014, the Human Capital Institute and International Coach Federation jointly defined a composite index to measure the level of development of coaching culture. Since then, several tools have been developed to measure the level of embeddedness and/or the strength of coaching culture (for example, Embark by Unlimited Potential).

As the number of internal coaches has greatly increased, the implementation of coaching culture has become easier and has grown accordingly. Furthermore, focus on the concept of coaching culture has increased sharply since pragmatic studies have shown a significant correlation between the level of development of a coaching culture and improved financial results of the company, as well as the engagement of their employees (ICF 2014).

The supervision of coaches, internal and external, who are involved in building a coaching culture, needs more co-ordination and control than the usual supervision of coaches working for an organization. Tools such as Embark could also be used for better supervision.

Organizational coaching

The third direction for transformational work is 'organizational coaching' (OC), which has grown significantly in countries like France where the concept of a coaching culture is not well known. For example, 25 per cent of coaches in France claim they practise organizational coaching, most of them having been trained in one of the 12 schools that specialize in this form of coaching and offer their programmes.

OC was first mentioned as early as 2006 in Hawkins and Smith (2013) but became fully developed in 2008 in the first edition of Moral and Henrichfreise

(2018). Since its first appearance, several books related to OC have been published in France and cover different aspects of OC, including: Vergonjeanne (2010) focusing on using Berne's Theory of Organizations, Motto (2013) relating to the use of Constellations in OC, Dugois et al. (2016) and Devillard (2018) who have separately developed a methodology for OC.

The definition of OC was initially included in a general definition of coaching proposed by Giffard and Moral (2007: 15): 'Coaching consists in helping a system so that it provides its own responses to challenges it faces. Such a system can be a Person, a Team or an Organization'. Recently, Kaj Hellbom (2018: 120) has described it as 'Organizational Development done with a coaching mindset. That means partnering with the client to help the client to achieve his goals by using his resources and strengths'.

Common to both definitions, the ambition of OC is to engage the whole system, even if it starts with only one of the elements, usually the corporate culture or the strategy. A number of elements were identified by Moral and Henrichfreise (2018) as being part of the system: vision, mission, what is at stake, strategy, action plan, leadership model, corporate culture, etc. In this formulation the organization constitutes the 'coachee' and therefore extends far beyond a person, a single team or a team of teams. The objectives of the coaching also develop far beyond the objectives set for an individual or team coaching, and, finally, what the organization is asking for is either a collective need, a desire for renewed governance, or sometimes a caregiver's prescription requested by a trade union.

In terms of methods, OC uses a combination of approaches such as individual coaching, team coaching, facilitation of large groups and coaching of 'teams of teams'. The notion of 'coach' extends beyond a single person and can be either a group or a team of coaches facilitated by a 'meta coach'. In practical terms this means that the group or team of coaches, which must function as if it was a single coach, is formed of external and internal coaches and is supervised using specific techniques.

Coaches involved in an OC mission should develop competences and skills over and above the current standards of their profession. Hellbom (2018) states that, beyond excellent coaching skills, the following additional skills are needed: systemic understanding, organizational dynamics skills and insights into social psychology.

Such skills are required by the market and are already included in the 'ECVision Competence Framework of Supervision and Coaching' (2015) and in the EMCC Supervision Competence Framework (2019). This shows a shift of the coaching industry towards more focus on organizational aspects.

Internal coaches

Internal coaches play a role in the coaching culture approach and are also used for organizational transformation when they are trained in OC. The role of supervision in internal coaching or coaching culture was studied and then presented during several international conferences, especially by various contributors to the Oxford Brookes supervision conferences. See also Maxwell (2011) and Chapter 22 by Champion Maxwell and Pinder in this volume. There are now two doctoral dissertations that discuss the role of supervision in internal coaching: Field (2014) and van Reenen (2014).

A number of concerns have been identified in the work of Van Reenen (2014) and St John-Brooks (2014, 2019), to which we add our own observations. The following are only some concerns that particularly suggest the need for supervision.

Most internal coaches are only coaching part time, which might cause problems with their professional role: when a manager coaches, are they still a manager? If they are alone this is easily handled by a supervisor. If they are in a group or team, the patterns of the organization are reproduced by parallel processes, and homeostasis is high.

The level of autonomy for internal coaches is another potential issue because it might be a sign of low independence, which could cause conflicts of interest. Depending on the organization where the coach is employed, there might be one or more areas where their autonomy is limited. Of course, supervision is an opportunity to explore how the coach could gain more autonomy when doing their job, but, again, when coaches are in a group or team, corporate patterns might prevail. For example, our experience shows that line management support drops when awareness of corporate functioning increases.

More specific issues noted by St John-Brooks (2014, 2019) also include the boundary between coaching and counselling, the client not being fully engaged and frustration. She pointed out lack of impartiality, augmentation of the scope for parallel process, contagion of emotion, more drama triangles and difficulty with groups of coaches who also form a team.

Role of supervisors in organizational transformation

In this section we explain the background to our approach to supervising organizational transformation and elaborate on the key concept of 'metaposition'. Then we discuss the role of internal supervisors and supervision of supervision in this context.

The purpose of two studies that we conducted was to:

* Understand how coaching and supervision are organized and how supervisors are selected
* Define a common view among organizational coaches and supervisors on what an approach to supervision of OC could be.

The result of the first work shows that very few companies or institutions have established a clear approach to coaching and supervision as a way to support their organizational transformation (Moral et al. 2017). Also, the control of the skills and professionalism of supervisors is performed through interviews and not on the basis of training, accreditation or proven experience. Clearly, supervision still appears very mysterious!

We know from Bachkirova et al. (2020) that evidence about reproducible impacts of supervision is scarce and conclusions from largely qualitative studies are tentative. This is probably why the people involved in the setting of coaching and supervision within 22 French organizations who were interviewed by Moral et al. (2017) declared that the quantitative benefits of supervision are still unclear.

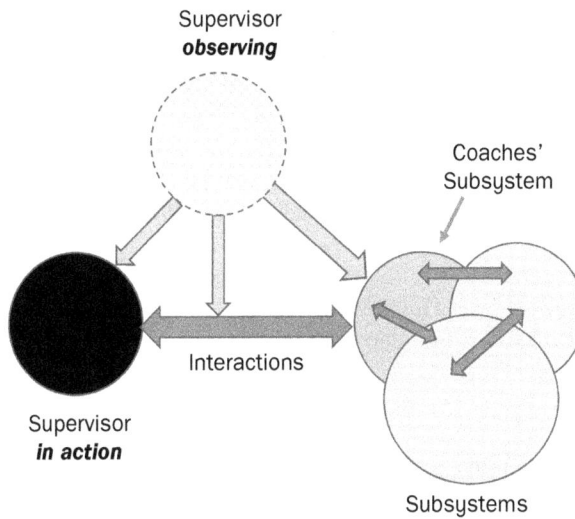

Figure 24.3 Metaposition in organizational coaching

Furthermore, the knowledge and understanding of the role of supervision by executives in the main ranges from very limited to none at all. However, despite the lack of quantitatively proven effect of supervision on the client and their organization, 'heads of coaching' generally believe it is important for the quality of coaching.

The second work consisted of six two-day seminars, which were held to explore how organizational coaches could be supervised. Trained supervisors who hold an ESQA certificate (EMCC Global Supervision Quality Award) worked in collaboration with organizational coaches trained in different schools, especially the HEC Executive Education programme on OC. The study started mid-2017 and ended late 2018. It included reflection on how to extend it to the whole supervision of organizational transformation. The outcome of these seminars is detailed below.

'Metaposition' in an organization

Ideally, in order to supervise the organization as a whole, the supervisor needs to work with not only the external and internal coaches but also the consultants. This is not always possible because the change subsystem is often separate from the coaches' subsystem and it reports to a different line of management. A key question is how to reach an agreement on the need to set a 'metaposition function' in the organization.

Metaposition is observation of the system while acting on the system. It requires the coach to dissociate themselves into an actor and an observer and is a fundamental approach to individual and team coaching. The principle is that if a system is able to observe its own functioning, then it is able to modify itself and, especially, correct dysfunctions.

In team coaching one of the objectives of the coach is to help the team implement metaposition. First, the coach shows how they are themselves in metaposition, and subsequently, the coach asks the team to assign one of the members to take the metaposition. Over time the team gets used to analysing how it functions rather than just acting. For reasons of circularity, the members in metaposition must be different at every meeting. Circularity is an important concept in systems theories, which has been operationalized by the Milan Systemic Centre Team (see Ceccin 1987).

The same occurs in OC: the coaches' subsystem must act if it were a single coach in metaposition. The role of the supervisor is to apply techniques that enable the group to act in unison as if they were one.

Box 24.1 A supervision technique

In individual coaching with horses, there is an exercise aimed at gaining the trust of the horse. The coachee stands in the centre of a riding arena and the horse is on the edge; the coachee must make the horse walk, trot, gallop, change direction, etc. If he does it without dominating, he will gain the confidence of the horse, which will join him at the centre of the riding arena.

The same exercise with a group at the centre of the arena only works if the group acts as one person, without the slightest disagreement, even in thought. When the group in the centre of the arena is the group of coaches, and possibly consultants, who are in charge of organizational transformation, this exercise helps the individuals to align with the collective intention. During the debriefing, the supervisor analyses the negative feelings of each participant about things that went wrong with the horse. Repetition of the exercise helps the participants to manage their negative emotions for the benefit of the group.

Ideally, once the coaches' subsystem is able to consistently be in metaposition, it has to transfer this skill to someone or to a group within the organization. It can either be the strategist, if there is one, or someone else close to the CEO.

Then, the second task of the supervisor is to observe the whole system and identify parallel processes between subsystems. In order to do this, a slightly different kind of metaposition is needed: when in observation mode the supervisor is looking at the coaches' subsystem and at the interactions between it and all other subsystems. These interactions can only be seen through the lenses of the coaches' subsystem.

Different techniques exist for working with subsystems that cannot be seen directly by the supervisor. Systemic constellations are considered very effective (supervision using constellations is discussed in more depth by Francis in this volume).

Box 24.2 Supervision techniques using a form of systemic constellations

To highlight the mechanisms involved between the different subsystems, the following exercise can be proposed to coaches:

The different subsystems are represented by sheets of paper on the ground bearing the name of their leader. The internal and external coaches stand on these sheets and play the role of the person written on the sheet.

The supervisor then introduces a task such as negotiating contract. They then operate the system by trying to reproduce the dynamics of a real-life situation. The result is surprisingly realistic.

Systemic constellations offer a wide variety of tools which can be used to explore what might be the intimate functioning of an organization. Persons, groups (for instance, the legal department), business units and even concepts like the strategic plan or a corporate culture can be represented. Furthermore, some important characteristics of these representatives can be shown, for instance power, influence, change potential, and leadership potential.

Another way to encourage coaches to adopt systems thinking is to undertake supervision sessions where it is not allowed to talk or ask questions about what is called Eyes 1 to 6, that is the different actors (client, coach, supervisor) and interactions between the actors (see Hawkins and Schwenk, this volume). So, for example, if one of the supervisees says, 'I would like to understand why I feel guilty when I coach the Human Resource executive', only Eye 7 is allowed during the discussion. Forcing the supervisee to look at the context will help them see what they don't usually pay attention to.

Finally, when the coaches' subsystem behaves as a single person and has a good feeling of how the organization functions, the supervisor can work on patterns of social interaction as suggested by Lawrence and Moore (2018). A careful analysis of stability and predictability might flag up a potential risk of chaos or the 'butterfly effect'.

Role of internal supervision

The possibility of internal supervision has been addressed by Long (2012) and Field (2014). Two questions are raised by these authors. First, who should be the main client of the internal supervisor? This, in turn, raises the feasibility of questioning of the organization by an internal supervisor. Second, the related question of what kind of contract is needed between supervisors and the organization, and between internal supervisors and the organization (see Figure 24.4).

The degree of real independence of the internal coach or internal supervisor from the sponsor or from the organization will determine who the real client is. This is something that the supervisor, external or internal, must decide with the

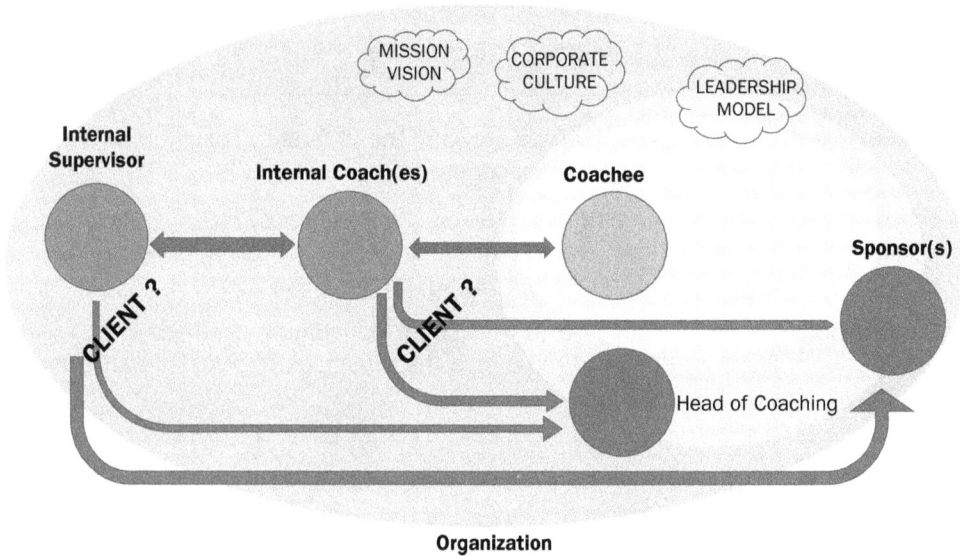

Figure 24.4 Who is the client for an internal coach or supervisor?

supervisee. This is particularly important when analysing ethical dilemmas. The same question exists for the internal supervisor.

The concept of a three-cornered contract (English 1975) might be useful for analysing the different situations that internal supervision creates:

- In hierarchical companies, there is a three-cornered contract, formal or not, between the coach, the client and the organization (represented by the sponsor).
- In matrix organizations, the sponsor can be either the line or functional manager of the client, or be represented by another function, for instance HR.
- In organizations with a 'strong coaching culture', in addition to the above, the sponsor might be the function or person in charge of coaching management (for example, a Chief Coaching Executive or Head of Coaching).

Depending on who is the sponsor, there are two possibilities, as represented in Figure 24.5: if the sponsor is the Head of Coaching or the HR executive, they can organize and co-ordinate the two three-way meetings and draft the three-cornered contracts in a balanced way. If the sponsor is the line manager of the coachee, they organize the three-way meetings between the coach, the client and themselves. The supervisor's relationship is with someone else in the organization, for instance the Head of Coaching or HR, who might not try to co-ordinate with the sponsor. Risks of imbalanced three-cornered contracts are higher in this case.

Micholt (1992) added the notion of 'perceived psychological distance' to the concept of the three-cornered contract. She analysed in detail how an imbalanced three-cornered contract can be the source of conflict and psychological games.

Finally, most authors agree that supervisors of internal coaches need more systemic skills than supervisors of external coaches. Another recommendation would be to supervise the supervisors (Moral and Henrichfreise 2018; Moral and Turner 2019).

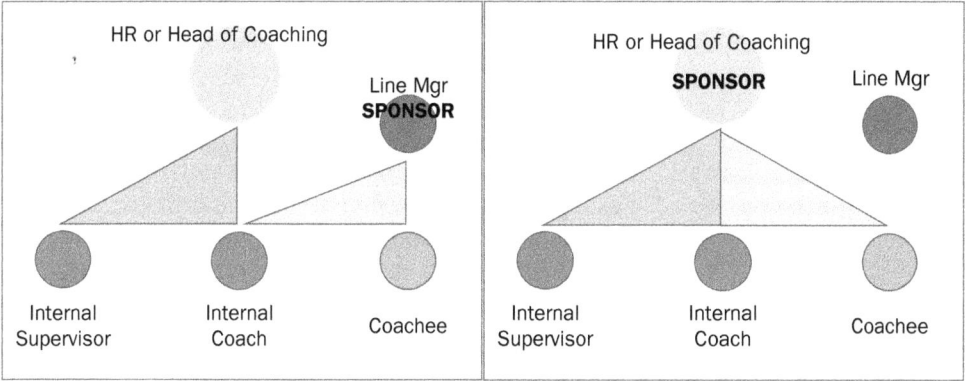

Figures 24.5 Contracts with the internal supervisor

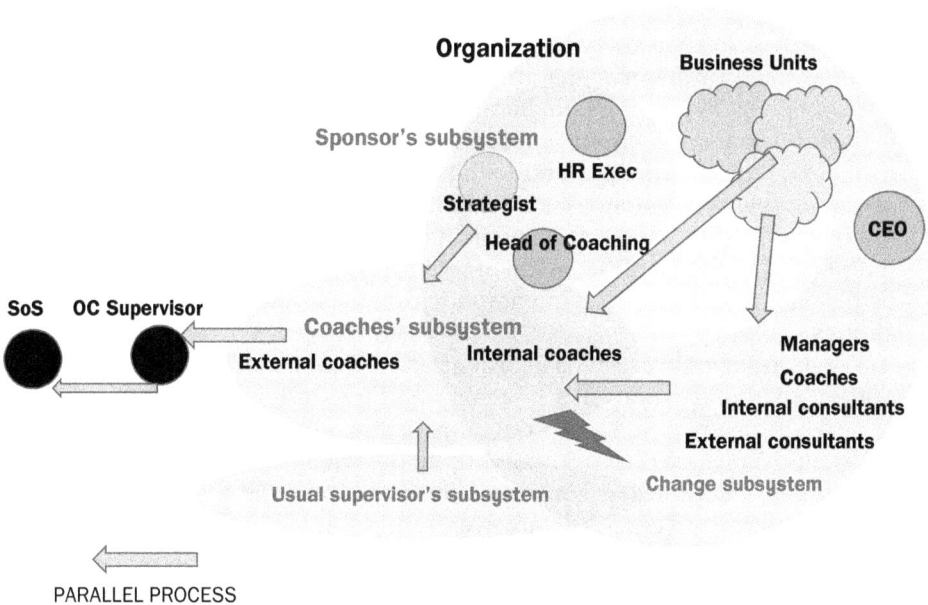

Figure 24.6 Systemic representation of subsystems and their relationships

Supervision of supervision in organizational transformation

During our assignments we have found that the supervisor can be personally affected by the intensity of parallel processes. Consequently, we experimented with introducing a Supervisor of Supervisors (SoS) in the system (Figure 24.6). It appears that a SoS is not only useful but necessary to contain the emotions and sometimes the confusion that the supervisor of OC receives from the subsystem of coaches. As the parallel processes flow from the stakeholders towards the coaches' subsystem and later towards the supervisor, their emotional and psychological impact increases and they also need the support of the supervisor.

Supervision of the OC supervisor helps reflect on the parallel processes that occur between the supervisor and the coaches' subsystem. Experience of both supervisors and organizational coaches shows there are some residual parallel processes between the supervisor and the SoS.

Supervision of supervision has been explored in depth by European practitioners (Van Kessel 2018) and more recently by Moral et al. (2018). If the supervisor of the supervisor has a good understanding of second-order systems and complexity theories, they could be of real help to the supervisor (Lawrence 2019).

Guidance for further learning and research

Supervisors need additional skills to supervise organizational coaches, and possibly consultants, either individually or in groups. It is critical that their systemic understanding is solidly established and covers first- and second-order systems theories as well as complexity theories (Lawrence 2019 and in this volume). They will also need to have knowledge of theories of organization.

As people in organizations are more and more linked through virtual networks such as the internet, an additional theorical framework may be needed in the future and an *energetic approach* seems to be appropriate: in systems and complexity theories people interact like magnets but are not interconnected. In energetic theories (Lamy and Moral 2018) everything is connected to everything else. Traditional Chinese medicine is an example of such theories where the solution might be far from the problem; for instance, treating the foot could be the cure for a headache. In energetic theories, systems are similar to living entities.

For professionals involved in organizational coaching, organizational development or the creation of a coaching culture, reflexive practice is key. As regards the complexity involved in organizational transformation, the supervisor should guard against oversimplifying the whole system. Another danger is the flow of emotion that converges on them and supervision of supervision can be a remedy. There are, however, not yet enough case studies and more research is needed to assess the impact of supervision on the transformation process.

Questions for reflection

- What prompts us (coaches and supervisors) to work with larger and larger groups (teams, teams of teams, organizations)?
- What are the differences between the functions of supervision and those of a steering committee in a change project?
- In what way might the organizations' patterns of culture be similar to individual personalities?
- From an organizational point of view, what are the risks of supervision?

Further sources

Hawkins, P. and McMahon, A. (2020) *Supervision in the Helping Professions.* London: Open University Press. This work shows the need for increasing awareness of the culture and a first step to leading some improvement but supervision. It describes the process that helps to identify dysfunctions and fix them.

Lawrence, P. (2019) What is systemic coaching?, *Philosophy of Coaching: An International Journal*, 4(2): 35–52. In this work system and complexity theories are articulated to understand how a team of coaches and/or consultants drive the change.

Moral, M. and Henrichfreise, S. (2018) *Coaching d'organisation*, 3rd edn. Paris: InterEditions. A reference book about organizational coaching. It includes a case study that illustrates how a team of coaches can organize the change and how this team is supervised.

References

Argyris, C. (1970) *Intervention Theory and Method: A Behavioral Science View.* Reading, MA: Addison-Wesley

Bachkirova, T., Jackson, P., Hennig, C. and Moral, M. (2020) Supervision in coaching: systematic literature review, *International Coaching Psychology Review*, 15(2): 231–253.

Bion, W.R. (1961) *Experiences in Groups.* London: Tavistock.

Burke, W. (2002) *Organizational Change: Theory and Practice.* Thousand Oaks: Sage.

Caplan, J. (2003) *Coaching for the Future.* London: CIPD.

Ceccin, G. (1987) Hypothesizing, circularity, and neutrality revisited: an invitation to curiosity, *Family Process*, 26: 405–413.

Clutterbuck, D. and Megginson, D. (2005) *Making Coaching Work: Creating a Coaching Culture.* London: CIPD.

Clutterbuck, D., Megginson, D and Bajer, A. (2016) *Building and Sustaining a Coaching Culture.* London: CIPD.

Crane, T. and Nancy-Patrick, L. (2007) *The Heart of Coaching: Using Transformational Coaching to Create a High-performance Coaching Culture.* San Diego: FTA Press.

Devillard, O. (2018) *Méthode de Coaching d'Organisation pour Piloter le Changement.* Paris: Eyrolles.

Dugois, P., Gauthron, T. and Béon, P. (2016) *La transformation permanente: Une introduction au coaching d'organisation.* Paris: Pratiques d'entreprises.

De Haan, E. (2012) *Supervision in Action: A Relational Approach to Coaching and Consultancy Supervision.* London: Open University Press.

ECVision Competence Framework of Supervision and Coaching (2015) Available from: www.anse.eu/wp-content/uploads/doc/ECVision/ECvision_e_book.pdf (accessed 27 July 2020).

EMCC Supervision Competence Framework (2019) Available from: https://www.emccbooks.org/product/supervision-competences (accessed 27 July 2020).

English, F. (1975) The three-cornered contract, *Transactional Analysis Journal*, 5(4): 383–384.

Field, C. (2014) *Impact of Supervision on Internal Coaching.* Sydney: Sydney University.

Giffard, M. and Moral, M. (2007) *Le coaching d'équipe.* Paris: Armand Colin.

Hawkins, P. (2012) *Creating a Coaching Culture.* Maidenhead: Open University Press.

Hawkins, P. and Smith, N. (2013) *Coaching, Mentoring and Organizational Consultancy: Supervision, Skills and Development.* Maidenhead: Open University Press.

Hellbom, K. (2018) Organisational Coaching – The New Frontier of Coaching, EMCC Mentoring, Coaching and Supervision Conference, University of Chester, 10–11 July.

ICF (2014) Building a coaching culture. Available from: https://coachfederation.org/research/building-a-coaching-culture (accessed 27 July 2020).

Jones, G. and Gorell, R. (2014) *How to Create a Coaching Culture*. London: Kogan Page.

Lamy, F. and Moral, M. (2018) *Les outils de l'intelligence collective*. Paris: InterEditions.

Lawrence, P. (2019) What is systemic coaching?, *Philosophy of Coaching: An International Journal*, 4(2): 35–52.

Lawrence, P. and Moore, A. (2018) *Coaching in Three Dimensions: Meeting the Challenges of a Complex World*. London: Routledge.

Lewin, K. (1951) *Field Theory in Social Science*. London: Tavistock.

Long, K. (2012) Building internal supervision capacity in organisations, *The OCM Coach and Mentor Journal*, 12: 2–6.

Maxwell, A. (2011) Supervising the internal coach, in T. Bachkirova, P. Jackson and D. Clutterbuck (eds) *Coaching and Mentoring Supervision: Theory and Practice*. Maidenhead: Open University Press.

McGregor, D. (1971) Theory X and theory Y, in D.S. Pugh (ed.) *Organization Theory*. New York: Penguin.

Micholt, N. (1992) Psychological distance and group interventions, *Transactional Analysis Journal*, 22(4): 228–233.

Moral, M. (2011) A French model of supervision, in T. Bachkirova, P. Jackson and D. Clutterbuck (eds) *Coaching and Mentoring Supervision: Theory and Practice*. Maidenhead: Open University Press.

Moral, M., Guerand, A., Desroches, J. et al. (2017) How to best organise supervision in a 'strong Coaching Culture' environment? *EMCC International Mentoring and Coaching Conference*, University of Edinburgh. Available at: https://www.undici.fr/wp-content/uploads/2017/04/Edimbourg_2017__How_to_best_organise_supervision_in_a_strong_coaching_culture.pdf (accessed 27 July 2020).

Moral, M. and Henrichfreise, S. (2009) Considerations on the emergence of organizational coaching: international perspectives, in M. Moral and G. Abbott (eds) *The Routledge Companion to International Business Coaching*. London: Routledge.

Moral, M. and Henrichfreise, S. (2018) *Coaching d'organisation*, 3rd edn. Paris: InterEditions.

Moral, M. and Turner, E. (2019) Supervision of supervision, in J. Birch and P. Welch (eds) *Coaching Supervision: Advancing Practice, Changing Landscapes*. London: Routledge.

Motto, C. (2013) *Coacher les organisations avec les constellations systémiques*. Paris: InterEditions.

Peterson, M. and Smith, P. (2000) Sources of meaning, organizations and culture, in N. Ashkenasy, C. Wilderom and M. Peterson (eds) *Handbook of Organizational Culture and Climate*. London: Sage.

Porras, J.I. and Silvers, R.C. (1991) Organization development and transformation, *Annual Review of Psychology*, 42: 51–78.

Schein, E. (1985) *Organizational Culture and Leadership*. New York: Jossey-Bass.

Srivastva, S. and Cooperrider, D. (1990) *Appreciative Management and Leadership: The Power of Positive Thought and Action in Organisations*. San Francisco: Jossey-Bass.

St John-Brooks, K. (2014) *The Inside Story*. London: Routledge.

St John-Brooks, K. (2019) Supervision for internal coaches, in J. Birch and P. Welch (eds) *Coaching Supervision: Advancing Practices, Changing Landscapes*. London: Routledge.

Vergonjeanne, F. (2010) *Coacher groupes et organisations – La Théorie Organisationnelle de Berne (T.O.B.)*. Paris: InterEditions.

Van Kessel, L. (2018) *Supervision on Supervision – An International Bibliography*. Available from: https://www.researchgate.net/publication/324454638_SUPERVISION_ON_SUPERVISION_-_AN_INTERNATIONAL_BIBLIOGRAPHY_I_Anglo-Saxon_II_Dutch_III_German (accessed 27 July 2020).

van Reenen, M. (2014) *Developing a Conceptual Framework for Coach Supervision of Internal Coaches at Organizations*. PhD thesis, Stellenbosch University.

25 | Supervision in mentoring programmes

Lis Merrick and Paul Stokes

Introduction

In the original version of this chapter, we argued that supervision in formal mentoring programmes is a form of supervision that has been under-researched and there was little evidence of good practice in programmes in the UK. Both authors design and develop mentoring programmes and have examined the relationship between the developing experience of the mentor against functions of supervision required in mentoring. We discuss the rationale for using supervision in mentoring, offer an updated conceptual schema linking mentor development and supervision and use it to examine supervision in two mentoring supervision case studies. Broader implications for mentoring supervision are also considered. We feel it is useful for the reader to consider how coaching and mentoring differ within organizational contexts and the impact this has on supervision, as well as the emerging needs of the mentor supervisee as they develop their practice.

The context and mode of supervision practice in mentoring programmes

Early research by Willis (2005) into mentoring and coaching standards undertaken by the European Mentoring and Coaching Council (EMCC) suggests that in practice there are more similarities than differences between mentoring and coaching. More recently, Garvey, Stokes and Megginson (2018) argued that, when comparing mentoring with coaching, mentoring activity is found in all sectors of society and includes both paid and voluntary activities. It is also associated with 'offline' partnerships. Here, we are defining mentoring as an offline developmental dialogue with mutual benefits but acknowledge many of the similarities with coaching (see Stokes et al. 2020 for a more detailed discussion of these similarities and differences).

When developing mentoring programmes, we have been faced with the challenges of how to support mentors at varying stages of development in order to facilitate their practice and progression as a mentor. This is complicated when mentoring is part of a wider organizational programme. Access to the mentors, resources (people and funding) and motivation to spend more time on the programme can all be very limited. Mentors are often volunteers who mentor as a small part of their work and have busy day jobs. In contrast to professional full-time coaches, selling the benefits of mentor supervision to part-time voluntary mentors can be a harder sell.

First, we need to address some key questions: What is mentor supervision? How does it differ from coaching supervision? What implications might these differences have for mentor development? These were the initial questions we sought to address when first exploring what mentoring supervision might mean for our practice as programme designers.

Our initial research, conducted in 2003, revealed the following functions of mentor supervision:

- Being a mentor to the mentors
- Being able to explore techniques and help with problems
- An opportunity to reflect on own practice
- To support a mentor who feels out of their depth
- As a mark of good practice for the profession
- To support with ethical issues
- To be available for the mentor as an emotional safety valve.

This echoed Barrett's (2002) work on the benefits of mentoring supervision:

- Preventing personal burn-out
- A celebration of what I do
- Demonstrating skill/knowledge
- Helping me to focus on my blind-spot(s)
- Discovering my own pattern of behaviours
- Developing skills as a mentor
- A quality control process
- Providing a different angle on an issue.

Barrett's (2002) work aside, there has been little attention focused on mentoring supervision in the mentoring literature. Nevertheless, the importance of the supervision role is apparent in other helping professions, including psychoanalysis (Kutter 2002), medicine (Marrow et al. 2002), education (Blasé and Blasé 2002) and social work (Maidment and Cooper 2002). These discussions may be due to changes in the way other helpers understand the supervision process. However, it is interesting to reflect on the mentoring theme that runs through this literature. For example, Lawton and Feltham (2000), when exploring counselling, argued that 'the original concept of supervision as primarily an element of training has altered and its role as a means of providing monitoring, support and education for counsellors throughout their careers has taken on greater significance' (p. 27). This suggested a more holistic view of helping through supervision than training or advising, so drawing it closer to mentoring in terms of its breadth of scope. In this vein, Feasey (2002) argued: 'The supervisor is very much a mentor and model for the counsellor in training. She models empathic attention and the ability to offer insightful reflection as well as to inculcate the values of the counselling code' (p. xi).

This widening of the notion of supervision in other professions coincided with increased concerns with how mentors might be developed within the mentoring community (for a useful discussion of educating mentors, see Garvey and Alred 2000). These concerns prompted us, in 2003, to develop a heuristic which linked together the needs of the mentoring supervisee with their development as a mentor.

It made sense to start with the literature on counselling development as Kram (1985) identifies counselling skills as an integral part of mentoring as part of its psycho-social function. See Stokes (2003) for a more critical discussion of the relationship between counselling and mentoring.

Hawkins and Shohet (2012) offer four categories of counsellor development listed below:

- The novice
- The apprentice
- The journey person
- The master craftsperson.

While it can sometimes be unhelpful to artificially compartmentalize human development, this framework offers a typology against which the helper can compare themselves and begin to identify what their development needs might be. Following this model, we generated some similar stages for mentor development to be used as a device for mentoring practitioners to aid reflection on their own practice and have used them in our own practice since then.

These mentor development categories are as follows:

- Novice mentor
- Developing mentor
- Reflective mentor
- Reflexive mentor.

For each stage we offer a description of each, summarizing the benefits and challenges and the role and responsibilities of the supervisor. We have refined these as shown below.

The novice mentor

A novice mentor is someone who may be new to mentoring, with little experience of mentoring in practice. This does not mean that they are untrained or unskilled, but that they have little experience of participating in a live, dynamic human mentoring process. They may have been mentored themselves or used mentoring skills in their work/profession but may not have thought of themselves as a mentor before. As a result, they may well have development needs that are different and distinct from more experienced mentors. For instance, they will need to become familiar with the protocols of mentoring within their programme and what its aims and objectives are. They will therefore need help and support in defining/refining their approach, so that it is consistent with their programme. They may also need help in gaining access to the models of mentoring that exist.

Implications for supervision – description of practice

One of the important functions of the supervisor at this stage is to ensure that the mentoring offered is congruent with the aims of the programme. This resembles what Hawkins and Shohet (2012) call the management/normative function of supervision.

This 'quality assurance'/audit function has two main purposes:

- To check the mentor's ability as a mentor, i.e. are they using acceptance, empathy and congruence with their mentee?

- To bestow what Feltham (2000) calls the 'aura of professionalism' to ensure programme credibility in the eyes of its sponsors.

Here, most supervision occurs through running focus group activity for the mentors at regular intervals. For example, a programme that has been set up for a year may bring mentors together every four months to review how the mentoring is going and to provide further education about the programme. The purpose of these groups will be to check progress on programme aims and objectives, to ensure the mentors offer the type of mentoring that the programme is advocating (e.g. developmental not sponsorship) and to equip the mentors to move to the next stage of their development.

Focus group questions may include:

- What has really gone well/less well in your mentoring relationship?
- To what extent do you feel you have contributed to this?
- Which stage of the relationship do you think you have achieved?
- What aspects of mentoring do you feel least confident about?
- Would any further support be helpful?

The developing mentor

In one sense, all mentors are developing, but in this context the developing mentor is someone who can no longer be considered to be a novice, as they have some experience of mentoring 'under their belt' and understand the 'rules' within their particular programme/context. They can use a well-known mentoring model/process (e.g. the seminal work of Kram 1983) and will have some of the skills and behaviours required by an effective mentor (see Clutterbuck and Megginson 1999 for examples of skills/roles involved). However, this repertoire of behaviours is basic and their ability as a mentor is confined to a small repertoire of behaviours.

Implications for supervision – description of practice

Here, the developing mentor needs to start to identify other ways of mentoring so as to expand their effectiveness as a mentor. The supervisor may need to pay more attention to supporting the mentor in their process development and in recognizing the dynamics within a mentoring relationship. This resembles what Hawkins and Shohet (2012) refer to as the educative/formative supervision role. The supervisor can model those behaviours needed to help the mentor acquire these skills and may even coach them in these areas where appropriate.

The supervisor needs to support the mentor in identifying a mentoring process that works for them and helps them enhance their understanding of the different skills required.

Some programmes provide one-to-one supervision where the programme organizer acts as supervisor or they may bring in an external supervisor. However, one-to-one supervision can be challenging due to resource constraints. Due to these constraints, most formal programmes will use focus groups to supervise mentors at this stage, or begin to bring in peer discussion and reflection around areas such as:

- Outcomes
  - Objectives for programme
  - Your own goals for relationship
- Processes
  - Have we met often enough?
  - Have we spent enough time in the meeting?
  - Have we challenged each other sufficiently?
  - Have we agreed actions?
  - What processes have worked best?
- Relationship
  - Have we established trust?
  - Have we created a 'safe protected space'?
  - Are we able to be honest with each other?
  - Do we give each other feedback?
  - What have we done to achieve this in our relationship?

One way to give developing mentors such support is to organize real play practice for them in trios, where a peer will give them feedback using a checklist of relevant skills. This identifies developmental needs that the mentor can then take back into one-to-one supervision support with the programme organizer or external supervisor.

The reflective mentor

The reflective mentor is someone who has a fair amount of mentoring experience and has extended his or her repertoire of skills beyond that of the developing mentor. They are aware of several different approaches to mentoring and have developed an awareness of context and their own identity as a mentor within the mentoring community. They are now in the position to begin to critically reflect upon their own practice and to develop their skills and understanding of different mentoring approaches, drawing from other mentors, their supervisor and from other helping professions.

This process should have begun within the developing mentor stage but becomes central at this stage. It is distinct from the developing mentor stage in that the reflective mentor has had an opportunity to reflect on some of their experience as a mentor through the lens of their supervisory discussions. Hence, the reflective mentor has begun to take some responsibility for thinking about and directing their own development as a mentor and has started to incorporate ideas developed within supervision and elsewhere into their mentoring practice.

Implications for supervision – description of practice

One of the important aspects of effective supervision for the reflective mentor is that the supervisor is able to demonstrate empathic attention and insightful reflection to the mentor. Mary Cox writes in Feasey (2002): 'What I want from my supervisor is intelligent listening, experienced reflection, realistic mirroring, perceptive confrontation and a sense of personal warmth and humour' (p. 141).

This development function is a combination of Hawkins and Shohet's (2012) role of educative/formative support and of a supportive function, where through reflecting on and exploring the supervisee's work, the supervisor focuses on developing the skills, understanding and ability of the mentor they are supporting. Therefore, there are two changes in focus here. First, the supervisor is focusing more on the mentee and the 'work' of the mentor while at the same time encouraging the mentor to begin to recognize how the mentor's own experiences (including those as a mentor/supervisee) are beginning to impact upon their mentoring work. Second, the supervisor is supporting the mentor to develop his or her own internal critically reflexive capacity.

The reflexive mentor

The reflexive mentor has considerable experience as a mentor and may even be a mentor supervisor themself. They have developed sufficient self-awareness, with the help of their supervisor, to critically reflect upon their own practice and to identify areas for their own development, as well as being more competent in detecting and using their own feelings within mentoring conversations to inform their practice. They are, however, astute enough to recognize that they need to continue with their development and recognize the dangers of complacency in terms of rigidity of approach. Hence, the reflexive mentor needs supervision to assure the quality of their helping skills and to prevent blind spots or damage being done through arrogant or careless interventions.

Implications for supervision – description of practice

Here, the supervisor would need to be a highly competent, flexible and experienced mentor themselves. The range of supervision required might go from gentle support when a problem occurs through to adopting a strong critical position in order to challenge the potentially complacent mentor supervisee. Also, the frequency of supervision may differ, depending on the varying needs of the supervisee.

With these four stages in mind, we will now examine two mentoring supervision interventions.

1. Associated British Foods (ABF) case study

Angie Price, Executive Development Manager

Associated British Foods is a diversified international food, ingredients and retail group operating in 52 countries. It is split into five segments: Sugar, Agriculture, Retail, Grocery and Ingredients.

The 'Two-way Mentoring programme' was developed in 2013 as a pilot activity to support gender diversity. The programme aims to aid long-term succession planning through the expansion of individual networks, support for personal and professional development and mutual learning experiences for mentors and mentees. It now supports many under-represented groups with over 260 mentoring pairs. There are currently 55 mentoring pairs working on a global basis, and over 25 per cent of the mentors are former mentees.

Mentor supervision is available to all mentors in the programme and is offered on a small group virtual basis or to individuals. The supervision provides:

- An ethical check
- A quality assurance intervention
- An educative intervention.

Since 2019, the mentors have self-selected into two categories of experience for their group supervision, based on Merrick and Stokes (2020):

1. Novice and developing mentors
2. Reflective and reflexive mentors.

For novice and developing mentors, the focus is on which roles/behaviours the mentor feels they are using in the relationship and how far the relationship has developed through the lifecycle. Frequency and mode of contact is discussed before each mentor has individual time to discuss their relationship. With a combination of input from peer mentors and the supervisor, each mentor is provided with challenge and support, depending on their needs. The session finishes with a presentation on a skills topic to enhance the mentor's ability.

For reflective and reflexive mentors, sessions are led by mentors' needs and supported by input from their peer mentor colleagues and the supervisor. Challenge is encouraged to develop the reflexivity of the mentor being supported. Each session ends with some educative input around techniques and models for the mentor to use in supporting resilience and adaptive capacity development.

Themes from supervision sessions are collected to help further programme development. Some of the recent challenges which have come out of the supervision and have been discussed in sessions include:

- Maintaining momentum in the relationship. Some mentors have experienced a lack of energy after two or three sessions and the mentee 'goes quiet' as they have received a lot of support and learning quickly and may need to assimilate this before they go back to their mentor for another session.
- Listening more effectively. Mentors are often conscious they can improve their listening skills and are self-aware after sessions they have talked too much. This is one of the most common issues that novice and developing mentors 'beat themselves up' about.
- Mentoring virtually. With all relationships working virtually during the COVID-19 pandemic, mentors who had used to face-to-face conversations previously, became more used to the virtual mentoring space.
- Requesting additional techniques and knowing when to use them. This request often involves becoming more comfortable with process models, such as the 'Three Stage Process' or a solution-focused approach. There is often a growing awareness on the part of the mentor that they can use other techniques
- How to provide structure and process in the conversations. It is useful for the mentor to introduce a check in and check out to the mentoring session and to understand what elements to include in both. This skill develops over time and novice and developing mentors find it helpful to discuss this concept again.

Conversations in the novice/developing mentor supervision sessions focus on developing their process, with mentors needing external validation that they are 'doing it right' and that their mentee is benefiting from it. Reflective/reflexive supervision tends to focus on learning new techniques and reminding the mentors about good process. They are aware of it, but they may have forgotten some of the concepts they once knew.

Case study discussion

Some interesting insights can be taken from the ABF case study. First, our model was intended to be an analytical lens through which mentor supervision might be characterized. However, ABF have explicitly employed this as a practical way of organizing their mentoring supervision needs. They have adapted the model to fit with those needs, combining supervision interventions for novice and developing mentors and then combining reflective and reflexive mentors. This recognizes the importance of seeing mentor development as being on a continuum rather than expecting there to be hard and fast distinctions between one stage and another. ABF's experience also suggests that, while the reflective/reflexive mentor's needs may have changed, the other functions of supervision – particularly what we call the 'training' function – is still present, shown by the fact that these more experienced mentors still value some educative input as part of their peer group supervision sessions.

The case also reveals supervision as a way of militating against regression in terms of the mentors' learning. In other words, both groups of mentors seem to use the supervision as a way of reminding themselves about the lessons and skills that they have already developed on their mentoring journey, in addition to identifying and embedding new learning. By engaging in giving and receiving constructive feedback and learning from others, group supervision at ABF seems to give mentors the opportunity to be supported in working through challenging issues and to identify solutions to take forward into their mentoring practice.

2. Group mentoring supervision in Médecins Sans Frontières (MSF)

Agnese Pinto, MSF Mentoring and Coaching Hub Co-ordinator

From the start, the MSF 'Mentoring & Coaching Hub' was committed to provide the best mentoring possible. We knew we had a great community of committed mentors, that wanted to do better, that had asked multiple times to gather and to share their learning, They were also asking for feedback on their performance: the more invested they were in mentoring, the more they wanted to know if they were providing quality support to their mentees. So how could we provide all that? How could we, at the same time, evaluate their performance, provide developmental opportunities and have them create a community? And achieve this with our own internal human capital and no budgetary implications?

I came across an article written by Paul Stokes and Lis Merrick, who provided a fresh perspective. What I took from it, was that evaluation of, and control over, mentors' performances, were not going to bring about quality. My role as a programme manager was to support mentors' development. I needed to provide ample, safe opportunities for mentors to open up and learn. And that's what we did.

Group Supervision – together with webinars, online social gatherings and an online learning platform/community of practice – was launched. We trained a few experienced mentors (who were also internal coaches and facilitators) to facilitate group supervision sessions. We launched two groups simultaneously. The structure had to be simple, and was as follows:

- **Who**: A closed group with a maximum of six. Diversity within the group and of mentors' experience were encouraged.
- **When**: Meeting up to four sessions of 1.5 hours, at six-week intervals.
- **How**: Based on the action learning set model. Every participant would have 5 minutes to introduce the topic and design how they wanted the group to support them (listening, providing guidance, advising, etc.). The group would have then 10 minutes to do so. The facilitator/supervisor would offer advice when needed, facilitate the discussion, and provide a wrap up of the session at the end.

One group was a great success, according to its members. There were only three members, after some dropped out from the start. They ended up meeting on a monthly basis over a seven-month period (ending in March 2020). They kept in contact and the two most experienced participants volunteered to facilitate other group supervision sessions in the future. They decided not to have more than four participants to keep the sessions to 1.5 hours. They also wanted to explore the possibility of working with external mentors from other organizations in the future. They felt that the diversity of the group was the source of the richness of their learning. The second group met twice, all participants were very committed; however, the facilitator had limited time to follow up on the logistics, which proved to be more time-consuming than expected, and the group didn't meet again.

We have launched a new group supervision (and a second will soon follow) specifically for mentors who offer short-term support for staff facing COVID-19-related challenges. Learning from our previous sessions, we have provided additional administration support to the facilitators, helping them hold the process and follow up on participants who drop out.

Case study discussion

Here, we also have some interesting lessons for mentoring supervision practice. First, the MSF Hub decided to use online methods of support, using an action learning set structure that prioritized the sharing of mentoring practice and issues. This support is important in MSF's context where both mentors and mentees can be placed in challenging environments within which to practise as part of their day job. Of the two groups discussed in the case study, it can be argued that both groups of mentors were probably at the developing mentor stage within our typology.

In the group that was less successful, the supervisor struggled to contain the group in terms of the logistics of the process. However, perhaps it is also the case that the group did not feel contained by the supervision process in a psychological sense and that the supervisory needs were not being satisfied in terms of quality assurance (i.e. knowing that they were doing 'the right thing' as mentors). This may also be true for those who dropped out of the first group. One of the challenges with online processes is that, while they can be relatively easy to access, they can also be relatively easy to withdraw from. When faced with competing pressures from their day jobs, it can be easy to prioritize that pressing work over one's own development. MSF's 'missions' are often conducted in an emergency context, which can encourage participants to see any activities that have a distal outcome in terms of patient care (like mentoring supervision) as being relatively unimportant and self-indulgent in relation to actions that have more proximal outcomes (e.g. work that directly influences patient care in the short term). It seems important that mentoring supervision in such contexts has clear boundaries concerning participation and engagement, thus emphasizing the importance of the first stage in our model.

Evolution of mentoring scheme supervision

In both cases, we can see the benefits and challenges of this sort of mentoring supervision. Despite the 'blurring' of hard and fast distinctions between the labels of coaching and mentoring (Stokes et al. 2020), mentoring still has associations with the use of personal experience and with the whole person and their values. We can see how mentors in both organizations were supported by the opportunity to reflect and analyse their mentoring practice. A similarity between the two supervision programmes is a desire to leverage individual learning from mentoring practice and to enable mentors to bring themselves fully to the mentoring process and to be able to offer their experience to their mentees. While this intention is not exclusive to mentoring schemes, this tendency seems more prevalent than in coaching schemes, which are more likely to involve process experts who do not necessarily have experience in the field in question. This tendency has some important implications for mentoring supervision.

As many novice mentors will say, they find it hard to resist the urge to give advice and to tell the mentee what they know; we have found that the supervision processes can be useful in helping the mentors find a suitable amount of professional distance from their own experience. This distance seems important in contexts where mentors give a lot of themselves and their experience. This enables them to be resourceful as mentors by avoiding the 'pendulum effect' of either pushing their experience onto the mentees or withholding their experience from them. Our experience of working with larger organizations suggests that some programme participants have healthy egos and often, irrespective of gender, espouse a tough guy/macho (Deal and Kennedy 2000) culture within their organizations. Hence supervisors also need to pay careful attention to the importance of challenging dominant assumptions about business and organizations with the mentors to avoid complacency. We feel that mentoring supervision enables mentors to offer their experience to the mentees on the one hand, but to resist, either consciously or subconsciously, developing clones of themselves on the other!

Research on mentor supervision still lags behind research on coaching supervision for a number of reasons. First, mentoring as a label often refers to more informal unpaid helping relationships, which can mean that mentoring supervision, in turn, is likely to receive less formal attention and recognition than coaching (which is more likely to be a paid activity). The majority of mentors do not have access to supervision, resources or financial incentives to support their supervision activities as the mentoring itself is often voluntary and unpaid. Hence, the professionalization of mentoring is less prominent than it is for coaching, as mentoring is much less commercialized. We argue that coaches can see supervision as another way of extolling their quality of professional practice. By differentiating themselves from non-supervised coaches, they are willing to pay for professional supervision from a coaching supervisor as they can then pass this fee onto the end client. This is not an option for volunteer mentors.

With the image of coaching (rightly or wrongly) as being more performance focused, manager-coaches are more likely to get organizational support and supervision for their performance coaching of staff rather than their mentoring activities. Volunteer mentors find it more difficult (a) to convince others to give more time for their own development as a mentor, and (b) to give them challenging feedback about their practice as a supervisor for fear of discouraging them to volunteer. Nevertheless, mentor supervision is still needed but is in short supply. While coaching supervision and mentoring supervision – like coaching and mentoring themselves – are very similar activities with almost identical skill sets, the context in which the labels get used can suggest different emphases for supervision. If we accept that mentoring is still often used to refer to someone more experienced helping someone less experienced in making transitions in their knowledge work or thinking, then mentoring supervisors must be prepared to pay extra attention to helping the supervisee to become aware of how they are using that experience alongside the other process skills that are common to both coaching and mentoring.

Guidance for further learning and research

As argued above, there is relatively little research on mentoring supervision in particular. However, the edited volume *Mentoring in Action* (Megginson et al. 2006) contains several case examples of mentoring programmes that are still pertinent in terms of how mentors might be supported in their practice, across a wide range of contexts. Similarly, Gopee's (2008) book focusing on mentoring and supervision is also helpful, although care must be taken to avoid confusing mentoring supervision with clinical supervision in the NHS. Both these texts contain a practical discourse on using mentor supervision. Finally, for a critical text on mentoring in context and the challenges facing mentors and their development, Colley's (2003) excellent critical text on mentoring for social inclusion is worth examining, particularly in terms of the psychological pressures that mentors face.

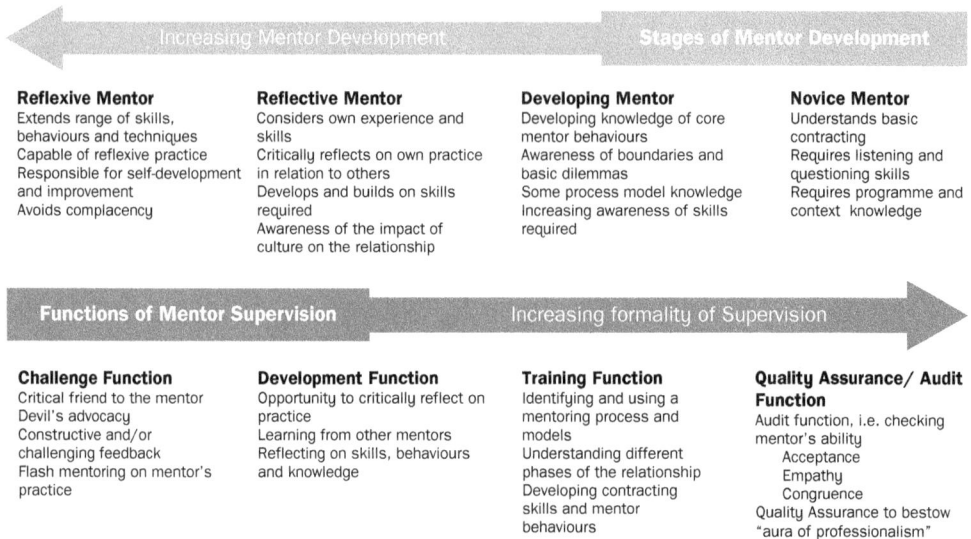

Increasing Mentor Development		Stages of Mentor Development	
Reflexive Mentor	**Reflective Mentor**	**Developing Mentor**	**Novice Mentor**
Extends range of skills, behaviours and techniques	Considers own experience and skills	Developing knowledge of core mentor behaviours	Understands basic contracting
Capable of reflexive practice	Critically reflects on own practice in relation to others	Awareness of boundaries and basic dilemmas	Requires listening and questioning skills
Responsible for self-development and improvement	Develops and builds on skills required	Some process model knowledge	Requires programme and context knowledge
Avoids complacency	Awareness of the impact of culture on the relationship	Increasing awareness of skills required	

Functions of Mentor Supervision		Increasing formality of Supervision	
Challenge Function	**Development Function**	**Training Function**	**Quality Assurance/ Audit Function**
Critical friend to the mentor	Opportunity to critically reflect on practice	Identifying and using a mentoring process and models	Audit function, i.e. checking mentor's ability
Devil's advocacy	Learning from other mentors	Understanding different phases of the relationship	Acceptance
Constructive and/or challenging feedback	Reflecting on skills, behaviours and knowledge	Developing contracting skills and mentor behaviours	Empathy
Flash mentoring on mentor's practice			Congruence
			Quality Assurance to bestow "aura of professionalism"

Figure 25.1 A schema for mentor development and supervision

To conclude, there are several pertinent questions that need to be explored further in the context of mentoring supervision:

- What sort of supervision do mentors need when helping people?
- How does mentor supervision differ from mentoring for mentors?
- How can mentors be supported in achieving an effective balance between using their knowledge to help the mentee and allowing the mentee to become self-reliant?
- Is mentoring supervision distinct from coaching supervision due to its different markets, contexts and participants?

Further sources

For further exploration of the relationship between mentoring and supervision, see Carozza, L.S. (2011) *Science of Successful Supervision and Mentorship*. San Diego, CA: Plural Publishing.

For an examination of the links between mentoring, supervision and organization development, see Schultz, J. (2012) Coaching and mentoring supervision: theory and practice, *European Journal of Training and Development*, 36(6): 666–668.

Our original model explores the connections between mentor development and supervision and can be found by reading Merrick, L. and Stokes, P. (2003) Mentor development and supervision: a passionate joint enquiry, *International Journal of Coaching and Mentoring* (e-journal): 1. Available from: www.emccouncil.org.

References

Barrett, R. (2002) Mentor supervision and development – exploration of lived experience, *Career Development International*, 7(5): 279–283.

Blasé, J. and Blasé, J. (2002) The micropolitics of instructional supervision: a call for research, *Educational Administrative Quarterly*, 38(1): 6–44.

Clutterbuck, D. and Megginson, D. (1999) *Mentoring Executives & Directors*. Oxford: Butter-worth-Heinemann.

Colley, H. (2003) *Mentoring for Social Inclusion: A Critical Approach to Nurturing Mentoring Relationships*. London: Routledge.

Deal, T. and Kennedy, A. (2000) *Corporate Cultures: The Rites and Rituals of Corporate Life*, 3rd edn. Cambridge, MA: Perseus Books.

Feasey, D. (2002) *Good Practice in Supervision with Psychotherapists and Counsellors*. London: Whurr Publishers.

Feltham, C. and Horton, I. (2000) *Handbook of Counselling and Psychotherapy*. London: Sage.

Garvey, B. and Alred, G. (2000) Educating mentors, *Mentoring & Tutoring*, 8(2): 113–126.

Garvey, B., Stokes, P. and Megginson, D. (2018) *Coaching and Mentoring: Theory and Practice*, 3rd edn. London: Sage.

Gopee, N. (2008) *Mentoring and Supervision in Healthcare*. London: Sage.

Hawkins, P. and Shohet, R. (2012) *Supervision in the Helping Professions*. Maidenhead: Open University Press.

Kram, K. (1983) Phases of the mentor relationship, *Academy of Management Journal*, 26(4): 608–625.

Kram, K. (1985) *Mentoring at Work: Developmental Relationships in Organizational Life*. Glenview, IL: Scott-Foresman.

Kutter, P. (2002) From the Balint method toward profession related supervision, *American Journal of Psychoanalysis*, 62(4): 313–325.

Lawton, B. and Feltham, C. (eds) (2000) *Taking Supervision Forward*. London: Sage.

Maidment, J. and Cooper, L. (2002) Acknowledgement of client diversity and oppression in social work student supervision, *Social Work Education*, 21(4): 399–407.

Marrow, C.E., Hollyoake, K., Hamer, D. and Kenrick, C. (2002) Clinical supervision using video-conferencing technology: a reflective account, *Journal of Nursing Management*, 10(5): 275–282.

Marrow, C.E., Macauley, D.M. and Crumbie, A. (1997) Promoting reflective practice through clinical supervision, *Journal of Nursing Management*, 5: 77–82.

Megginson, D., Clutterbuck, D., Garvey, B. et al. (2006) *Mentoring in Action*, 2nd edn. London: Kogan Page.

Merrick, L. and Stokes, P. (2003) Mentor development and supervision: a passionate joint enquiry, *International Journal of Coaching and Mentoring* (e-journal): 1. Available from: www.emc-council.org.

Stokes, P. (2003) Exploring the relationship between mentoring and counselling, *British Journal of Guidance and Counselling*, 32(1): 25–34.

Stokes, P., Fatien Diochon, P. and Otter, K. (2020) Two sides of the same coin? Coaching and mentoring and the agentic role of context, *Annals of the New York Academy of Sciences*. doi:10.1111/nyas.14316.

Willis, P. (2005) *European Mentoring and Coaching Council, Competency Research Project: Phase 2, June*. Watford: EMCC. Available from: www.emccouncil.org (accessed 23 June 2020).

26 Supervising virtually

Eve Turner and Damian Goldvarg

Introduction

Advances in technology and the need for supervisors to consider how the exercise of their practice may be undergoing major changes is only heightened by concerns about personal and planetary health. This chapter will draw on existing literature on supervising virtually, as well as our own research, and personal perspectives as experienced practitioners.

We adopt the definition of virtual work from Pullan (2016: 3), as

> work done by people who are geographically distributed, working together despite the fact that at least one person is not in the same location as the others . . . supported by communications technology that helps people to connect when far apart.

In the last decade, alongside the growth in supervision (documented by, for example, McAnally et al. 2019; Hawkins and Turner 2017) there has been a growth in technologies that have made working virtually increasingly possible and popular and made access to supervision globally easier, beyond the use of the telephone, text or email.

This has been accompanied by increasing internet usage by up to 4.57 billion people worldwide, which equates to a global penetration of 59 per cent (Clement 2020) in 2020 compared to less than 7 per cent in 2000 (Roser et al. 2020). While forms of video-telephony have been in use for 150 years, the twenty-first century has seen a proliferation of video-conferencing, made possible by the improvements in internet connectivity in many parts of the world. Skype hit 100 million downloads in 2005, the first FaceTime was developed in 2010–2011, Zoom's software and Hangouts (Google) were launched in 2013 and many other types of videoconferencing have been developed (including WhatsApp, Lifesize, Remo, BlueJeans, Signal, Jami, GoToMeeting, Adobe Connect, Cisco WebEx and Microsoft Teams).

In spite of this growth in usage, the area of virtual coaching and supervision has seen relatively little research. Much that is available relates to alternatives to face-to-face contact, such as phone, chat and email. For this reason, the chapter also introduces original research to consider how widely virtual supervision using video is happening and what might be the benefits and disadvantages for working remotely in this way, consisting of a survey of supervisors and coaches from various networks. The research was conducted during the global coronavirus pandemic and therefore includes responses relating specifically to experiences of turning a practice into a virtual mode under those circumstances. In total, 128 supervisors and 87 coaches took part in the study. The analysis generated a number of themes that will be discussed together with the themes of the literature.

We start this chapter with exploring the nature of the virtual modality of supervision, drawing both on the available literature and on our own research. Then we examine what are perceived as the benefits and advantages of virtual supervision, followed by challenges and disadvantages. We end the chapter with useful strategies that can be offered to those supervising virtually and provide guidance for further learning and research.

Virtual modality of supervision

Since Murdoch (2010: 137) suggested a decade ago that 'The potency, flexibility and cost-effectiveness of virtual working is an enormous benefit to coaches, mentors and supervisors, and I am sure that as the virtual landscape develops, there will be more of it', the growth in literature specifically related to virtual coaching supervision has remained relatively limited (Murdoch 2010; Downing 2020a). Therefore for this chapter we have drawn on the wider literature, particularly that on therapy/counselling even though this has often concentrated on phone and internet-based chat or email supervision, rather than video-conferencing (for example, Allsbrook 2016; Bolton 2017; Ghods and Boyce 2012; Martin et al. 2017; Murdoch 2010; Rousmaniere 2016; Rousmaniere and Renfro-Michel 2016; Speyer and Zack 2003). Pullan (2016) focused on research and practice in virtual leadership and much of her guidance is relevant; and there is increasing literature in the field of coaching and mentoring which also has some relevance for supervision (for example, Ahrend et al. 2010; Beddoes-Jones and Miller 2006; Clutterbuck and Hussain 2010; Geissler et al. 2014; Hawkins and Turner 2020; Ribbers and Waringa 2015; Williams et al. 2012).

The wider helping professions literature advocates protecting confidentiality and ensuring legal and ethical practice, providing safeguards for service interruptions and having robust codes of practice for virtual working (such as Allsbrook 2016; Bolton 2017; Martin et al. 2017; Rousmaniere 2014) though with limited specific guidance on virtual safeguards. While there is reference to the limit of visual clues (Rousmaniere and Renfro-Michel 2016), the overall view is that virtual work is convenient and makes it more accessible to all, regardless of location (Speyer and Zack 2003). However, there has to be a recognition that virtual work may have implications for developing a strong personal relationship. For example, Murdoch (2010: 131) talks of the increased importance of the supervisor's 'capacity for profound listening' and the supervisee's need to have access 'to the supervisor who is a true match for them'.

There is another element of the discussion on virtual work brought about by attitudes to technology in different generations from baby boomers to successive generations, Generations X, Y and Z. Davidson (2020) points out this can lead to different expectations. She uses a global online platform that offers 30-minute coaching sessions that are relatively inexpensive, describing how

> with their thirst for instant knowledge they enjoy the 30-minute sessions fitted in promptly to their schedule with sometimes only an hour's notice, when they can access quality coaching or mentoring with a qualified coach to focus on an immediate need.

As Ahrend et al. (2010) point out, technology makes it possible 'to move beyond a focus on executive-level coaching and give everyone valuable work-related coaching support' (2010: 44). To date, the context has been coaching, but this could extend to supervision, and substituting the word supervision for coaching in Davidson's description could illustrate elements of future supervision.

In the first half of 2020 the coronavirus pandemic brought the issue of virtual work to wider attention. Virtual working had already been increasing for some supervisors, often dictated by an increasing desire for supervision in locations where there were few or no supervisors. While this meant some supervisors had an almost entirely virtual practice, that was not the case universally and the advantages, disadvantages and challenges were new territory to some, and findings from research were not widely available.

"Popular video-conferencing app Zoom has seen its revenues skyrocket as second quarter profits more than doubled due to the coronavirus crisis. Revenues leaped 355 per cent to $663.5m (£496.3m) for the three months ending 31 July, beating analysts' expectations of $500.5m. Profits soared to $186m, while customer growth rose 458 per cent, compared with the same period in 2019" (BBC, 2020). This growth was greatly influenced by the social distancing measures, which led to surging demand for remote solutions, although there was some falling back because of the privacy and security concerns. This raised questions for all of us as we work virtually, in how we create safety for our supervisees and ourselves. What then do we need to have in place for supervising virtually to be effective, safe, robust and reliable? And what strategies can we develop to deal with any challenges we might experience? As Pullan (2016: 89) makes clear, 'It is important to understand that technology is only an enabler. Alone, it does not make virtual working effective'. And we are probably all familiar with what is described as the most used phrase during the 2020 lockdown in various countries: 'You're on mute'!

The key findings from our survey reflect the literature with limited difference between supervisors and coaches. Participants were asked to offer five advantages, five disadvantages and five challenges (there was considerable overlap between the latter two), and then suggest any ways around the challenges. These themes are picked up below.

The coronavirus pandemic affected professional practices and virtual work became a requirement rather than a choice. Professionals who were already working virtually did not find their practices so significantly affected. Most coaches and supervisors, in our follow-up survey, agreed the transition had been smooth and better than expected. One coach told us:

> I have experienced very little change as I have been encouraging remote working for the last 2 years, mainly due to climate considerations. Clients who previously resisted that way of working have found it beneficial to be able to access support flexibly. Personally, it means I can focus wholly on delivery vs logistics/travel, etc.

But others, like this supervisor, noted that:

> Creating an open and trusting environment when not sitting 'knee to knee' requires additional presence and holding the group's expectations . . . and having

to adapt tools to be usable is challenging. Overall, working virtually is a good experience but one that requires extra vigilance and adaptation by a supervisor.

One supervisor wrote that 'It's been a revolution to virtual work only!' Another felt that supervisees who have previously resisted remote one-to-one work have 'embraced the technology and adapted to ensure they continue to get the supervision they need through this time of crisis'. For most supervisors, working virtually was surprisingly constructive and positively useful.

However, there was another side, with one supervisor also expressing the feelings of loss associated with lack of in-person contact with each other: '[working] virtually can be an impediment to some people and they just are not able to move ahead with this possibility'. We note that while virtual work seems set to be the predominant supervision strategy, there will always be professionals who would rather work in person, resisting technology and virtual relationships.

The advantages of virtual working

In the literature and in our research study, there were similar themes from coaches and supervisors relating to the advantages of virtual working. They found key advantages in time-saving, convenience, flexibility and being able to work globally. Coaches, in particular, appreciated the possibility of working with supervisors located in different countries and who may sometimes be more experienced than local supervisors. Supervisors appreciated the possibility of supervising coaches around the word, enriching their practice and, according to one, 'making relationships with people I would normally never meet'. Other advantages included cost-saving, flexibility and being more eco-friendly through less travelling. The main themes were as follows:

Time-saving – This was the most repeated advantage across the board. Coaching virtually saved travel time and the cost of the traveling and parking. If working from home, there was also potentially a saving on office accommodation. Another advantage was a reduction from the stress of travelling: 'Not having to get in my car to go to a venue', 'Allows me to choose my own safe, comfortable space', 'I don't have to travel miles to get to the people I'm working with', 'avoid transit in the City'. This mirrors Kanatouri and Geissler's finding (2017: 714) that individuals can receive coaching as and when the need arises reducing travel time so providing 'time savings, cost efficiency and flexibility in coaching delivery'.

Working globally – Accessibility was frequently mentioned with no geographical constraints and worldwide access for coaches to supervisors and vice versa. 'Working globally increases the potential range of clients and thus experience'. This reflects Ribbers and Waringa (2015: 5), who talk of 'a technological response to society's demand for care that is unrestricted by geographical, physical, psychological and/or financial obstacles'. Supervisors talked of being able to work with clients 'from anywhere to everywhere in the world'. Coaches said: 'choosing the supervisor that I want without worrying where they are based' with 'Easy access to world class supervisors' and 'Able to work with supervisors I respect that are not available in my country'. As Murdoch (2010: 131) says, 'coaches and mentors have access to the supervisor who is a true match for them'.

Flexibility and cost-saving – Practitioners experienced flexibility of work location, scheduling (more time since there is no wasted time in travelling and more options for session dates and times), and of personal choice – 'I can stand or sit and wear comfortable clothes'. All this is at 'No additional cost for travel/location/space'.

Efficiency – Respondents described how working virtually allows for the 'Ability to be centred and present in my own surroundings' and hence 'can feel safer'. There was a perception that working virtually makes it easier to 'Work straight to the point' and have an 'ability to focus more quickly on the work'. It also allows for 'emergency sessions'. Also, there may be less distractions from office surrounding, although as Hawkins and Turner (2020) point out, these can increase too in home settings from dogs to deliveries, giving us more of an insight into the world of our clients of course!

Eco-friendly – Some respondents mentioned reducing their carbon footprint. 'On the big picture, less carbon pollution for commuting'.

Miscellaneous – A session can more easily be recorded and shared with the supervisee. 'I can record and play back the session'. This was noted by Downing (2020a) in her doctoral research who ensured that 'agreements on the uses and retention of recordings were explicit'. How they are stored securely, though, is a consideration.

The disadvantages/challenges of virtual working

The survey highlighted key issues associated with disadvantages and challenges that are treated together because of significant overlaps, and are also mirrored in the literature: issues of technology, effect on personal connection/rapport, managing distractions, reduced creativity, security, privacy and confidentiality considerations and a personal preference for face-to-face working on the part of the coach and/or supervisor.

Issues of technology were the primary concern. This included having a reliable internet connection, the right equipment, and an understanding of how the platforms work. Some professionals face power outages in their countries that are beyond their control: 'It may be frustrating if technology fails to work properly'. 'In [my country] we've had extensive power outages impacting telecoms.' And as respondents note, 'Technology is not always perfect. Poor virtual/digital connection and can be unreliable'; '(quality of sound, internet stability, etc.) can compromise the quality of the meeting'. Ghods and Boyce (2012: 518) also urge coaches to understand 'client/mentee and coach/mentor comfort with and competency in the technology deployed; evaluating availability, functionality, and feasibility of technology used'.

The effect on personal connection/rapport – A common theme for coaches and supervisors was around communication and the possibility of missing nuances: 'You may miss nuances of body language and some body language and non-verbals are lost.' 'Coaching and supervision are about human interaction and reading the body and the mood which can be lost virtually.' There was also concern that some topics affecting relationships might only be brought face-to-face: 'There are topics I wouldn't talk about online: its value and significance can be underestimated.' 'Some things are better revealed face-to-face in person.' However, in her doctoral research, Downing (2020a) found that having video compared to audio made a difference: for example, the 'gallery view' gives a sense of being in a circle together and seeing facial and some body expressions led to greater intimacy being experienced. Pullan (2016) believes that through an understanding of the system in use the individual supervisor can maximize security available and that this is a factor in the ability to develop a strong personal relationship.

The third common theme was *managing distractions*, such as interruptions from children, unexpected visitors, pets, sirens, doorbells, for both parties. Respondents talked of interruptions and the 'Need to pay greater attention', admitting that, 'Concentration is sometimes not so good'. 'I have often had clients who were working from home and had personal distractions such as children and pets.'

Both groups of professionals in our research believed that virtual work can *reduce creativity*, although more supervisors than coaches brought this as a concern. This particularly applied to working somatically, with constellations, and other methodologies that they perceived required working in person. 'The supervisor might feel limited in what tools they can use with me', 'Could be more superficial?' 'Use of co-creative intervention, e.g. constellation limited or harder to set up'; 'Some exercises that require equipment/material (magic box for instance) are less easy to use'. Lahad (2000) advocates a range of approaches to harness creativity and as the pandemic continued there was more evidence of this happening, for example, in the use of virtual perceptual positions and constellations (Box 26.1).

Security, privacy and confidentiality – Respondents pointed to a number of concerns: 'I'm in the UK, so security has no such high surveillance that I think it's possible that your session could be monitored in some way that you don't know about.' Another worried that 'privacy might be hacked'. In the literature protecting confidentiality and ensuring legal and ethical practice is a widespread concern (Bolton 2017; Martin et al. 2017; Rousmaniere 2014), along with security. Pullan (2016) divides this into two areas: building security into the infrastructure and technology used (passwords, encryption and firewalls); and remaining personally vigilant. She suggests that tools with lower costs may offer less control on how the user's data is used and shared.

Finally, for respondents, *personal preferences and beliefs* came into play: some professionals do not like working virtually with comments describing 'the magic of the face-to-face encounter', noting that virtual 'is not right for everyone'. And there is also a money issue: 'face-value is less, so remuneration is less'. A few coaches also mentioned time zone differences. Pullan (2016) highlights practical complications of virtual working across time zones and cultures. She points out that while we may all be aware of the challenges of overlapping working hours when practising globally, clocks change at different times and directions depending on hemisphere. Working weeks also differ (the Middle East generally favours Sunday to Thursday compared to the UK, USA and Australia where it is generally Monday to Friday) and there may be different statutory holidays, for example, national public holidays, Eid, Christmas. Annual holiday practices also differ, with USA residents generally having two weeks leave while many European countries may take six weeks, in some cases with an almost total shutdown in August.

This expansion into culture, diversity and ethics, while not present in the surveys, is though picked up in literature. Ryde et al. (2019: 42) point out that ethics is affected by a number of factors, not just 'nationality or race but [. . .] geographical cultures such as countries and regions; social cultures such as race, class, sexual orientation and gender and organisational cultures'. Pullan (2016) discusses how differing responses to a dilemma can all be considered 'correct' by different cultures, because how we solve dilemmas draws on national cultures. She mentions several elements that might be impacted, from status and views on working time to the focus on face. And while they not mention virtual work explicitly, Iordanou et al. (2017) raise points around ethics, from confidentiality to contracting and trust to culture, that are applicable.

Useful strategies for working virtually

As many of the strategies are indicated together with challenges in the previous sections, here we only mention additional pointers for managing virtual working. Drawing on their experiences of running virtual sessions globally for some years, Hawkins and Turner (2020) produced guidance for virtual working at the start of the pandemic. After watching a videoed meeting where a health worker's wine collection was the backdrop, they advocate considering the appropriateness of what people see behind you. Our visibility is another theme, arranging screens so we are high up in the frame with hands in shot (we have probably all experienced many cut-off chins!). Light can also play a role in people's experience on virtual calls, so they suggest we pay attention to how light falls at different times of day, so we are not too bright or too dark.

As technical problems are entirely predictable, they urge assuming these will occur, so they do not 'throw' us at the time. In fact, Downing (2020a) describes in her doctoral research that when technology issues happened, the calm, accepting response by the supervisor was a key element of creating and maintaining the safe container for the group. Pullan (2016) describes how there are fewer 'water cooler' moments, so we need to create planned ways to have informal conversations to build relationships. Hawkins and Turner (2020) suggest starting meetings early to allow for personal and social bonding time, so that we act as if we are in the same room as much as is possible. One of the authors has also subsequently found that as people arrive early, putting them into breakout rooms for 'coffee' to break the ice before meetings start is successful. Hawkins and Turner end with a few process suggestions such as ensuring sufficient comfort and drink breaks, contracting well including on aims and to ensure everyone's voice is heard.

The need to acknowledge barriers/potential issues at the beginning and to re-contract around technology is echoed by Downing (2020a) who writes that contracting on the utilization of the technology was explicit, including whether video capability was required for all participants. Ghods and Boyce (2012) discuss setting ground rules around desired behaviours or example, not multi-tasking during the session. One respondent described a specific instance that makes a broader point around the degree of informality:

> I once had a supervisor for my therapy work, who dialled in from her bed, where she was laid up with a bad back. I was very uncomfortable as the supervisee, it felt intrusive into her private life, and I felt uncomfortable about sharing my case work in those circumstances. I addressed this with her in a later session.

Alongside being prepared oneself with the technology, one respondent described providing 'detailed instructions for operating the audio and video, so that they can participate with relative ease the first time'. The need for mental and psychical preparation, mirroring face-to-face work, was also mentioned by coaches and supervisors, from closing down other applications to 'Investing some time before the call starts to get myself into the best possible state for holding the virtual session'.

The need for creativity was underlined: 'Ask clients to do something creative like draw a metaphor'; 'Be creative, attending to possibilities rather than seeing the technology as offering limitations'. The work of Lahad (2000) is as relevant to virtual work as face-to-face, and with a degree of care, most of the ideas he suggests such as drawings, objects, cards, using metaphors and journaling, are possible to adapt, to which can be added using an online whiteboard, live quizzes, polls and word clouds, bringing in avatars (Clutterbuck et al. 2016) or constellating.

Box 26.1 Case illustration

One of the authors, Eve, was working with a supervision group on virtual creativity, when Natasha shared this story from her practice as an example. While this was done using a laptop, on reflection Natasha said that had the client been using a PC she would have got them to stand up and take different positions within view to inhabit the positions or use their phone to move around the room.

My client is running a team that has been widely praised for their successful response to the transition and changing business needs of the organization during the pandemic. Despite this, she experienced persistent criticism and undermining behaviour from her line manager, going into a 'childlike state' when dealing with him. I wanted to explore the relationship dynamics that were causing her such anxiety she was considering leaving her much-loved job.

My client is cerebral by nature and is very interested in models and theory. I decided to try the NLP perceptual positions/ORSC Third Entity exercise for her to work somatically, and despite scepticism about this working virtually, she agreed to move around her living room with her laptop camera on. She stood in position A and talked as herself to her boss (position B), as if addressing him directly by saying what she felt and what she wanted. I asked her then to shake herself off and inhabit the body language and the mindset of her boss (position B). How does he stand and speak, what are his verbal tics? What are his priorities and world view? As position B she addressed position A directly by saying what he felt and what he wanted. She then moved to position C as the voice of the system, knowing both these people with their best interests at heart. I asked her 'How do you feel watching these two people? What do you know that they don't know? What do you need from them?' On reflecting what she had learnt my client saw that the relationship was in her words 'rather amusing and faintly ridiculous', in that her childlike behaviour and defensiveness was feeding into her manager's 'apprehending parent' behaviour. She began to understand her own accountability for the skewed relationship with her boss and wondered what triggered her child-like behaviour with a particular kind of authority. The exercise lost none of its power by being carried out virtually.

Guidance for further learning and research

The results from our study are consistent with the literature review and also showed consistency between coaches and supervisors. Virtual work is seen to save time, money, and natural resources and allows professionals to work with colleagues from all over the world, but may face challenges regarding internet stability, technology literacy (how to navigate software), distractions, and personal preferences.

Following her doctoral research Downing (2020b) offers these reflections that contain suggestions for further research:

1. What are desirable lengths of sessions – in my research all of the sessions were 90 minutes? That is our working assumption about the length of time one can stay present and focused.
2. What assumptions and reactions are related to the physical settings one is in while participating on Zoom? How does the background shift the way a person is perceived by the others?
3. What are best practices in contracting about recording the supervision sessions and ensuring appropriate data management?
4. How do supervisees experience virtual supervision as contrasted with in-person supervision? [This question would be useful as we consider how to refine and enhance our virtual supervision experiences.]

As we move to an increasingly virtual world, there are further themes that have emerged from both our literature review and our research. Training programmes and ongoing learning in basic technology is a clear need, as is ensuring security and confidentiality in a world where new technology is frequently becoming available. Professional coaching bodies will also need to embrace this area in future iterations of codes of practice. But technology is just a starting point. Training could consider how to pick-up nuances from listening to the voice and with limited body language, and to find ways to incorporate somatic experiencing within virtual work.

> ### Questions for reflection
>
> - What additional considerations are there for contracting when working virtually?
> - How might the impact of technological issues be minimized?
> - How might we ensure we work as creatively virtually as we do face-to-face?
> - What additional resources do we and our supervisees need to ensure we work effectively and maintain our health and well-being?

Further sources

Kanatouri, S. and Geissler, H (2017) Adapting to working with new technologies, in T. Bachkirova, G. Spence and D. Drake (eds) *The SAGE Handbook of Coaching.* London: Sage. The chapter provides a strong background including a rich overview of research and purpose-built technologies.

Pullan, P. (2016) *Virtual Leadership – Practical Strategies for Getting the Best Out of Virtual Work and Virtual Teams.* London: Kogan Page. This book has breadth and covers a wide range of topics relevant to supervisors, from how we show up to cultural assumptions we might have.

Ribbers, A. and Waringa, A. (2015) *E-Coaching: Theory and Practice for a New Online Approach to Coaching.* Abingdon: Routledge. This book is the most comprehensive in the field to date, covering technology, different models and processes, and a short discussion on ethics.

References

Ahrend, G., Diamond, F. and Webber, P.G. (2010) Virtual coaching: using technology to boost performance, *Chief Learning Officer,* 9(7): 44–46. Available from: http://www.w.cedma-europe.org/newsletter%20articles/Clomedia/Virtual%20Coaching%20-%20Using%20Technology%20to%20Boost%20Performance%20(Jul%2010).pdf (accessed 11 December 2020).

Allsbrook, D. (2016) *An Ever Changing World: The Ethical Use of Technology in Supervision.* Unpublished dissertation, University of New Orleans. Available from: (accessed 1 September 2020).

BBC (2020) Zoom profits double as revenues skyrocket. Available from: https://www.bbc.co.uk/news/business-53979632 (accessed 1 September 2020).

Beddoes-Jones, F. and Miller, J. (2006) 'Virtual' mentoring: can the principle of cognitive pairing increase its effectiveness?, *International Journal of Evidence Based Coaching and Mentoring,* 4(2): 54–60. Available from: https://radar.brookes.ac.uk/radar/items/6da67d83-5539-4e71-bb7c-017356b3869e/1/ (accessed 1 September 2020).

Bolton, J. (2017) The ethical issues which must be addressed in online counselling, *ACR Journal,* 11(1): 7. Available from: http://www.acrjournal.com.au/resources/assets/journals/Volume-11-Issue-1-2017/Ethical_issues_in_Online_Counselling_1-15.pdf (accessed 1 September 2020).

Clement, J. (2020) Worldwide digital population as of July 2020. Statista. Available from: https://www.statista.com/statistics/617136/digital-population-worldwide/ (accessed 1 September 2020).

Clutterbuck, D., Whitaker, C. and Lucas, M. (2016) *Coaching Supervision – A Practical Guide for Supervisees.* Abingdon: Routledge.

Davidson, C. (2020) *Private correspondence.*

Downing, K.M. (2020a) *Creating the Container for Reflective Practice in Virtual Small Group Supervision*. Unpublished Doctoral Dissertation. London: Middlesex University.

Downing, K.M. (2020b) *Private correspondence*.

Geissler, H., Hasenbein, M., Kanatouri, S. and Wegener, R. (2014) E-coaching: conceptual and empirical findings of a virtual coaching programme, *International Journal of Evidence Based Coaching and Mentoring*, 12(2): 165–187. Available from: https://radar.brookes.ac.uk/radar/items/585eb4f9-19ce-49e1-b600-509fde1e18c0/1/ (accessed 1 September 2020).

Ghods, N. and Boyce, C. (2016) Virtual coaching and mentoring, in J. Passmore, D. Peterson and T. Freire (eds) *The Wiley-Blackwell Handbook of the Psychology of Coaching and Mentoring*. Chichester: John Wiley.

Hawkins, P. and Turner, E. (2017) The rise of coaching supervision (2006–2014), *Coaching: An International Journal of Theory, Research and Practice*, 10(2): 102–114.

Hawkins, P. and Turner, E. (2020) Working from home, in K. McAlpin and D. Norrington (eds) *Surviving the Coronavirus Lockdown and Social Isolation*. Cardiff: Wordcatcher Publishing. Available from: www.wordcatcher.com/LetsResetNormal

Iordanou, I., Hawley, R. and Iordanou, C. (2017) *Values and Ethics in Coaching*. London: Sage.

Kanatouri, S. and Geissler, H. (2017) Adapting to working with new technologies, in T. Bachkirova, G. Spence and D. Drake (eds) *The SAGE Handbook of Coaching*. London: Sage.

Lahad, M. (2000) *Creative Supervision – The Use of Expressive Arts Methods in Supervision and Self-Supervision*. London: Jessica Kingsley.

Martin, P., Kumar, S. and Lizarondo, L. (2017) Effective use of technology in clinical supervision, *Internet Interventions*, 8(June): 35–39. https://doi.org/10.1016/j.invent.2017.03.001. Available from: https://www.sciencedirect.com/science/article/pii/S2214782917300131 (accessed 1 September 2020).

McAnally, K., Abrams, L., Asmus, M. et al. (2019) *Global Coaching Supervision: A Study of the Perceptions and Practices Around the World*. Available from: https://coachingsupervisionresearch.org/wp-content/uploads/2020/02/Global_Coaching_Supervision_Report_FINAL.pdf (accessed 1 September 2020).

Murdoch, E. (2010) Virtual coach and mentor supervision, in D. Clutterbuck and Z. Hussain (eds) *Virtual Coach, Virtual Mentor*. Charlotte, NC: Information Age Publishing.

Pullan, P. (2016) *Virtual Leadership – Practical Strategies for Getting the Best Out of Virtual Work and Virtual Teams*. London: Kogan Page.

Ribbers, A. (2015) *E-Coaching: Theory and Practice for a New Online Approach to Coaching*. Abingdon: Routledge

Roser, M., Ritchie, H. and Ortiz-Ospina, E. (2020) Internet. Published online at OurWorldInData.org. Available from: https://ourworldindata.org/internet (accessed 1 September 2020).

Rousmaniere, T. and Renfro-Michel, E. (eds) (2016) *Using Technology to Enhance Clinic Supervision*. Alexandria, VA: American Counseling Association.

Rousmaniere, T. (2014) Using technology to enhance clinical supervision and training, in C.E. Watkins, Jr. and D.L. Milne (eds) *The Wiley International Handbook of Clinical Supervision*. Chichester: John Wiley.

Ryde, J., Seto, L. and Goldvarg, D. (2019) Diversity and inclusion in supervision, in E. Turner and S. Palmer (eds) *The Heart of Coaching Supervision – Working with Reflection and Self-Care*. Abingdon: Routledge.

Speyer, C. and Zack, J. (2003) Online counselling: beyond the pros and cons, *Psychologica*, 23(2): 11–14.

Williams, S., Sunderman, J. and Kim, J. (2012) E-mentoring in an online course: benefits and challenges to E-mentors, *International Journal of Evidence Based Coaching and Mentoring*, 10(1):109–123. Available from: https://radar.brookes.ac.uk/radar/items/a7c21f50-3d18-4112-b279-946c3c1ef1d6/1/ (accessed 1 September 2020).

Index